NEIL JORDAN: WORKS FOR THE PAGE

Neil Jordan
Works for the page

VAL NOLAN

First published in 2022 by
Cork University Press
Boole Library
University College Cork
CORK
T12 ND89
Ireland

© the author, 2022

Library of Congress Control Number: 2022932570
Distribution in the USA: Longleaf Services, Chapel Hill, NC, USA

All rights reserved. No part of this book may be reprinted or reproduced or utilised in any electronic, mechanical or other means, now known or hereafter invented, including photocopying and recording or otherwise, without either the prior written permission of the publishers or a licence permitting restricted copying in Ireland issued by the Irish Copyright Licensing Agency Ltd., 25 Denzille Lane, Dublin 2.

British Library Cataloguing in Publication Data
A CIP record for this book is available from the British Library.

ISBN: 978-1-78205-495-5

Printed in Poland by BZ Graf.
Print origination & design by Carrigboy Typesetting Services
www.carrigboy.co.uk

COVER IMAGE – Photograph of Neil Jordan, Express/Getty

www.corkuniversitypress.com

Contents

ACKNOWLEDGEMENTS	vi
PERMISSIONS	vii
INTRODUCTION	1

1. A Writer who just happens to make Movies: Neil Jordan's literary life — 11
2. The Ending of the Day brings Release: *Night in Tunisia* — 38
3. Making Sense of the Present: Looking to *The Past* — 64
4. Transformative Myth: Interpreting *The Dream of a Beast* — 89
5. A Place where each Statement has Two Meanings: *Sunrise with Sea Monster* — 114
6. Observation is all I am: Narration and recurrence in *Shade* — 139
7. Jordan's Film Stories: The uncollected collection — 167
8. Bad Fairies and Strange, Unrealised Desires: *Mistaken*, *Carnivalesque* and the many Neil Jordans — 195

CONCLUSION	222
NOTES	229
BIBLIOGRAPHY	253
INDEX	263

Acknowledgements

Writing a book like this is not a solitary journey. The present volume evolved from a doctoral thesis that I wrote at National University of Ireland, Galway, and I am very grateful to John Kenny for fine support, honesty, common sense and loyalty throughout that process. The advice and encouragement of Adrian Frazier was also of immeasurable value. I find it difficult to imagine myself as an academic if not for their examples.

Friends and colleagues at Aberystwyth University have also been an indispensable source of encouragement. I would like to express particular gratitude for the support provided by Louise Marshall and Malte Urban, with additional thanks to Tasha Alden, Neal Alexander, Richard Marggraf Turley and Matthew Jarvis for shrewd advice in the later stages of the project.

This work has benefited from the support of many people. I wish to express specific thanks for practical help, interest and worthy counsel to Jen Smith, Ira Ruppo, Daniel Kennedy, Liam O'Donoghue, Patrick Heffernan, Garret O'Malley, Sarah McCann, Cathy Wagenschutz, Elizabeth Wagenschutz, Craig Salvona, John Enos, Anne Karhio, Dermot Burns, Ciaran McDonough, Anthony Cantor, Katrin Urschel, Meg McDonald and Tiffani Angus. I am grateful too for the input of Mike McCormack and Kim Stanley Robinson, with whom I had a number of very helpful conversations when I was formulating my ideas. I also wish to extend my gratitude to the anonymous readers whose appreciative responses offered both reassurance and useful suggestions for improvement.

Finally, I wish to thank Esther Le Mair for her unfailing support, and my parents for their generosity and goodwill. I could not have completed this work without them.

Permissions

My thanks for kind permission to excerpt from the following:

Anonymous, 'Neil Jordan: Return to form', *Books Ireland*, vol. 183, February 1995, pp. 5–6; quoted with permission of Ruth McKee, Editor, *Books Ireland*.

Cahalan, James M., *The Irish Novel: A critical history* (Dublin: Gill & Macmillan, 1988); quoted with permission of Linda Murphy, Gill Publications.

Dillon-Malone, Aubrey, 'Transmogrification', *Books Ireland*, vol. 79, December 1983, p. 230; quoted with permission of Ruth McKee, Editor, *Books Ireland*.

Evans, Georgie, '9 Most Anticipated Books of 2017', *Cultured Vultures* (online); quoted with permission of Jimmy Donellan, Editor, *Cultured Vultures*.

Foster, John Wilson, 'Neil Jordan: Night in Tunisia and other stories', in Seamus Deane (ed.), *The Field Day Anthology of Irish Writing*, vol. 3; quoted with permission of Ciarán Deane, Field Day.

Fox, Caoimhe, 'From Captain America's to Hollywood and Back', *Books Ireland*, vol. 367, May/June 2016, pp. 18–19; quoted with permission of Ruth McKee, Editor, *Books Ireland*.

Haslam, Richard, 'Neil Jordan and the ABC of Narratology: "Stories to do with love are mathematical"', *New Hibernia Review*, vol. 3, no. 2, summer 1999, pp. 36–55; quoted with permission of David Gardiner, Editor, *New Hibernia Review*.

Jesse, Neal G., 'Contemporary Irish Neutrality: Still a singular stance', *New Hibernia Review*, vol. 11, no. 1, spring 2007, pp. 74–95; quoted with permission of David Gardiner, Editor, *New Hibernia Review*.

Lanters, José, '*Nightlines* by Neil Jordan', *World Literature Today*, vol. 70, no. 3, summer 1996, p. 692; quoted with permission of *World Literature Today*.

Murphy, Neil, *Irish Fiction and Postmodern Doubt* (New York: Edwin Mellon, 2004); quoted with permission of Edwin Mellon Press.

Shumaker, Jeanett, 'Uncanny Doubles: The fiction of Anne Enright', *New Hibernia Review*, vol. 9, no. 3, autumn 2005, pp. 107–22; quoted with permission of David Gardiner, Editor, *New Hibernia Review*.

Wondrich, Roberta Gefter, 'Survivors of Joyce: Joycean images and motifs in some contemporary Irish fiction', *Studies*, vol. 90, no. 358, summer 2001, pp. 197–206; quoted with permission of Cecilia West, Director, Messenger Publications.

Introduction

The question was once put to me, 'Why study Neil Jordan's fiction? Surely the films are what's important?' It is a query that has recurred throughout the duration of this project and one which deserves to be addressed at the outset of this volume. Simply put, those only casually interested in the investigation of Irish history and identity by one of our most prominent contemporary artists are satisfied with *Angel* (1982), *The Crying Game* (1992), *Michael Collins* (1996) and so on. Significant works all, products of Jordan's tremendous skill as a filmmaker, but easily accessible. By contrast, those who take a chance on *The Past* (1980), *Sunrise with Sea Monster* (1994; published in North America as *Nightlines*), *Carnivalesque* (2017) and so on discover a more personal working-through of themes and concerns which Jordan the writer has long conducted in parallel with the similar – but not identical – concerns of Jordan the director: the struggle to define oneself against the weight of Irish history, both political and artistic; the quest to understand and contextualise the nation's violent efforts to transcend and process its colonial past; a fascination with the hidden, the speculative; and – drawing the two Jordans together in a novel like *Mistaken* (2011) – the conflicted nature of the artist operating across multiple media.

For, like the protagonist of that book and his uncanny doppelgänger, it often seems as though there are two Neil Jordans. Both men look the same, both sound the same, people confuse one for the other, and, occasionally, they switch places. The current study focuses on the literary half of this diptych in an effort to redress the lack of attention paid to Jordan the writer over the past four decades. It reframes the shot, to borrow a cinematic metaphor, so that its subject appears as an author in the same way previous work has presented him as an auteur. This is not to denigrate those volumes from a Film Studies perspective, far from it. Much essential work exists on the topic of Jordan's films, valuable and, more often than not, insightful and readable contributions to contemporary criticism. The purpose of this study is not to situate itself in antagonistic opposition to such work but instead to complement it. As Eileen Battersby, one of Jordan's strongest advocates among literary journalists, said several times: filmmaking gained substantially from Irish fiction's loss.[1] This is especially true when one considers the depth of feeling and artistic merit found in Jordan's novels – work which many people suspect he has produced in his spare time.

Part of the current volume's purpose is therefore to unveil a person sometimes perceived as merely 'dabbling in prose-writing' to be a serious author.[2] From this vantage, the director of eighteen highly regarded feature films becomes the acclaimed writer of nine original and challenging books.[3] The Academy Award-winning screenwriter (1993) is transformed into the recipient of the *Guardian* Fiction Prize (1979); the winner of the Silver Bear at the Berlin Film Festival (1998) for his adaptation of *The Butcher Boy* (1997) becomes the winner of the Rooney Award for Literature (1981) for *The Past* (1980), a book named by critic D.J. Taylor as one of the forty most important novels of that decade.[4] A filmmaker with multiple nominations for Golden Globes, BAFTAs (including wins in 1993 and 2000) and a wide variety of festival and critics' association prizes becomes the recipient of a Lifetime Achievement Award from the Irish PEN association (2004), an honour which, in previous years, has been bestowed upon writers such as John B. Keane, Edna O'Brien, William Trevor and John McGahern who have made an outstanding contribution to Irish literature. Readers and scholars now discover that the once well-mapped landscape of contemporary Irish fiction has been altered by the sudden appearance of a most remarkable figure: a mature novelist who has gone largely overlooked by the academy and reading public; a writer with identifiable periods, an established back catalogue and solid links to the literary establishment. Jordan the director may work with the Tom Cruises and Jodie Fosters and Nick Noltes of the world, but Jordan the writer is a fellow traveller of contemporary greats such as Patrick McCabe and John Banville, and was characterised by Fintan O'Toole in *The Irish Times* as a significant asset for Irish writing on the basis of his early fiction.[5]

Should this sound too much like guilt by association then one need only look to the remarkable vision of the work itself. From overtly political narratives like *The Past* and *Sunrise with Sea Monster* to the allegorical fantasy novella *The Dream of a Beast* (1983, regarded by Banville as Jordan's masterpiece)[6] and even the more personal volumes such as *Night in Tunisia* (1976), *Shade* (2004), *Mistaken* and *Carnivalesque*, Jordan's fiction is underpinned by an interrogation of politics, identity and representation in a specifically Irish context. Considered as a body of work, Jordan's writing aligns with the traditional objective of much Irish fiction which, in the view of Colm Tóibín, is to boldly engage with questions of national identity.[7] In the process, Jordan raises political figures such as Éamon de Valera to the level of mythology and lowers supernatural races like the Tuatha Dé Danann to seedy carnival attractions. He tells and retells the story of the Irish twentieth century, with the current volume shaped in turn by the ebbs and flows of this oeuvre. A deliberate choice has thus been made to follow the general direction of much Irish criticism by relating the fiction directly back to that which it is critiquing. Therefore, an approach primarily considering individual novels or groups of stories is preferred throughout *Neil Jordan: Works for the Page*.

The purpose of this is to reveal the variety of critical entry points to Jordan's writing and the fact that his work, as Seán O'Faoláin wrote in the introduction to *Night in Tunisia*, delivers personal and distinctive stories in highly original fashion.[8] Simultaneously, *Neil Jordan: Works for the Page* is intended to demonstrate the not insignificant fact that the author's core concerns eventually lead those who know him only as a filmmaker towards recognisable thematic and autobiographical material. Consider Jordan's uncollected 'film stories' or his depiction of early cinema in the pages of *Shade*; consider the repurposing of his own formative English expatriate experiences as backdrops for the interiority of characters in crisis in his powerful short story 'Last Rites' a decade and a half before his Oscar-winning film *The Crying Game*. A closely related benefit of this wide-angle approach is the manner in which it shows how, from the beginning, Jordan the fiction writer has revelled in a willingness to expand traditional constructions of Irish identity and to break away from, as O'Faoláin saw it, dull and overused language and symbols.[9] Jordan achieves this through an absorption of the fantastic and eventually even the science-fictional into his work, an assimilation of themes and tropes so organic and so complete that it is utterly essential to many of his books. While Jordan is typically categorised as a writer of historical realism, novels such as *The Dream of a Beast*, *Shade* and *Carnivalesque* are undeniably fantasy, arguably even broaching the realms of science fiction, in how they marry Gothic weirdness, body horror, ghosts, time loops, changelings and even gravitational theory to their keenly observed – and very Irish – narratives. The work further displays a consistent awareness of the external world. Novels such as *Sunrise with Sea Monster* and *Mistaken* eschew insularity to depict an Ireland perturbed by the influence of everything from world wars to the social and economic policies of British colonialism, the cultural subversion of American popular culture and the unavoidable consequences of globalisation. (While, on the surface, Jordan's 2016 novel *The Drowned Detective* would seem to satisfy this last criterion, its Central European focus pushes it largely outside the scope of this study.)

Closely related to this is Jordan's fascination with those events of the Irish twentieth century where the relationship between this island and its neighbours – both archipelagic and continental – was at its most strained. His fiction repeatedly circles around the collapse of Anglo-Irish influence, the war of independence and the 'Emergency' (the Irish euphemism for the Second World War), and all this from a writer who belongs to the first generation of modern Irish artists with no first-hand experience of large-scale war or conflict. However, it is not just political turmoil that attracts Jordan's interest but also the associated artistic tensions. Along with the upheavals of the Irish civil war, the above periods provide the backdrop for 'A Love', *The Past*, *Sunrise with Sea Monster* and *Shade*, with at least the fingerprints of another kind of Irish national trauma, that of the recurring recessionary experience, visible in 'Last Rites' and *Mistaken*. Readers of early work such as *The Past* will discover an idiosyncratic response to the formation of the Irish Republic just as those of *Sunrise with Sea Monster* encounter an interrogation of the state's subsequent isolationist stance; *Shade* offers a sweeping depiction of the first half of the twentieth century while *Mistaken* offers the same for the latter and *Carnivalesque* casts Jordan's fictional eye even further back to a mythologised version of the Great Famine.

Of course, in practice, the Irelands of *Night in Tunisia*, *The Past*, *The Dream of a Beast*, *Sunrise with Sea Monster*, *Shade*, *Mistaken* and

Carnivalesque are all different countries and, as fiction, constitute a body of work in dogmatic conflict with itself. This is less a grappling for, or a lack of, coherent artistic vision on Jordan's part than it is a purposeful rejection of coherence or imposed continuity in an historical context. As he has written of his generation, the idea of a single imaginative nation was, in his opinion, a mistake.[10] In a piece published in Richard Kearney's *Across the Frontiers: Ireland in the 1990s* (1988), Jordan describes his belief that violent ideologies and the conceptualisation of history as a straight line to idealised destiny were fodder for a notion of home that could never truly exist.[11] Much of his artistic practice, especially in fiction, subscribes to this principle, to the idea that writers have a moral responsibility to challenge withered ideologies and, indeed, to experience exile even within their homeland.[12] Such is the exilic disaffection afflicting Donal Gore in *Sunrise with Sea Monster* and the labourer in 'Last Rites', as well as that of the narrators of *The Dream of a Beast*, 'Remote Control' (1993) and 'The Berkeley Complex' (2003). All are characters whose sense of home and identity – national, artistic and even biological – is in radical flux; all are figures who have become lost in what Jordan deems the *u-topos*, the place that cannot be, within us all.[13]

It would be too easy to regard Jordan's fiction as occupying a similar no-place on the map of Irish literary criticism. But, like the markers and structures of Nina Hardy's childhood in the latter timeframe of *Shade*, evidence of prior industry is apparent when one investigates the critical responses to Jordan's fiction. Evoking the ruined factory built by Nina's father, much of this is dated and unmaintained; it has become overgrown like the Dublin of the *Beast* and its hard edges are seen to have crumbled over time. Like Kevin Thunder's city in *Mistaken*, the Gothic nooks of criticism's dirty old town have been overlain by the shining modernity of a bright new metropolis populated by a generation that often does not even realise that Jordan writes novels. Yet, dig a little deeper and one can see where the current edifice which houses the film critic is built upon the foundations lain by the literary scholar and journalist. For instance, studies such as that of Kevin and Emer Rockett begin with an emphasis, albeit brief, on Jordan's background as a writer. Remove the façade of film scholarship entirely and many would be surprised to find that the early criticism of Jordan's work most often discusses him alongside Desmond

Hogan, Aidan Higgins and, particularly at the start of his career, John Banville. Nor is this work originating merely on the margins. Previous discussion of Jordan's writing has come from established literary critics as varied as John Wilson Foster, George O'Brien, Gerry Smyth and Roberta Gefter Wondrich.[14]

The first chapter of this volume therefore situates the key critical writing on the fiction against the larger context of the literary Jordan's life and reception, though it is worth noting here that the tailing-off of scholarly engagement since the 1980s has resulted in a present meagreness of critical material on Jordan's fiction. To offset this, close analysis is used throughout *Neil Jordan: Works for the Page* in order to generate the body of readings necessary for detailed discussion of the work. The multitude of extant interviews – both filmed and in print – from across the author's career have been considered as another important corpus of material. Thus, this book provides a substantive 'first reading' of Jordan's writing, as well as the media presence of Jordan *as* a writer. As such, *Neil Jordan: Works for the Page* is a volume that uses literary theory only lightly. For instance, the term 'postcolonial' is used in several places in this study (particularly with regard to *The Dream of a Beast*), but it serves primarily to position Jordan's work in terms of temporality: he writes from a modern, post-independence Ireland, and this inevitably informs his perspective on Irish history, drawing our attention to unexpected tendencies such as how the protagonists of *The Past*, *Sunrise with Sea Monster* and *Shade* are all descended largely from the ranks of the Protestant Ascendancy. Indeed, Jordan has said that quite a lot of beautiful objects in Ireland derive from British rule in the eighteenth century and that a greater part of national energy since independence has been devoted to tearing these down.[15] However, this is an aesthetic rather than a political statement, and one that is regularly confounded by the fiction. Jordan is interested in the ambiguities inherent in the moments of transformation which lie between idealised beauty and the magnificent imperfections of reality. While this is readily apparent in the fantasy elements of *The Dream of a Beast* – the protagonist of that novel undergoing a transformation into something at once monstrous and divine, even as the land seems quite literally to throw off its colonial bonds – it is also central to the plots of *The Past*, *Sunrise with Sea Monster* and *Shade*, arguably even *Mistaken*, where the fates of Jordan's characters are defined by the compromises they make in the independence struggle, the Emergency, the First World War and the Celtic Tiger era respectively. In each case, the 'Irishness' of the protagonists – be that a Protestant or Catholic, upper- or lower-class, imperial or postcolonial, interpretation of the term – is a crucial determinant of their actions.

In the case of *Night in Tunisia*, examined in Chapter 2, the three tent-pole stories of the collection are considered on just this basis of their protagonists' troubled relationships with their homeland. These stories, 'Last Rites', 'Night in Tunisia' itself and 'A Love', further serve as exemplars of Jordan's early fictional preoccupations with Irish politics and with the tension between social and pop-cultural influences from home and abroad. Chapter 3 carries this investigation further, interrogating the intersection of history, theatre and nostalgia in Jordan's first novel, *The Past*, and how it consciously acknowledges history as a narrative subject to the whims and aims of its authors, a series of stories to be told and retold across three generations of a nationalist family. Here, as throughout his writing, the novel form allows Jordan to indulge his protracted investigations of Irish history in all its nuanced, contradictory dispositions, in a manner often denied by the broad appeal necessitated by the highly commercialised nature of cinema.

Yet, as highly realistic as Jordan's first books are, the aforementioned strain of the fantastic soon creeps into his fiction. Growing steadily in importance throughout his career, this is typified by the transformative myth of *The Dream of a Beast*, the breakdown of objective reality in Ireland during the 'Emergency' in *Sunrise with Sea Monster*, as well as the time-travelling ghost story *Shade*. These novels are the subjects of Chapters 4, 5 and 6 of the present study. Chapter 4 considers *The Dream of a Beast* from the perspective of 'postcolonial biology', the modernisation of Irish society through the literal mutation of the protagonist and the changes occurring in both the urban and rural landscapes around him. Chapter 5 deals primarily with Jordan's questioning of Irish life as being insular – meaning both isolationist and island-based perspectives – during the Second World War as depicted in *Sunrise with Sea Monster*. It combines historical and geographical readings of the novel in order to demonstrate the value of both disciplines to Jordan's evolving conception of Ireland.

Carrying this analysis both forwards and backwards, Chapter 6 then considers the question of time and causation in *Shade*, a novel that combines the stylistic sensibilities of the Jordan who writes capital-L literature with the Jordan who is interested in genre and speculative approaches to questions of identity and politics.[16] That book contrasts a prelapsarian depiction of colonial Ireland with the drudgery and disappointments of life in the Free State, but the technique adopted by Jordan in *Shade* is no mere compare-and-contrast. Instead, the two eras are figured as an interplay of life and death. The story Jordan tells is an endless, Möbius strip style recurrence centred on an atemporal spirit, the titular shade, whose very presence, and the hint of uncanny violence that surrounds her, would seem inadvertently to engender the murder of her physical self before the cycle of disappointment, violence and death begins anew; as damning an indictment of post-independence Ireland as Jordan has yet produced.

Finally, Chapters 7 and 8 return to the disparity between Jordan the writer and Jordan the filmmaker. The structure of Chapter 7 echoes the earlier discussion of *Night in Tunisia* in that it is again focused on three short stories. In this instance, the three pieces are uncollected fictions which depict aspects of a world belonging to the other Jordan: stories of filmmakers and actors drawn from the breadth of Jordan's career. This blurring of lines between the two aspects of the artist also forms the central concern of Chapter 8. The discussion here centers on *Mistaken* and *Carnivalesque*. Unlike the singular focus of earlier chapters, Chapter 8 discusses a pair of novels on account of their thematic similarity and their relevance to our understanding of how Jordan sees himself as an artist. In *Mistaken* we meet Kevin Thunder, a Dublin architect and so a creative practitioner whose works, like those of a filmmaker, are visually impactful projects completed only by the co-operation of vast teams. Kevin is constantly confused with his double, Gerald Spain, a writer. It is no great stretch to thus identify *Mistaken* as Jordan's most autobiographical work to date. Nor is it difficult to draw a through line between it and *Carnivalesque*, wherein the adolescent Andy loses his way in a hall of mirrors only for a simulacrum to emerge and take his place. Andy, now Dany, is rescued by one of the fairy folk, themselves masquerading as carnival acrobats and roustabouts. He discovers a secret world of whimsy and wonder even as questions of what is real – is he the genuine article? is life as he understood it the full story? – are problematised in a manner of direct bearing on our study of Jordan's bifurcated career.

Taken together, these two novels provide the ideal end point for *Neil Jordan: Works for the Page* because they compel the reader to ask again the questions that motivated this study to begin with: are Jordan's fictions simply a funhouse reflection of his work for the cinema or are they an authentic and artistically credible secret history concealed in plain sight? What is the relationship between Jordan the writer and Jordan the director? To what extent does fiction allow Jordan the freedom to pursue the hidden Ireland, to dally with the disenfranchised political and social subcultures beneath a surface too often depicted as homogeneous and twee? As cinema scholar Ruth Barton reminds us, the challenge, particularly for local critics of Jordan's work, is to balance traditional, essential notions of Irish identity against the stereotypes which too often accompany the same, while simultaneously asking the question of what exactly is unique about being an Irish artist.[17] Jordan's fiction casts fresh light on this line of inquiry, as well as on his own interactions with Ireland and the Irish experience. It is unsurprising, therefore, that he claims to regard writing as the more self-reflective and more private of his creative affairs, being less about an examination of the world and more about an inquiry into his own mind and imagination.[18] As such, there is a dialogue between his books which allows them to tell stories collectively: the stories of individual characters struggling against the limitations of their lives, the story of Ireland in the twentieth century, and of course the story of Jordan himself, at first a young man weighed down by national history and symbol, later an established artist obsessed with image and description, and finally a mature novelist emboldened by the possibilities of genre.

Given Jordan's obvious and longstanding creative division, it is amusing to see how each time he publishes a new novel it is hailed as a 'return to form' when in fact it is a return to *the* form, a coming home to the artistic activity where he first began to develop a vision and a voice of his own.[19] For Jordan, writing continues to be 'an amazing experience ... like rediscovering an entire part of myself that I'd forgotten, the attention to words and what words can actually do'.[20] Yes, his films are his most obvious contribution to Irish culture, but it is the medium of fiction that most allows him to challenge the accepted consensus of Irish identity. The present study aims to put right the critical imbalance in this regard. It exists because there is a gap in contemporary Irish literary scholarship, because there is a prospect of building bridges between traditional fiction studies and Irish film criticism, and because there is a lost opportunity in the field of Irish Studies more generally to engage with a rich, imaginative and significant aspect of the work of one of our most important artists.

CHAPTER 1

A Writer who just happens to make Movies: Neil Jordan's literary life

THE CHILD THAT BOOKS MADE

Unlike the characters of Kevin Thunder and Gerald Spain in *Mistaken* (2011) – two identical boys from widely divergent socio-economic backgrounds – the literary Neil Jordan and the filmic Neil Jordan are undoubtedly the same person. They were brought up in the same home by the same parents, played with the same friends, were exposed to the same influences at the same time, and yet they blossomed as artists in two different fields and have enjoyed differing levels of recognition and productivity across the breadth of their careers. While in practice their stories are as dissimilar as those of Kevin and Gerry, the fact that the two Neil Jordans *are* the same person presents a challenge to the critics of both fiction and film. For instance, an extensive account of Jordan's early life and career is provided by Emer and Kevin Rockett in *Neil Jordan: Exploring boundaries* (2003), a study of his films up to and including *The Good Thief* (2002), but – along with volumes by other cinema scholars such as Carole Zucker's *The Cinema of Neil Jordan: Dark Carnival* (2008) and Maria Pramaggiore's excellent *Neil Jordan* (2008) – this is the biography of a film director, a kind of scholarship that necessarily differs in emphasis from that of a literary biography.[1]

Jordan himself has stated that there should not be any issue in pursuing two artistic paths.[2] Any effort to critically engage with his literary output and persona must therefore remain mindful of the ongoing necessity of reviewing the literary Jordan's place not only vis-à-vis the filmic Jordan, but against the context of the unified artist. Thus, the figure of Jordan the filmmaker remains present throughout this volume, albeit in a background capacity, an important supporting player in a story focused on another. The narrative presented here is not intended to replace existing accounts of Jordan's cinematic life but instead to balance them, to complement that work by integrating it with a substantial new study of interview material and Jordan's own non-fiction in order to provide what is, in essence, a writer's life. Though the following biographical and bibliographical account is offered as the basis for a work of literary criticism, and so is weighted to emphasise the literary aspect of Jordan's upbringing, early career and reception, it is also something that can be read alongside the existing, cinematically focused studies to provide some semblance of the complete Neil Jordan.

Born in Sligo in 1950 as the second of five children, Neil Patrick Jordan was initially brought up in Rosses Point, which he would later describe as then being almost the same as when Jack Yeats had painted the village but which, nowadays, seemed mostly to have been cannibalised by a golf course.[3] His father, Michael Jordan, was a teacher and school inspector with research interests in the field of children's literature. The family lived in Sligo until Jordan was five, before relocating to Dublin and taking a house opposite St Anne's Park on Mount Prospect Avenue in Clontarf when his father was appointed to a job educating trainee primary-school teachers at St Patrick's College in Drumcondra.[4] This move from one coast to another would have several noteworthy impacts on the writer and filmmaker's representations of Ireland. For one, it left him with an early fascination for the sea which, as John O'Mahony observed, continues to be an aspect of Jordan's art throughout his career.[5] Equally, the summers Jordan spent in east-coast holiday villages such as Howth, Portmarnock and Bettystown would eventually form the backdrop for much of *Night in Tunisia* (1976), including, most evocatively, the title story itself.[6] Jordan ties the seediness of these resorts to his early-teenage protagonists' growing awareness of sex and the sliding moral scale of the adult world. By contrast, the Irish west in Jordan's writing is more traditional. From his earliest short stories right up to *Carnivalesque* (2017), his fiction displays a compulsion to return to the west. It is a place people go to in order to regain their youth, a place of purity where families are reunited and miracles are possible. It is a prelapsarian space which colours everything from 'A Love' to *The Past* (1980) to *Sunrise with Sea Monster* (1994), and it is no stretch to associate this with the author's early separation from his childhood home.

Nonetheless, the relocation to Dublin brought an early literary connection for Jordan. His father Michael was novelist John McGahern's school inspector, and Jordan recalls the infamous controversy that followed McGahern's publication of *The Dark* (1965), though as the book was banned he was unable to read it at the time.[7] He was nonetheless struck by the unsavoury rumours which surrounded the teacher's work and the fact that McGahern did not return to work one day and the students were left to wonder why.[8] An explanation would have to wait until publication of *The Leavetaking* in 1974, which Jordan felt was the perfect encapsulation of the school atmosphere, right down to the smell of sour milk in the concrete yard.[9] In fact, McGahern would base the character of the school inspector in *The Leavetaking* on Jordan's father and, though Jordan himself would never fictionalise the incident, it represents an early illustration for him of the profound impact writing could have on society and individuals.[10]

Despite such lessons, Jordan admits to being a slow learner at school, though he acknowledged the irony of this to John O'Mahony given that his father was an educationist.[11] As a boy, he says he did not play many sports and claims to have had a dislike for football in particular.[12] Influenced by his mother, who was a painter, he gravitated instead towards artistic pursuits.[13] Like the protagonist of 'Night in Tunisia', the young Jordan played music (though in his case it was classical guitar), and though he says he could seem somewhat inhibited, he in fact used to be relatively social, preferring the company of women and girls, with whom he used to form quite deep attachments.[14] In this way the young Jordan, who claims his parents granted him remarkable freedom as a child, drifted through the 1960s.[15] For secondary school, he attended St Paul's College in Raheny but remembers largely being bored by the experience.[16] Yet, there was an imaginative benefit to the school's location on the grounds of St Anne's estate, which contained a crumbling Guinness family mansion.[17] Jordan found the house, if not the school, to have a magical quality, recalling its tunnels, overgrown statuary and mock-Grecian follies as a fantastical landscape which would influence not just the lush visuals of his films but also the idiosyncratic landscapes of prose work such as *The Dream of a Beast* (1983).[18]

Like the Dublin of that book, this magical place also provided a site of transition. He has stated in interviews that he became aware of his own childhood ending at the point when all his friends wanted to go play football, something Jordan believes they did in order to avoid entanglements with girls.[19] He further disconnected from his peers when, as they grew older, they began to substitute realistic concerns for more imaginative ones.[20] Meanwhile, the only things he claims he had interest in were reading and writing.[21] Already he was consuming vast quantities of adult books, and, though he has often mentioned a difficult relationship with his father, Michael Jordan used to encourage his children to read enormously.[22] The elder Jordan, at the time Neil was at the age of reading comics, was researching and writing a thesis on children's reading for a master's degree in Education.[23] This work involved analysing the syntax and speech of comics to gauge the effect they might have on children's literacy.[24] Between this project and his father's library, Jordan recalls that he grew up in a house that was filled with books. In a short piece of memoir for *The Guardian*, he recalled moving through Nicholas Monsarrat, Orwell, P.G. Wodehouse, Gogol and Mickey Spillane in turn.[25] He says he read books such as those by Sergeanne Golon which he did not understand at the time and regrets not being able to return to them with an adult's comprehension of the world.[26] Most intriguingly, he remembers encountering the works of George Bernard Shaw in collected editions, though, lacking an appreciation of theatrical playscripts at the time, read them as stark and descriptive works of novelistic fiction.[27] Shaw (who would later appear as a character in *Shade*, 2004) was a particular draw for the young Jordan because he believed that *Man and Superman* had something to do with the superhero stories published by DC Comics.[28] It was therefore ironic, as Jordan later observed, that his father was in his study with a wonderful selection of comic books to which his children were not allowed access.[29]

Michael Jordan, his son says, was an articulate and educated individual, but one who grew up within the narrow restrictions of an Irish society dominated by the Catholic Church.[30] He was an educationist who contributed to broadening the school curriculum in Ireland.[31] Despite this, Jordan told Marianne Brace that his father observed strict limits on how far he allowed his imagination to go.[32] He was a conservative man by nature and was later somewhat concerned that one of his children was publishing in the public eye.[33] Jordan says that when he began to write fiction it caused a certain amount of alarm for his father.[34] He told Brace that his writing engendered a tension between the pair as there were subjects that his father was unwilling to engage with.[35] Yet, Jordan has no difficulty speaking about a man he describes as brilliant, a student of mathematics who later went into education which, at the time, was dominated by the church (though Jordan suspects that his father also had some difficulty with how church control rendered entire areas of intellectual activity troublesome).[36] He recalls in *The Guardian* that his father held a variety of educational theories but that John McGahern claimed the younger Jordan lived his life as if in refutation of them all.[37] Though the elder Jordan kept diaries, his son has thus far refused to read them as they would, he says, make him feel queasy.[38]

None of which is to say that Jordan experienced a discontented home life when growing up. In fact, he would dedicate his first novel, *The Past*, to his mother and father. He frequently reminisces about his happy childhood in interviews,[39] though acknowledges that his adolescence was more turbulent.[40] At school he was reserved without necessarily being a loner, according to Jordan's former second-level English teacher, Father Joseph McCann.[41] It was around this time that the future writer began dabbling in stories, though he recognises now how difficult a path he had set for himself, seeing a novice writer's greatest challenge as committing to the idea of *being* a writer, admitting that vocation not just to editors or publishers but also to themselves.[42] In his *Guardian* essay, Jordan reflected on the need for creative practitioners at the beginning of their careers to learn how to trust the validity of their own experiences.[43] He gives the example of the bluebells in St Anne's or watching the sea from the Bull Wall and how, at the outset of his journey towards writing fiction, he found it difficult to believe that the private value they offered him would be of interest to anybody else.[44] This assessment, as it transpired, was both right and wrong. The young Jordan's first English compositions were, in McCann's opinion, largely conventional for a writer of that age.[45] Nonetheless, the teacher maintains that close assessment of these pieces usually offered interesting perspectives and, in his final year at St Paul's, Jordan won the school president's prize for a short story entitled 'Sunday'.[46]

As he grew older, Jordan took to roaming Dublin in mod gear and listening to bands such as The Yardbirds, Manfred Mann and, later, the likes of Jim Morrison and other performers on the intellectual and artistic fringes of popular culture.[47] The latitude extended to the teenager even encompassed trips abroad, with a bemused, sixty-year-old Jordan later recalling being in a pub in London in 1966 (before his Leaving Certificate) when England were playing Germany in the World Cup.[48] He had a summer job on a building site and had joined other Irish people to cheer on Germany in the final.[49] Looking back on it, Jordan had cause to wonder what on earth he was doing in London at the age of sixteen.[50] Though such independence also had more pedestrian consequences. It was around this time that he began to go to the cinema by himself and started to develop a legitimate obsession with movies.[51] Yet, the notion that he might one day become a director was still subservient to his literary ambitions because of a belief that filmmaking was not an Irish art form.[52] Instead, he believed at the time that Irish people were supposed to write books, get banned, and then have to leave the country in disgrace. (He recalls walking on Dollymount strand with a girlfriend and telling her that he wanted to be a writer, a disclosure that was received with disgust!)[53]

Completing secondary school, Jordan enrolled in University College Dublin, where he first studied English literature. There, he continued to compose stories, poetry and plays but says he lacked confidence in his work, suffering from pervasive feelings of shame or embarrassment when he contemplated the results of his writing.[54] He was similarly despondent over what he found to be the depressing academic approaches that he encountered during his study of English, maintaining in interviews that the coherent analysis of highly personal works of art was something he found very strange.[55] He has said that he found the process clinical and has likened it to the dissection of a piece of meat.[56] Consequently, he turned to medieval Irish history. The dearth of records there, he told *The Independent*, meant that he saw history as requiring certain elements of invention, that the discipline thus shared some characteristics with fiction, and so it is perhaps no coincidence that in his writing for both the page and the screen (for instance *The Past*, *Carnivalesque*, or even *Michael Collins*, 1996), Jordan repeatedly interrogates the questionable nature of histories fictionalised by memory, nostalgia or by the absence of objective accounts.[57]

At university, Jordan was regarded as a good-looking young man, says playwright and filmmaker Peter Sheridan, who thought his friend's sallow skin and long, dark hair were reminiscent of a youthful W.B. Yeats.[58] Nonetheless, Sheridan remembers Jordan as a shy and withdrawn individual, one who was less obviously outgoing than others in his peer group but who compensated with an air of mystery that drew people to him.[59] Jordan also struck up a productive friendship with Peter's brother Jim, later the Oscar-nominated writer and director of films such as *My Left Foot* (1989) and *In America* (2002).[60] Together, this trio partook in a variety of theatre and music projects, work that for Jordan consisted of scribbling down fragments or scenes and providing musical accompaniment, mainly on the saxophone.[61] The trio even travelled as far as the United States to put on plays by Samuel Beckett and Seán O'Casey for Irish-American audiences in Chicago. The experience was to have a lasting effect on Jordan which would colour both his books and his films for the rest of his career, and he would later write about the strange familiarity he felt towards the American landscape in contrast to how he thought of the Irish one.[62] Jordan found himself reflecting upon how deserts and skyscrapers, due to the proliferation of American popular culture, were better known to him than the green fields and medieval ruins of his own country.[63] In the process, he began to consider the exciting potential of how the Irish landscape could be made to resonate equally with the consumer of film, television and fiction.[64] Such a perspective continued to develop upon returning to Dublin with the Sheridans, where they often performed Yeats' plays in schools and in public parks. Jordan also completed a minor thesis on the lives of the saints, graduating to dubious employment prospects with a bachelor of arts degree in 1971.[65] He found that 1970s Ireland provided him with little to do except to read and write, though he did place a radio play, *Miracles and Miss Langan*, with RTÉ and the BBC in 1972.[66]

The poor economic situation necessitated that Jordan and his new wife Vivienne Shields, who he had met at UCD, decamp to England.[67] In London they lived in a squat and held a variety of casual jobs as they became available.⁶⁸ Jordan frequently took employment as a manual labourer while continuing to work on the short stories that would eventually comprise *Night in Tunisia*. Of these, one of the best known remains the vivid and eerily observed opening story, 'Last Rites', which depicts the bleak life and suicide of an Irish labourer in London. In fact, Jordan's expatriate experiences would go on to inspire the creation of many exilic characters in both his fiction and films. In addition to the labourer, strong examples are to be found in Neil from 'A Love', Fergus in *The Crying Game* (1992), Donal Gore in *Sunrise with Sea Monster*, Nina Hardy in *Shade* and Kevin Thunder in *Mistaken*. In the case of the labourer, the exile depicted is psychological as much as it is physical, a distancing effect of repressive Irish society amplified by the expatriate community he finds himself living in. Meanwhile, Donal Gore chooses exile, as do Neil, Nina Hardy and Kevin Thunder. In Kevin's case – and, to a lesser degree, Nina Hardy's – this decision is based on economic realities. Donal Gore is more interesting in that his choice to go and fight in the Spanish Civil War is a deliberate rebellion against the insular conflicts of his parents' generation. On a thematic level it is a means of escaping the civil war in his own household, true, but in terms of the character it is the act of an ungrateful youth determined to spite his father even at the cost of his own life.

Situating Jordan within the wider context of Irish fiction, Roberta Gefter Wondrich considers *Sunrise with Sea Monster* (alongside Desmond Hogan's *Farewell to Prague*) to be a contemporary myth of exile, a narrative of voluntary expatriation.⁶⁹ She hails the novel for how it attempts to reframe the typical Irish obsession with history, and for its efforts to critique the pieties of Irish society.⁷⁰ *Sunrise with Sea Monster* also typifies the defining aspect of exile in Jordan's writings: the return. Or, if one prefers, another instance of art imitating life, for Jordan and Shields only remained in London until 1974 when they came back to Ireland to attend the funeral of Shields' aunt, who was killed in the Dublin and Monaghan bombings perpetrated by loyalist paramilitaries.⁷¹ They decided to stay and, initially, Jordan spent time on the dole before Shields secured work in the legal sector and he took a job as a night-watchman.⁷² He claims that he wrote initially in the absence of anything else to do and that he soon began to use this work to support his family.⁷³

The first of this writing for which he was paid consisted of several episodes of the long-running RTÉ children's television series *Wanderly Wagon* (though he cautions against making too much of this), however his interests in the early 1970s remained primarily with theatre business.[74] Along with Des Hogan, David McKenna and Jim and Peter Sheridan, Jordan was involved with the agreeably chaotic Children's T Company and the SLOT (St Lawrence O'Toole) Players.[75] The intimate knowledge of the acting life which Jordan acquired at this time would, like his exilic experiences, percolate through much of his future writing, particularly *The Past* and *Shade*. In the former, Jordan connects theatre to the posturings and performance of politics in Free State Ireland during the 1920s and '30s. Una, that novel's grande dame, is a politically ambitious actress of little talent whose rise and fall in the nationalist movement fuels the earliest portions of the narrative. Rene, her daughter, later discovers a sublime talent for the theatre, and though she actively shirks the political associations of her mother, her life as an actress is destined – *pre*destined, the novel seems to imply – to intersect with that of the state's greatest actor, Éamon de Valera. *Shade* too owes much of its narrative drive to Jordan's early theatrical interests, with Shakespeare's *As You Like It* informing the love quadrangle of Nina, Gregory, George and Janie.

Theatre as it appears in both novels further speaks to Jordan's interest in the way real life is reflected by the stage and vice versa. An early example of this fascination can be found in *Journal of a Hole* (1971), one of the more notable productions of Jordan and the Sheridan Brothers. An original play written by Jordan and Jim Sheridan, and directed by Peter Sheridan, it portrayed the lives of students at the Artane industrial school, the 'hole' of the title.[76] The show was staged in the Project Arts Centre in Dublin (before later transferring to the Little Theatre at UCD) and followed a character named Robert Nolan from delinquent schoolboy to inmate of the infamous Christian Brothers institution, which was presented as a violent, sadistic prison.[77] *Journal of a Hole* featured scenes of graphic physical and emotional abuse.[78] At one point, Robert is punched in the nose by the head brother, who sends the boy away to clean himself up before punching him again because he has not cleaned off all the blood from the first assault.[79] In pursuit of what Peter Sheridan called an honest, socially engaged and immersive audience experience, and in a genuine effort to stimulate debate, the cast included an audience plant who stood up at the end to accuse the play's authors and performers of being biased against the Catholic Church.[80]

But Ireland in the 1970s was not yet ready for these truths. In particular, Michael Jordan claimed *Journal of a Hole* was repellent, something that led to a resurgence in the tension between father and son.[81] Speaking to the *Sunday Independent*, Jordan is nonetheless keen to contextualise such conflict as occurring during Ireland's emergence from long decades of censorship (the McGahern scandal, for example, had occurred only ten years before).[82] He says he was interested in explorations of interior sexual worlds and writing without barriers or constraints, whereas his father could not reconcile himself to the idea that his son was eschewing the respectability of employment or academia.[83] Michael Jordan, his son said, eventually changed his opinion after the publication of *Night in Tunisia* and, by the time of his death at sixty-four, had even expressed admiration for *The Company of Wolves* as it engaged with literary concerns drawn from fairy tales and myths.[84] Doubtless Michael Jordan was also more at ease with the classical material of *Oedipus Rex*, which his son and the Sheridan brothers also performed. The reviews, Jim Sheridan recalled, were less than spectacular, though he praised Jordan's performance as Tiresias which, rather than acting in the traditional sense, required Jordan merely to forcibly portray his own personality.[85] Whether anyone involved later appreciated the irony of an artist who would become known for his descriptive prose and highly visual filmic style starting out as a blind prophet is not recorded.

What was clear to everyone, however, was that Jordan was determined to pursue all avenues in bringing his work to an audience, even if he had to create these distribution channels from scratch. His most notable effort in this regard began in 1975,

> in the unlikely mise en scène of Captain America's on Grafton Street, [where] Jordan and a number of other ambitious writers and literary activists, including the late Steve McDonogh, Desmond Hogan and Fred Johnston, established the Irish Writers' Co-operative with a view to supporting and facilitating Irish writing and authors through a new style of co-operative publishing.[86]

The group, along with the likes of Dermot Bolger, Leland Bardwell, Lucille Redmond and Ronan Sheehan, envisioned the venture both as a way of supporting aspiring authors and a means to campaign against the Irish Censorship Board.[87] Jordan himself has said that he saw the co-operative – and, for that matter, writing itself – as an offensive in the culture wars against the patriarchal rigidity of Irish society in the 1970s and '80s.[88] The Writers' Co-operative went on to prove a valuable boost for new Irish writers at a time when British publishers showed little or no interest in their works. Interviewed in *The Guardian*, novelist Dermot Bolger discussed just how important the co-operative was, as well as the tough, uphill struggle which its members faced from the outset.[89] He recalled the very great difficulties of publishing at the time and how they sold only one copy of Jordan's first book in London, there not yet being a wider awareness of the vibrant new Ireland which was then emerging.[90]

For Jordan's part, writing was – in contrast to other activities – something that he felt that he was good at.[91] The sustained work ethic which would later become the hallmark of his career soon paid off and David Marcus eventually published one of his stories (called 'On Coming Home') on the New Irish Writing page of the *Irish Press*.[92] As Jordan told Michael Dwyer, he remembers visiting the *Irish Press* office where Marcus asked him to remove a rude word from the story, which Jordan did.[93] The author found Marcus to be a delightful individual, and was keen to acknowledge his importance to creative practitioners of the time (Marcus is later mentioned in *Mistaken* as an early supporter of Gerry's writing).[94] Jordan's successes would continue to build towards the end of the 1970s and he became one of many Irish authors 'poached' by London houses as interest in Ireland by the UK publishing industry strengthened again.[95] When *Night in Tunisia* was republished by the Readers' and Writers' Co-operative in the UK in 1979, it was joint winner of the *Guardian* Fiction Prize (along with Zimbabwean novelist Dambudzo Marechera for *The House of Hunger*), something which heavily contributed to Jordan's emerging profile as one of the leading young Irish writers of the period.[96] Later that year *Miracles and Miss Langan* was filmed by director Pat O'Connor as a television drama for RTÉ (O'Connor would later direct an adaptation of 'Night in Tunisia' for the station in 1983).[97] Already working on his first novel, *The Past*, Jordan also applied for and was awarded an

Arts Council Film Script Award in 1979 which eventually resulted in *Traveller*, a 1981 film directed by Joe Comerford.[98] Jordan further wrote four of the thirteen episodes of *Seán*, RTÉ's adaptation of Seán O'Casey's autobiographies, which aired in 1980.[99]

Writing for the screen, a more profitable undertaking, was thus occupying a larger part of Jordan's time as the 1970s came to an end. Yet, the filmic Jordan's most important break derived from the work of the literary Jordan, with the visual qualities of *Night in Tunisia* bringing him to the attention of film director John Boorman.[100] Boorman engaged Jordan first to collaborate on an unrealised script project (*Broken Dreams*, adapted from a French science fiction novel) and, subsequently, as a creative associate on the Arthurian epic *Excalibur* (1979).[101] In what has been called a private apprenticeship of an extraordinary kind, Boorman released £25,000 from the *Excalibur* budget for Jordan to undertake a documentary entitled *Excalibur: Myth into Film* about the making of the film.[102] It was an experience that gave Jordan the confidence – as well as the industry contacts (especially in terms of Boorman's role as a member of the Film Board) – to tackle a motion picture of his own with *Angel* in 1982.

Jordan's move from the writing desk to the director's chair was largely motivated by his frustrating experience with how Comerford had filmed *Traveller* (certainly if 'She: An Unfinished Story' is any indication). It was not the film he had originally written, Jordan said a few years later.[103] Though he has since stated that he is satisfied with his contribution to Comerford's film, his involvement with the project motivated a new determination to stay in control of his own work.[104] *Angel*, the initial treatment of which was completed within months of publication of *The Past*, was a first step on that road.[105] Thus, with two well-received books to his name and a burgeoning film career, the early, defining period of Jordan's writing career was complete. From this point on the literary and filmic Jordans would cross over when it suited them (such as the relationship between *Night in Tunisia* and Jordan's 1991 film *The Miracle*); however, like the two boys of *Mistaken*, they would lead largely separate lives. Indeed, those readers who discover Jordan's writings after knowing him only as a film director are often surprised by how small a role the cinema plays in his fiction. Only a handful of uncollected stories and the final sections of *Shade* discuss the process of filmmaking, and in the latter case they are portrayed more as an offshoot of the theatre than as a legitimate and independent art form.[106] Surprisingly, that novel's Nina Hardy is one of the most autobiographical of any of Jordan's characters prior to *Mistaken* or *Carnivalesque*, an early-century mirror of sorts to the author and to how he too is long haunted by another version of himself. What's more, in a book predicated on time and cycles it is impossible to overlook the most trivial of biographical coincidences: Nina dies in the year Jordan was born.

Not that the autobiographical content of Nina's make-up is unusual given how Jordan has displayed an interest in autobiographical protagonists throughout his fiction. He typically writes aspects of his life into his texts as a journey from containment to creative fulfilment. The boy in 'Night in Tunisia', Neil in 'A Love', the narrator of *The Past*, the diptych of Kevin and Gerry in *Mistaken*, and of course Nina Hardy, can all be read as at least partially autobiographical creations. In Nina's case, her cinema experiences are a cause of frustration. She compares the early film studios to glasshouses, and the fact that she is later murdered in a glasshouse makes clear just how damaging this career path was for her.[107] Despite the presence of her half-brother Gregory as her manager, Nina's life in cinema is largely unsatisfactory from an artistic point of view. Her rescue by George Bernard Shaw, who restores her to the stage, depicts filmmaking as a diversion from its more literary relative, the theatre. Jordan too understands the kind of distraction that comes from being dragged in two separate artistic directions. For instance, eleven years passed between *The Dream of a Beast* and *Sunrise with Sea Monster*, with Jordan himself acknowledging how time-consuming his filmmaking career has been and how novel writing requires a different, deeper form of concentration.[108] It is an observation on the author's part that acknowledges the necessity for a different creative process – a different creative persona – for each of his two art forms. Jordan has said that he writes scripts very quickly, occasionally over the course of a fortnight, but when he comes to prose he might only write a handful of sentences a day.[109] The latter work may take longer, it may be conducted in relative isolation (as opposed to the highly collaborative process of filmmaking) but in that lies its power to connect its readership with Neil Jordan in a more intimate fashion than even his most personal of films.

THE FICTION IN ITS CONTEXT

Writing, Jordan has claimed, is simultaneously a wonderful undertaking – largely because of the freedom that it affords the artist – and also among the most difficult work he knows of.[110] He has frequently expressed the belief that the act of creation, of producing something good when one sits down to write, is something that defies straightforward explanation.[111] He suggested to Gay Byrne that a writer's job is to ensure that these mysterious moments of inspiration are expressed in language that is as clear and as honest as possible.[112] While such hard work, enthusiasm and success has translated into critical acclaim for Jordan's career as a screenwriter and director for cinema, the effect is less immediately apparent in the reception of his fiction. His writing for the page requires a radically different critical approach, paradoxically a more conventional approach, than his writing for the screen. The characteristic concerns of his films – gender, race and the Northern Ireland Troubles, for instance – are largely absent from a prose more interested in recognisable tropes of Irish literary fiction such as disenchantment with post-revolutionary politics and society in Ireland, the so-called Big House, and the aforementioned recurrence of exilic motifs.[113] Those approaching the fiction with analytical purpose thus need to do so as literary scholars and not, accidentally or otherwise, as film critics. Yes, the literary and filmic Jordans are the same person; however, the thematic disparity between their work necessitates that extra care must be taken not to let impressions of one colour analysis of the other.

This is especially true given how the filmic Jordan's output and international profile can often threaten to overwhelm consideration of his literary counterpart. He has in the past remarked on how his name is as associated with filmmaking as that of Heinz is with baked beans, and, despite the seeming proliferation of low-budget filmmaking in Ireland during the Celtic Tiger era, it has been difficult for new Irish directors to challenge the prominence of the country's two established filmmakers: Jim Sheridan and Neil Jordan (though the likes of Lenny Abrahamson are more and more making their presence felt).[114] In the resulting situation there is, of course, an element of resistance to acknowledging the artist's dual identity, even an occasional reluctance on the part of film critics to share Jordan with the field of literary scholarship. Not even journalists are immune from this effect, and such imbalanced reception of Jordan's work was, for example, nowhere more apparent than at the Dublin launch of *Sunrise with Sea Monster* in January 1995. Though the event was attended by heavyweight literary figures such as Richard Kearney, John Banville, Ronan Sheehan and Seamus Heaney, the author nonetheless found himself upstaged by that supporting character never known for his chattiness, the filmic Neil Jordan.[115] He says that though journalists in attendance ought to have been asking him about the novel, most just wanted to talk about his *Michael Collins* film, and it is a media tendency that has never quite abated.[116] Almost fifteen years later, in a television interview with Gay Byrne, Jordan appeared eager to talk about fiction, making repeated reference to writing or to one who writes, though Byrne focused on filmmaking and mentioned writing only once.[117]

Despite this journalistic belief – that there is more to discuss in his films – also pervading in the academy, there does exist a body of scholarly responses to Jordan's writing.[118] Beyond the presentation of his fiction as an interesting origin story in volumes of film criticism (for instance how the Rocketts' *Neil Jordan: Exploring Boundaries* covers Jordan's early work in prose with brevity and exactness), his writing, in particular the early stories and *The Past*, is frequently mentioned in guides or introductory volumes to contemporary Irish fiction from a variety of theoretical approaches. Neil Murphy, for example, treats Jordan's writing in terms of the epistemological crisis in modern fiction in a chapter of his 2004 book *Irish Fiction and Postmodern Doubt*.[119] Concluding that study, Murphy makes the point that Jordan's work 'merits consideration beside that of Higgins and Banville because his work too, in both media, is occupied with the dilemma thrown up by developments in contemporary literature'.[120] Indeed, these figures (usually in list form) provide comparisons again and again for the literary Jordan, particularly for the manner in which their fiction reveals the tensions between tradition and modernity. It is a point echoed by Maurice Harmon, who classifies Jordan's writing – again alongside that of Banville and Higgins – as possessing a noticeable strain of modernism.[121]

Meanwhile, by applying approaches drawn from postcolonialism and feminism, American academic Lori Rogers has produced a comparative analysis of the work of Jordan and McGahern in her succinct 1998 monograph *Feminine Nation: Performance, Gender, and Resistance in the*

Works of John McGahern and Neil Jordan.[122] Though a perceptive study in its own right, the standout feature of Rogers' volume is less the critical framework and more her detailed and valuable discussion of Jordan, specifically *The Past* and *The Dream of a Beast*, within the wider context of Irish literature. A similar, though briefer, examination of Jordan's fiction is to be found in Christina Hunt Mahony's useful survey *Contemporary Irish Literature: Transforming tradition* (1999). Devoting several pages to Jordan, she describes how his fiction records the contemporary Irish cultural experience while simultaneously gesturing towards the genre's future.[123] While the form of Mahony's volume denies her the opportunity to focus on Jordan's writing with the depth found in Rogers, what is again noteworthy here is context, the manner in which Mahony unquestioningly places Jordan within a broad selection of living Irish writers. Given the constraints of space, she limits her focus to 'Night in Tunisia', along with more concise assessments of two more stories, 'Skin' and 'A Love', though it is enough to demonstrate how Jordan's themes and modes of expression fit comfortably alongside the nation's best post-war fiction.

Richard Kearney too, in a 1988 discussion of contemporary Irish literature, identifies Jordan as belonging to a counter-tradition of late twentieth-century Irish novelists.[124] He groups Jordan with the later Francis Stuart, Flann O'Brien and Banville as a writer who has taken up Joyce and Beckett's radical challenge, and who shares with them modernism's basic impulse to transform traditional quest-style narratives into a more self-critical and self-questioning form.[125] His observation is based mainly on *The Past*, though a similar interrogation of the self is immediately apparent in the protagonists of *Sunrise with Sea Monster*, *Shade*, *Mistaken* and *Carnivalesque*. Kearney's counter-tradition stems from what he calls the imaginative crisis instigated by Joyce and Beckett, and, while we will see how efforts to write 'around' these figures (Joyce in particular) have certainly influenced the shape of Jordan's fictions, they are not the sole explanation for the preoccupations of the novelist or his contemporaries. One cannot overlook the manner in which developments in society and politics during the period Jordan, Banville, Higgins and others emerged transformed public attitudes, and so if there was an imaginative crisis in the Ireland of the 1970s and '80s it was rooted in a search for new metaphors by which these developments might best be articulated in fiction. In Jordan's case, such transformations were expressed as mutations in *The Dream of a Beast* and, much later, as distortions within the sideshow funhouse of *Carnivalesque*, something which ought not to surprise us given how James Cahalan has written in his critical history of the Irish novel that Jordan's work 'inspects past realities through refracted mirrors'.[126]

As such, when portions of *The Past* first appeared under the Joycean title of 'Fragment from a Novel in Progress', published by Peter Fallon and Seán Golden as part of their *Soft Day* miscellany of contemporary Irish writing in 1980, the editors made the prescient decision – though it would take several decades to come to pass with work such as *Shade* and *Carnivalesque* – to place Jordan among those young prose writers most likely to transcend the then recognisable tropes of Irish fiction.[127] Alongside Dermot Healy and John Banville, Fallon and Golden hailed Jordan as an innovative author of unselfconsciously Irish writing which seemed to portend renewed openness and verve for the field, an assessment which was at the time based mainly on the contents of *Night in Tunisia*.[128] The irony, of course, is that as Jordan's oeuvre developed, he began to explore more traditionally Irish material; it would be difficult to describe *The Past*, *Sunrise with Sea Monster* or *Mistaken* as anything but self-consciously Irish. In fact, though it may not have been apparent in his early years, any critic approaching Jordan's fiction now must acknowledge that the majority of the work is resolutely traditional in terms of subject material (take *The Past* or *Sunrise with Sea Monster*, for example). The author largely confines experimentation to the thematic level (*Night in Tunisia*'s break with established depictions of Irish identity, say, or *The Dream of a Beast*'s slow transition from realism to phantasmagoria). Arguably, it is not until three and a half decades after Fallon and Golden's assessment that *Carnivalesque* – with its fantastical narrative cloaking repeated gestures towards the science-fictional – sees Jordan come closest to shedding the trappings of mainstream Irish writing. But even that novel's emphasis on historical events such as the Great Famine, on the impact of repeated economic downturns, and on a recognisable idealisation of the west of Ireland grant the material an undeniable familiarity.

Meanwhile, on a structural level, Jordan's most successful attempt at actualising experimental notions occurs in *Shade*, where the surface narrative of hauntings and murder suggests a subtle circular story in which the atemporal presence of Nina's ghost is at least partially responsible for driving George to murder her in the first place. As repeated emphasis on this novel may have already suggested, *Shade* is an important work for Jordan. The novel's sundering of Nina's soul (destined to repeat the events of the novel) from her physical body (washed into the river at the story's conclusion) opens the door for the more jarring conceit of *Mistaken*: two physical selves who share the same soul. 'I was his lost soul ... and ultimately, his ghost', as the cover of the first edition proclaims. Yet, *Shade* and *Mistaken*, along with the thematically related *Carnivalesque*, have yet received little in the way of critical engagement beyond newspaper reviews and author interviews. A shame, for these novels are arguably his most accomplished to date. *Shade* and *Mistaken* in particular also wear two of the literary Jordan's strongest influences proudly, with *Shade* circling around a Yeatsian amalgam of a Protestant Big House, supernatural goings-on and civil strife, while the Dublin wanderings of *Mistaken* draw on both a Ulyssian portrayal of the city – in terms of narrative, if not formal expression – and Jordan's own memories of feeling the streetscape of *Dubliners* induce a kind of creative claustrophobia during his youthful meandering around the city.[129]

Nonetheless, the novelist admits that the Irish literature he read as a student moved him in profound fashion.[130] He began to seriously engage with Yeats and Joyce in secondary school and made immediate connections to both the landscape he himself knew well from Rosses Point and Dollymount strand.[131] He has confessed in interviews to a profound sense of inadequacy when reflecting upon how Yeats and Joyce generated so much internal drama from the everyday comings and goings of their lives, but also how so much of what they described remained recognisable to him. In particular, he remarks that Dublin seemed to have changed little since *Dubliners* or *A Portrait of the Artist*; as he recalled to Gay Byrne, it was a place where everyone was Catholic except for the few people one did not meet who were Protestant, as well as a handful of people who were Jewish.[132] This constant presence led to a dilemma noted by several critics and acknowledged by Jordan himself: the difficulty of writing about contemporary Irish urban life in the creative shadow of Joyce's language and mythology.[133] The young writer's solution involved embracing popular culture and developing an interest in jazz, a non-native musical form evoking sexual and imaginative freedom, to great effect throughout his early work.[134] His use of the saxophone over, say, the fiddle is of a piece with, as Heather Ingman puts it, the openness to cosmopolitan outside influences characteristic of the Irish generation that came of age during the 1970s.[135] Yet, for all of that, the major inspirations for Jordan remained the overwhelming influences of Joyce and Yeats.[136]

Pramaggiore, for her part, sees in Jordan's work a resemblance to that of James Joyce and Samuel Beckett despite Jordan's rejection of European exile for a return to Ireland.[137] That said, their influence on Jordan is most apparent in the work he partially completed during his own period of exile, the stories of *Night in Tunisia*. Comprising Jordan's own take on the paralysis afflicting Irish characters, the stories are, in Derek Hand's view, potentially the best realised vision of Irish short fiction since Joyce published *Dubliners*.[138] Meanwhile, Ingman sees specific evidence of Joyce's influence in the story 'Skin', a reimagining of the Gertie material from *Ulysses*, this time from the perspective of a sexually curious middle-aged woman.[139] Moving into the later work, Gefter Wondrich, writing in the *Irish University Review*, interprets *Sunrise with Sea Monster* as an intentional tribute on Jordan's part to how Joyce utilised the coastal regions around Dublin in liminal fashion.[140] Should one wish, it is also possible to read a tip of the hat to the cyclical, endless structure of *Finnegans Wake* in *Shade*'s implied lack of a true beginning or genuine end (and not inappropriately so, for it is a novel filled with expressions of recognition and gratitude towards the author's literary predecessors).

Jordan's most effective rebuttal to what he has acknowledged as the all-encompassing influence of Joyce would not arrive until *Mistaken*.[141] Emphasising the geography of Dublin via careful incorporation of place names, distances and literary reference, that novel acknowledges Joyce's technique while responding directly with a very different take on the national and fictional capital. *Mistaken* takes the search for an imaginative identity in Joyce's city as one of its central concerns. Which should not surprise readers as Jordan is in fact one of a number of post-war Irish authors, among them John Banville, 'partly John McGahern', Patrick McCabe and Desmond Hogan, whose writing, by 'privileging themes such as the relationship between fiction and history', attempts to assimilate 'a wide range of Joycean references in terms of interrelated themes, motifs and imagery'.[142] In the case of *Mistaken*, Jordan extrapolates multidimensionally from these motifs. He offers the reader a Dublin which is not simply Joyce's city but a city of literature full stop (and it is perhaps no coincidence that, in the year prior to *Mistaken*'s publication, Dublin did in fact hold the title of 'UNESCO City of Literature'). Hence, the vampire figure that haunts Kevin Thunder's imagination, though ostensibly rooted in the fact that the character grows up near Bram Stoker's house, is in essence not just Stoker's Dracula (though his presence serves the atmosphere of the novel) or even Joyce's Leopold Bloom (whose shadow is impossible not to see in the protagonist's wanderings): it is the entire heritage of literary fiction in the city given form. The extent to which it threatens to suck the imaginative lifeblood from any young creative types lies at the root of the novel's anxieties.

Which might be the reason Jordan maintains that poetry, in many respects, has been more important to him than prose.[143] In particular, the writings of W.B. Yeats represent an influence and source of inspiration which has received less attention than that of Joyce. Jordan has been engaged with Yeats' work since he performed in a version of *The Cat and the Moon* on Dollymount strand with the Sheridan brothers in the early 1970s.[144] In a 2004 lecture delivered at the National Library as part of a celebration of the poet's work, Jordan mused aloud as to the degree to which his own imagination had been formed by Yeats.[145] He determined that it had, though it was difficult for him to define exactly how.[146] Though he was keen to emphasise the manner in which Yeats – arguably the definition of a literary stereotype – also repudiated the cliché image of genius.[147] In particular, Jordan found that the poet's lack of academic proficiency, such as the misspellings in his diaries and journals, made him far more accessible as an individual and as a writer.[148] Zucker emphasises a further link between Jordan and the poet: both their childhoods were influenced by the quasi-mythical west of Ireland landscapes, particularly those of a near-fabulised Sligo.[149] Certainly, the accompanying romanticisation is of a piece with how Jordan's narratives tend to look always towards the mythopoetic west, a return to which (in 'A Love', *The Past*, *Sunrise with Sea Monster* and *Carnivalesque*) is often necessary before his characters can find peace.

Evidence for Jordan's love of Yeats, especially the later Yeats, is apparent everywhere in the fiction. It occurs thematically – his emphasis on the Protestant contribution to the Irish state, say, as well as through more direct reference. It will not be lost on readers that the demise of Una in *The Past* alludes directly to 'Sailing to Byzantium',[150] while the novel's opening quotation, 'Eternity is passion', is lifted from the poet's 'Supernatural Songs'.[151] Such reference continues throughout later work, with Jordan's 1999 film *In Dreams* borrowing its title from the epigraph to Yeats' 1914 volume *Responsibilities* ('In dreams begins responsibility'[152]) while another quotation, this time from 'In Memory of Eva Gore-Booth and Con Markiewicz', provides Jordan with the epigraph of *Shade*, where 'dear shadows, now you know it all' allows him to establish the omniscience of the novel's dead narrator.[153] Meanwhile, the release of the animals from the Bray circus at the end of Jordan's film *The Miracle* is both a real and a metaphoric reference to the poem 'The Circus Animals' Desertion',[154] with Jordan's own creative difficulties (which led him home from Hollywood at the end of the 1980s) lensed through Yeats' similar inspirational concerns.[155] When quoting from the body of Yeats' work, however, Jordan is at pains to stress the deliberate thematic relationship with the works in question. For example, 'Whence Had They Come?', the relevant section of 'Supernatural Songs', bears a direct correlation to the sexual, dramatic and generative concerns, even the plot, of *The Past*, the novel it precedes:

> Eternity is passion, girl or boy
> Cry at the onset of their sexual joy
> 'For ever and for ever'; then awake
> Ignorant what Dramatis Personae spake;
> A passion-driven exultant man sings out
> Sentences that he has never thought;
> The Flagellant lashes those submissive loins
> Ignorant what that dramatist enjoins,
> What master made the lash. Whence had they come,
> The hand and lash that beat down frigid Rome?
> What sacred drama through her body heaved
> When world-transforming Charlemagne was conceived?[156]

The Christian character of 'Supernatural Songs' may seem an unusual preface to a book where the only real Christian representative, Father Beausang, is, as we shall see, a Euclidian and delinquent student of both philosophy and mischief, and hardly the typical fictional representation of a clergyman. But, then again, Jordan's relationship with religion in general and Christianity specifically has always tended towards the contradictory.

Jordan claims to have been very religious in his early years, though he says the experience left him without significant scars and, in the end, mostly evaporated.[157] He even told Marianne Brace that as a child he considered becoming a priest but that his mother, in her wisdom, refused to allow it.[158] Describing the religiously restrictive nature of Ireland in the 1950s and '60s, he is keen to emphasise the sense of the ridiculous which accompanied it, citing the propensity of Irish people to believe that the wooden statues they pray to are capable of talking back to them.[159] Since then he has acquired an aversion to religion and instead claims to be more like the classical Romans in his beliefs, seeing ghosts in everything but one single God in nothing.[160] He has further stated that a dislike of absolutes has led to a dislike of the Catholic Church.[161] In conversation with Byrne he said that he did not believe in the notion of going to Hell because one has transgressed a church rule and that, should his soul be lost, it will be because of some action he has taken by and for himself.[162] In Jordan's eyes, God is a creation of the human imagination, indeed he believes the concept to be one of the greatest works of human creativity, rivalling physical descriptions of existence such as Einstein's general theory of relativity.[163] This scepticism translates readily into the work of both the literary and the filmic Jordan: think *Shade*'s shirking from doctrinal Catholicism's afterlife or the haunting of *Sunrise with Sea Monster*. Equally, consider the supernatural implications of films like *The Company of Wolves*, *High Spirits*, *Interview with the Vampire* or *Byzantium*.

These depictions are clearly rooted in the manner whereby, as Jordan says, Catholicism in Ireland has more to do with magic than with religion.[164] He has said that he views it as a set of superstitions which one learns during childhood, the practice of which is easy to abandon as an adult even if the ingrained sensibility remains.[165] In his writings, this imprinted superstition manifests as a series of permeable barriers between this life and the next, but also as a discernible non-linearity, a cyclical conception of time and existence which is, as mentioned, at times almost Yeatsian in its rejection of progress as it is typically imagined by Christianity. Often, Jordan's fiction is at its best when, as in *Carnivalesque*, it embraces the 'magical' element of Irish belief as a means of subverting the certainties of top-down religious doctrine; or when it shines a light on what the society of his characters teaches to be the limits of ethics, sexuality, or the nationalist conception of an Irish state so closely tied to Catholic thought. The title of Jordan's story 'Last Rites' is a case in point: the ceremony enacted by the protagonist is a preparation for a death which he feels is necessary only because of the sexual repression of his Catholic upbringing. Equally, the funeral scene of *Shade* is very literally an empty ritual, there being no body to bury and a sexual assignation going on upstairs (*Shade*, 311–12). And yet, in spite of the scorn afforded to rite and ritual, Jordan's portrayal of Catholicism's more spiritual aspects in his fiction can often be surprisingly sympathetic, with *The Past*, *Sunrise with Sea Monster* and *Shade* all featuring characters who have converted from Protestantism and found some measure of meaning in the process.

Such protagonists are frequently the scions of Anglo-Irish dynasties. 'A Love', *The Past*, *Sunrise with Sea Monster* and *Shade* all feature Protestant families, characters who have converted from Protestantism, or the vestigial remnants of the Ascendancy. Examples include the Vance family of *The Past*, the heirs of Baltray House in *Shade*, and the Gore family in *Sunrise with Sea Monster* reduced to living in a house that belies their background.[166] Again, something that Yeats would certainly have approved of, the emphasis on the continued existence of Protestants in Free State Ireland and beyond is a crucial aspect of Jordan's fiction. The present, his novels imply, comprises elements of the past – quite literally, in the novel of that name – and so his Protestant characters serve as an important acknowledgement of the contribution made by the minority, and as a further repudiation of restrictive nationalist narratives. Consider the employment and modernisation provided by the delft factory owned by the Vance family or the seafood plant operated by Nina Hardy's father. Furthermore, the fiction openly acknowledges the fate that befell this minority during the independence struggle, with the balance of the region's Big Houses being burnt by republicans during the War of Independence (*Shade*, 269).[167]

Beyond the dominant presence and characteristic concerns of Joyce and Yeats, however, there is one further influence on Jordan which opens up rich comparative possibilities for critics: that of John McGahern. Rogers, in her comparative monograph, sees McGahern and Jordan as having a similar claim to the themes of shedding institutional Irishness, and this in spite of a critical ecosystem which at least in the past tended to position McGahern as an established elder of Anglo-Irish literature and Jordan as a scrappy novice.[168] Her appraisal illustrates not just the similarities between Jordan and McGahern but, in case we become too comfortable with the comparison, also the potent generation gap between the two. The contrast between Jordan and McGahern, says Fintan O'Toole, is suggestive of exactly the kind of social transformation that the younger writer and his work came to embody.[169] McGahern was after all sacked from his teaching job by the Catholic Church after the banning of his novel *The Dark* (1964) and his registry office marriage to a foreign, Protestant, divorcee.[170] Yet, just over a decade later, Jordan was being celebrated for publishing a sexually frank collection of stories which depicted how Irish culture's edifice of nationalism and Catholicism had begun to crack apart.[171] Linking the two demonstrates the radical changes that occurred in Irish society between the 1960s and '70s and, though it would be unwise to force any sense of baton-passing, it is clear from reading the fiction that the literary Jordan often draws on McGahern both thematically and, on occasion, via direct allusion.

For example, work on Jordan from a Film Studies perspective often cites his review of *Wheels* (1976), the short-film adaptation of McGahern's story by director Cathal Black, as an early example of the future director's engagement with the mechanics of the medium. Of more relevance here, however, is Jordan's *Irish Times* review of McGahern's short-story collection *Getting Through* (1978). Titled 'A Rural Irony', the review is a short, deft piece of criticism in which Jordan focuses on what might be read as his own greatest debts to McGahern: the tension between the necessity of love and the impossibility of perfection in the same, the drama of triangular relationships and affairs (in stories such as 'Sierra Leone'), and the gulfs across which even the shared experiences of family members, friends or romantic partners cannot reach.[172] Indeed, David Malcolm sees in McGahern's 'The Beginning of an Idea', the opening story of *Getting*

Through, a strain of ambitious cosmopolitanism which reverberates through the work of younger Irish short-fiction writers such as Jordan, Hugo Hamilton and Mary Dorcey.[173] John Wilson Foster further sees in 'Night in Tunisia', which he selected for the *Field Day Anthology of Irish Writing*, an 'equation between the end of a son's boyhood and a father's way of life' which echoes that of McGahern's 'Korea'.[174]

More broadly speaking, Jordan's 'Last Rites' can be read as an evolution of McGahern's thoughtful (and first-hand) understanding of mass emigration's traumatic impact on Irish society, along with his sympathetic depictions of those emigrants in stories such as 'Hearts of Oak and Bellies of Brass' or 'Faith, Hope and Charity'.[175] As developed by Jordan, this becomes a focused study of despair and acute loneliness. The success of 'Last Rites', in Ingman's view, therefore derives from Jordan's precise depiction of the labourer's interiority.[176] For her, 'Last Rites' is simultaneously an Irish fiction and a work from which notions of Irishness have been peeled away, with the labourer's recollections of home transmuted into broader, more universal longings. (Ingman notes too how Jordan's inclusion of African immigrants anticipates an opening up of Irish fiction to other cultures in the 1990s.)[177] Like McGahern's London Irish, the labourer is trapped between worlds, a limbo space physically delineated by the shower cubicle in which most of the story takes place but metaphorically encompassing the character's national and sexual ambiguities.[178] Further echoes of McGahern, specifically his great novel *Amongst Women* (1990) and, for that matter, his short story 'Wheels', are clearly visible in Jordan's *Sunrise with Sea Monster* where a widowed war of independence veteran takes a younger, second wife named Rose. As with *Amongst Women*, much of *Sunrise with Sea Monster* is told through flashbacks and considers themes of nationhood and isolation, while, as in 'Wheels', Jordan's novel explores the manner in which father and son swap roles as time moves on, with sons becoming carers to their parents and fathers in old age becoming like children once again.[179] The same kind of familial disloyalty which Eamon Maher identifies in the McGahern story is also apparent in 'A Love'.[180]

Jordan's debt to his literary predecessors will therefore be readily apparent to those familiar with McGahern, Yeats and Joyce. It is visible in the exilic experiences or predilections of Jordan's protagonists

('Last Rites', 'A Love', *Sunrise with Sea Monster*, *Mistaken*), triangular relationships ('A Love', *The Past, Sunrise, Shade, Mistaken*), the dynamics between fathers and sons ('Night in Tunisia', 'A Love', *The Past, Sunrise*), Dublin (*The Dream of a Beast, Mistaken, Carnivalesque*), and the legacy of Protestantism or the Anglo-Irish (*The Past, Sunrise, Shade*). Having absorbed these influences, Jordan deploys them against a backdrop of his own construction, claiming that an escape into an alternate landscape lies at the root of all his fiction, and that this is a deliberate effort to map times or spaces beyond the traditional concerns of Irish writing.[181] The most obvious of these loci include the grim east-coast seaside holiday towns of *Night in Tunisia* or the Bray of *The Past* and *Sunrise with Sea Monster*, the urban fantasyland of *The Dream of a Beast* and its realistic counterpart in *Mistaken*, the Boyne marshlands and the First World War battlefields of *Shade*, or the fairgrounds and hidden cultures of *Carnivalesque*. Together, these form a country of the imagination constructed from many repeated elements which Jordan returns to again and again throughout his fiction, elements that, as he has said, derive from the influences of Irish literature, folklore and theatrical tradition.[182]

It is an admission true of not just his fiction but also his films. For Jordan has drawn on Irish literature, history and superstitions for pictures as varied as *Angel* (1982), *High Spirits*, *The Crying Game*, his Patrick McCabe adaptations *The Butcher Boy* (1997) and *Breakfast on Pluto* (2005), his version of Beckett's *Not I* (2000), and his modern take on a Selkie story, *Ondine* (2009). *The Miracle* is closely related to the stories from *Night in Tunisia*, while *Sunrise with Sea Monster* exists as a kind of temporally offset companion piece to the movie Jordan was making at the time, *Michael Collins*, and is frequently discussed in Jordan's *Michael Collins Film Diary* (1996). Expand again beyond the local frame of reference and Jordan remains the most literary of filmmakers. *Interview with the Vampire* (1994) and *The End of the Affair* (1999) are both based on novels (by Anne Rice and Graham Greene respectively) while *The Company of Wolves* (1984) is based on the stories of Angela Carter's collection *The Bloody Chamber* (1979). He has written the vast majority of his feature-length films as well as twenty out of twenty-nine episodes of *The Borgias* (2011–13), a television series he created for US cable network Showtime. There is thus considerable truth in the assessment of the then *Irish Times* literary correspondent Eileen Battersby that Jordan is, at his core, a gifted writer who just so happens to also make films.[183] Or, as Jordan himself states, he began as a novelist and it has remained a crucial aspect of his existence as an artist throughout his career, so it is a curious experience when people tell him that they never knew that he writes books.[184]

In 2009, Jordan was asked how he would like to be remembered. He responded, simply, that he would like to be thought of for what he does.[185] What he does is make movies *and* write fiction, and though clearly very much a part of the filmmaking scene, Jordan has succeeded in also remaining part of the literary community in Ireland, a world of poetry and cigarettes and manuscripts in various states of disarray about which he has written very fondly.[186] For O'Toole, Neil Jordan's work represents more than just a single individual's creativity and ambition, but rather a momentous realignment of the national culture.[187] O'Toole frames Jordan's evolution from author of literary fiction to director of motion pictures as symbolising a much more dramatic transformation in the way Ireland sees itself.[188] It is an astute observation, yes, but one must also acknowledge that, like the protagonist of *The Dream of a Beast*, Jordan's new form retains more than a little of his prior incarnation. He continues to publish novels, win awards for his fiction and, arguably, is producing the best writing of his career with books such as *Shade*, *Mistaken* and *Carnivalesque*, all alongside the rigours of an ongoing directorial career. For, like the characters in his best short fiction, Jordan has been changed: changed by experience, like the labourer in 'Last Rites'; by contact with mentors, like the boy in 'Night in Tunisia'; and by maturity, like Neil in 'A Love'. It therefore seems appropriate to begin the discussion of Neil Jordan's writing with his first published book, the story collection *Night in Tunisia*.

CHAPTER 2

The Ending of the Day brings Release: *Night in Tunisia*

It seems to amuse Neil Jordan that people consider sex and violence to be his primary themes.[1] He has said in interviews that he considers sex and violence – how people live, love and eventually die – to be *everybody's* themes.[2] His generalisation, while accurate, disguises the full scope of his own fiction's engagement with specifically Irish themes of identity and tradition. Indeed, the stories of *Night in Tunisia*, his 1976 debut volume, unearth a tightly bound psychic and emotional structure which revels in sex and violence, yes, but sex and violence inseparable from questions of Irish history, identity and the transformation of Irish society in the 1970s.[3] The collection draws heavily on its author's memories of holidaying in the shabby seaside resorts surrounding a post-war Dublin that was fundamentally Catholic and sexually troubled. He has said that when he composed those stories he imagined that he was writing about somebody else, though, of course, looking back on them today he is forced to concede that they are indeed highly autobiographical.[4] Throughout the collection, the fresh-faced author places an emphasis on young people, teenagers in particular, a demographic that, with the exception of some work by Frank O'Connor, was not a serious focus of Irish short fiction prior to the 1970s but which, alongside Jordan's work, is explored from this point onwards by writers like Julia O'Faolain, Desmond Hogan and Kate Cruise O'Brien.[5] Quite clearly drawing on his own experiences, *Night in Tunisia* explores a life familiar to Jordan.[6] He tackles the building sites of London and the music halls of small-town Ireland in turn – places well known to him – before, in the concluding story, blurring the line between author and character entirely by giving the reader a narrator named 'Neil'. Jordan now admits that this closing piece, 'A Love', is a naked text and one in which he did not try to conceal anything.[7] His father, of course, considered the material quite shocking, says Jordan, though evidently changed his mind when it was well reviewed by *The Irish Times*.[8]

In fact that newspaper reviewed the collection twice: first in a piece by Adrian Vale in 1977 (where Jordan's promise and talent was heavily praised)[9] and then in a short article by Kate Cruise O'Brien upon the volume's re-issue in 1979 (with O'Brien seeing the stories as exemplars of short fiction's formal strengths).[10] These followed the broadsheet's glowing profile of Jordan by Caroline Walsh in December 1976, which again stressed the richness and the value of the collection.[11] Other critics were equally impressed. Literary tastemaker Gerald Dawe, writing in 1980, saw *Night in Tunisia* as the work of an author disinterested in conventional depictions of Irish experience, one who instead pursues modern approaches to the concept of Irishness with a paucity of recycled or recognisable images.[12] Moreover, Dawe praised Jordan's efforts to understand the contemporaneous Irish experience by differentiating between the traditional literary inheritance and what is subjectively important – and, for that matter, *not* important – to the collection's characters (Dawe singles out the final story, 'A Love', for particular approval in this regard).[13] The protagonists of *Night in Tunisia*, Dawe maintained, perceive the grandiloquence of the past through the prism of the present which, though it seems concrete, in fact remains largely improvised.[14] Their experiences are rooted in the everyday but looming behind them is a set of semi-mythical nations: the heroic Ireland, the religious Ireland, the creative Ireland, and so on; historical and social constructions which weigh upon the characters as much as the country's literary heritage weighed on their young creator.

When he first began writing, Jordan says, he was troubled as to how he ought to confront these notions of Irishness in his work.[15] It is, he claims, only once a novice writer begins to shed such paralysingly self-conscious questions of identity that they are in a position to see the specifically Irish traits of their imagination.[16] The stories of *Night in Tunisia* are a case in point. The collection's characters, the author has claimed, are all trying to escape from their established personas via seduction, suicide or simply walking into the sea.[17] These actions, he says, are a means of redefining who the protagonists are by breaking down the barriers separating who they are from who they want to be.[18] Yet, in taking flight like this, the movements of his characters delineate the boundaries of the very anxieties that they, and the young writer, seek to avoid. The narratives of *Night in Tunisia* consequently draw attention to a thematic negative space wherein sex finds its counterpoint in death, and doubt seeks out belief. In attempting to elude the established tropes of Irish short fiction by foregrounding elements such as jazz music and young people, the collection finds itself returning again and again to prototypical concerns such as the regenerative properties of the west, the conflict between fathers and sons, and paralysis of both the personal and national variety. Thus, while *Night in Tunisia* is a collection rightly celebrated for its freshness and energy, it would be a mistake to separate it entirely from the wider context of Irish literature, a valuable scaffolding which adds strength to the collection's interrogation of modern nationalist mythology, gender politics and acute cultural change.

In his foreword to the volume, Seán O'Faoláin framed *Night in Tunisia* as the work of a gifted writer with a talent for rendering feelings and responsiveness in striking images and words, and, in light of the emergence of the directorial Jordan, it is nowadays tempting to see the book's obsession with visual description as cinematic in nature.[19] His prose, though quite different from the films he would go on to direct, relies on similarly lush visual qualities. It is therefore unsurprising to learn how *Night in Tunisia* helped to launch Jordan's filmmaking career by bringing him to the attention of director John Boorman in 1979.[20] Certainly, the stories of *Night in Tunisia* share Boorman's interest in repressed sexualities, and in the secret and personal mechanics of desire. The title story, for instance, considers themes of sexual longing and identity, intergenerational conflict and intercultural difference, in a manner reminiscent of Boorman's own work. Moreover, Boorman, like Jordan, is a screenwriter with a keen sense of place and its connection to character, and the landscapes that predominate in *Night in Tunisia* – the shabby east-coast holiday resorts, the bareness of the Burren, the Victorian bathhouses of London – all sharply mirror the sensitivities and alienation of the volume's protagonists in a manner reminiscent of Boorman pictures such as *Deliverance* (1972) and *Excalibur* (1981).[21]

Combined with the quality of his meticulous prose, these aspects of Jordan's work would also catch the attention of critics. *Night in Tunisia* was awarded the 1979 *Guardian* Fiction Prize, an award with a certain abstruse prestige when compared to better-known accolades such as the Booker.[22] This prize entitled Jordan, according to the wry 'Irishman's Diary' in *The Irish Times*, to five hundred pounds in cash, afternoon tea in the Waldorf Astoria hotel and a brief intelligent feting among the literati of London.[23] Joking aside, reviews of the book at the time tended to focus on individual stories and to an extent this is understandable when one imagines the arresting effect of reading 'Sand' or 'Skin' for the first time. Yet, with the benefit of time one can appreciate the careful structure of the collection as a whole. *Night in Tunisia* is a volume that lends itself to a division into two thematic halves. The first five stories, 'Last Rites' through 'Night in Tunisia', deal overtly with physical and emotional loss, while the second group, 'Skin' through 'A Love', consider loss more in terms of spoiled dreams and vanquished aspirations. A careful mirroring of the yearning and uncertainty displayed by 'Last Rites' and 'A Love' stresses the unified structure of *Night in Tunisia*, a symmetrical design within which the shorter stories serve as connective tissue. The collection's architecture is most apparent when 'Last Rites' and 'A Love' are considered alongside 'Night in Tunisia' itself, the book's highly regarded central story. These three texts, virtuoso performances on the part of Jordan, are the most substantial, successful and moving of all the stories in *Night in Tunisia*. Though they are often quite dark for a twenty-five-year-old writer, as Jordan himself acknowledges, they represent some of finest writing which the author has produced.[24]

BEYOND MOODY, ARBITRARY, ADOLESCENT BOREDOM: 'LAST RITES'

'Last Rites', the opening story of *Night in Tunisia*, is atypical when compared to others in the collection. Thus, it announces the book to the reader – who has most likely come to Jordan's debut with expectations based upon its well-publicised focus on tawdry resorts and adolescent angst – as a volume that intends to subvert preconceptions. The imagery of seaside towns and teenage longing characteristic of the collection as a whole is entirely absent here, while its English setting is unique among *Night in Tunisia*'s otherwise Ireland-based stories. 'Last Rites' also represents a touchstone for Jordan's own work in both fiction and film. The central character's extreme dissatisfaction with life hints at themes which will recur in *The Dream of a Beast* (1983), while the British cityscape of the expatriate worker is a landscape that will be seen again in *The Crying Game* (1992) and, more briefly, in *Breakfast on Pluto* (2005). Indeed, the building sites of 'Last Rites', along with the shower cubicle, prefigure a sustained interest in marginal zones up to and including the space between life and death which Jordan will display throughout his work for page and screen (seen in this story; in *High Spirits* (1988); *Sunrise with Sea Monster* (1994); *In Dreams* (1999); and *Shade* (2004)).

For its part, 'Last Rites' chronicles the final hours of an Irish immigrant labourer in London who chooses a public bathhouse, a place combining elements of an unemployment exchange and a hospital ward, as the site to take his own life (*Night in Tunisia*, 9). The labourer buys his admission ticket, queues, washes, masturbates, and finally slits his wrists, with most of the story taking place inside his shower cubicle itself. Despite the intimacy of how the protagonist is presented, the labourer is never given a name. Such anonymity is not an unusual trait for the characters of *Night in Tunisia*, though, while the collection's other protagonists struggle with the mantles of everymen and women, the labourer carries it securely enough to guarantee an instant, avataristic identification with the many thousands of Irish who sought work in Britain in the 1960s and '70s. Jordan himself worked those building sites and ascribes the genesis of the story to his experience of being in London without good prospects.[25] Like the story's protagonist, he too used the showers at the Kensal Rise Baths, formerly the Kensal Rise Tontine and Workingmen's Association, a public wash-house that, at the end of the working week, became the focus of labourer attention in that area of the English capital.

As much as anything else, the disillusioned construction worker's weekly visit to this bathhouse is an act of rebellion: every Friday he washes the dust off himself and gains the brief pleasure of cleanliness along with a metaphorical independence from the building site, from the oppression of labouring life on the one hand and, on the other, the greater metaphorical project of empire-building. Nonetheless, he knows that, come Monday, the dust will return to cake his body once again, lingering until his next rebellion. The cyclical nature of this patience and revolt, redolent of so much of Anglo-Irish history, serves to politicise the emigrant experience. Further traces of the political structure beneath Jordan's haunting story are evident in the dichotomy of attitude between the Irish labourers and those originating in other countries. The labourer listens to the rich, loud voices of the African and Afro-Caribbean labourers but, by contrast, there is caginess and even bitterness to the Irish voices that he hears (9). This comparison is drawn throughout, with Jordan utilising modes of relaxation as an illustration of national characteristics in the same manner as he will do in *The Past*, where the nominally Ascendancy characters of the Vance family occupy themselves with painting, photography and excursions, while native characters 'rebel' against them in the highly politicised amateur theatre.

If 'Last Rites' can be said to have a stage, however, it is the constrained dais of the protagonist's shower cubicle. In it, the labourer finds a respite from external pressures and an arena in which he can resolve his own internal conflicts. The design of the bathhouse cubicles, all identical, allows each occupant a moment of peace and separation. They are a luxury to the London workmen as much as they are a necessity. Yet, they are also a taunt to the labourer's desires: as he passes each cubicle he hears splashes and movements from within and is sorely aware of the fact that each thin door conceals a naked man (10). His subsequent arousal quickly turns to frustration as he cannot act upon his urges in a manner that involves any satisfying human connection. The best he can do is masturbate to the anonymous sounds of water splashing against a body in an adjacent cubicle (18). Characterised by a deep sadness, this is the first instance of the homoeroticism Jordan will utilise elsewhere in the *Night in Tunisia* stories ('Seduction', 'Sand', and the sand-dune masturbation scene in 'Night in Tunisia' itself are the more obvious instances) as well as throughout his fiction and films. It is underscored here by the bittersweet evocation of the labourer's sensual longing and sexual isolation, elements that have earned 'Last Rites' a place in at least one anthology of gay fiction.[26]

Neither fully public nor fully private, the shower cubicle is an ideal site for the labourer to confront what he considers to be both public and private humiliations. Yet, its liminal nature requires the imposition of an external, elemental force – in this case water – to transform it fully from its communal context into a cloistered space where he can be himself. When the labourer switches on the water, he seals himself off from the outside world (13), though in doing so he further separates himself from human contact of any kind, and the disappointment he experiences when he realises no one could have witnessed his act of masturbation contributes substantially to the suicidal depths of his disillusionment. The story goes on to present the act of washing as a transitional activity which exists between workdays and weekends, and which has, until now, punctuated the repetitive existence of the labourer with something that both is and is not pleasurable (8). In the space between asbestos black and eerie white (13), the shower scene draws attention to the terminator between grime and cleanliness, between the stereotypically unclean act of masturbation and the impossible moral standards which have contributed to the labourer's demise. As he strives for complete physical and psychological cleanliness, the character is essentially washing himself out of existence. His over-familiarity with the space and with the process, apathy beyond any experienced by Jordan's bored seaside teens, is key to his suicide. But, in spite of this, there is a part of the character that tries to see life with fresh eyes again.

While the story makes clear from the outset that the labourer is seeing his environment – and himself – for the last time, the character's focused attention reads as an effort by his self-preservation instinct to rattle his suicidal resolve, an attempt that ultimately fails. Considering himself in the mirror, the utilitarian gaze of the labourer finds nothing of value: he considers his own body the way he might assess the usefulness of a trowel (10). Now the labourer realises what he really is: a tool, a person used by another for his own ends. He is, in fact, what one might call a poor tool, an unskilled workman or a shiftless person.[27] The need to deliberate over the usefulness of the hypothetical trowel tells the reader as much; if the tool were any good, there would be no need to gauge its usefulness at all, an experienced workman would know at once. If it were worth keeping, one would not have to make the choice. Of course, alongside this there is a further connotation here: 'tool' as slang for the penis, or what Jordan ungenerously portrays in flaccid terms as the labourer realises he has arrived at the point where he will masturbate. The story explains that the character always arrives at this decision in different ways, though the implication is that repression and loneliness provide the mainstay of his approaches. The bleak, unaccompanied nature of his sexual act is emphasised in two ways. First, the intense moment of silence which marks his climax is interrupted by a conversation between two of the Black labourers outside, an exchange of warm colloquialisms from which the labourer feels forever barred. Second, as if to reinforce the absence of any sexual partner, the labourer's discharged semen is swept clinically down the drain. Water, the principal elemental medium of *Night in Tunisia*, has struck for the first time.

It is at this point, with the labourer essentially removed from the surrounding universe, that Jordan introduces the first of the many quasi-Joycean narrative strategies which upset the reader's expectations about the *Night in Tunisia* stories. In the case of 'Last Rites', this manifests as a series of italicised flash-forwards to the events following the labourer's suicide. Jordan intersperses five of these throughout 'Last Rites' and the effect is as though the reader has joined the labourer in an out-of-body experience (in itself a foreshadowing of how Jordan will use the character of Nina in *Shade*). In these sections, the lifeless labourer is watched over and tended to by his fellow workmen, a multi-ethnic, multi-linguistic group bound together not by occupation or resolve, but by a common appreciation of the loneliness and misery that drove this everyman to his death. It is a simple and effective means of presenting the after-effects of the suicide and one which preserves the story's principal point of view. Jordan allows the labourer's dead body to be read as another kind of text by the audience in the flash-forwards – uneven muscles speak to years on the sites carrying heavy loads, and so on (11) – and it is in these scenes, rather than those focused on the living character, that the life history of the labourer is told most poignantly. This workman's wake augments the funerary atmosphere which defines the story as a whole. The careful choreography of the participants hints at the ceremonial nature of proceedings where each movement and statement possesses a meaningful ritual quality (8).

Counterpointing this air of formal observance is the titular last rite performed in the story. It is not a religious undertaking, nor is it occult or even (as might be appropriate to a group of builders) masonic. It is in effect the opposite of fraternal: a ceremony conducted by and for the labourer alone, *le petit mort* of his regular masturbatory orgasm followed by the very real death of his final, suicidal act. He has found himself living with boredom and apathy as a condition of life and he can continue no longer. It is fitting then that he should die alone. The onlookers see his body in the aftermath, of course, but they are not privy to the details revealed to the reader by the omniscient narration. Instead, these workmen themselves, by and large immigrants from Commonwealth countries and former colonies, consider the approach to the bathhouse via red-bricked streets passing beneath a green bridge (7). They understand elements of what has led to the labourer's misery, but, crucially, they fail to comprehend the manner in which the labourer's psyche has fallen beneath the weight of national stereotypes, poverty and sexual repression. These elements combine in 'Last Rites' to create a condition of inferiority, worthlessness and inhibited sexual desires in the labourer, and, while his contemporaries may understand the root cause, they cannot hope to grasp the peculiarly Irish illness to which the character succumbs.

The peace that the labourer eventually finds in death can thus be considered the logical extension of his isolation in the shower cubicle – part womb, part grave – which is itself a kind of social death. The nature of the cubicles is underscored when the labourer enters the bathhouse and passes the rows of white doors. Behind each, another naked man is embryonically contained but socially isolated. Far from being just an incidental detail garnered from Jordan's own visits to Kensal Rise, these sequestered bodies represent the near-at-hand inaccessibility of the labourer's desires. The resulting frustrations stand as a key determinant in both his decision to end his life and in his choice of the location in which to do so. The marginal aspect of the showers means that the labourer is both accompanied and alone. It allows his death to make a point about his life, and as he lies dying in the cubicle, the blank empty space demands a recollection from his mind. He remembers the story's initial images: an old man with a bowed back standing beneath the green bridge and red-brick façade of the Victorian bathhouse (19). That there is nothing more significant than this in his life is the ultimate measure of his existence, the final thought which passes through his mind before his anti-climactic expiration in a pool of blood thinned into a weak rosé hue by the shower water (8). Naturally, this colour is not chosen lightly. Jordan offers it as if to say that dilution is the final fate of the strong, vibrant red which the labourer saw outside. Thinned by the grey water of the showers, it assumes its final post-mortem pigmentation.

In this, 'Last Rites' represents the first and one of the most obvious uses of water in Jordan's work. It does more here than simply wash away the grime of the building site or the semen and blood of the labourer's final moments; it also washes away the last of his doubts. The shower is crucial in a liminal, ritual sense, something echoed in the labourer's own mechanical masturbation. It is a preparation, an antechamber, a ceremonial embarkation prior to his demise; it is neither part of the material world nor the hereafter. To pass into one he must first remove the marks of the other. The shower water washes away the paint on his cheek which, like an erased birthmark or a tattoo removed, wipes out the visible identity of his life (16). With soap and scrubbing he removes grime and dust and all evidence of his work on the building sites in the pursuit of a final bleak cleanliness. His grim trajectory cannot end with simple spotlessness, however, as to do so would be to submit again to the cyclical recurrence of misery in his life that brings him back to the same location at the end of every week. His suicide, from this point of view, is therefore inevitable. Soap may be suitable for dirt and paint, but the labourer requires death to remove the stains and marks beneath his skin, those of an impoverished Dublin childhood which Jordan evokes with cramped and suffocating tenement imagery (11), and presents as a series of metaphorical life lessons which went unlearnt.

Nonetheless, it is the lessons that *have* been learnt – both by the labourer and by Jordan – that mark 'Last Rites' most deeply. It is perhaps worth nothing that Jordan presents the labourer's discharge as seed, something that provokes another return to Joyce, in this case *Portrait of the Artist as a Young Man* (1916) where, in Chapter 3, St James is quoted as saying that 'from the evil seed of lust all other sins had sprung forth'. In 'Last Rites', the labourer's lust very clearly expresses what Joyce in *Portrait* calls 'envy of those whose vices he could not reach to' and, in turn, engenders the act of suicide which is itself held to be a sin. In one final rebuttal to both the tenets of Catholic Ireland and the self-perpetuating cycle which the character has initiated, Jordan closes the story with what is essentially a secular prayer, an act of talismanic faith from one of the

Caribbean labourers who, standing over the dead body on the tiles, confesses to his fellows that he thinks every day about committing the same suicidal act and that every day he drowns his sorrows in a bottle of wine in order to forget that urge (19). His admission reflects a sentiment Jordan has expressed elsewhere, that characters and writers alike must accept the reality of transience, must accept that home is in many ways an impossible notion, before they are able to find true peace.[28]

OH, PLAY THAT THING: MUSIC AND MOTIVE IN 'NIGHT IN TUNISIA'

Emblematic of how many stories in the collection bring the purity of water and the beachfront into direct conflict with the tawdriness of the settings and the characters, 'Night in Tunisia' fulfils – in fact is responsible for the creation of – the stereotypes associated with Jordan's debut volume: a seaside setting, an adolescent protagonist with a strong sexual yearning, and an authorial interest in popular culture. The story is a cornerstone of Jordan's early career and, along with *The Past*, is one of the texts most frequently discussed by critics engaging with his work for the page. In *Contemporary Irish Literature: Transforming tradition*, for example, Christina Hunt Mahony is keen to praise 'Night in Tunisia' as an outstanding example of modern Irish fiction.[29] The story, as she points out, has been made canonical by its inclusion in *The Field Day Anthology*, a publication that itself describes 'Night in Tunisia' as casting 'familiar, even hackneyed, themes of a boy's sexual growth in a new light for Irish fiction'.[30] A version of the story was adapted for RTÉ television by director Pat O'Connor in 1983, while the essential part played by jazz music and lyrics here (including an early reference to the song 'The Crying Game') grants the story a strong connection to one of the defining aspects of Jordan's later work for the cinema, including his debut film *Angel* (1982), *The Miracle* (1991) and *The Crying Game* (1992) itself.

Indeed, music is essential to the structural and the thematic arrangements of 'Night in Tunisia'.[31] The story takes its title from a Dizzy Gillespie song subsequently made famous by Charlie Parker and centres on a love and a talent for jazz being passed from generation to generation. It depicts a summer spent by an adolescent boy with his father and older sister, renting a green corrugated-iron chalet in an east-coast holiday town not far from Mosney holiday camp. The children's mother is never mentioned and, as their father plays in a band all night for the older holiday-makers at Mosney and does not get up until late in the day, the children are mainly left to their own devices. With his sister having grown distant since the onset of puberty, the boy (as in the case of the labourer, the reader never learns his name) becomes enamoured of Rita, an older teenage girl and a native of the resort town. He also takes up with a group of older boys whose respect he earns by playing simple ditties on an old clubhouse piano as a means of compensating for his relative youth (70). The boy's pursuit of musical proficiency is further motivated by his father, who is galled by what he sees as a waste of his son's musical talent. He wants him to learn the saxophone, but the boy, in search of his own identity, refuses despite obvious skill and desire, going so far as to practise secretly while the elder musician sleeps, and deliberately hitting wrong notes when he knows his father is listening.

Throughout 'Night in Tunisia', music is therefore integral to both the boy's conception of himself and his interaction with the world. In his first weeks in the town, music provides the means by which he deals with his adolescent longings, guilt and confusion, a state of mind captured in one of the story's most poetic images, the protagonist imagining himself inside a tin drum he possessed as a child as the rain hammers against the iron roof of the family's holiday cottage (49). Jordan finds in his protagonist's obvious skill a means of expressing his helplessness and, throughout the first half of the story, it is as though life is playing the protagonist rather than vice versa; he has no control, no agency of his own. Later, as he becomes disenchanted with the teenage boys and their lecherous, adolescent interest in Rita, he begins to reassert himself through musical means. His previous inability to unlock his own potential, symbolised by the broken keys of the piano, is now replaced by the freedom and security of the stronger metal keys by which he plays the alto saxophone (52, 69). Though he insists he is only practising the saxophone because his father is paying him, he gives himself completely to the instrument and so to the fullness of post-adolescent individual contentment.

In his introduction to the volume, Seán O'Faoláin singles out the music of 'Night in Tunisia' as the kernel of Jordan's imaginative language, and jazz music as another character – arguably even the hero – of the story (interestingly, O'Faoláin picks out the use of 'The Crying Game' in particular as a central Jordan metaphor a decade and a half before the author utilised it so effectively in the film of the same name).[32] Indeed 'music', says John Wilson Foster in the *Field Day Anthology*, is the protagonist's 'half-articulate correlative language, appropriate in its mere suggestiveness to the melancholy of the adulthood he is soon to enter'.[33] Certainly, music is both the means by which the character best communicates and a grease to the wheel of maturation. Yet, Foster's 'melancholy' is but one of many possible adulthoods which the boy may yet attain; the latter portion of the story suggests a more optimistic future for the character – rejecting the false promises of the teenagers for a mastery of the saxophone. However, Foster chose to omit this final portion of the text in his selection for *Field Day*, and so the canonical presentation of 'Night in Tunisia' denies the reader the final fifth of the story. In actuality, the boy's eventual embrace of his musical talent opens new vistas for him, a beautiful country of rolling green hills stretching off – an early invocation of the infinity Jordan will later play with in *Shade* and *Carnivalesque* – towards the vanishing point (68). The closing image then, a metaphor which conflates the mouthpiece of a saxophone with the lips of a lover – imagines a future where the protagonist's musical and worldly ease is finally transmuted into sexual fulfilment (73).

Yet, Foster does make an astute observation when, in his brief introduction to 'Night in Tunisia', he compares the arrangement of the story's paragraphs to musical 'riffs' as though 'music might also be a structural matter for the author'.[34] In fact, Jordan's use of jazz to create an initiation rite for his young protagonist derives from a deep personal interest in the genre.[35] During the period he was composing the *Night in Tunisia* stories, Jordan was himself learning to play the saxophone.[36] He also played guitar and banjo in a band which had been formed by Niall Stokes (later editor of *Hot Press* music magazine). Stokes recalls the young Jordan as a competent musician, though not in the same league as the gifted protagonist of 'Night in Tunisia'.[37] The band performed material with a vaudeville energy to which Jordan's banjo was well suited.[38] Subsequent to 'Night in Tunisia', Jordan would draw on his musical experiences to inform the narratives and stylistic choices which define so much of his work for the screen. The impact of music, jazz in particular, is typically most apparent in those pictures which, like 'Night in Tunisia', are built around the interrogation of liminal or – as the story deems them – crepuscular spaces.

The boy's sacred summer between childhood and adulthood takes place in a town that marks the meeting of the land and water (a favourite location of the literary Jordan and one to which he will return in *Sunrise with Sea Monster*, *Shade* and eventually *Carnivalesque*). Outside the boy's chalet, the texture and movement of the sea evoke both cloth and glass, and the youngster dreams constantly of a way by which he might bridge the competing realms and combine these two materials, of a means through which he might yoke his childish enthusiasms to his adult desires (52). As if subconsciously aware of his own transitional state, the boy becomes preoccupied with twilight: he begins to experience it on a sensuous, almost spiritual level the way one might a religious sacrament (49). The boy's imaginings carry him through this dark night of partial crisis to dawn and the literal promise of a new day. It is only then he realises how morning is a repetition and a reversal of an evening's twilight (52). Thus, his budding responsiveness to the adult world is implicit in his realisation of life's cyclical nature, and in the fact that the sky never becomes completely dark (72). Most importantly, liminal spaces are delineated by the boy's burgeoning awareness of sexuality, in particular with regard to the character of Rita.

A permanent resident of the seaside town, Rita represents the type of recreational lifestyle to which the seasonal visitors aspire, but the endless, almost claustrophobic nature of her days are shown to have no positive benefits. She lives mostly on her own, as her father is always away working, and her existence tends towards boredom, delinquency and suicidal ideation. Despite her symbolic domicile in one of the green chalets, Rita is no Cathleen ni Houlihan. Her wrists are rumoured to bear the evidence of self-harm and she twice attempts suicide by drowning (47, 71). Rita is one of *Night in Tunisia*'s more angst-ridden characters, closer to the disposition of the labourer from 'Last Rites' than to her fellow teenagers. Paradoxically, she is also very much at ease in the seaside town and in her own skin, something remarked upon by the boy, who wonders what the cost of such ease might have been (57). He interprets her comfort as the result of some kind of Faustian bargain; yet the boy's reading of her character is central to his re-conception of his own identity and, in the final pages of the story, he begins to conceive of himself – in adolescent fashion – as a hero who can save her, specifically, as a lifeguard who can rescue her from drowning. To the boy, Rita is all the more alluring for the adult knowledge she seemingly possesses. Maguy Pernot-Deschamps goes so far as to suggest Rita is a young sex worker, but, despite her jaunt in a car with an overweight man, there is little evidence that her behaviour has been thus formalised outside of local gossip (56).[39] She was, the story reveals, an individual about whom people in a small town would talk regardless of fact (48). The story's omniscient narrator is not immune from this and describes Rita as venal three times in the opening section of the story (47, 50, 57). Much of 'Night in Tunisia' and, for that matter, much of the critical discussion around it, therefore pivots between the opposing poles of virgin and whore to which men confine women throughout the story, something David Malcolm and Cheryl Alexander Malcolm find especially visible in the comparison between Rita, as the protagonist's object of romantic desire despite the salacious rumours which swirl around her, and the statue of the Virgin Mary with her hands stretched out towards the sea.[40] Though, as the Malcolms say in their *Companion to the British and Irish Short Story*, neither option offers the story's women a role beyond that of a male voyeuristic fantasy.[41]

Emer and Kevin Rockett also assess the depiction of women in 'Night in Tunisia' as a function of adolescent, masculine insecurities; the boy here, like many of the male characters in *Night in Tunisia*, is trapped in a messy matrix of clichéd desires and assumptions, something that allows little room to acknowledge the agency of the women themselves.[42] Of course, balance will later be created by the second half of the collection where many of the stories involve more progressive depictions of women. 'Skin', 'Her Soul' and 'Outpatient' examine the female perspective in similar depth to the title story's concentration on the male. In the case of 'Night in Tunisia' itself, however, the overt masculine gaze exhibited by the protagonist and implicit in the narration should not surprise us given that the protagonist is the product of Jordan's typical fractured family. Foreshadowing 'Seduction', 'A Love' and *Sunrise with Sea Monster*, the household here lacks a mother or any significant mature female presence.

The boy has only his sister to provide female influence, but even she proves unwilling and distant. Her increasing alienation from their childhood camaraderie pushes the boy more squarely into his father's sphere of influence just as the promise and significance of the boy's musical ability becomes obvious to both of them. Though, as with the majority of Jordan's father/son relationships ('A Love', *The Past*, *Sunrise with Sea Monster*), the boy is in danger of squandering his potential to outshine his elder through pride and stubbornness.

Some commentators have attempted to identify a weakness in the somewhat thinly characterised figure of the father, though Mahony acknowledges that his depiction shares similarities with Jordan's later directorial intentions.[43] Samuele Grassi's article specifically on father/son relationships in Jordan's fiction claims the boy's father is, like Rita's, an alcoholic, and that his primary ambition is to play music with his friends in a local bar, though there is little evidence of this character being a drunk, as he is repeatedly described by Grassi.[44] Additionally, his musical interest is a professional engagement as part of a band committed to nightly entertainment at Mosney holiday camp. Grassi's portrayal of the father's relationship to his saxophone as being more important to him than his relationship to the boy is also misleading. Grassi presents the father's love for music as greater than that for his own son, but in actuality the father's love for his son is overwhelming to the point of self-destructiveness.[45] The father begs and pleads with the boy not to waste his talent, knowing that he is at the right age to learn easily if correctly taught (66). His devotion is such that he is willing to give of himself so that his son can fulfil his promise and exceed him.

As in 'Last Rites', it is water that provides a means by which the protagonist can externalise his internal struggle. Whereas in the opening story it served to make real the labourer's isolation, here it functions as a filter through which the universal music of the world is channelled. For instance, when the boy is at the sink and Charlie Parker's high-speed playing comes on the radio, the song is accompanied by the falling water of the tap (62). The result is a music that only the boy can hear, and this use of water to convey secrets to correctly attuned characters foreshadows, say, water's supernatural associations in Jordan's film *In Dreams* (1999). Crucially, where the damaged characters of that film can divine only malignancy, longing and psychic instability from the medium of water, the innocence of the boy in 'Night in Tunisia' insulates him from such negativity. Water in this story serves as a positive, metamorphic element which contrasts with other stories in the book. In 'Last Rites', for instance, water helped to literally erase the labourer's identity. Here, however, it functions to reinforce the protagonist's individuality, no more so than when he dispatches a fat boy from the raft for spreading rumours about Rita and so metaphorically assuring his dominance on the tiny craft (61). Conversely, and as with the characters of *In Dreams*, Rita's conspicuous lack of innocence taints her relationship with water. At the end of the story she attempts to drown herself twice, both times having to be rescued by the local lifeguard. The boy fantasises about saving her from the sea himself, about pushing the salt water from her lungs, but the story ends without fully resolving the ambiguity of his feelings towards her.

By contrast, the story's most enigmatic character is consciously landlocked throughout 'Night in Tunisia'. The boy's sister is a surly presence in the background of the narrative. Like Rita she gains knowledge of the adult world ahead of the boy but, unlike the local girl, she is evidently perturbed by the revelations. For the first few days both she and her brother remain mired in childhood and unable to escape established familial routines. The boy walks around with his sister proper and correct alongside him, but her transformation is already in progress and so their conversation is minimal. The turning point comes when they pass Rita on the road. The boy recalls earlier visits to the town when all of them used to play together, lying naked and innocent on the golf links without truly being aware of their state of undress (49). Why, he asks his sister, did she not greet their former friend on this occasion (49)? But for the sister, that memory has been tarnished by her growing awareness of sexuality. The boy has not yet made that leap but is becoming conscious, however hazily, that it exists, and so their relationship comes to echo that of the brother and sister in 'Sand', one of the preceding stories. While in 'Sand' the brother's education comes from an attempted sexual assault, here the boy's knowledge stems from the teenagers with whom he spends his days, the same boys who, at night, watch hungrily as his sister walks through town. Her ephemeral presence, moody disposition and awakening yet idle sexuality combine to create the suggestion that Jordan sees similarities to

Rita in her future (though the author's gestures towards the complexities of female adolescence are never a primary component of the story).

The boy, for his part, exhibits episodes of almost comical innocence which illustrate how far removed he is from the prosaic reality that surrounds him. For example, he is familiar with words like 'tautology' but not with terms like 'whore'; he witnesses a boy masturbating into a condom but is more intrigued by an inflated contraceptive floating on the sea, described in almost escapist terms as being lifted and carried by the wind (55). He is afforded only associate membership of the teenage group yet he listens to the talk and the jokes of the older teens with a musician's ear, intent on learning and imitating what he can. Physical immaturity, however, is something he cannot yet overcome. His lack of an Adam's apple, his thin arms and his hairless body are all apparent when he accompanies the older boys on swims to the raft anchored off the beach. This is their observation post, their place from where they can watch the action of the strand as though it were a theatrical performance (51). Mahony sees in this scene a suggestion of bathing sequences from other fictional journeys from innocence to experience such as Joyce's *Portrait of the Artist* and F. Scott Fitzgerald's 'Winter Dreams'.[46] But Jordan's use of the raft is more consciously developmental, portraying it as a maturation tank of sorts, a final staging-area before the teenagers' assault on the (literal) land of adulthood, and a place where, for the time being, they can conceal their sporadic erections from society at large.

Also concealed, this time beneath the appearance of a traditional coming-of-age story, is a structural idiosyncrasy whereby run-on sentences form distinct isolated paragraphs. Typographically, 'Night in Tunisia' is presented via brief, individual vignettes, the majority of which exist on the page as long, lonely paragraphs. This authorial organisation serves to focus the reader's attention on the blank spaces as much as on the printed text, creating a meditative effect which is crucial to the success of the narrative. The reader is gently subsumed into a flow of images and intuitive responses to an increasingly jarring world as the omniscient narrator represents the adolescent's consciousness. Within the limitations of space, this stylistic choice is preserved in the story's 1990 appearance in the *Field Day Anthology of Irish Writing*, where each section is presented as its own paragraph.[47] This arrangement was also maintained in the most recent edition of *Night in Tunisia*, though the paragraphs were compressed to a more traditional spacing when the collection was reprinted in *A Neil Jordan Reader* (1993). The latter presents a rare simultaneous outing for both Jordans, collecting the early short fiction (*Night in Tunisia* and *The Dream of a Beast*) alongside the screenplay of *The Crying Game* for an American readership for whom the pop-culture references of 'Night in Tunisia' would have been more familiar than the distinctly Irish political backdrop of, say, the collection's closing story, 'A Love'.[48]

SHOUTING 'UP DEV!': 'A LOVE' AND THE END OR THE BEGINNING OF HISTORY

On the day they buried Éamon de Valera, one of the architects of Ireland's transition to independence, Neil Jordan was driving through Dublin city centre.[49] It was, says Fintan O'Toole, a day as symbolically rich and significant for Irish people as the funeral of Winston Churchill had been for their counterparts in Britain, but as the cortège passed down O'Connell Street, Jordan found his attention drawn to those in the crowds watching the funeral indirectly, through the television sets on display in shop windows.[50] From this experience sprung *Night in Tunisia*'s great closing story 'A Love'. The last of the collection's tent-pole offerings, 'A Love' employs the same meditative paragraphical breaks as 'Night in Tunisia' to frame a pensive tale of love, conflict and acceptance. It offers the reader a narrative of modern Irish history from the civil war to the death of Éamon de Valera but, as if to compensate for the near-parochial concentration on Irish politics, the story utilises an internationalised, almost Americanised, language to set its scene (de Valera, for instance, is depicted simply as the President, 103). 'A Love' is particularly notable for two reasons: it represents Jordan's first use of a fictionalised de Valera character, an important element of his most notable work in both film and fiction from *The Past* to *Sunrise with Sea Monster* to *Michael Collins*; and it begins Jordan's fascination with sexual triangles involving a father and a son both obsessed with the same woman, a persistent element which recurs throughout his writing and a vehicle for Jordan's ongoing exploration of personal and political betrayal across the Irish twentieth century.

'A Love' thematically unifies *Night in Tunisia* and is the point at which the architecture of the collection is fully apparent. That the protagonist is an emigrant recently returned from London allows 'A Love' to bookend the volume and present another take on the experience described in 'Last Rites'. Like many of the stories in the second half of the collection, 'A Love' concludes with the characters turning inwards in search of healing. The story, and so the entire book, comes to an end in Lisdoonvarna and thus offers the reader a perspective on missed opportunities for renewal by concluding at what is essentially a seaside town without a sea (122), which also serves as a further mirror to Kensal Rise in the opening story, the book's original bathing place with curative properties. The central character too combines elements of the labourer and the boy from the previously discussed stories. In this case, the central character is a twenty-something Irishman who returns from self-imposed exile on the day of de Valera's funeral to meet an unnamed older woman who, years previously, had initiated him into an adult world of sexuality and love.

Complicating our reading of the text, Jordan chose to name the protagonist here Neil and so the story invites one to consider if the character's rejection of, and alienation from, Irish historical concerns is shared by the author (though it should be made clear that subsequent projects, including *The Past, Sunrise, Michael Collins, Shade, Carnivalesque* and 2021's *The Ballad of Lord Edward and Citizen Small* testify to the fact that Jordan has anything *but* rejected Irish historical concerns).[51] Neil is a notable authorial imposition, especially given Jordan's deliberate choice to avoid the word 'I' as much as possible in *Night in Tunisia*.[52] Grassi has proposed an autobiographical correspondence between the narrator and the author on the basis of Jordan's established interest in autobiographical references throughout his work.[53] Yet, this identification can be minimised in light of Jordan's own vision of the stories as autobiographical only insofar as, in almost every case, they describe things that he had seen or witnessed in real life and are presented in a photo-realistic style.[54] Choosing to set the story on the day of de Valera's funeral is a case in point, with Jordan saying that he was intrigued by the manner in which people responded – or did not – to the occasion, and how the funeral seemed to signify a (self-)questioning aspect of Irish consciousness rather than one rooted in surety or certainty.[55] The Neil character is therefore defined by an ambiguity of identity directly connected to the changing nature of modern Ireland. The adult character is unsure if he belongs in modern Ireland while the flashback sequences depict his teenage self as equally conflicted about his sexual and national concerns.

Neil has arranged to meet his former lover because he desires a means by which he can finally understand his relationship with her, but the occasion of the funeral transforms what follows and affords him the opportunity to truly understand the nature of de Valera's Ireland itself. Watching the cortège pass, he feels (with a nod to Yeats) as though he is watching the death of a great animal, one that was monstrous, murderous and paradoxical in equal measure (111). In one notable passage, Neil realises he will always be out of tune with the history that has defined him, and wonders if he would rather be an outsider in London where, at least, he has experienced passions that are more rational in nature (105). 'A Love' thus proffers a metaphor for the violent turmoil of Ireland's independence struggle, the ramifications of which reverberated through fifty years of life and politics. De Valera's death offers the nation a chance to dispense with the hegemony of his difficult mindset (though of course Jordan himself, notably in *The Past*, *Sunrise with Sea Monster* and *Michael Collins*, has proven unable to step out from the shadow of the so-called Long Fellow). In 'A Love', more so than in his other appearances, Jordan's de Valera character is representative of all that has gone before. He is representative of what is both best and worst about modern Ireland (113). Even Neil, with some difficulty, confesses to once idolising him, recalling how his father brought him to political meetings to wave the tricolour and shout Dev's praises (113).

The story begins with eight lines describing a deserted Dublin as though to illustrate the emptiness of Ireland without its political titan, before quickly segueing into a recollection of a teenage Neil smashing two greenhouse windows with a gun, a civil war pistol belonging to the woman's father (103). This immediately phallic image counterbalances an otherwise reflective opening narration with a tone of awakening, boyish sexuality the reader recognises from 'Night in Tunisia' and other stories in the collection such as 'Seduction' and 'Sand'. In the story's present day – 1975 – the woman is dying and requests that Neil accompany her to the sulphur waters of Lisdoonvarna, a place presented as for those beyond the prime of their lives (110). The story alternates between their journey and flashbacks to the protagonist as a teenager in conflict with his father over the affections of the woman. Intensified by his mathematical father's identification with de Valera, father of the nation (as he will again be portrayed in *The Past*), this violent quarrel culminates in humiliation for the boy during an attempt to shoot his father dead. Their conflict comes to mirror the clash between an Ireland defined by the civil war era and one characterised by the concerns of the 1970s. As if to emphasise this generational gap, the band accompanying de Valera's cortège is composed of brass musicians playing archaic nationalist tunes, our understanding of their performance having been modified by the collection's insistence in its title story that brass music is a dead genre, one seldom played and which is only distantly recalled (48, 109).

The affair of the young Neil and the woman is depicted in similarly loaded political terms. Carrying a message from his father, the boy is quickly seduced by the metal solidity of a real gun and by the real bullets of the woman who owns it (103). His sexual imagination is ignited by the machinery of violence and he is readily enthralled when the woman takes the gun from him and conceals it within her blouse. Her longing is described in terms of a woman whose husband left for fighting, and she takes the teenage Neil as her lover despite the erstwhile courtship of his father. In doing so she rejects the abstract love, what one might call the nationalist love, of her own generation for the physicality of a more concrete affair. As in 'Night in Tunisia', the sexual education of the boy occurs within sight of that pervasive Jordan symbol, the sea, as the woman is the proprietor of a Greystones guesthouse where the boy and his father have taken a room. Yet, the transition to adulthood experienced by Neil here is altogether more pointed and more carnal than the lessons learned by the 'Night in Tunisia' protagonist. In the title story, the boy is an observer; he studies the older teenagers to learn from them and he watches their cavorting acted out (50). Neil, on the other hand, becomes a participant, a literal actor on the stage. In doing so he gains valuable sexual experience from the woman which, during his time in London, serves him as a performer of theatrical sex in the city's clammy revues (109).

There is a particular musk too to the café where the grown-up Neil and the woman meet, a smell redolent of Dublin, and one which is typified by the women who, not unimportantly, wait as a passive audience for the passage of heroic, virginal, old, dead men (105). Ireland itself, its history and people, are rendered as little more than some gigantic funeral procession. The women on the street are said to have waited all their lives for such things, for funerals or for the return of a child or husband. They are contemporaries of both Neil's father and his former lover, women of the years when both de Valera and the country were forged and when waiting for funerals was a significant national pastime. But now that older country is dying, its citizens weakened by their figurehead's demise. Neil's lover is not immune; she looks sick and worn in the quiet manner of cancer (106). She is clearly dying in the way the author wishes us to see that de Valera's nation is expiring, though some critics have chided Jordan for falling prey to what Richard Haslam calls 'the centuries-old tradition drawn on by Irish writers (usually male), in which a female character functions to a greater or lesser extent as a representation of Ireland'.[56] It is, of course, a connection that de Valera himself often stressed, 'happy maidens' (usually misquoted as 'comely maidens' due to an initial misreporting) and whatnot. The woman here, therefore, represents de Valera as much as she does the idea of Ireland. So intimately is the relationship between her and the protagonist connected to a country steeped in de Valera's influence that Neil's response to the president's name is to recall the nights he spent lying in her creaking bed overlooking the sea, their movements a kind of shocking revelation to him at the time (107).

If readers accept, as well they should, Haslam's proposal that the woman in the story 'functions' as Ireland, then it is possible to read her manipulation of the boy's 'awkward adolescence' and, importantly, their furtive lovemaking, as symbolic actions on her part. Her choice of Neil as her lover, rather than his father, is an attempt to banish everything that the father and de Valera created. Again, via Neil's recollections, emphasis is placed on the seductive, revolutionary femininity of clandestine trysts rather than on the more material aspects of womanhood. The boy's mother is seen only in photographs which have faded to brown, her absence creates a void both in the boy and in the father in a much more corrosive way than the absent mother of 'Night in Tunisia' did. Indeed, the father/son relationship here is closest in tone to that of Donal Gore and his father in *Sunrise with Sea Monster*. As in that novel, the characters of 'A Love' are incapable of resolving their complex relationships on the east coast and require instead the assumed simplicity of Ireland's west. Here, it is the woman who declares that she and Neil will go to Clare, taking charge of their final encounter as once she had taken charge of their first. Lisdoonvarna is her preferred destination.

The woman desires in her final days to become part of the pseudo-religious and mythic west: the Burren, the sulphur springs and the unfamiliar flowers which grow nowhere else in the country. As she describes this, she takes on some of the more clichéd characteristics of Cathleen ni Houlihan; Neil sees her as both young and old simultaneously, and he is struck by the deep desire for happiness that afflicts her. Their departure for the west makes it apparent that Neil, despite his cultural and physical exile, is more a product of de Valera's Ireland than he wishes to acknowledge. He cannot drive, yet would like to escape by feeling free in mechanistic fashion; he still exhibits the same inability to control the life he struggled against as a teenager (112–13). In fact he remains imprisoned, emotionally and culturally, and when the woman asks him if he is happy he cannot give a firm answer to the question. Tellingly, his failure occurs as they pass Portlaoise and see the towers and barbed fences of the prison, along with the walls of the psychiatric hospital (115). They move across the country until they reach Limerick as if re-enacting the push of the Free State troops across the country in opposition to the republicans during the civil war. Yet, instead of proceeding south, as the original fighting did, they turn west, for Clare. The earlier implication of the woman has been that the west remains the natural dying ground for those of the civil war generation, though as Jordan demonstrates in other *Night in Tunisia* stories such as 'Outpatient' and 'Tree', these are in fact the places where the battle for the soul of modern Ireland is played out.

In Lahinch they take lodgings in a B&B which mirrors that of the flashbacks and, pointedly, it is the woman who pays for their accommodation. As they undress and re-consummate their earlier affair it is as though Neil is prostituting himself for her youth. As they re-enact their bygone days, the mind of the protagonist drifts back to the conclusion of their previous relationship. The scene is the Great Northern Hotel, and the teenager watches his father and the woman waltz, drinking their leftover sherry. The sight causes him to see his father anew. He is no longer, like de Valera, a man who scribbled mathematical notions deep into the night. Rather, he is someone who shares the boy's yearning. The teasing superiority of adolescence fades and Neil's own blood becomes his rival. His public chastisement at the hands of his father touches off a civil war of his own and, later, while sleeping in the woman's bed, he hears his father in the bathroom. Arming himself in an echo of 1922's dissent, he retrieves the woman's pistol and fires four shots at his father, though none successfully penetrate the mahogany door. Thereafter, everything is, as the woman makes clear, ended (121) and the son's victory over the father is questionable at best. The resolution of the young Neil's conflict with his father goes beyond that which occurred between the Free Staters and the republicans; he has lost all and gained nothing in return, the reason for his exile finally becoming clear. Yet, as Mahony has written, his relationship with the woman is more genuine and, arguably, more long-lasting than the repressive, over-idealised conception of Irishness proffered during the independence era and its aftermath (such virtue being symbolised by a luminous statue of the Virgin Mary which Neil sees by the guesthouse wall).[57]

The next day Neil buys a newspaper, but the former president is relegated to the small print now, a meaningful detail which – alongside the repetitious focus on change throughout the story – Mahony sees as anticipating Ireland's future.[58] The increased fragmentation of the passages here (similar to 'Night in Tunisia') suggests the narrator's own apprehension at a national narrative robbed of its through-line. Ireland has lost its founding father and so the character cannot help but relate this to his own parental estrangement. Final release from this considerable burden of guilt occurs in Lisdoonvarna, an eerie, silent ghost town. Where the other holiday villages of *Night* are lively, youthful places in sight of the sea, this is a fossilised place seemingly populated entirely by old people (122). Neil finds he cannot even communicate with the inhabitants of this topsy-turvy world, who themselves exhibit considerable bewilderment as to what is going on. Confused as to whether the woman will bathe in the waters or drink them, he shouts the question to a passing couple, but the only response is an old man feigning confusion (123). Neil imagines both scenarios but his conclusion is the same: this is definitely the end of what has come before (124). His extended boyhood, like that of de Valera's nation, has finally reached its conclusion. His civil war is over.

For Jordan, however, the sustained investigation of modern Irish history, through both his fiction and his films, was just beginning. He has said that what fascinated him most during the real-life de Valera funeral was the struggle people had in looking their history in the face and how much easier it was for them to watch it, for example, on a television screen.[59] In one of his most important early interviews, he told Colm Tóibín that Irish cultural inheritance is one defined by questions and, in the kind of paradox that only a writer can truly relish, by an ambiguous relationship to ideas of memory and conceptions of what has come before.[60] Thus, while it is a rich and multifaceted text, 'A Love' nonetheless proved incapable of resolving what it was that de Valera embodied for either the nation or for Jordan personally beyond the faded photographs in school textbooks (105). That investigation would wait until Jordan's first full-length novel in 1980, a book which itself begins by extending a postcard image beyond its serrated frame.[61] That novel, which considers the importance of de Valera from political, theatrical and nostalgic perspectives, grows logically out of 'A Love'. A book concerned with the presence and significance of family memory, it is called simply *The Past*.

CHAPTER 3

Making Sense of the Present: Looking to *The Past*

Speaking almost twenty-five years after its publication, Jordan has described his debut novel *The Past* (1980) as a dense and difficult text, one which many people (including, he suspects, his own children) have not read.[1] The book's defining characteristics are Jordan's overwhelming devotion to descriptive imagery and his dedicated effort to utilise Ireland's past as a way to make sense of the nation's present.[2] The novel follows an unnamed narrator as he searches for the truth about his parentage. It comprises a conscious effort on the protagonist's part to reconstruct his *own* past by researching the lives of his grandparents – Free State hero Michael and flamboyantly bad actress Una – along with that of his mother, Rene, a girl whose affairs with an Anglo-Irish father and son, James and Luke Vance, resulted in the narrator's conception. With the help of his family's elderly friends, the narrator attempts to assemble a coherent narrative, eventually journeying west to see where he was born under the watchful eye of Éamon de Valera. Spanning the turbulent years of the early Irish state, *The Past* is Jordan's first sustained effort at untangling the nation's foundational myths. It explores the ways in which history and memory are processed, manipulated and commodified by individuals in general as well as by politicians and artists specifically. In the process it questions the notion of there ever being a single, definitive past which can be rediscovered, the recollections of the characters invariably coloured by nostalgia and political leanings, and the available photographic evidence subject to interpretation and reinterpretation. As Gerald Dawe observed, it is a novel that is firmly rooted in the particularities of a late 1970s Irish creative awakening.[3]

For Eileen Battersby in *The Irish Times*, Jordan's debut novel was already a mature and masterful piece of work.[4] She singles out *The Past* as perhaps the most underrated Irish novel of the twentieth century, but her point needs clarifying.⁵ In fact, *The Past* is rated quite highly by many critics, among them D.J. Taylor, Seán Golden and Christina Hunt Mahony, the latter considering this first long-form effort to be very impressive.⁶ Battersby herself states that contemporary reviews for the novel bordered on encomium, and so we are left with a novel that is publicly overlooked rather than critically underrated.⁷ Though the fact that *The Past* is remembered fondly is not inappropriate, for it is, in many ways, a nostalgic novel. Its first image is a yellowed postcard from a honeymoon, and its first paragraph is a meditation on the passage of time. Its concern is the representation of history, principally through photography, theatre and politics, all of which, as we will see, are constructions which upset the presumed impartiality of factual historicism. The use of these devices is Jordan's clearest signal that the narrative, a mixture of recollection and imaginings, is itself untrustworthy. In fact, the protagonist's attempt to settle the mystery of his mother's *real* past through the *fictional* narratives of her friends' reminiscences, only to discover that historical fact and aesthetic fantasy are – in every sense of the term – intimately linked, is one of the principal reasons why Richard Kearney places Jordan in his post-Joycean counter-tradition.⁸

While many of the author's works, including 'A Love', *Sunrise with Sea Monster* and *Shade*, along with some of his best-known films, have been inspired by modern Irish history, *The Past* differs in the manner in which the characters relate to history itself. All are performing roles, whether in front of the camera lens, on the drawing-room carpets of early Anglo-Irish theatre, or on the wider stage of national politics. The narrative of *The Past* is propelled by the narrator's inability to discern one true narrative from these varying interpretations of history. The use of the definite article in the novel's title implies an authentic history yet the past of the novel is no more definite than the past of memory. New events and information constantly shift the way-markers of the narrator's heritage, transforming the past into a process rather than a series of fixed points, a stack of photographs rather than a motion picture. As a result, critic James Cahalan has labelled the novel's approach to history an examination 'of fairly traditional materials ... in a thoroughly non-traditional way'.⁹ This, he maintains, is primarily a function of narration:

> The narrator presents his fantasies about the lives of his ancestors, moving from confusion to hypothesis to doubt, finally implying that he can be sure of neither who his father is nor who he himself is. He can look at photographs and other emblems of the past but can never clearly solve them.[10]

Such actions are not so far removed from the practices of professional historians themselves, something of which Jordan, as a graduate of a university history programme, can claim an awareness of.

Indeed, before he reaches his interpretative stage, the novel's narrator undertakes the kind of research any historian might carry out: he interviews surviving participants, visits relevant buildings and places, and performs an assessment of primary material such as contemporary photographs. Empirical research is therefore, illogically, the foundation of his uncertainty. That being said, the novel's Father Beausang insists that fiction possesses a semblance of truth (*The Past*, 136). The remark offers a valuable perspective on the narrator's search for the truth about his family and, by extension, the reader's expectations about the historical novel as a genre. On an immediate level, the narrator of *The Past* is faced with the question of whether his father is James Vance, a photographer, or his son Luke, a theatrical stagehand. More broadly, the mysteries of the affairs these men conducted with the narrator's mother are rendered immaterial by the arrival of Éamon de Valera who, by the coincidences of level crossings and halted trains, delivers the narrator into the rich swaddling of Irish history only moments after the child is born. Thus, as the narrator looks back on his life and heritage, he experiences three distinct versions of an earlier Ireland, three separate visions distorted in turn by the principal concerns of each potential father figure: photography, theatre and politics.

Before that, however, and again after the fashion of respectable historical practice, Jordan offers the grandparental context out of which these contesting perspectives on Ireland emerge. Beginning with a picture-postcard representation of a lost time and place, and reaching its climax amid the wondrous Burren of Clare's west coast, *The Past* is a novel structured as a progression away from England and imperialism. Though it takes Ireland and Irish identity as its primary themes, the story nonetheless begins in Cornwall, in 1914, on the esplanade of a small holiday town in the south-west of England (9). Thereafter, the narrative moves in successive jumps to Dublin, 1921, Bray, 1922, 'The Provinces', 1934, before culminating in Lisdoonvarna, which Jordan's readers will remember from 'A Love' as a kind of landlocked spa town (*Night*, 119). It is perhaps disappointing to realise that the relentless drive westwards, to the soul of Ireland, terminates in a place not so different from that which it sought to define itself against. Despite the regularity and propriety of its Edwardian façades vis-à-vis the bare rocky landscape of west Clare, Cornwall is already the edge of civility as far as the English are concerned (15, 215). Its harbours shelter rows of the simple paddle-boats which amuse the Irish (though not the jaded remnants of the Protestant Ascendancy) and, like the later depiction of Lisdoonvarna, the out-of-season English resort is filled only with the elderly, the infirm and a smattering of locals (10, 21).

The Cornwall similarities are nonetheless insufficient for an Irishman, even a Redmondite home ruler such as the narrator's grandfather Michael, to feel at ease in England. Though characterised by the fusion of naivete and insistent idealism which was in fashion at the time, Michael is shown to be insecure about how to act and how his behaviour marks him in English society (13, 16). As a consequence, he resorts to mimicry for the first but not the last time in the novel, becoming a pastiche of the imperial gentlemen he sees around him. He graduates from *The Times* to *The Manchester Guardian* to *The Telegraph* even while his wife regresses into Irish nationalist cliché in order to cement her own identity in such mercurial surroundings (19, 22). Una, the actress, contorts her whole being into a personification of the Irish struggle. Her prone form on the bed suggests the island itself while she allows the Cornish wind to rustle her clothes as though they are the banner of a newly born nation (20). She shuns the English while Michael, at this point in his life, actively seeks their acceptance. He travels to the core itself, to London, even as Una withdraws altogether from the conventions of imperial society, even from the diurnal hours themselves as if protesting against that sun which refuses to set on the British Empire (17, 21).

Yet, Jordan grants neither character their desired ease. Una is reduced to a chain-smoking recluse, an Irish wraith haunting the hotels at the edge of the imperial world, while Michael finds in London neither the order nor the pageantry of empire that he sought and is instead tormented by the frenzied High Gothicism of St Pancras station (21, 22). The city's Irish expatriate community is similarly disordered and divided: Michael encounters acquaintances from his students days now decked out in khaki uniforms, he briefly considers joining up with the Irish Guards but, at the same time, he hears the term home rule thrown around as a glib insult (21). He can never be British, let alone English; at best he can only hope to be an Irishman *in* Britain, tolerated but never embraced. As such, his attempt to become the perfect home ruler leads instead to a struggle with his own Redmondite nature (24). Unable to either support or deride the imperial war effort, Michael becomes politically impotent even as he neglects his wife for the pleasures of June, a Cornish prostitute; as the reader is told, he suffers a loss of resolve before regaining his ideological composure once again (23).

Confounding the staid poetic trope of Ireland as a woman, de rigueur for artists and activists in the period being described, Jordan here utilises two different characters to represent two very different Irelands and two very different futures (46). Una, embodying an ill-treated nation, naturally represents the prospect of violent struggle for independence while June, with her aura of Protestant correctness, personifies a continued legislative arrangement with the empire (27, 29). The potential of each is inherent in the children they carry, each of which has been fathered by Michael. Both are the children of Ireland but they could not have been conceived more differently. With Una the act occurs in an Amiens Street hotel room following a Conradh na Gaeilge meeting, while with June it is in the gaudy canvas tent of a British holiday resort (26, 41). In day-to-day experience, the alternate Irelands jar further: life with Una, and so independence, is closeted and lonely, an isolated existence where Michael is removed from ordered thought and outside learning (24). With June, however, he acts out a multitude of imaginative fantasies while engaged in the affair. He is a doctor or a cattle exporter; she is an actress or a governess (31). This whimsical play is more than mere masquerade. It reveals, to Michael at least, the multitude of possibilities – economic, social, artistic and romantic – presented by home rule, futures richer and more varied than the isolated alternative of an independent Ireland. And yet, considering

Una and June in their respective domiciles, considering both possibilities for Ireland, Michael realises that both were of his own creation (38).

Ironically, it is his sense of familial, personal propriety that lends itself not just to the end of his affair but also to his involvement in the later, greater impropriety of civil insurrection. Michael cannot leave his pregnant wife for a pregnant prostitute, and so he pays for June to terminate the baby. With that child dies the alternative possibility for Ireland's future, Michael's commitment to constitutional home rule, aborted by the city-centre guerrilla fighting of the Rising just as June's child is aborted by a back-street doctor, an operation that occurs at the same time as the arrest of Roger Casement in London (36). That future lost forever, Michael returns to Una, a burgeoning *grande dame* of Irish republicanism, and so adopts the tenets of violent rebellion (69). Their daughter Rene is born awash in blood and so the path of the nation has been determined (39). That all this should occur on British soil is not so anomalous as it might appear, because Dublin, in the early sections of the novel, is a problem for both the Irish and the British. To Fenianism it remains an imperial city (12, 21). To British eyes it is just as easily dismissed, of a piece with the outermost reaches of their own island, marginal places connected to other marginal places as though by the frigid wind which chills the Cornwall esplanade (24). Dublin is a jigsaw of emblematic sites and names, appropriated and misappropriated by all sides in the independence struggle, with *The Past* leaning heavily on the symbolism of the GPO in particular. The site of the Republic's proclamation is, twelve years later, where Una – that lost Republic's most vocal defender – suffers a fatal cardiac arrest (129). The Free State has, literally, broken her heart.

Neither truly Irish nor successfully English, the Dublin of *The Past* thus spawns satellite colonies of its own: Sandymount, which is presented as the internal exile of anti-treaty characters such as Una during the Free State years, and Bray, home of fallen Protestant families such as the Vances, who continue the pantomime of Ascendancy despite the waning of both their social and their economic status in the country. Each grouping slowly comes to resemble the other despite their outward differences, with Una becoming accustomed to a touch of aristocracy in her life just as the Vances develop a concern for Irish politics and culture (66). Dublin's ability to encompass protean communities makes it the perfect capital for a contested state which even its native sons, for instance the home rulers of Michael's era, consider to be a peripheral, backwards and uninformed space filled with little more than rumour and where everyone is related to each other (23). The latter point is emphasised by James Vance – scion of the guilty Protestant perched on horseback to whom Una compares every enlisted Irishman – when he leaves Bray and travels through the provinces (27). The careful, ordered genealogies of his heritage have left him unprepared for the chaotic multitudes of cousins variously removed, and of knotty families who await him at every turn, and, tragically, the character never appears so utterly alien as when adrift in the landscape where his son Luke and his lover Rene feel most at home (212).

In spite of this, Ireland remains a country that he loves (76). James shares the self-conscious embarrassment of a broken gentry, a class that is aware of its own shame. He realises that he cannot truly be an Irishman as the decrees of history have forever alienated him from such a life (76). Consequently, the story of the Vance family foreshadows that of the Hardys in *Shade* by being the story of Ascendancy decline and the fate of Protestants in the Irish Free State. Once the owners of a small ceramics factory whose home bordered on the lands of Lord Meath, the Vance fortune shares its brittleness with the delft they traditionally produced. Eventually put out of business by mechanised ceramics production in England, the Vance estate decays. By the time of *The Past* they have become artists and photographers and stagehands, side-lined by a rising tide of cultural nationalism despite their best efforts to engage with it. The Vance grandfather – and by association James and Luke – is regarded by the Bray establishment as Bohemian, and therefore foreign. In Catholic, nationalist Ireland, he cavorts with Jewish models and his art exalts no one politics or movement. His only government is that of his desires, a constant source of clerical vexation. Son of such a household, James Vance is at pains to be less outlandish. Of a mind to bring together Irish discourse with the contemporaneous European framework (77), this Protestant has swapped his horse for a sense of moral integrity (144). His concerns, somewhat naively, are with public improvements, with the documentation of tenement poverty and the stuff of social geography. He devises various schemes, allying himself to Æ's agricultural movement, and buying a school in Connemara to introduce east-coast slum youth to the west of Ireland (144). Essentially a tragic character, all of James' plans are failures and, as if to undermine his commitment to the project, Jordan relates only those excursions that take James to the most British-sounding areas of the capital itself such as Gloucester Diamond (77).

His chosen home is also suspect, one of those gloomy Edwardian frontages arrayed along the promenade in Bray mirroring to the Cornwall esplanade across waters shared by their little fleets of paddle-boats. Decades of imperialist impulses on the part of the Anglo-Irish have made this area a colony of sorts, at best a playground littered with the exotic evidence of British imperial expansion. Eucalyptus trees – transported from the far side of the world by Victorian adventurers, Jordan says – predominate along the seafront (80, 83). Though useless in Irish weather, they nevertheless shelter the remains of the Ascendancy, frequently James Vance himself. Even in the 1920s depicted by the novel, Protestantism's transformative zeal continues in the area, with the artistic aim of the Vance grandfather being to make an Italianate bay out of a dull, grey Irish sea (61, 81). The old man is intolerant of geographical truth (81). It is only upon meeting Una's daughter Rene and seeing in her an Irish future characterised by cultural nationalism that this fervour is itself transformed, softening into a Hibernicising of the Hellenistic mural he has painted in his hall (98, 99). Over time this image becomes less a yearning for distant lands and more a portal through which the Vances can escape to the mythical Irish west (180).

However, Rene is not a child of the nation in the same way the narrator, her own son, is. She is an intermediate figure; Rene is Ireland's journey, not its destination, an association emphasised by her obsession with train tracks (123). In that vein, her involvement with the Vance dynasty is a healing act, an acceptance by the new state of its eccentric progenitors. Travelling to see them, via rail of course, Rene carries in her hands a tattered English–Irish dictionary, its pages whirling under her fingers as if it is up to her alone to heal the multitude of wounds between the islands (156, 157). Joining them on the Bray promenade, which Jordan will again use heavily in *Sunrise with Sea Monster*, Rene enacts a pseudo-Ireland with the family, a fantasy that is part-Protestant, part-Catholic, and which reflects the Vance progression from the religion of the coloniser to that of the colonised. Least diluted by the native influence, the grandfather is surest of his identity and, until Rene appears, is wilfully ignorant of Irish culture and language. James is more complex, being pulled by an ungainly integrity towards everything he cannot ever be (75, 82). He entertains nationalist sympathies, enters a Catholic marriage (though his wife dies young) and, at her insistence, their son Luke is christened a Catholic (83). The conversion of the family from English to Irish culminates in this boy, one who prefers the company of priests and cattle, and who may well be the biological father of a narrator who assumes the role of child of the nation (167, 191).

Travelling with Rene, the gatekeeper who allows him access to the true Ireland, Luke joins MacAllister's theatrical touring company as a stagehand, carrying flats decorated with Grecian pillars which hint at the original incarnation of his grandfather's mural (187). In this capacity he helps bring, among others, the works of Shakespeare – the literature of the empire – to the so-called provinces, though all accuracy of period is gleefully ignored, with Celtic, Roman, Elizabethan and Edwardian influences blurring into one another until the past is an undifferentiated whole counterpointed only by the present (178). As if in further acknowledgement of the breakdown in the old colonial order which has sustained him for so long, MacAllister himself abandons the grand plan of his usual touring schedule in light of Rene's advanced pregnancy (185). He adopts instead a mysterious reasoning that leads the troupe from small town to small town at their own pace, with Jordan favouring an almost religious language throughout the passages describing their journey, creating an atmosphere of expectation appropriate for the company's leading lady (191). Travelling through places like Clones, Birr, Ballina, Boyle, Gort and Lisdoonvarna, moving from community to community in the manner of early Christians, the fervour surrounding the travelling performance reaches its zenith in the unlikely environs of Strandhill, County Sligo – just across the water from Jordan's own childhood home – where their show is reviewed by a critic from *The Irish Times* in an article dense with the symbolic language of emeralds and wonders (184, 185, 196, 200).

Within the final, undated section of the novel then, the colonial Ireland of the opening chapters is finally, and fatally, deconstructed. Myth and industry collapse together, the biblical encounters the contemporary and the empty differences between Catholic and Protestant, Irish and Anglo-Irish are made meaningless (221, 230). The Cornwall birth is re-enacted, but freed now from the shadow of alternate possibilities. In one of the most positive depictions of the character anywhere in Jordan's work, there is to be only one future for Ireland: that of Éamon de Valera. The leader of the new state gives his benediction to the child in a west that is said to have awakened (196). While the narrator's wonderment at the Lisdoonvarna setting for this hints at his own intricate heritage (he wonders, for instance, how a holiday without sand, beaches or promenade can ever be enjoyable, a question posed equally to the tastes of his particular Protestant and home rule forbearers), the closing chapters look to the future, not the past (215). In the end, the west becomes a land of renewal and regeneration, with the narrator – just as his mother was – born near rejuvenating sulphur waters (222, 223). The appearance of de Valera only serves to highlight the transformation. By the conclusion of *The Past*, the arts of photography, theatre and politics have reshaped Ireland entirely.

GHOSTINGS ON A CLEAN PLATE: THE ART OF PHOTOGRAPHY

It is the spirit of the photographer that, to paraphrase the novel's introduction of James Vance, initially impels *The Past* (75). On the very first page the reader is presented with the image of a yellowed postcard, a photograph of an esplanade, which offers a frame within which the narrator can construct the story of his grandparents' honeymoon. The photograph has a tangible effect on his spatial sense of Cornwall, especially as so much else of Michael and Una's story is imaginary. Though he has never been to that part of England, the narrator is able to tell much from the photograph, extrapolating a sense of the holiday town's urban layout which provides a suitable stage for the story he had devised. It is what Kevin and Emer Rockett interpret as the contemporary tendency to use photography as a replacement for memory and history.[11] In this way Jordan uses the photograph as a form of delineation between the protagonist's timeframe and the pre-independence story of Michael and Una. Though *The Past*'s narrator tries to break through this barrier via imaginatively extending the image beyond the photograph, his attempt is unsuccessful and the serrated edges of the postcard remain a constant reminder of the scene's artificial nature. The author, say the Rocketts, seems to consider photography a fiction like all representations, something that is especially true when such documents are offered as objective evidence of reality.[12]

As Jordan himself saw it, *The Past* is a novel hobbled by just this preoccupation with the filtration of history through intermediate layers with the potential to manipulate and distort.[13] He told *The Independent* that the prevalence of visual description in the novel, of photographers and photography, was an effort to steer the novel form in a direction it did not want to go and thus marks the beginning of his turn to filmmaking.[14] Given the importance of *The Past* to the filmic Jordan's divergence from his authorial counterpart, it unsurprising to find that a motion picture appears in *The Past* at a moment when a character is contemplating their future direction. Increasingly unsure about his commitments to both his politics and his wife, a contemplative Michael attends a film and marvels not at its plot, but at its technical and artistic attributes, recalling nothing of the story but mesmerised by how it ranges freely across space and time (37). This collapse of realistic temporal progression occurs as a result of how the filmmaker's edits remove protracted, real-life stretches of tedious activity in order to retain the interest of the audience. Though Michael may understand how such edits shape the scenes of drama with which he is preoccupied, his own story remains, in his eyes at least, plodding and without a strong narrative through-line.

These feelings of monotony are compounded by how Michael's visit to the cinema follows quickly on the heels of his brief encounter with nationalist adventurer Roger Casement. Here is a man who, seemingly, lives the eventful cinematic life. Michael deems Casement's undertakings worthy, be they African exploits, the anti-war effort or the intrigues that led to the cancellation of his London speech. Like the film, Casement's life can be seen as cutting rapidly from one episode to the next, not from the dining-room to the garden but instead from the jungle to the parliament to the unruliness of a hotel lobby. It is no coincidence that after the Casement debacle, and inspired by the uninterrupted stream of incident in the film, Michael begins to make himself more active in republican circles. The manner in which he became involved remains uncertain, although the narrator has already fictionalised enough history to allow both him and the reader to infer that Michael's involvement stemmed from his London experiences, from a conscious attempt to increase his feelings of agency by the application of cinematic conventions in his own life (38).

Evidence for this is provided by Michael's stated skill at the emulation of others. He begins to wear the trench coat and cap ensemble characteristic of the guerrilla movement's upper leadership, and even takes to writing verse, a republican practice popularised by men such as Pádraig Pearse (46). This Michael is a contrast to the younger man whom the reader originally meets, sitting in a suit, in an oak-lined room reading *The Times*. After London, he undertakes a reinvention of himself in order to bridge the gulf between the man he is and the man he wants to be. He is contemplating the promises of Redmond and the potential of home rule, says the narrator at Michael's introduction. Later, his thoughts turn to Arthur Griffith and the issue of conscription, later again to de Valera and militarism (19). These views originate in the moving-picture palace, and in the monotonous existence of a seaside town which he is consigned to endure for the duration of Una's pregnancy. It is only in the cinema that Michael can finally acknowledge the unfulfilling conventionality of his approach to life. The editing process of the motion picture itself comes as a revelation regarding the limited pattern of his existence, a state of stagnation and isolation exemplified in the two identical stills of Cornwall shown as unchanging when, in fact, between the two postcards the Archduke Ferdinand was shot in Sarajevo and Europe itself has been turned on its head.

Later in the novel, James Vance's photographs also depict an attempt to capture and preserve a staid vision of reality. His theatrical portraits result from the uncomfortable union of photography, still less than a hundred years old, and the long-standing conventions of the stage. He photographs actors against flats and he encourages them to adopt exaggerated poses in order to communicate the attributes of their characters. The effect is stilted and, as is Jordan's intention, it destroys any pretence of realism. A photograph of a stage is just that, and it elicits little imaginative response from an audience trained to respond to the animation of actors in a full theatrical illusion. As a result, Vance's photographs are less a record of cultural endeavour and more an indication that this was a transitional age caught, as Nina Hardy will be in *Shade*, between the waning dominance of the stage and the advent of popular cinema. Vance's photographs are artefacts of a specific and historically localised moment, in this case the Irish literary revival and its attendant nationalist trappings. The evolution of that moment's modes of expression can be seen in the most prominent incidence of photography in *The Past*: the tri-partite frieze of Chapter VIII.

The first of these three images shows Una holding a spear in the guise of a female Celtic warrior. She wears a costume of pleated skirts described as vaguely Grecian but for the elaborate Celtic signifiers, a detail that foreshadows the conflation of Hellenistic and Hibernian influences seen later in grandfather Vance's mural (43). The improvised stage for this event appears to be the drawing room of a large residence, very elegant and proper, reflecting how, in the early days of Irish amateur theatre, it was not uncommon for performances to be held in private homes for an invited audience. This dichotomy between stage and scene is troubling enough, but the real artificiality of the photograph is shown by the emphasis on Celtic in the description. Always a problematic ethno-cultural construction, the word's appearance here serves to underscore the eventual futility of this type of carpet show in general and of Una's theatrical career in particular. This form of drama would soon be rendered obsolete by new styles of performance, particularly the peasant realism of the Abbey which largely signalled the death of pseudo-Celtic presentations in the theatre.

Yet, for a time the new and the old co-exist in a transitional state. Dating from this intermediate period, the second photograph of the frieze captures Una as Cathleen ni Houlihan between caricatures of John Bull and Kaiser Wilhelm II. The foreign figures are grotesquely comedic, an exaggeration of national stereotypes displaying a potbelly and a comically large top-hat, and a goatee and a spiked Prussian helmet respectively (43). Between them, Una's Cathleen is depicted as a poor woman in a shawl at the gable of a thatched cottage. She is the embodiment of another consistently evoked Irish stereotype, the mythical dignity of the starving peasant. Again, this image is designed to fuel insurrectionist feeling and the narrator is unimpressed. His previous asides about her dreadful acting ability here become specific. His critique of the photographs veers more towards personal commentary on his grandmother's appearance. It is as though he is embarrassed by the continued existence of evidence that testifies so absolutely to her limited talent and, not for the first time, the reader suspects that the narrator is himself involved with the arts.

The final photograph is the most modern, which is to say that stylistically it is the most easily understood by the contemporary eye. It appears to be a rehearsal shot from a fully fledged theatrical production, the narrator firm in his belief that it is Seán O'Casey's *The Shadow of a Gunman* on the stage of the early Abbey theatre (44). Within the frame, the character of Donal Davoren sits at his typewriter while Una, as Minnie Powell, is seen over his shoulder having completed both her own artistic journey from drawing room to stage, and the metaphorical transformation of Cathleen ni Houlihan from violent pseudo-Celtic princess, through peasant rabble-rouser, to the urbanised heroics of the modern Irish woman. Exhibited together, both to the narrator and to the reader, these photographs provide a reminder of the fallibility of historical interpretation, highlighting again the delicate boundary between fact and fiction along which Jordan the writer so often walks. Irish history is a contested arena, the formational years of the state more than any other, and the figures captured by the photographs in *The Past* do not necessarily represent an accurate record of events. Snapshots like James Vance's staged pictures are insufficient for Jordan's engagement with Irish history. They seem unreal; they lack life, motion and the implicit link to politics which both Jordan and the narrator seek throughout *The Past*. It is a desire that can only be satisfied by bringing the images to life. For Michael, this animation took the form of a motion picture projected on a distant screen, but for most of *The Past*'s characters it is more immediate, a literal stage on which art and politics collide in search of answers to the many questions of Irish identity: the theatre.

PEASANT IN EMPHASIS, NATIONALIST IN THEME: THEATRE AND POLITICS IN *THE PAST*

A stage is not a neutral space and an audience is not a neutral gathering. Jordan, who in his youth sought the controversy of the footlights with provocative productions such as *Journal of a Hole* (1971), is well aware of how powerful theatre can be when it comes to asserting or redefining self and society.[15] It is therefore unsurprising to find the theatrical life as one of the central components of *The Past* (and, later, in 'The Berkeley Complex' and *Shade*). Theatre, particularly the amateur carpet shows and early Abbey productions, functions in the novel as a means of regulating the pent-up nationalism which characterises the early portions of the storyline. In this way, *The Past* reflects the prominent use of theatre at the time as a means of swaying cultural identities through allegory and suggestion. As Thomas MacAnna wrote, popular theatre at the time offered a parade of thinly sketched Hibernian heroes on the run from the clichéd villainy of murderous British authorities while shawl-clad red-headed Kathleen Mavourneens lamented their menfolk's incarceration, exile or melodramatic demise.[16] Figures such as Robert Emmet ascended the stage and hanging scaffold alike, often twice nightly.[17] In *The Past*, this aspect of the theatrical world is portrayed through the character of Una, a parody of Maud Gonne who, despite her imperfect talent, attains a pre-eminent position amongst nationalist actresses (46).

Una resumes her earlier stage career – interrupted by the need to hide her pregnancy – in mid-1915, less than a year before the Dublin Rising. Her journey to prominence is assisted by what the newspaper reviewers refer to as her quintessential Irishness, her Gaelic majesty, and by what the narrator derogatorily christens her fortunate *blas* (41, 42). When she is challenged by the other *grande dames* of republicanism, it is this cloak of nascent national identity that ensures her dominance. Within the novel she serves as an embodiment of the nationalist zeitgeist, and her involvement in the era's theatrical revolution serves as a powerful echo of the rolling political upheaval which provides the narrative backbone of *The Past* as a whole. The reader will note, for instance, the growing technical sophistication of the performances captured in the frieze of Chapter VIII discussed above. These photographs reflect not just Una's growth as an actress or the increasing narrative sophistication on the Irish stage during the revolutionary era, but also the development of the nationalist movement from posed concern through unsophisticated political agitation to genuine engagement. The relative speed of change can in turn be taken as an indication of increasing instability in the lives of Una and Michael on their return to Dublin, as well as in the political movement to which they pledged their allegiance.

Moreover, the images of the theatrical frieze – in particular the Greco-Celtic *mise en scène* and the John Bull/Kaiser Wilhelm propaganda piece – are essentially examples of *tableaux vivants*, a theatrical grouping of silent, motionless and costumed performers posed and lit for the purposes of displaying a 'living picture', often a recreation of a painting or a set of sculptures. In many routines, a series of *tableaux vivants* would be grouped together to form a narrative series without the need for the more technical aspects of theatrical performance. Instead of a script, plot or characters, these sequences were linked usually through a thematic or a literary connection (in Una's case cultural nationalism). Of course, it is important to note that the theatrical photographs of Chapter VIII do not constitute a tableau series *per se*, merely snapshots of individual tableau, and so it is as though Jordan is playing a theoretical game with the form. He offers a non-sequential tableau which nonetheless follows a thematic progression. The sequence is only readily apparent from the removed perspective of the reader for, within the novel, Jordan is using the *tableaux vivants* in their most straightforward fashion: the simple demonstration of a scene. Nonetheless, the manner in which they combine the evolution of theatrical form with its use as an implement of cultural nationalism enacts a far more complicated performance as, within one short chapter, the author has encapsulated a myriad of *tableau vivant* usage from multiple perspectives.

It is this very flexibility of the form that illustrates why *tableaux vivants* were historically important tools for organisations such as Inghinidhe na hÉireann (the Gonne-led 'Daughters of Ireland'), and why they would appeal so much to a character such as Una. Inherent in their conception of spectacle and performance is the idea of a tableau as a learning aid. American and European tableaux of the nineteenth century bore strong connections to the instructional manuals of etiquette, particularly for women, which were popular at the time. Tableaux describing how to descend a staircase or board a train are often cited examples of the era.[18] However, in the situation detailed by *The Past*, the instructional nature of the tableaux has been dramatically co-opted by the needs of cultural nationalism. The Greco-Celtic tableau teaches its audience an interpretation of Ireland's cultural origin which legitimises the independence struggle, while the John Bull/Kaiser Wilhelm performance is a republican reading of the

First World War political situation distilled for the benefit of an audience on the periphery of the conflict. In this context, *tableaux vivants* function as a kind of primitive nationalist educational system, or, perhaps more accurately, as a form of intellectual conscription. Una's prominence in these activities is at least partly responsible for her later notoriety in republican circles.

However, Una's finest role is not to be found among these photographs of plays and carpet shows. It is instead tied up in the elaborate masses, receptions and state funerals at which she is an obligatory guest after Michael's murder (69). Her costume is a black cape and veil, her character is the widow of the nation (69) and, again, the basis of her success is her ability to capture the country's mood. Where Michael's IRA involvement during the 1915–19 period contributed to Una's credibility in only a minor fashion, his death during the civil war is infinitely more suited to her needs. As the surviving family of a prominent political figure, even Una's grief is stage managed and promoted in the manner of a theatrical production: James Vance photographs Una and Rene in the days after Michael's murder and when the picture is placed in the newspapers it serves as an advertisement for Una O'Shaughnessy's performative mourning. Even James Vance appears unconsciously aware of the irony and regards the photograph's publication in the way a publicist might view a successful campaign: pleased to see his work so prominently illustrating poignant coverage in the national broadsheets that would be read by thousands of people (90). For a time, Una is rendered sacrosanct in the republican social hierarchy, though her strength is also the root of her greatest weakness. Beneath her aggrieved dignity she remains only a mediocre performer, and the part she crafts for herself after Michael's death – her talk of plots and conspiracies – is a limited repertoire which blinds her to further changes in the zeitgeist and to the fact that the young country will not long tolerate the aging widow.

Yet, even this does not represent the novel's greatest entanglement of political and theatrical themes. For that, Jordan requires the character of Éamon de Valera, a figure whose political machinations are presented in *The Past* as yet another exercise in dramaturgy. Though, one must be careful to emphasise the differences between Jordan's fictional de Valera and the historical persona here (as one must with Jordan's *Michael Collins*).

Any representation of de Valera is already fraught with conflicting performances: he is an American, with a Spanish name, playing at being an Irishman; in the Rising he acts the military hero, though really he is the lean schoolteacher concerned with numbers as much as nationalism (45); after the treaty he projects an air of principled political abstinence, but drops this as soon as he sees an opportunity for power as he did by taking the oath of allegiance when he eventually entered Dáil Éireann. De Valera was seen by many to have betrayed his nationalist principles with this act, and this despite declaring the oath an 'empty formula' as though it were a poor script in need of revision. Among those furious at de Valera's decision to sign the king's book of allegiance are Una, who offers condemnation more vocally than anybody else (71). But her protests go unheard as her marginalisation from the centre of nationalist opinion has been completed. The final flourish of this is provided by de Valera himself, who snubs Una's opening night in Denis Johnston's *The Moon in the Yellow River*. It is a perceptive move by which Jordan demonstrates the sharpness of his character's political instincts. By rendering his most vocal critic irrelevant, the de Valera of *The Past* paves the way for his own comeback on the national stage. Years later, or so the narrator imagines, Una will develop a sense of humour to accompany her political exile, and her anger at de Valera's change of position will eventually become amusement. She will revise history herself and claim that it entertained her greatly when de Valera entered the Dáil at last and signed his name performatively with one hand over his eyes. More importantly for Una, she will manage to amuse her friends in republican circles too (113).

For two characters whose earlier connection had been so strongly insinuated, the rift between Una and de Valera is an unpleasant argument which is never put to rest. At her funeral, de Valera is represented only by a mass card. His adversary had been fully defeated long before her death and so this funeral lacks any of the trappings associated with Michael's burial. The ceremony went unmentioned in the newspapers, the character of Lili, his mother's friend and fellow actress, tells the narrator (129). In this vein, the funeral signifies something more than Una's passing. It closes the novel's treatment of Ireland in the age of militant insurgency, with Una as its fictional muse. From James Vance's perspective, it is clear that the makers of history are gone. He looks around for the politicians and the soldiers decorated in medals but does not find them, forced to conclude that all the great events of history are passed (131). Whereas the state funeral of Jordan's earlier story 'A Love' marked the end of the de Valera stranglehold on Ireland, Una's funeral marks its foundation. Una's death occurs in 1931, when Rene is sixteen years old. Less than twelve months later, the 1932 general election would elevate de Valera to the leadership of the country, a position then known as president of the Executive Council. By the opening of the next section of the novel, 'Bray, 1933', he has solidified his control of the country with a snap general election, a melodramatic gesture which returned a majority Fianna Fáil government to power.

Thus, Una's funeral is reduced to an epilogue, a coda to her more famous performances and yet another show that the good and the great of Ireland cannot be bothered to attend. Years later, de Valera's snub of Una's opening night, if not her funeral, will be reversed in the politician's surprise appearance during Rene's last performance on the provincial tour which dominates the latter portion of the novel. Lili, who was afraid of the murmur in the audience which announced his arrival, tells of de Valera sneaking in during the performance. Again, the allusion to de Valera's entrance to the Dáil, the most notorious of Ireland's theatres, is clear (228). The backdrop to his performance, however, has undergone a radical transformation and the focus of the novel has moved west again with significant symbolic purpose. Throughout *The Past*, as well as in 'A Love' and *Sunrise with Sea Monster*, Jordan depicts the west as the spiritual heartland of Ireland. For his de Valera character too, the west is more than another province. It has a mythological, spiritual, indeed even a religious quality. Jordan paints it as a fabled realm, a place beyond mere history where the lineage of the inhabitants runs not just through Irish heroes such as Brian and Niall, but back through Moses and Adam and directly to God himself (231).

CHILDREN OF THE GODS: THE DENOUEMENT OF *THE PAST*

The seventh and final section of *The Past* is simply titled 'Lisdoonvarna'. That it takes place in the year 1934 is clear from earlier events, yet Jordan's omission of the date from the heading (in contrast to all previous sections) grants the occurrences here a sense of mystery and timelessness. Rene, pregnant now with either James or Luke's child, has joined MacAllister's Emerald Theatre Company in what Jordan terms 'The Provinces'. Her maternal radiance, disguised under loose-fitting costumes, proves to be the defining aspect of the tour and is widely praised. The eyes of the audience were magically drawn to her, the reader is told, with her movements rendering the lines themselves irrelevant. She has inherited all her mother's faults, yes, but whereas Una tended to transform every role into a public address, Rene's gift is to transform each character into the essence of herself (188). While there are concerns that a pregnant but unmarried actress will cause controversy in small-town Ireland, this proves not to be the case. Instead, the effect of Rene's pregnancy is transmuted into her performance. Theatregoers were blinded to her pregnancy by her resplendence, and the favourable reviews poured in (189). Though the narrator implies that the exuberance of *The Irish Times* is as much to camouflage their reviewer's dalliance with a Roscommon widow as it is to extol a worthy show, the newspaper's article generates considerable publicity for the troupe and, as Lili explains, all sorts of theatrical critics subsequently began to show up in the most curious of places.

Such reviews are intrinsic to the denouement of the novel, for the publicity generated in the media is key to James Vance's discovery of Rene and Luke's whereabouts. Eventually, Rene's collected devotees become so numerous that James only has to ask in the streets in order to garner information on the troupe as the tour pushes westward with an almost religious fervour (202). Foreshadowing the end of *Carnivalesque*, it is as though the tour is the vanguard of a great pilgrimage towards some immense historical revelation – an event for which the logical candidate is the narrator's birth at the climax of the novel. Jordan positions the narrator as the representative of a new generation. If the reader accepts the novel's implied continuation of the civil war by other means throughout the political wrangling of the 1920s, then his is the first generation to enjoy a cessation of the extended hostilities, a calm generated by de Valera's consolidation of power in the early 1930s and his subsequent dismantling of the divisive Anglo-Irish Treaty. The narrator, progeny of such an illustrious nationalist heritage, is therefore heir to a largely new conception of the Irish state. As if to reinforce the political genealogy that links de Valera to the narrator, it soon becomes apparent that Jack, de Valera's driver, is the same man who served as a chauffeur for Michael. He is the man who informed Rene of her father's death and his presence now, at the birth of Rene's child, is both a cathartic end for a figure earlier reduced to a sorrow characterised by tears on his face and a cap in his hand, and an important symbol of the continuance of the earlier nationalist movement within the independent Ireland (71).

A generation later, in the narrator's chronological present tense, continuity with the familial past is replaced by a representative of the other stereotypically restrictive power in Ireland, the Catholic Church. An enigmatic priest who never seems to rise above the rank of curate despite his long service to the parishes of the greater Dublin region, the character of Father Beausang is, like de Valera, part mathematician. He provides counsel to James Vance before the arrival of Rene, and, years later, provides a similar assistance to the narrator himself. The pun in the character's Norman-derived name is intentional: *Beau sang* translates from French as 'beautiful blood', with the meaning of *beau* extended to 'fine', 'handsome' or 'lovely looking'. If anyone is going to assist the narrator in his search for the history of his own noble bloodline, it is fitting that his guide should be so appropriately named. In becoming his confidant, Beausang contributes to the rationale for the narrator's journey west. The search, at this point, becomes his as much as it has thus far belonged to the narrator and to Lili. All three are tightly connected to the story, and yet none has ever revisited the site of the birth. The narrator himself seems to realise the importance of this only slowly, at first merely promising to report back to the priest on his findings in the west (182). Beausang though makes the journey by himself, begging the forgiveness of the narrator for his inability to stop himself (219). The final locations of Rene, Luke and James' drama loom in his imagination: Quilty, Ballina, Strandhill, Knock (220), all places James marked for him via postcard, the same way Cornwall is marked for the reader at the opening of the novel. The further west the adventure takes them, the more exotic the locations become for Beausang, a man for whom the west coast was a stroll in Salthill (220).

There is also the company of Lili, with whom Beausang strikes up an immediate and affectionate relationship, and while the trio's journey provides one narrative branch to the story, its conclusion is never really much in doubt: they are destined to reach their goal. Dramatic tension throughout the final sections of the book is therefore provided by James Vance's search for Rene and Luke in flashback. Here, the younger Beausang is also the impetus for that journey, providing James with the newspaper cutting from *The Irish Times* and leaving the reader to appreciate the ironic twist of how the reviewer's scandalous dalliances provide the clergyman with the information necessary to reunite this most atypical of families. As at every other point in the story where he has helped expedite matters, Beausang appears to know exactly what he is doing. If the narrator embodies Irish politics and history, then Beausang personifies the concept of historical progression itself. His role in the novel is like that of a theatrical director: he prompts the actors of history, from James to the narrator, towards their marks.

More than this, however, Beausang is the mischievous externalisation of the narrator's desires. When they first meet in the Bray house that once belonged to James, Beausang's introductory act is to rip the wallpaper from where it covers the mural painted by the grandfather Vance. Passing through the house, the narrator has just commented on how the mural has been covered up with green and orange paper (138). Beausang makes short work of this propriety, relishing the destructive act and the revelation of the faintly erotic Greco-Celtic painting on the wall beneath. He then goes on to make the narrator complicit in both the vandalism and the pretence of innocence they must adopt when two families arrive to view the property, which is for sale. A refreshing portrait of a clergyman, Beausang presents himself as everything the narrator is not: he drinks (139), lies (160), sleeps when he wants to (174, 180) and has a certain improper fondness for women (228). Furthermore, Beausang is involved in a curious incident involving a chairlift soon after meeting the narrator, one which can be considered the book's only concession to the supernatural (or, if one prefers, the beginnings of Jordan's interest in the fantastical). As they walk along the Bray promenade, beneath the remains of a disused chairlift, Beausang muses on life, death and rejuvenation, ending with the philosophical flourish that the neglected cable will yet hoist another passenger through the sky (146). The reader shares in the narrator's surprise as immediately, and as though by Beausang's command, his desire to see the chairlift move is fulfilled: with a creak of the cable, the whole contraption comes back to life, grease glittering like blood in its veins as a yellow chair passes overhead (147). Its sudden appearance is by far the most inexplicable occurrence within the novel, though it is camouflaged by the narrative's quick onward momentum. The reader is fooled, by sleight of literary hand, into agreeing with the narrator's logical, if forced, summation that the summer season was close to beginning and that surely the chairlift's revitalisation was the work of a canny local businessman (147).

While some of the incidents surrounding Beausang, such as falling asleep at the Eagle's Nest or on the train, can be attributed to the priest's age, it is more useful to imagine the character as the ironic embodiment of the narrator's repressed self. The narrator is too proper and too refined to indulge these desires himself. Instead, when he encounters temptation, it is, ironically, the priest who appears to sway him. Essentially, Beausang is the id component of the less than holy trinity who journey to Clare in the contemporary era of the novel's finale. He is 'the inherited instinctive impulses of the individual, forming part of the unconscious and ... interacting in the psyche with the ego and the super-ego'.[19] If one continues to map out the constituent psychology of this triumvirate, then Beausang's advisory role to the narrator is balanced by that of Lili, who acts out the role of the super-ego, 'that aspect of the psyche which has internalised parental and social prohibitions or ideals early in life and imposes them as a censor on the wishes of the ego; the agent of self-criticism or self-observation'.[20] Lili's censorship can be seen throughout the novel, having taken on board her mother's closeted disapproval of Una (34), and developing a dissatisfaction of her own which she focuses on the character of James, who she claims she never really liked (200). Yet, in spite of this, she wonders if she loves him as an extension of her love for Rene and Luke. The short, self-questioning sentences of this realisation reveal the discomfort caused to her by her infatuation with what was, essentially, a *ménage à trois* in all but name. This fascination with the others threatens Lili's belief in social order and conventions, and is the opposite of what might be considered Beausang's comfortable familiarity with the tenets of unconventionality. Bringing this interpretation to its conclusion, the narrator, standing between Lili and Beausang, and receiving guidance and information from both, is identifiable with the psychological role of the ego, 'that part of the mind which is most conscious of self ... that part which, acted upon by both the id and the super-ego, mediates with the environment'.[21] This mediation constitutes the narrative thrust of *The Past*, and a pattern soon develops whereby the character receives some new information from Lili or Beausang, applies it to his search for information, and derives a fresh reimagining of the historical reality from the experience.

The apotheosis of this collaboration occurs during the novel's conclusion where the trio make the trip to Clare and, in the process, invoke the events of 1934. As Lili tells the story, James finally catches up with the Emerald Touring Company in the town of Gort. To Lili, James' very being is defined by his profession; he spies them through a lounge window, much as he might frame a picture of them through a photographic lens (202). Crucially though, James has travelled to the west without his camera. The performances he witnesses here are recorded only in his memory and imagination which, as the novel has proposed several times, are the only true stages of history. At first James regrets his decision not to bring his camera, but soon he comes to see that this is not the disaster it first appears to be. He finds that all the images he has taken exist in his mind. His revelation is similar to that of Michael, sitting in the London moving picture palace twenty years earlier, though where Michael underwent 'death of time' and all its associated longings, James' mind treats him to an acceleration of temporal experience. If the cinematic lexis is greater than its photographic equivalent, then the mental lexis must be boundless indeed, for all the scenes he has captured return to him not as photographs but as memories flickering at speed as they move through the years, a mental picture palace with James' soul for a projector (202).

His realisation is that he, and not the black box of his camera, is the real lens by which history is recorded. His photographs exist in the form of prints, yes, but they exist too in his mind and they are all the more vivid there for their interconnectivity. James sees Luke age from child to man, and Rene jump to womanhood in a series of quick cuts, leaving the reader to wonder if James should in fact become a filmmaker on his return to Dublin (202). Consequently, it is easy to read Jordan's future interest in film into James' revelation, as it is to see aspects of it in *The Past* as a whole.

Not unlike a photographer, be it of stills or motion pictures, Jordan here captures a succession of historical, theatrical and political images in the language of the novel and, despite the vibrancy of their individual nature, it is only through assembly into a cohesive unit that they truly come to life. Despite his own statements that *The Past* struggled under the weight of visual imagery, Jordan succeeds in crafting just such a coherent whole with the novel.[22] *The Past* is a book whose complex engagements with the notion of 'Irishness' provide a thematic baseline for Jordan's future fiction. Through his novels, Jordan builds on the explorations of *The Past* to consider the Irish individual as a figure against a changing backdrop: the fallen Ascendancy of this novel finds a companion piece in that of *Shade*; its political machinations directly underpin the isolationist state of *Sunrise with Sea Monster* as well as providing background and context for the postcolonial nation of *The Dream of a Beast*, let alone the ballet of shared misunderstandings in *Mistaken* or the hidden narratives of *Carnivalesque*. Dressed and redressed by Jordan in this fashion, the nation's history itself becomes one of the more expansive and intriguing stages in mainstream Irish contemporary fiction. In this way at least, *The Past* proves key to all the work Jordan would write in the future.

CHAPTER 4

Transformative Myth: Interpreting *The Dream of a Beast*

The Dream of a Beast (1983) is possibly Jordan's least read work after his uncollected film stories. A novella-length hallucinatory fantasy, the volume stands alone among the author's fiction as something different, a postcolonial allegory described by the *New York Times Book Review* as a feverish evocation of Joycean Dublin as though seen through the eyes of Franz Kafka.[1] It follows the transformation of an unnamed protagonist from suburban family man to animalistic beast against a backdrop which is itself metamorphosing from a recognisable cityscape to a surreal grassy vista (*The Dream of a Beast*, 102). It is a story of both generic and genetic mutation, one that offers a critique of social and political, even economic, developments in the Ireland of the early 1980s. Though it lacks the temporal or geographical range of Jordan's other long-form fiction, it is the work that seems to travel the furthest distance from its starting point. Perhaps on account of its unusual subject matter and all its inherent ambiguities, criticism of *The Dream of a Beast* swings widely 'between awe and befuddlement'.[2] The *Financial Times* considered it a beautiful work which accomplished the difficult task of telling a fantasy story for adults that was unsettling without slipping into ghoulish territory.[3] By contrast, Christina Hunt Mahony sees the book as a nightmarish bestiary which holds a macabre mirror up to the structure and intention of Lewis Carroll's *Alice in Wonderland*.[4]

Many critics and reviewers overlook the book entirely, and while the novella is often listed among Jordan's works in profiles, it is rarely addressed in any great detail. The primary exception to this is Lori Rogers, who considers the novella's representation of bodily secrets in a *Critique* article and, subsequently, in her monograph *Feminine Nation: Performance, gender, and resistance in the works of John McGahern and Neil Jordan* (1998).[5] Rogers argues that the narrator's transformation into a non-human beast is engendered by his growing realisation that he is a man with a highly developed if stereotypical feminine side to his personality, one combining creativity and passivity (and in this way the novella echoes the concerns of Jordan's more visible work for the screen).[6] A similar approach is taken by Keith Hopper in his consideration of the novella as part of an examination of *The Company of Wolves* (1984), Jordan's contemporaneous Angela Carter collaboration to which *The Dream of a Beast* bears an interesting kinship. In the main, however, references to *The Dream of a Beast* are mostly offhand. Alain Chouinard touches on the novella as part of a larger examination of how Jordan uses water in his work, but does not investigate it in great detail.[7] Meanwhile, Matthew Ryan sees in it a search for authenticity.[8] For Pat McCabe, the most striking characteristic of Jordan's novella was its use of language.[9] Aubrey Dillon-Malone, in a review for *Books Ireland*, deemed it a 'work so solipsistic, so rich and profound and yet so mind-bogglingly obscure that the layman could be forgiven for calling it purple'.[10] For John Banville, meanwhile, it is simply Jordan's masterpiece.[11]

In many respects it is easier to categorise *The Dream of a Beast* by how it does not fulfil its comparisons rather than by how it does. For instance, while comparison to *The Metamorphosis* by Kafka is almost inevitable, Jordan's protagonist is rooted in the desires of a postcolonial, post-*industrial* backdrop. While it is true that both texts highlight the judgemental nature of society when faced with someone – perhaps some*thing* – different, Kafka's dream, as Roger McHugh put it, foregrounded the horror of transformation and the human inability to hold it at bay whereas Jordan's tends towards a celebration of change (though, as he notes, the novella itself is not lacking for scenes of disquiet or destruction).[12] *The Metamorphosis* also deals with the ramifications of the transformation, not the process of change itself, whereas *The Dream of a Beast* is more concerned with the protagonist's emotional response to the slow but inevitable progression of his mutation. Jordan himself dismisses the Kafka connection in place of more cinematic inspirations, being inclined to compare it to films such as *Creature from the Black Lagoon* (1954) or *The Fly* (1958).[13] The horror element of those films suggests a further tempting comparison with another transformative novella (as well as investigation of split personalities): Robert Louis Stevenson's

Strange Case of Dr Jekyll and Mr Hyde (1886). Again, however, this bears only superficial similarities to Jordan's story. Though *The Dream of a Beast* sees an inner beastly form come forth, in the course of which one side of the protagonist's identity slowly comes to dominate the other, the transformation is not resisted. It is less a reflection of the protagonist's inner conflict than it is a consequence of incomprehensible changes in the wider world impacting on his sense of self. After all, Jordan's protagonist is not a vector of infection – be it biological or ideological – but instead represents the effect of larger changes occurring in the world. He may be a beast, but he is not a monster, and that distinction grants him an uncommon perspective.

This use of an outsider figure in such a fashion is of a piece with Jordan's other work. For though his writing is steeped in the realistic tradition, a defining aspect of his fiction (especially going forward) is his repeated inclusion of inexplicable events coupled with privileged observers. Reality, he has said, is not as important to him as the world that we imagine.[14] He claims to enjoy stories that depict the collapse of rationality, narratives that force characters beyond the point of intellectual explanations for their circumstances, and further states that he likes to tell stories involving imaginary, often monstrous beings.[15] It is therefore not without cause that many critics have identified a strain of magical realism in Jordan's writing, as Gefter Wondrich has with regard to *Sunrise with Sea Monster*.[16] Somer and Daly, in their introduction to the *Anchor Book*, position *The Dream of a Beast* as a kind of Celtic contemporary to South American experimentations in magical realism, a style of writing which they intriguingly loop back to certain episodes of Joyce's *Ulysses* and which they see as a rejoinder to postmodern cynicism.[17] *The Dream of a Beast*, they say, evokes images from humanity's deepest psychic recesses and seeks to connect with the reader on an almost subconscious level.[18] Such an effect can also be seen in *Sunrise with Sea Monster*, at the return of the father's ghost from the ocean, in *Shade*, where the entire narrative structure is (dis)ordered by the posthumous perspective of its narrator emerging from the septic tank where her remains have been disposed of, and in the slowly unfurling history of the Tuatha Dé Danann which occurs in *Carnivalesque*. In the case of *The Dream of a Beast*, these speculative elements are best explored alongside Jordan's film *The Company of Wolves*

(1984), both of which draw heavily on the Gothic in terms of both imagery and intention.

Indeed, the compositional proximity of *The Dream of a Beast* and *The Company of Wolves* offers interesting avenues for interpreting Jordan's novella. The book's transformational subject matter becomes much less surprising when one considers the transformation which the author himself was undergoing at the time. Since the publication of *The Past* he had completed *Angel* (1982), his first feature film as writer and director, as well as embarking on co-writing *The Company of Wolves* with Angela Carter. He had, in other words, begun to shed one creative skin and adopt another. It is telling that the human form of the Beast works in advertising – itself a hybrid of words and imagery – and so is engaged in a creative practice with elements of both writing and filmmaking. His partner Morgan is the pen-man, contributing drawings and pencil sketches of central concepts, while the narrator himself is said to possess an imagination figured in cinematic terms and is described as though he were a director putting a scene together (16, 17). Morgan's expression of concern that the duo's collaboration will someday be forgotten (72) speaks to Jordan's own transition from pen to picture at the time, though in much the same way that the Beast retains his human cognitive and emotional abilities, the author's transmutation into a filmmaker did not involve the loss of Jordan the writer, but rather his incorporation – like the boy the Beast assumes into himself (100) – into a new *gestalt* identity. For instance, *The Dream of a Beast* follows stylistically from *The Past* (1980) in that this novella is again composed mostly of description rather than dialogue.[19] But unlike that story, which fits comfortably within, arguably even profits from, the formal constraints of the novel, Jordan himself admits that *The Dream of a Beast* could quite easily have developed into a screenplay.[20] As much as metaphor and symbolism, it is the visual image that holds Jordan's interest in this work, and in a far more striking way than in *The Past*. *The Dream of a Beast* is therefore a particularly good example of the overlap between the fictional and the filmic Jordans, as well as the manner in which, as Des O'Rawe has put it, the author has a crucial relevance to the discussion of the relationship between literary and visual cultures in modern Ireland.[21]

Much later, exploration of that same divide would drive the plot of *Mistaken* (2011), a novel which offers the reader a version of the author split into two creative identities, the textual and the visual. Yet, where the identical central characters of *Mistaken* are able, much like Jordan himself, to swap identities on occasion, the titular Beast in this book enjoys no such luxury. He is undergoing a transition, moving from a state of being where he understood his limitations to one that, though he retains elements of his prior identity, is of more mysterious, even frightening, potential. In the course of this change the Beast is repeatedly judged and misjudged in a way that, ironically, prefigured the novella's reception by readers and critics. Though he already had two books to his name when he published *The Dream of a Beast*, Jordan told *The Independent* that he recalled the novella being reviewed as though he were a filmmaker who had now decided to try his luck with prose.[22] That said, *The Dream of a Beast* is very much the work of an artist in transition, a writer who is becoming a filmmaker and, in the process, growing more distant from the writing community of which he was heretofore a part. As Jordan himself has stated, the novella was a true expression of his feelings at the time.[23]

Of course, as potent as Jordan's professional metamorphosis is to any consideration of *The Dream of a Beast*, one would be remiss to overlook a more prosaic inspiration for much of the novella's transformational imagery. In a public interview with Pat McCabe, Jordan recalled living in the Dublin suburb of Marino and suffering from eczema.[24] He spoke about the difficulties of – like the Beast – trying to conceal the changes to his skin from family and friends, and about the revulsion he perceived from others when they noticed his condition.[25] *The Dream of a Beast*, he said, was an effort to express that experience in words. Be that as it may, the author still considers the novella's themes to be far from uniquely personal. As he has written elsewhere, Jordan perceives the effort to envision different states of being and living to be an intrinsically Irish act.[26] He is unsure as to the ultimate cause of this but suspects it is the result of – as we will see again in *Carnivalesque* – an historically derived Irish necessity to think ourselves into new places and situations.[27] Critics too see a thematic breadth to *The Dream of a Beast* which extends far beyond eczema sufferers on the northside of Dublin. For the Rocketts in particular, the novella reflects issues recognisable from Jordan's wider work including a concern for the body, for love in both familial and sexual terms, for estrangement, difference and, obviously, for transformation.[28]

This final contradiction – an exceptionally personal work with a nonetheless universal appeal – is reflected on multiple formal, generic and symbolic levels within *The Dream of a Beast*. For example, Jordan's use of fantasy reaches an intensity here which is unseen elsewhere in his prose, one which is potentially off-putting to mainstream audiences, though the book's brevity ensures that the demands it makes on the literary reader never outstay their welcome. The novella is a work that combines a precise and chillingly evocative physical description of Dublin city and its environs with a willingness to confront reality's more indefinable concerns (the protagonist hides out on the roof of the then Central Bank building on Dame Street, seeking solitude in the midst of Dublin city, an isolated figure in the middle of Ireland's largest population centre).[29] The Beast exhibits a joy at leaving his humanity behind, which some critics found themselves quite disturbed by (perhaps because of its implicit celebration of Jordan's own flight to motion pictures) and yet it is precisely this capacity to relish beauty and to experience the moments of true happiness which his transformation brings that elevate the character into a figure of almost mythological scale.[30] Ireland, in turn, is shown as an increasingly alien space as the story progresses but, in practice, the narrator is already privately alienated from the rules and norms of his society long before the mutations of the novella take hold. There are consequently a variety of ways to interpret *The Dream of a Beast*, with the readings presented here concentrating on defining the novella as a work of fantasy, reading it as an allegory of postcolonial Ireland, and contextualising it as the work of a writer who is in the process of becoming a filmmaker.

DO YOU WISH TO FLY? FANTASY AND *THE DREAM OF A BEAST*

Given that it is a story of genetic mutation, one might expect *The Dream of a Beast* to fall under the genre umbrella of science fiction. Yet, the novella is more comfortably of a piece with the conventions of fantasy, particularly Gothic fantasy, and in that light aligns more readily with the work of Jordan the director who to date has never made a science fiction film (having once dismissed *Star Wars* by George Lucas as a space-based homage to Second World War fighter pilot films[31] and noting a silliness in *Star Trek*, though acknowledging that franchise's entertainment value).[32] Indeed, science fiction elements are rare in Jordan's work, with the exception of the time-travel component of *Shade* (a structural choice as much as anything else), the gravitational theory underpinning much of the imagery and metaphors of *Carnivalesque*, and the fractal graphs and viral events which texture his COVID-19 story 'Easter 2036'.[33] For the most part, Jordan largely eschews the scientific – the search for fact-driven exploration – in favour of the potent uncertainties of the fantastic. He has stated a dissatisfaction with scientifically approved and accepted descriptions of the universe[34] and, instead, favours things that defy rational explanation.[35] He told *The Independent* that he is drawn to narratives where characters are transformed and where people's motivations lie deeper than they themselves realise.[36] Furthermore, fantasy as a mode allows considerable scope for Jordan's allegorical intentions and, given how often and how successfully he has utilised it on screen – typically as a means of bringing unconscious desire to the surface in highly stylised fashion – it would in fact be more surprising if it never surfaced in his fiction.[37] He has, for example, frequently linked the Gothic to fantasy (and, for that matter, to horror). He has professed a liking for the Gothic, and stated in interview with Michael Dwyer that many of the things he finds most interesting and visually engaging on screen have been accomplished within the realm of fantasy and horror.[38] Thus, as Des O'Rawe put it (about the films, though it is equally applicable to the fiction), Jordan's Gothicism is informed by a longstanding and perceptive appreciation of the genre within a specifically Irish context (and indeed, beyond *The Dream of a Beast*, this will be key to engaging with later work such as *Shade* and *Mistaken*).[39]

Of course, for many readers the genre classification of *The Dream of a Beast* is open to debate, not only because the novella seems so antithetical to pure realism from the outset, but on account of its close compositional relationship with the warped fairy tales, as Richard Haslam puts it, which comprise *The Company of Wolves* (a twisting we will see again in *Carnivalesque*).[40] Other critics, such as Marianne Brace, see the story as riffing on and reversing elements of *Beauty and the Beast*.[41] Such readings are given weight by the multitude of fairy-tale references within the text, primarily in scenes to do with children. The protagonist's daughter, for instance, begs her father to read her a story of magical and mythological creatures (7). Later, the boy caring for him shares tales straight out of fairy stories about potions and magical practitioners and enchanted kisses (70). Yet for all of this, a close examination of the text suggests that it draws more on the fantastic than on the folkloric backdrop which Haslam and Brace's observations imply. In fact, unlike the fairy tale, *The Dream of a Beast* is obviously fantasy in that it dramatises the kind of hesitation that Tzvetan Todorov considered a central aspect of the genre, that experienced by a person confronting an event inexplicable according to the known parameters of the world.[42] Moreover, the story is not set in a never-never land but in a recognisable Dublin, and this definite location – which, as we shall see, is crucial to a postcolonial reading of the text – stands in direct opposition to a key feature of the fairy tale, an unreal world, as defined by Stith Thompson.[43] Neither is the story a retelling or a look back at the folktales of the past but instead, as characteristic of much of the best fantasy, simultaneously correlates with and abstracts from notions of modernity, something that is true of *The Dream of a Beast* in the constant presence of turbines and trains, in its wire-filled hall and its urban setting (74).

The novella's classification as fantasy becomes clearer again when one considers how the genre derives mostly from Romanticism's idealisation of the child and its refutation of the Enlightenment's scientific rationalisation. Such characteristics are clearly recognisable in *The Dream of a Beast*, ranging from Jordan's use of William Blake in the novella's epigraph, to the story's scepticism of reason and analysis in the face of the unexplained, and to its exaltation of children in the form of both the protagonist's daughter and the young boy who cares for him during his transformation. Equally, says Maria Nikolajeva, the eclecticism of fantasy derives from how it blends together the seemingly discordant tropes and traits not just from the obvious storybanks of fairy tales and mythology, but also from chivalric novels and romances, the mysterious sensibilities of the Gothic, the roguishness of the picaresque, as well as the genres of mystery and science fiction.[44] Clear traces of such appropriations are visible in *The Dream of a Beast* and, to pick prominent examples from Nikolajeva's list, it is not difficult to identify at least touches of myth (in the manner in which the novella tells of the creation of a new world), romance (between the narrator and both his wife and his female client) and the Gothic.

More specifically, *The Dream of a Beast* is what Farah Mendlesohn defines as an intrusion fantasy, a narrative where the accepted normality of the world is breached by something beyond the everyday.[45] A typical intrusion fantasy requires that a character negotiates or overcomes this disruption to the assumed integrity of the storyworld.[46] Sometimes the outside power may be victorious but, in almost every case, narrative closure takes the form of a return.[47] Mendlesohn cautions that her taxonomic schemata are a tool for understanding forms rather than an end in and of themselves, though they provide a useful yardstick by which Jordan's use of genre conventions can here be measured. *The Dream of a Beast* clearly corresponds to the paradigm of an intrusion fantasy in that it begins with a relatively normal, 1980s suburban setting. This normality is increasingly disrupted by both the changes which the protagonist himself is undergoing and the ecological transformation gathering pace around him. Eventually, the protagonist leaves his home for a period of adjusting to – negotiating with, if you will – his new state of being. In this instance the intrusion wins; the world and the protagonist are irrevocably changed. However, there is still a kind of return, as Mendlesohn puts it, with the narrator and his family reunited at the end of the novella. Likewise, the intrusion fantasy is a form that depends on a protagonist's naivete and on their cognisance of how the inexplicable can bleed into the everyday, an awareness usually rooted in sensory stimuli rather than dry factual knowledge.[48] Again, these characteristics are an almost perfect fit for a protagonist who describes himself as less intellectual than those around him (2), and who grows increasingly reliant on animalistic senses as his transformation quickens.

The fantastic as a genre and authorial choice, Mendlesohn says, allows for the introduction of chaos and, in an image ideally suited to this text, is like a monster hiding at the bottom of a garden (the Beast here spends a short chapter skulking around the bottom of his former garden after being cast out of that hostile Eden; 83, 84).[49] While not chaos *per se*, there is certainly considerable disorder implied in the text from the outset through the presence of soldiers on the streets, the heaps of uncollected garbage everywhere, and the constant discussion of how things – in the broadest sense – are getting worse (1). Against this backdrop, both the reader and the protagonist undergo a typical intrusion fantasy journey from repudiation to acceptance, the former forced to recognise that this work does not sit readily alongside the realism of Jordan's earlier writing, the latter realising that nothing will bring back the existence, even the body, which he once enjoyed (70).[50] Yet, it is the ending of the novella that makes it more of a fantasy than a fairy tale, and which provides the real revelation of the author's speculative intentions. The final three chapters of *The Dream of a Beast* take place in an undeniable fantasy landscape with none of the resemblances to reality which one might expect from a fairy tale. Here, Jordan's descriptions of the city forsake traditional depictions of Dublin for a fugue-like account of ruinous structures crumbling into dust. The protagonist and the boy similarly abandon the city and, instead, find themselves in a more primitive, much warmer and wetter environment (98). They spend time on the shore of a new sea (100), a seemingly brackish body implying the inundation of the land by a colossal upsurge (99), a tidal wave, in other words, sweeping the landscape clear for the Beast and those like him.

For his part, Jordan told Brace that he sees the novel purely as a work of fantasy.[51] Of course, fantasy is often an easier sell on the screen than between the covers of mainstream Irish fiction, especially when the author has an established reputation for well-received literary writing. This perhaps explains some of the unwillingness of critics to engage with the novella. It is easy to see how the use of non-realistic subject matter here confounded preconceived notions of Jordan as an author of serious fiction conversant with Irish history while, simultaneously, demonstrating the attendant and genuine genre expectations of a fantasy text. Not that this should be a sticking point for anyone coming to Jordan's fiction with a knowledge of his work for the screen. Seen as the product of the unified artist, *The Dream of a Beast* becomes far less of an outlier. Jordan gravitates towards the supernatural, not just here or in *Shade* but in films such as *The Company of Wolves*, *High Spirits* (1988), *Interview with the Vampire* (1994) and *Byzantium* (2012), work that conflates supernatural evocations of religious imagery with his previously cited interest in stories portraying rationality's collapse.[52]

This question of religiosity is interesting in that it often plays into how science fiction and fantasy can be read as the products of differing spiritual philosophies: critics such as Adam Roberts see science fiction as intrinsically 'Protestant', while fantasy is inherently 'Catholic'.[53] Roberts is just one of the more recent scholars to put forward this admittedly coarse binary whereby the magical – and for that read supernatural – aspects of fantasy are contrasted with the technological characteristics of science fiction.[54] Essentially, it is a divide between stories of cryptic or impenetrable novelties and those that are more tangible and cogent. Though Jack Fennell, in his study of Irish science fiction, rightly maintains that religiosity is not an effective means of analysing genres in their entireties, Roberts' generalisation does have its uses.[55] *The Dream of a Beast*, unconcerned as it is with the scientific causes of the mutations it depicts, offers further confirmation that what we are dealing with is a work of fantasy: the flirtation with modernity which helps rule out the novella's identification as a fairy tale is not enough to tip the book into the realm of science fiction. More than that, and despite its indifference to the theological implications of its protagonist's transformation, it is still one which betrays the fact that, as Angela Carter once pointed out, Neil Jordan was raised in the traditions of Irish Catholicism.[56]

Even though he is not a believer in that faith, the symbolism imparted by his background looms as large in a text like *The Dream of a Beast* as it does elsewhere in Jordan's work. At one point, the protagonist's wife notes an auroral glow around him resembling a halo, a piece of religious iconography typically associated with holy or sacred figures such as saints or prophets or angels (9). Is the Beast worthy of such adornment? Arguably yes. As stated, he may be becoming monstrous but he is no monster. He is in fact a man of peace. He cares for children and lives by a doctrine of acceptance, inclusivity and forgiveness. His metamorphosis enables him to reach a grace state, a spiritually loaded turn of phrase which implies a closer union with, if not God in this case, then at least the natural world.[57] The Beast is a Christ figure who metaphorically dies (in this instance shedding his original form), spends a period of time in a place that resembles a tomb (76), and is eventually reborn as the avatar of a new age. Though rarely as overtly religious as this, notions of personal development inform much of Jordan's writing. He has expressed a belief that fiction ought to be transformative (though not necessarily in terms of a moral purpose).[58] In fact, according to the Rocketts such transformative elements are of central concern in Jordan's body of work.[59]

Whatever the religious influence on the author's worldview, Jordan's Beast combines his moral standing with, as is the case for Mendlesohn's typical intrusion fantasy protagonist, an intrinsic sensitivity towards the true landscape – both the suburban setting and that of the storyworld more generally – which transcends that of the supporting characters.[60] This aspect of *The Dream of a Beast* is not just apparent in a spiritual sphere but also resonates with the novella's postcolonial subject matter, its effort to depict a new Ireland. The strange flowers on the streets (1, 4) and the increasing dereliction of the cityscape speak to an established tradition of portraying imperial collapse through the decay of infrastructure. Indeed, there are occasions when *The Dream of a Beast* resembles a fresh spin on, of all things, J.G. Farrell's *Troubles* (1970) with its crumbling streets roamed by quasi-feral cats and overgrown by tropical vegetation. Yet, where a novel like *Troubles* examines the problems of a very different timeframe, as well as parodying aspects of its own genre,[61] *The Dream of a Beast* looks at the long-term consequences of colonialism on newly independent populations while also fully embracing the established principles of fantasy. Jordan uses 'a rhetoric of nonchalance to transcribe the quiet desperation of the nullified universe his narrator inhabits'.[62] Instead of conflagration, the story ends with water, scattered with wreckage yes, but overall tranquil (100). This washing away of the past is a cleansing act rather that one of complete destruction, and the widespread nature of this change at the novella's conclusion is a final reminder that the mutations depicted throughout *The Dream of a Beast* are not simply confined to the protagonist but also to the country which he inhabits.

REIMAGINING IRELAND: POSTCOLONIAL BIOLOGY

Within *The Dream of a Beast*, Jordan the writer's established interest in Irish history and politics is subsumed beneath layers of symbol and allegory. His conscious use of fantasy, particularly its Gothic elements, is a significant gesture for Keith Hopper in terms of how the national narrative is expressed, one which stresses the rich union of the political and the fantastic in Jordan's work.[63] Hopper, by both literally and figuratively devolving a discourse preceding and presaging the literary impact of Joyce and Yeats, quite rightly sees Jordan as gaining access to an entirely dissimilar aesthetic and indeed political palette.[64] Thus, as radical as the intersection of geography, politics and the supernatural will be in the more mainstream *Sunrise with Sea Monster* or *Shade*, it is in *The Dream of a Beast* that Jordan presents his most ambitious speculation as to the fate of the postcolonial nation. The novella offers Jordan's ultimate parable of a landscape and society transcending colonial impositions and returning to an imagined prior state of being. *The Dream of a Beast* presents an Ireland in the throes of sweeping transformation: the urban geography – Jordan's most substantial use of the city in his fiction until *Mistaken* – is devolving into a primal state of unsettling blossoms and eerie, alien leaves (1). Dublin itself is seen to cast off the shackles of imperialism, such as when the swelling timbers of the railway sleepers cause the metal tracks to buckle and break open (1). Thereafter, the trains, symbolic of the British transformation of the island into an ordered, productive colony, become more delayed than ever, eventually ceasing to run altogether. Even the people have begun to part ways from foreign notions of civility, transforming slowly, as the protagonist does, into lumbering primates.

Such a reading of the novella is less far-fetched in light of Hopper's assertion that the multifaceted, and occasionally contradictory, politics underpinning Jordan's 'Irish' work – that being those fictions and films set in, or about, Ireland – can only be fully appreciated through the lens of the author's serious interest in the fantasy genre and its allegorical potential.[65] For Rogers too, the premise of the novella is expressly political, an exploration of how contemporary society subjugates and rejects individual desire and even individual physical form.[66] This is to say that *The Dream of a Beast* is of a piece with how, as Haslam points out:

> Bodily transformations of every kind feature in Jordan's fictions and films. In *Angel*, *Mona Lisa*, *We're No Angels*, and *The Crying Game*, the body is transformed from the outside in; in *The Past*, *The Company of Wolves*, *The Dream of a Beast*, *High Spirits*, and *Interview with the Vampire*, the body is transformed from the inside out.[67]

In this case the novella draws heavily on the medieval image of the body as the state, a notion later suggested by *Sunrise with Sea Monster*, where the paralysis of Sam Gore reflects that of the nation as a whole during the Emergency. Bodies – beginning with the narrator's – are being transformed as the state itself finally has the opportunity to become something new in the early 1980s. As such, *The Dream of a Beast* can be read as a highly stylised, metaphorical response to decades of repression in Irish society, a prose-poem guided by a kind of self-critical mood prevalent within artistic segments of the population.

This is something that Roger McHugh also identified in his *Irish Press* review of the novella, stating pessimistically that the physical and societal disintegration depicted would seem to anticipate the eventual end state of then contemporary trends.[68] Yet, for him, the dissolution of society portrayed in the texts is not so calamitous as would be the experience of that collapse. Thus, as Lori Rogers says, the dilemma of the narrator is one that reflects questions of national importance, though she focuses primarily on the critique of gender roles which occurs through the character's expression of feminine traits within the context of traditionally patriarchal Irish society.[69] While her argument and associated close reading of the text is compelling, the importance of the Beast's transformation for Irish society more generally should not be overlooked. The alienation exhibited throughout the novella, as well as the tentative steps its protagonist takes towards a new life, are therefore best contextualised by Jordan's own feelings that the 1980s were an unsettling period in Irish history.[70] As Brian McIlroy puts it, the intimate knowledge of horror apparent in Jordan's particularly Irish version of Gothicism – read, if you will, *fantasy* – is one which recognises the suffocating threat conservative, curatorial cultures pose to the healthy human imagination.[71]

While on the surface *The Dream of a Beast* would seem to have very little to do with the postcoloniality of modern Ireland, the political element is – as in much of Jordan's work – certainly present, and in that way the novella is true to what Hopper has portrayed as the author's endless rephrasing of national origin stories.[72] For example, an allegorical concern with political events is flagged from the very start of the novella with its narrator recounting the climatic and administrative deviations from the norm, hinted at by undulations in the usual organisation of the environment, the atmosphere and even the earth itself, which have all begun to affect his early 1980s Dublin (1). Later, the changes become more revolutionary (in all senses of the word), occurring so quickly as to deliver sometimes wondrous, sometimes terrifying new developments on an almost daily basis (95). While much of the extant discourse on the novella considers the story in relation to the narrator's home life, these wider developments deserve consideration. One prominent example is the response from the political administration to events taking place, which in this case is the reactionary and militaristic ordering of soldiers onto the streets (2). The reality of previous colonial experience is represented by this authoritarian effort to hold the process of change in check, whereas the Beast's new life represents the almost magical possibilities of the postcolonial. After all, as readers are told in *The Past*, Ireland is an entirely different country in the heat (*The Past*, 148).

Transcending the hybridity usually associated with postcolonialism (as in *Sunrise with Sea Monster*) and traditional Anglo-Irish culture and society (as in *The Past*), the narrator proves to be the vanguard of something genuinely new. He begins to slowly but inevitably shed his skin, his very identity, as if in preparation for the beginning of a new era (23). This character, and the new environment of which he is emblematic, posit an alternative construction of national identity, one which recognises the debilitating influence of British authority on the character of Irish landscape and society. His metamorphosis into a more animalistic, if more docile, nature and appearance problematises his notion of identity; he hides himself, first under gloves and bandages, and, later, in a semi-abandoned storeroom (62). Here, it becomes apparent that the Beast's real transformation is to be psychological. He must learn to embrace his true self, that which has been constrained by exactly the type of suits and waistcoats and starched shirts adopted by Michael in *The Past* when that character was aping an English way of life (33). Now, the protagonist must answer a question with particular resonance for Irish nationalism: how is it fair to possess cultural memory of things as they were, and a collective desire for the way things might be, when one's society is consigned to endure things as they are (88). Yet, as he transforms, the Beast's perception of those involved in the everyday drama of human lives begins to change (26). He witnesses the existing population move through life in a mercantile, urban sleepwalk (22). The Beast observes people who seemed luminous for the briefest of moments before diminishing once again, but his own radiance is more permanent, promising less fleeting prospects than those who merely queued in lines or made small talk or enjoyed transitory flashes of sexual gratification (21). The halo which his wife sees around him identifies the narrator at last as a harbinger of a new order, though as soon as that connection is made, she becomes fearful, growing more distant as his transformation quickens (9).

Nevertheless, the Beast's appearance and behaviour are not just degenerating, they are devolving, a crucial distinction given the importance of the term 'devolution' – the transfer or delegation of power from a centralised authority to a regional level – in the context of these islands. Thus, it is not just political choices, but now, after the colonial and immediately post-independence periods, biology itself that has been returned to local control, and which responds to this new freedom with a vengeance. As his change progresses, the Beast returns to sleeping on the ground, forsaking the implied civility of the bed for a symbolic carpet of green (13). In the Phoenix Park, the Beast hears approaching hooves and readies himself to hide in case he meets a rider upon a horse, a subservient, colonial response which has become innate. Yet, the Protestant on a horse depicted in *The Past* does not appear here; instead, the Beast is faced with an image of freedom, a loose deer whom he feels is calling him to emulate its ways (37). Journeying deeper into the park, the Beast subsequently comes to the presidential residence, Áras an Uachtaráin, which was, during the colonial period, the Vice-Regal Lodge, home of the chief British administrator in Ireland (37). This opulence is rejected by the Beast in favour of nearby Dublin Zoo, where he hopes to find the archetype of his new form, though for a moment he conflates the two and imagines the caged animals lined up along the avenue to the presidential palace (37). It is as though an honour guard has appeared to herald the arrival of the postcolonial state.

As such, the Beast proves to be a vanguard of a political as well as a biological revolution, and, like any revolutionary, he must conceal himself, first under bandages, and later in storerooms and on rooftops. The Beast becomes nocturnal as shadows themselves offer him a further disguise (58). His self-consciousness about his present and coming changes leaves him feeling as though his efforts to hide are more pathetic than anything else but, nonetheless, he persists with them (26). As his transformation accelerates, his behaviour becomes all the more subversive: he walks to the city along the railway tracks, but, in doing so, he is not just rebelling against the colonial infrastructure, he is usurping the need for it altogether (14). In the city centre he sees statues celebrating the heroes of the past pointing towards nothing (36). He imagines a landscape without human beings and ponders the potential of such a radical change (36). In essence, the Beast becomes a political terrorist, though one as aware of his own terror as he is of that which he inspires in others (55). He becomes a disgusting figure in the eyes of those around him, an embodiment of shame for wider society (46, 50); he is shunned even by those he loves until the transmutation becomes a widespread event.

It is therefore fitting that, for his chrysalitic hermitage, the Beast chooses the Central Bank building on Dame Street, the masterpiece of Sam Stephenson, an architect well known for his antipathy towards the colonial fabric of Dublin city.[73] Chapter 17 of the novella describes the building in detail as (with a nod to Kafka) a kind of giant beetle looming over the tightly knotted streets of Temple Bar (60). It is described as a seat of power, a castle of sorts, and, from its parapet, the Beast overlooks Dublin like an Irish Quasimodo (60, 70). It is a location as obvious to the book's initial reviews as it is today.[74] Its thin rectangular windows are like those of a tower or a keep (62). Lest one is tempted to see this as too sanitised a fairy-tale element, the narrator reminds us that it is nonetheless a savage place (77), which is certainly a damning indictment of economics. It is here that the Beast meets the boy, Alarth (86), who tends to him during the latter stages of his change the same way the Beast comes to care for the boy in turn after the final metamorphosis of the world. The boy, like the protagonist's daughter, is an innocent in this world but, as with the narrator's dream of the grown-up Matilde, the reader is left with the impression that this purity is soon to pass. The boy enjoys fairy stories such as Jack and the Beanstalk, but he is not merely content to retell these stories (92). He is on a quest for knowledge, interrogating both the tales he has been told and the evolving narrative of the Beast's transformation (66, 67). The boy possesses a longing for a friend yet initially lacks any realistic understanding of the obligations that friendship might entail (92), which is arguably a common desire of both fantasy characters and newly independent nations slowly shedding their former colonial identities and allegiances.

Jordan's creature, like Yeats' 'rough beast', spends much of his time 'waiting to be born'.[75] Apotheosis, as in *Sunrise with Sea Monster*, is realised only after the breaking of a storm. Swiftly following this downpour is a further intensification of not just the narrator's mutation, but also a transformation of landscape and culture (54). There is a noticeable erasure of infrastructure, such as how the city's bridges are overwhelmed by great masses of luxuriant vegetation (58). The Beast witnesses the return of horses to Dublin streets, a rejection of modern ideas of urbanity (88). He even gains the ability to fly, something that offers him a new perspective from which the whole sprawling urban fabric becomes just a dot on the wider landscape (92). Reflecting changing critical perspectives in the postcolonial age, the intimate dynamic between character and setting, which is a hallmark of Mendlesohn's intrusion fantasy, here finds a new relevance.[76] That the buildings of Dublin eventually crumble can be read as an indictment of the unnecessary complexity often inherent in state apparatus. City spaces towards the end of the book are – and this of course *is* fantasy – obsolete in the new order and, in a similar fashion to Donal's dream in *Sunrise with Sea Monster*, the city that the Beast inhabits is eventually washed away (*Sunrise*, 99; *Dream*, 99). The country which awaits the novella's characters afterwards is a pastoral and prelapsarian grassland (102). This new landscape evokes and anticipates quieter periods of history (102). The Beast and his now mutated wife reunite, both carrying the physical forms of rescued children inside them as a symbol of the innocence and imagination lacking in the stagnant reality they have superseded. It is of a piece with how Jordan would later write that every child dislikes their own present and thus tends to imagine more exciting and alluring alternatives (*Sunrise*, 27). It is further true of his characters more generally, with those of *The Past* dreaming of the free, independent Ireland that so frustrates those of *Sunrise with Sea Monster*. Equally, Donal in *Sunrise with Sea Monster* dreams of something to give his life meaning, as does Kevin in *Mistaken*. Meanwhile, the narrator of *The Dream of a Beast*, arguably undergoing the most significant change in all of human history, is dismayed, and hides himself away for he understands that there can be no going back (55).

At the end, however, Ireland is at once something old again and something new, with the clean slate Jordan offers his readers revitalising traditional sensibilities in a modern guise, the genetic transformation of the landscape and protagonist pre-empting the *genre* transformation of the fiction. *The Dream of a Beast* concludes in a manner quite unlike a typical work of Irish writing, with the environmental transfiguration nearing its conclusion and what animalistic beings remain congregating quietly to see what this new future brings.[77] Because the message of *The Dream of a Beast* is that change begets life and new life in turn begets hope. The book's narrator – an Irish everybeast – eventually attains his long-desired freedom through transformation and self-actualisation (94). He brings to the Irish landscape a new sense of possibility and anticipation based on the erasure of urban civilisation. That he does so in such allegorical, metamorphic, indeed impressionistic fashion – particularly in terms of the emphasis on changing light, on a singular perception of events, and a blurring of reality – makes sense given *The Dream of a Beast*'s compositional proximity to Jordan's collaboration with Angela Carter on *A Company of Wolves*, a surrealistic motion picture adapted by the pair from Carter's slight but tautly structured eleven-page story.[78] The novella, though it appeared before the film did, shares its DNA with this collaboration, with monsters and lessons in morality abounding against a backdrop of reminiscent language and imagery. It is therefore not unreasonable to divine a close relationship between *The Dream of a Beast* and *The Company of Wolves*, two texts of transformation which define a transitional moment in Neil Jordan's career.

THE COMPANY KEPT BY BEASTS

The Dream of a Beast looks to the future and *The Company of Wolves* looks to the past. What ties them together is a significant transition in the life of their author and director, the moment when Neil Jordan the writer began to disappear from the public consciousness and Neil Jordan the film director took his place. As if in illustration of this, the novella has long been below the radar of contemporary critics while the film has quite rightly attracted much scholarly attention since its release, recognised as an early example of Jordan's efficacious transformation of literary energies and inspirations into an idiosyncratic cinematic vision. It is clear, however, that Jordan's work on the adaptation also fed into his own self-reflective attraction to the formal potential of written and visual artistry, a creative loop which is less confounding when one considers how closely the composition of both works overlapped. Some critics, such as Hopper, read this as the film drawing on key themes and images from the fiction, though given the chronological crossover between the composition of the two works, it is perhaps more useful to read them as influencing each other.[79] The relationship between *The Dream of a Beast* and *The Company of Wolves* therefore becomes an object lesson in how Jordan was – for that matter, how *both* Jordans were – preoccupied with career-relevant themes of transformation at this time. In such fashion, Richard Haslam sees the 1983 novella as a work in which Jordan 'reconnoiters the metamorphic dream terrain' of the 1984 film,[80] and, as the Rocketts observe, both works obviously probe the sliding scale between man and monster.[81] Therefore, with an eye towards the future interactions of the two Jordans, it is useful here to consider how the themes of the novella and the film exist interobjectively with each other.

For, much in the same way that the ghost of the older Nina Hardy will haunt and influence herself as a child in *Shade*, there is a dynamic relationship between *The Dream of a Beast* and *The Company of Wolves* whereby examination of either text consistently enriches our understanding of its counterpart and vice versa. Some of the connections are almost too perfect. The first line of Carter's story 'The Company of Wolves' already mentions a beast, and metamorphosis is a theme all across *The Bloody Chamber*, the collection in which it is published.[82] In the stories of that volume – many of which influenced episodes of *The Company of Wolves* – the reader encounters the word 'beast' or 'beasts' almost ninety times across the book's 120 pages, some examples being the beast of 'The Courtship of Mr. Lyon' and that of 'The Tiger's Bride', as well as that mentioned in 'Puss-in-Boots'.[83] Moreover, though it has long been regarded as the Jordan film least conversant with the typical concerns of Irish Studies (*Time Out* went so far as to position it as an

English horror movie in that tradition's Gothic mode),[84] *The Company of Wolves* appears less surprising when viewed alongside *The Dream of a Beast*. In an astute and convincing close reading of the film, Sharon McCann sees a confounding subtext of Irish nationalism (which she links to Jordan's sensibilities as an Irish Catholic, and to the Northern Ireland Troubles) pulsing beneath the Anglo skin of *The Company of Wolves*.[85] She focuses on Jordan's use of the name 'Rosaleen' in the film, which she reads as a deliberate appropriation of the Irish *aisling* poem 'Róisín Dubh' in a similar manner to how centuries of Irish writers have reached for the image of 'Dark Rosaleen'.[86] While this may not initially appear pertinent to *The Dream of a Beast* and its unnamed protagonist, it is worth noting that the Irish word *aisling* means 'dream' or 'vision' and that the genre of *aisling* poetry is itself heavily connected to concepts of literary and even political subversion.[87] Thus, the contemporaneous film solidifies our understanding of Jordan's thinking at the time and supports the notion that we read *The Dream* – the *aisling*, if you will – *of a Beast* as an allegorical representation of Ireland.

Like the novella, the film's origins are grounded in the socio-economic conditions of late 1970s/early 1980s creative industries. The screenplay's authors, Neil Jordan and Angela Carter, first met in 1979 when she was part of the jury that awarded him the *Guardian* Fiction Prize for *Night in Tunisia*.[88] They met again accidentally during a week of Dublin festivities marking the centenary of James Joyce (in 1982). Jordan recalls that he had been shown Carter's story 'The Company of Wolves' and asked to read it with an eye towards adapting it into a feature film.[89] Though impressed with the material, and acknowledging that it would have made a wonderful short, he thought there was not enough in the text for a full feature.[90] Simultaneously, Carter had been commissioned by Walter Donohue at Channel 4 in the UK to write a short script based on her story, the initial draft of which was based upon her radio play version (which introduced the additional tales told by the grandmother into the narrative). Jordan found that this draft radiated all the brilliance of Carter's original story.[91] This version later found its way to Steve Woolley at Palace Pictures who expressed interest in expanding it into a full-length feature film.[92] Once a production deal was in place, Jordan and Carter began their work together on a story which incorporated elements from across *The Bloody Chamber*. In an interview with *Time Out*, he recalled setting up in London for the duration of the collaboration and cycling to Clapham each morning to meet with Carter at the latter's house.[93] Over many cups of tea, the pair would work on the script in businesslike fashion throughout the day.[94] Jordan claims to have appreciated the sense of near-puritan rigorousness which Carter imposed on her working life (and, by extension, his), saying he was reminded of surrealist artist René Magritte's habit of dressing impeccably, packing his things for the studio, briefly walking around the local streets, and then returning home to begin the day's work.[95] Jordan, for one, found this approach fruitful and exciting, if markedly different from the protracted isolation he normally associated with writing.[96] Indeed, he says that working with Carter reminded him of the more exhilarating aspects of stretching one's imaginative muscles.[97] He describes an almost intoxicating process of delving into the suggestiveness of fairy tales alongside Carter, progressing through intimations of Little Red Riding Hood, Tom Thumb and Beauty and the Beast, as well as their own previous writing.[98] Together, Jordan and Carter drew on what Hopper cannily frames as a genetic inheritance from Jordan's masculine novella and Carter's feminine collection.[99]

Jordan himself admits that he derived many of the film's more striking images – such as the babies emerging from the eggs – from the recently completed *The Dream of a Beast*.[100] Hopper in particular notes how the film and the novella share a palate of motifs and imagery (he also notes the influence of Yeats, specifically 'Leda and the Swan', 1923, on Jordan at the time).[101] Such imagery includes not just the clear emphasis on metamorphosis, both physical and psychological, but also the use of dreams, anthropomorphised animals, strange plants and growths, a child working the furnace of his father (in the film's case a blacksmith; in *The Dream of a Beast* a boiler fire) and a conclusive symbolic rebirth. The Rocketts too draw explicit comparisons with *The Dream of a Beast* in how both are fantasy texts which nonetheless allow Jordan to retain one artistic foot in the realistic world.[102] Both texts also share a destabilisation of human/inhuman characteristics, something Maria Pramaggiore alludes to, and to which Jordan will return in *Interview with the Vampire* (1994) and *Carnivalesque* (2017).[103] Both intersect with material aspects of the body horror subgenre[104] and, in the process, both feature characters enacting the same shedding of respectable clothes upon their transformation into something far more animalistic.[105]

That said, the differences between the two texts are telling. Carter's Wolf, the very incarnation of intelligent carnivorous ferocity, is the opposite of Jordan's Beast, who eats corn (77) and is largely unsure about his place in the world.[106] While both derive tonal and narrative elan from, ironically, their strong sense of ambivalence, the novella is in no way as transgressive at the film.[107] *The Company of Wolves* is more overtly concerned with its protagonist's sexuality.[108] In fact, where Rosaleen/Red in *The Company of Wolves* challenges the patriarchal model of female sexual passivity, the more passive protagonist of *The Dream of a Beast* – whose feminised masculinity has already been discussed – finds himself repeatedly at the mercy of women stronger than himself, such as his wife and his client.[109] The narrative of self which he creates is an acknowledgement of social change, a dream of political devolution; that of Rosaleen/Red is more of a personal polemic, a story of sexual maturation. In many ways Jordan's Beast is in opposition to that of Carter. He is a gentle being who eschews the predatory, hyper-masculine behaviours of beasts found in *The Bloody Chamber* or *The Company of Wolves*. Where the creatures of the film proffer a specific kind of violent, consumptive, sexual masculinity, the novella's Beast articulates anxiety about the same. He shirks and hides, he submits more than he initiates. Despite the sobriquet bestowed on him by the novella's title, the Beast is not one of the highly sexualised Carter-esque animal-human hybrids from whom the world can never truly be safe.[110] Yet, neither is he a version of the human-as-monster which dominates in postmodern horror films.[111] He enjoys sex but in a participatory rather than a predatory fashion. He seeks to share small pleasures where he can, not spread disquiet with his presence. His new state of being is not enticing, as for instance that of the protagonists of Jordan's *Interview with the Vampire*, but it is inevitable. Most importantly, the Beast is not a human monster, he is a post-human being.

This, perhaps, is the most significant divergence between the feminist significance of *The Company of Wolves* and the masculine scepticism of *The Dream of a Beast*.[112] The film famously depicts the emergence of the wolf form from that of a man, the animalistic snout literally squeezing out of an open mouth. It is a violent act. By contrast, the Beast form of the novella protagonist develops incrementally. Change for him is slow. It is ponderous rather than painful. It is less phallic than it is uterine, with the Beast at the end even absorbing the young boy into his new self in a kind of reverse birth, carrying him as an embryonic form who kicks to indicate delight and life (102). Lori Rogers believes that the narrator is transforming into a feminine creature (107, 109) and, given water's traditional associations with the feminine and the supernatural within Irish myths, the narrator's affinity with water underscores his gradual acceptance of his new body's fluidity and otherworldly powers. As a result of this transformation, he begins to perceive water sites as heterotopias in which he can escape the city's claustrophobic atmosphere of urban decay. His connection with water is again foregrounded when he submerges himself in a hotel's pool and assumes its elemental power (68). His literal dream flight above the sea within the novella's final chapters further confirms his symbiotic relationship with water.[113] More than that, it echoes Jordan's original ending for *The Company of Wolves* (which was abandoned given the limitations of special effects technology at the time), a conclusion where Rosaleen would have dived into the floor and disappeared, completely abandoning the realistic world of the film's frame story for the kind of pure fantasy that Jordan executes at the end of *The Dream of a Beast*.[114]

All of which is to say that for a largely forgotten and overlooked work, Jordan's *The Dream of a Beast* proves to be a rich and beguiling text. For an instant, the co-dependency of Jordan the writer and Jordan the director was laid bare in a multifaceted creative dialogue. Not even the film stories – lacking a silver screen equivalent – or the inspirational relationship between *Night in Tunisia* and *The Miracle* – separated by fifteen years – offer the kind of symbiosis on display here. *The Past* may have been Jordan's first novel, and *Angel* his first film, but the shared emphasis on transitional forms and states-of-being in *The Dream of a Beast*/*The Company of Wolves* make this the first – and last – time the two Jordans truly overlap. Hereafter, the filmic Jordan would go on to more and more international acclaim with releases including *Mona Lisa* (1986), *The Crying Game* (1992) and *Interview with the Vampire*. Meanwhile, the literary Jordan would, like the Beast on his rooftop, enter a protracted period of hibernation. When he emerged, eleven years later, it would be with a novel combining the attentive appraisal of Irish history found in *The Past* with a softer version of *The Dream of a Beast*'s fantastical energy, a book in which he tempers the flirtation with fantasy on display here and begins to move towards depicting both Ireland and his characters through metaphors of a more mathematical and scientific nature.[115] Such an approach will carry Jordan through *Shade* and *Carnivalesque* in due course, but it begins with *Sunrise with Sea Monster*.

CHAPTER 5

A Place where each Statement has Two Meanings: *Sunrise with Sea Monster*

In 1976, Neil Jordan received a bursary of £2,500 from the Irish Arts Council. Shortly after the award, he travelled to the south of Spain with his then wife Vivienne and their baby daughter, his intention being to research a novel concerned with the Spanish Civil War.[1] As explained to Caroline Walsh in *The Irish Times*, the couple initially went to Malaga and to nearby towns such as Fuengirola, though Jordan did not find what he was looking for there and so they came to Nerja, on the road to Almeria.[2] Though it would take almost twenty years to come to fruition with 1994's *Sunrise with Sea Monster* (published in North America as *Nightlines*), the idea of writing about the Guerra Civil Española never seems to have left Neil Jordan. That the novel which resulted opens in the Spanish desert, very distant from the liminal, littoral terrain so beloved of Jordan's characters, is a measure of how far that book's protagonist has strayed. Nonetheless, Donal Gore is of a piece with characters such as Neil in 'A Love' and the narrator of *The Past* in that his conception of Irish identity was formed in the shadow of the independence struggle's mythic figures, in particular Éamon de Valera and his own father. His is a story tied to the social, political and economic circumstances of Europe and Ireland in the mid- to late 1930s, backdrops that Jordan renders with his established care and attention to detail. *Sunrise with Sea Monster* is therefore a novel that enlarges the boundaries of Jordan's fictional world beyond its previous archipelagic constraints, and one which, simultaneously, re-emphasises the insular – in all meanings of the term – focus of the literary Jordan's imagination. Moreover, the novel's narrative restraint, arguably including the quasi-fantastical finale which reveals the book to be merely masquerading as a work of realism, serves to temper the rush towards pure fantasy with which Jordan experimented in *The Dream of a Beast*. In that way, *Sunrise with Sea Monster* sets the pattern for later Jordan work such as *Shade* (2004), *Ondine* (2009) or *Carnivalesque* (2017): a realistic story and setting enlivened by a frisson of speculative energy.

One of his 'most accomplished novels',[3] *Sunrise with Sea Monster* is at once a work of historical fiction, a love story (showcasing the author's by now recognisable preoccupation with triangular relationships), a meditation on the theme of uncertainty in its many mutable forms, and an object lesson in civil wars (and not just the Spanish conflict, though it dominates the opening section of the book). The reader will recognise familiar themes from both Jordan's previous writing and from his films, including 'the impact of the past on the present, the inextricable interconnection of the political and the personal, and the inevitability of betrayal'.[4] The novel's narrator Donal Gore is at war with his father just as, a decade earlier, his father fought with de Valera. Ironically, that divisive struggle brought together the elder Gore and his wife. Even after her death – which, like Una's in *The Past*, prefigures the beginning of the end for violent republicanism – the father's gun (like the firearm of 'A Love') remains evocative of their marriage. Sam Gore keeps it with his late wife's things, though it is later misappropriated by his son in an act of rebellion against the politics that brought him into being. Yet, as victorious as the pro-treaty side was, the civil conflict in Ireland does not rest in the 1930s of *Sunrise with Sea Monster*. Post-independence politics in the country is merely the continuation of war by other means. While in a fascist prison, a soon-to-be-executed fellow republican notes that Donal cannot sleep, hinting that the ghosts of even the notoriously violent Spanish conflict at least lie down quietly when they're killed (62). The Irish dead, on the other hand, define the living.

As narrated in flashbacks, Donal has left Ireland in the fashion of many younger men in the 1930s out of a need to forge their own destiny beyond the shadow of the independence struggle generation.[5] The real-life historical background against which Jordan writes is that approximately 900 Irishmen fought in the Spanish conflict. Though, unlike Donal, three quarters of them fought for Franco on the nationalist side of the conflict (largely due to the perception of the republican side as being anti-Catholic, and on account of Blueshirt leader Eoin O'Duffy's staunch commitment to the cause of fascism).[6] Yet, for those Irishmen on the republican side, as Diarmaid Ferriter has written, it was a defining experience, even though they were largely shunned and scorned in their homeland on account of their actions.[7] Donal joins one of these *Brigadas Internacionales* (International Brigades) not out of any ideological commitment but because of a dispute with his father over Rose, the woman they have both fallen in love with, a young piano teacher who joins their household some time after the death of Donal's mother (56). As recollected by Donal, their dramas are played out against the idiosyncratic world of 1930s Ireland, a place where statements tended to have both ostensible meanings and actual ones, a country of hushed voices where they censor the past as well as the post (74, 75, 156). As he describes it, he takes the route in life most likely to upset his father, signing up to the republican ideals which the elder Gore has abandoned and practising the politics most likely to upset and embarrass him (58, 59). In the process, Donal flees an island for a continent or, more accurately, for a peninsula. For though Iberia is about eight times the size of Ireland, it is still not the complete sundering from the sea – and hence from the influence of his fisherman father – that Donal perhaps intends it to be.

With the novel rightly seen by some to be representative of how the theme of self-imposed exile is treated by Irish novelists, it is fitting that *Sunrise with Sea Monster* looks to Irish fiction's paterfamilias of exile and return, John McGahern.[8] This is perhaps the Jordan novel that most keenly expresses and acknowledges the influence of, to paraphrase Declan Kiberd, Ireland's foremost writer of prose fiction since the death of Beckett.[9] In particular, the kinds of repetitive narrative rituals which Peter Guy identifies as one of the defining features of McGahern's 1990 masterpiece *Amongst Women* are reflected from the outset of *Sunrise with Sea Monster*.[10] It is apparent in both the religious rites accompanying the executions in the fascist prison, the Latin of which provides a structural refrain to the opening section of the book, and in Donal's memories of the ritualised fishing, laying the nightlines, which he conducted with his father as a child. Independence struggle veteran Old Moran's devotion to the Rosary in *Amongst Women*, which later takes the form of his second marriage to Rose, is again echoed in *Sunrise with Sea Monster*, not just in the emphasis on Catholic ritual, be it Irish or Spanish, but also in independence struggle veteran Sam Gore's own war of independence memories (14) and his own second marriage to a woman named Rose. Like Moran's wife, Rose here is said to have finally brought a measure of peace to her new household, though of course the truth of Jordan's narrative is far from this, with his Rose being a focus of conflict between father and son (15). Where McGahern's novel embeds the religiosity of its patriarch in its title – literally a quotation from the Hail Mary prayer – Jordan takes as his title a paraphrase of J.M. Turner's unfinished and abstruse 'Sunrise with Sea Monsters' (*c.*1845). Turner's painting is notable for its suggestions of pagan, sublime and dangerous things in the water (to which we will return later in the chapter), but what is perhaps more immediately relevant is its small section of hatch lines which have been occasionally interpreted as representing fishing nets, arguably even reminiscent of the nightlines Jordan depicts in the novel. Closing the loop, *Nightlines* is not only the title under which *Sunrise with Sea Monster* was published in North America, it is also a reference to McGahern's 1970 short story collection of the same name.

That said, *Sunrise with Sea Monster* is undeniably a Neil Jordan work. It retains the stylistic fingerprints of Jordan's earlier writing 'and it may be this attribute that allows him (albeit barely) to get away with something of a magical-realistic ending to an otherwise realistic plot'.[11] However, as with *The Dream of a Beast*, this push to classify the novel's denouement as magical realism is not an ideal fit. It might more profitably be identified as eerie in the sense described by Mark Fisher as demonstrating an aesthetic of unease fundamentally connected to notions of the outside.[12] The eerie, says Fisher, is seldom to be found in interior, enclosed or domestic spaces.[13] Such an atmosphere is more readily found in landscapes bereft of human beings.[14] So it is with Jordan's novel, where magic is a thing of freedom, of the coastal world, and every interior space (be that domestic or geographical) is a literal prison – such as the Spanish monastery used by the fascists to hold prisoners of war – or a trap: the barred windows of the hostel run by nuns where Rose stayed on first coming to Dublin, the seminary accommodation Donal's friend Mouse must sneak in and out of, and the Gore house itself in the aftermath of Sam Gore's stroke. By deliberate contrast, the fantastical conclusion of the novel occurs outside on a deserted beach at night. Here, the interface between land and sea further overlaps with that between the world of the living and the world of the dead (unlike, say, the earlier depiction of the war-time Spain as an Eliotesque deathscape of rubble piles and bomb craters and aimless lines of refugees walking in confounding directions with no destination in mind, 67). Whereas *The Dream of a Beast* offers an obvious intrusion narrative as we have discussed, the finale of *Sunrise with Sea Monster* draws its ambiguous fantastical energy from Donal's comprehension of what Fisher interpreted as realms beyond everyday reality.[15] Donal reflects on having fallen out of his place in the world as he drunkenly sets the nightlines on the sand one last time (172). It is only then, in a *Shade*-foreshadowing atemporal space or *Beast*-recalling dream or hallucination, that the character can finally commune and reconcile with the spirit of his now dead father. In the eeriest aspect of the novel, this encounter is never explained to the reader.

Yet, one should not be surprised by this development (though several reviewers, such as José Lanters, clearly were) for such uncertainty has been prepared for.[16] The character of Sam Gore has been a personification of eerie affect throughout, having suffered his stroke during Donal's Spanish sojourn (with his resulting similarity to the mannequins in Dublin shop windows being noted by his son, 109). In the same way that the dead's unseeing gaze or an amnesiac's bewildered eyes provoke a sense of the eerie for Fisher, the novel's elder Gore is paralysed but for his eyes, which flicker and stare in his only indication of movement.[17] It forces Donal into modes of speculation different from those he engaged with as a child (be they about his father's past or Rose's present). This absence of presence is most keenly felt in his silence, his inability to speak or respond. The stroke has silenced him, a former government minister, Trinity College graduate and eloquent speaker at the Royal Dublin Society. In the microcosm of the Gore household, the stroke is Jordan's expression of the invasive and heavy-handed censorship which defined Ireland during the Emergency.[18] It is a peering outward without context. It is an act of observation without the concurrent action of expression. Yes, the timing of his stroke may be attributed to his distress over Donal's departure for Spain, but it is emblematic of the following Emergency period and its severe censorship which limited Irish knowledge of events beyond its shores. For censorship is a silence. It is a void into which is installed an unsatisfactory imitation of the real thing, a state-sponsored simulacrum of reality beyond Irish shores. In this environment – let alone that of the war – certainty itself becomes a fragile concept for Jordan's characters in a manner this chapter will explore.

That Fisher considers the eerie to have a fundamental connection to issues of agency adds another layer to our understanding of Sam Gore's relationship with Ireland.[19] Similar questions about who or what is responsible for fate will recur in *Shade* (where, arguably, the answer is the authorial God of Jordan himself), though in *Sunrise with Sea Monster*, the question is less easily answered. The concealed agent of fate or history, which seemed to guide the action of *The Past* in particular, is here more focused, and seems to change throughout a novel in which agency – personal, political or supernatural – is a mutable concept at best.[20] Nevertheless, part of the book's eeriness comes from how, to adopt Fisher's perspective again, free will is absent, or at least is severely compromised by the authoritarian tendencies of the Irish state during the Emergency years (and worse, one imagines, by the warring parties on the continent).[21] This is apparent not just in censorship – such as how Donal's mail is clearly being read – but also by the presence of detectives from Dublin Castle (104), the government agents sent to spy on and handle him. It is only by reckoning with questions of agency (in this case literal Irish and German government agencies) that Donal is able to assert his free will at last. That Donal's sense of self-determination would finally manifest in positive fashion was never guaranteed. Where earlier this sense – itself an allegory for that of the nation at the time – had been clumsy and adolescent, his double-cross of the Nazis in the moonlight off Spanish Point is almost sophisticated, and his choice to save Hans, his Abwehr contact, is humane. If nothing else, Donal is finally making choices that are adult, realistic and engaged in a way his dalliance with the *Guerra Civil Española* was not. He has finally inherited his father's understanding of the threats facing Ireland, though, in Oedipal fashion, the cost of this new awareness is his father's life.

Or is it? Sam Gore's cryptic and suggestive reappearance in the closing pages of the novel transforms, to paraphrase the perfectly named Mark Fisher, the absence of presence into a presence of absence; it converts a cost into literal return.[22] Donal's father should be dead and gone but is somehow resurrected and present (166), the coast of Ireland clearly being one of those domains of unlikely revelation which Donal (and, for that matter, Jordan in his earlier work) previously alluded to (63). If Sam Gore has become a guardian spirit of some kind, as shall be discussed below, that is one thing, and a narrative choice of a piece with how Jordan will sprinkle his prose work with elements of the fantastic from here on out. However, the interaction becomes altogether different if the appearance of Sam Gore is drawn from the memories of Donal, be that via sleep or inebriation; he does after all admit that, after his father's death and Rose's return to her family in the west of Ireland, he overindulged in alcohol almost every night (166). A drunk or dreaming Donal disappearing into either a space of memory or an entirely imaginative state represents an attempt to reconstruct his father's presence from the void within himself. Though there are similarities between *Sunrise with Sea Monster* and *The Past*, the reconstruction of family here offers a variation on the earlier narrator's search for answers from without.

In an emotive conclusion, Donal sees his drowned father reappear from the sea, appearing both younger and older than the last time Donal saw him and, crucially, somehow more alive (174). Together they gather Donal's nightlines and return to their house where the ordinary domestic setting of all their quarrels becomes temporarily divorced from base reality. For the period between two tides they exist beyond the linear tick-tock of reality's clock. They speak over a breakfast of fish, in particular one mystical fish whose flesh, in biblical fashion, never seems to run out (173). But, crucially, Jordan does not relay direct dialogue here. The reader only learns the content of the conversation through Donal's reporting of it (176). Their reunion occurs between the past and the future, in an ongoing present moment (179), until they have said everything they need to say, everything they never said to each other. Father and son find forgiveness. The independence and post-independence generations achieve détente. Donal finds a peace which has eluded him through a childhood of war stories, an adolescence of domestic strife, and an adulthood of foreign conflict and Emergency. That the text is so ambivalent about what actually happens here is what grants this final section its power and, perhaps, engenders the desire for some to call it magical realism. Donal may indeed be witnessing a spectral apparition, the return of a lost loved one, or he may just be dreaming. In many respects, the symbolism is more important than the substance of this triumphant visitation. Certainly, Jordan himself, when asked in public interviews about the father's seeming resurrection in the book's finale, is always keen to mischievously turn the question back on his interlocutors, asking what the reader consensus on the matter is and if people ever reach any agreement.[23] It is not so much Jordan abdicating authorial responsibility but more him reinforcing audience obligation to complete the work of the artist by determining meaning for themselves. He is willing to give the reader a map but he asks them to take their own journey through his work.

A GUIDEBOOK TO THE TERRITORY: IRELAND AS ISLAND

In several interviews, Jordan has stated that he can never end a story until he gets it to the sea, and in this novel – as with 'A Love', *The Past* and, later, *Carnivalesque* – that journey serves as a structural device around which he builds his narrative.[24] The political, though not the personal, plot of *Sunrise with Sea Monster* concludes with an ambitious passage through the heart of Ireland to the fabled, though inevitably bogus, authenticity of the country's west coast. While more cynical about the west than in his earlier work – the wishing trees and seventh sons are here joined by Nazi submarines and altercations with the Local Defence Force – Jordan is still susceptible to the sentimental tide of the sea. Talking to Marianne Brace in 1995, he mused on why Irish writers had not written more about the sea.[25] He described how, in his early fiction, he could only conclude stories if his character managed to get into the water (something apparent throughout *Night in Tunisia*).[26] The sea, he told Brace, offers a union between the present and the vast spaces of memory.[27] Yet, the coast as Jordan uses it in *Sunrise with Sea Monster* represents more than a mere straight horizon line or geographical boundary. It is a place where life and death can coexist and where violence is sometimes quite literally just beneath the surface, the liminal becoming synonymous with the littoral, and the biblical allusions which overshadow the conclusion of *The Past* are here tempered with something much more elemental. Despite this murderousness, signified by the presence of battleships and submarines, the *Sunrise* coast is a source of uncanny serenity and detachment for many of the characters. The novel's Second World War setting does more than comment on the conflicts of the novel's protagonists; it reinforces the sense of Ireland as *island*, isolated from Europe and the world, a new nation warily divining a separate destiny from the empire across the Irish Sea. It is on the edges of this insular space that the eeriest aesthetic experiences of *Sunrise with Sea Monster* play out. It is here that the greatest threats to Donal and to Ireland more generally are to be found. Thus, geography, specifically that of the Atlantic Archipelago, is essential to the story of *Sunrise with Sea Monster*. As Neal Jesse puts it, 'Ireland's geographic isolation from the European continent – shielded by the bulk of the English mainland – provided it with a natural barricade from the last century of European conflict' including the Second World War.[28] Donal's Abwehr contact acknowledges the Irish claim on the country and its surrounding waters, as if Britain does not continue to dominate the archipelago, as if the Germans do not seek to usurp them, and as if the Irish coast eludes whatever semblance of logic prevails elsewhere in the European theatre (160).

In the literary Jordan's earlier work, propinquity to British colonial power typically begat an adoption of British styles and mannerisms among his characters, with geography having a direct bearing on their perspective and experience. Michael, in *The Past*, apes upper-class British behaviour. His English-cut suit sits awkwardly on an Irishman's frame but is yet worn willingly by a self-avowed Redmondite for whom parliamentary home rule – not complete political autonomy – is the goal of the nationalist movement. Representative of an act of union, Michael's attitude reflected that of the Irish population in the years prior to the execution of the Rising leadership in 1916. As Redmond said at the outset of the First World War in 1914: 'Ireland has been transformed from what George Meredith described a short time ago as "the broken arm of England" into one of the strongest bulwarks of the Empire.'[29] The subsequent awakening of Michael's nationalism and his reluctant participation in an armed struggle directly inspired by the Easter insurrection, a struggle culminating in wars of independence and civil dissonance, reflects the massive transformation of Irish political opinion between 1916 and 1919. Jordan's heavy concentration on a strictly urban milieu in that novel –

the burning of the Custom House, the metaphorical mapping of the treaty boundary onto the Bray promenade, and the murder of Michael himself on Trimelston Road (*The Past*, 12, 61, 69) – signals the continuing limitations of Dublin as an imperial city. The Irish capital is too close to London to authenticate the fledgling nation; it is only in the travels of Rene, Michael's daughter, throughout 'The Provinces' in the mid-1930s – the cultural moment in which the unconnected *Sunrise with Sea Monster* begins – that *The Past*'s paradigm of Irishness is fully realised.

The Past, in paralleling the journey of Irish nationalism towards self-determination with Rene and the narrator's journeys towards the west coast, creates an explicit link between modern Irish political identity and the evocative, romantic sense of place to be found there.[30] The heroic realm sought by generations of that narrator's family comes into being only as the characters move *away* from Britain (one is put in mind of Yeats recommending that J.M. Synge move to the Aran Islands). Furthermore, it is a compulsive journey, one that *must* be undertaken, a rediscovery of identity contingent on the geographical impetus to move west, and one which underpins Jordan's whole mythology of Irish nationhood from 'A Love' to *Carnivalesque*. Yet, where Ireland in the earliest section of *The Past* was an integrated imperial territory, a willing constituent of an empire at war, the island nation of *Sunrise*, politically, economically and socially detached at the outset of the Second World War, is very much sundered from the archipelago. This wilful isolationism in the face of geographical proximity prompted the much-disliked real-life British representative in Dublin during the war, Sir John Maffey, to call on de Valera's government to restore the strategic unity of the islands.[31] But such a plea underestimated the resolve of Ireland's leader, who, not unlike his fictional counterpart in *Sunrise with Sea Monster*, was firm. It further underestimated the widespread support for neutrality in Ireland, support engendered by a variety of factors including but not limited to a desire to avoid another destructive conflict so soon after the war of independence and the civil war.

It is thus natural that, when Donal returns to Ireland, his impression is that nothing has changed either politically or socially; only his father, now silenced and incapacitated by a stroke, is different (83). The colonial artifice of *The Past* has been shed, yes, but the Ireland of *Sunrise with*

Sea Monster is still very much at a transitional stage. Vestiges remain. Despite the symbolism of naming streets after heroes of the rising such as Pádraig Pearse, Dublin, pointedly, is still described as a city of Victorian architecture where citizens continue to exude a glamour redolent of the Edwardian era (18, 21, 143). Elsewhere, the landscape is more stable and more integrated. The anarchic seaside of Bray depicted in *The Past* is here presented in more consistent terms. It is more clearly incorporated into the rest of the Irish landscape, both rural and urban, than the Ascendancy resort town of the earlier novel. The coast too has expanded from the constrained, snapshot images of *The Past*. Donal, who becomes a fisherman, roams a territory which stretches between Donabate and Wicklow Head (108). In this intermediate, immediately post-independence era, transformation is ongoing. De Valera has gone so far as to change the country's name, which became Éire under the 1937 constitutional plebiscite, a crucial development in that the new national designation is in Irish, a language that, like that of the nation's political neutrality during the Second World War, was neither spoken nor understood beyond Irish shores. This sense of isolation is a central theme of *Sunrise*, a novel of islands and constant reminders that the state itself is an island nation (and how, for islanders, the ultimate outside is the ocean).[32] East coast islands such as Lambay are often mentioned in descriptions of Donal's fishing trips, though other islands are less obvious; after the storm of Section II, the Gore home stands above the flooded promenade and bowling green like a proud outcropping in a murky sea, while Rose's initial arrival at the house, laughing and sheltering herself as waves crash and burst around her, itself conjures images of a rough approach to some western isle (25, 117, 121).

While further changes in personal and political situations, as in *The Dream of a Beast*, are heralded by disruption to the leftover colonial infrastructure, for instance the absence of the train which Donal and Mouse imagine would lead to romance between Rose and Donal's father, it is in fact Sam Gore, Donal's father, who most embodies the halting progress which has occurred since independence. As a character, he is best thought of as a more engaged incarnation of *The Past*'s James Vance, and it is of note that Jordan returns again and again (as he will in *Shade*) to this conflicted form of character crossing religious and socio-economic boundaries in the early Irish state. It evokes, as much as anything, Elizabeth Bowen's comment on the potential authorship of any so-called Great Irish Novel during the Emergency, a project she believed could only be undertaken by a Protestant who has entered into a mixed marriage with a Catholic.[33] In *Sunrise with Sea Monster*, as in *The Past*, Jordan has done the next best thing: he has made such characters the subject of his own fiction. Sam Gore, though brought up in the Protestant faith, converted to Catholicism at the time of his marriage to Donal's mother (35). His father, says Donal, betrayed his class and the Ascendancy more generally by giving his allegiance to the republican cause (35) before later taking the treaty side in the civil war. In that part of his life he accepted a role in the first Cosgrave administration and oversaw the incarceration of his former comrades (35). He ran for election again in 1932 but lost his seat when the incumbent Cumann na nGaedheal party, which had governed since 1922, was defeated by Fianna Fáil. The metaphorical paralysis of the Irish state's society, economy and, for that matter, ideology which accompanied that transition is given form by how the elder Gore is thereafter consigned to a wheelchair staring out on the Irish Sea from his window on the Bray promenade, trapped in a rigid, changeless state (83).

It is, in Jordan fashion, only by going west that the characters here can affect substantive change on their circumstances. More than even 'A Love' or *The Past*, Jordan's depiction of the west in *Sunrise with Sea Monster* is an act of reconstruction by someone who spent his childhood there. Rose's recollection of growing up in Sligo, among the breakers and dunes in Strandhill (39), places her origins just across Sligo Bay from Jordan's own in the village of Rosses Point (and offers a further oblique link to McGahern via his story 'Strandhill, the Sea'). When the Germans agree to meet the IRA it is also in a storied location, this time Spanish Point on the west coast of County Clare (128). The place name is not just a reminder of Donal's Iberian misadventure but also of the wrecking of ships from a previous continental effort to invade the Atlantic Archipelago in 1588: the Spanish Armada (the blood of the Spanish sailors, Donal is told, turned the sea itself red, 128). En route to his betrayal of both the Nazis and republicans, Donal – like Neil in 'A Love' or the narrator of *The Past* – traverses the barren, Jordan-haunted western portions of County Clare, visiting towns where his father campaigned with de Valera (149). We know by now that any journey west in Jordan's writing, especially to the restorative waters of Lisdoonvarna, will be a fateful one. The Burren is a prominent space of change and transformation, and his use of the region is not limited to *The Past*. Equating the rocky, ruined landscape of the west of Ireland with the vanquished hopes and aspirations of his *Night in Tunisia* characters, Jordan sets several of his short stories in or around the region, a land of unexpected fantasies and magical possibilities. This question of the west and its role in the Irish imagination lies at the heart of 'A Love', a story that follows the Yeatsian assertion that an understanding of the west is essential to any understanding of Ireland as a whole (*Night in Tunisia*, 110). Making her final pilgrimage across the country, the old woman in 'A Love' emphasises a traditional usage of the region in literature and culture: the west is the land of the dead and to go into the west is to die. Yet, in *Night in Tunisia*, Jordan makes journeying to the west, especially in the final three stories ('Outpatient', 'Tree' and 'A Love'), a voyage of self-discovery, one undertaken by characters wishing to transcend physical or personal constraints amid a magical, elemental landscape, or to escape a confused, often irrational world of everyday perception into a country where past incidents serve always as catalysts for physical, emotional and interpersonal catharsis.

The same is true of *Sunrise with Sea Monster*. Strained by the vagaries of Free State politics, the relationship between the war of independence allies turned civil war enemies Sam Gore and Éamon de Valera eventually disintegrates into a bitter electoral conflict which takes the form of a political landscape realised on the physicality of the country's streets and roads. Jordan evocatively renders his description of electoral detritus which persists long after the balloting is complete and, while this imagery of election posters appears also in *The Past*, its use there lacks the unity with the landscape that is so apparent in *Sunrise with Sea Monster*. The posters of the earlier novel flutter in the wind as if they are merely tied loosely onto a countryside which politicians are arguing over from their Dublin strongholds (*The Past*, 205). There, the dry summer climate of a Burren September contributes to this impression, and the posters can sometimes seem like just another dead thing parched and wind-burnt by the peculiar Clare environment. By contrast, Jordan's use of posters in *Sunrise with Sea Monster* is more organic. The first notable difference is their vastly increased occurrence, with nearly every lamppost bearing a poster of Sam Gore's face (35). In *The Past*, James Vance is forced to search out posters and their valuable information, whereas in this novel they are defined by their unsettling omnipresence. Additionally, the faces in *Sunrise with Sea Monster* come alive through the appearances of the candidates on bandstands and behind megaphones (36). Theirs is a living campaign, played out on the streets of the nation and in direct opposition to the faded representations of *The Past*. Most importantly, the posters here decompose, while those of the earlier novel seem to endure in a hermetically sealed artificiality. Such festering allows the imagery of the election, which has first grown *onto* the landscape, to now grow *into* it, the posters becoming rain-sodden and torn, decaying into the brick and stone and becoming a material part of the promenade itself (38). Donal narrates a process whereby his father is subsumed within the very permanence of the streetscape (38) and, having already become one with modern Irish history (in the mind of his son at least), the elder Gore thus begins his union with the Irish landscape itself.

Yet, his electoral failure in the face of de Valera's Fianna Fáil juggernaut does not result in his erasure from the political scene. On the contrary, his resultant close identification with the Bray constituency and, in a social geography sense, with his Protestant heritage effects a post-electoral rapprochement. Even the strict deity de Valera softens towards his former opponent, installing him as under-secretary for external affairs to add a weight of experience and continuity to the new administration (38) during the period when the taoiseach served as his own minister for external (now foreign) affairs. Of paramount importance during the pre-war years, the office of external affairs oversaw the implementation of Ireland's neutrality in the face of strong – primarily British – opposition. It is therefore appropriate that Donal's father and de Valera, two men who had superimposed their political ideals symbolically onto the landscape, themselves in turn take on the roles of that landscape's protectors. Emphasised towards the end of the novel, this idea of Donal's father as a geographic protector of the island of Ireland reaches its apotheosis when he disappears into the Atlantic during the incident with the German submarine (162). He becomes part of the waters themselves, a guardian spirit of the seas separating Ireland from the rest of the European conflagration. In the altercation, Donal is knocked unconscious. When he recovers he finds his father's wheelchair empty by the beach and the old man gone, lost to an elemental realm which perhaps suits him better than most. It is in this supernatural being that the full potential of Jordan's revolutionary/politician/father-thing (with the Philip K. Dick short story of the latter title eventually referenced directly in *Carnivalesque*) is finally liberated. It is in this guise that Sam Gore's phantasmagorical reappearance in Section IV takes place. It was the day after de Valera controversially presented his condolences to the German embassy on the death of Adolf Hitler, and so it is on the eve of peace throughout the continent that the father at last returns to make amends with his son (166). If the sea-spirit apparition witnessed by Donal is genuine, then it suggests that his father has indeed a supernatural role in the geographic isolation, and therefore protection, of Ireland during the war years, a commitment that precludes their reconciliation taking place until the conclusion of the war. It is perhaps no harm here to remind the reader of Keith Hopper's observation, mentioned in the previous chapter, that it is only through Jordan's serious interest in fantasy and its allegorical power – in this case the mysterious reappearance of the father – that we can fully understand the multifaceted, and often contradictory, politics underpinning his writing about Ireland.[34] With regard to the Emergency setting of *Sunrise with Sea Monster*, such politics comprise the idea and the execution of Irish neutrality.

WE MUST KEEP AN EYE ON THINGS: NEUTRALITY AND EMERGENCY

When it comes to the terminology of Irish neutrality, Ronan Fanning observed that the interests of historians and academics typically range wider than those of politicians and professional diplomats.[35] Arguably, the concerns of the literary critic are quite different again, with neutrality offering a powerful allegorical device for the author of Irish literature, especially for work concerning or composed during the Emergency period.[36] Writers for page and stage have long made use of the contradictions and ambiguities of the war years in Ireland, from Louis MacNeice's poem *Autumn Journal* (1939) to Arthur Riordan's musical comedy *Improbable Frequency* (2004), to Neil Belton's novel *A Game with Sharpened Knives* (2005). What Jordan's novel shares with the best Emergency fiction is a sense of uncertainty which oozes through the narrative. He depicts neutrality as an uncanny situation for Ireland at the time, not just the Irish solution to an Irish problem, but a de Valerian calculation in response to the vastly complex equation of a Second World War in which Ireland both was and was not enmeshed. De Valera is, after all, said to have run the country according to Euclidean principles (170), deriving his theorems of governance from a small series of nationalist axioms which were intuitive to him at least (as he once famously remarked, 'If I wish to know what the Irish want, I look into my own heart').

In the coarsest understanding of history, Ireland's stance during the Second World War was one of doing nothing (though this fails to account for the so-called benevolent neutrality practised by the country in favour of the Allies, or for the tens of thousands of Irish people who fought in the Allied armed forces). Yet, doing nothing is in fact doing something, an ambiguous state of being that suits Donal Gore perfectly. When the reader first encounters Donal they find him in a figuratively uncommitted state, having volunteered for the Spanish Civil War not out of ideology but solely to annoy his father (16). In this way he represents the literal uncommitted state, that of Éire itself, which will adopt de Valera's policy of neutrality as the novel progresses.[37] Like the nation, Donal is unwilling to take a firm philosophical or doctrinal stance lest it constrain his ability to express his personal sovereignty. His involvement with the Spanish Civil War is obviously not neutral, and neither is his unwilling dalliance with the German Reich, though they do grant him an independence from his father's political and personal policies. Nonetheless, he remains – as does Ireland until unified by the censorships and practical requirements of the Emergency – obsessed with his own history and with his father's service in the independence struggle. While this is more reminiscent of Neil in 'A Love' than the narrator of *The Past*, Jordan has again created a character who is a child of the nation. In this case, Donal embodies how, as Diarmaid Ferriter says, the 1930s offered the illusion of Ireland setting its own direction on the international stage but, simultaneously, the hard truth that the nation could not operate on the basis of entirely unshackled independence.[38]

Indeed, the German interrogator is perplexed by Donal's incarceration in the Spanish prison, confounded by the presence of an Irishman in a conflict that has nothing to do with Britain (55). Mainland Europeans, the novel implies, cannot possibly separate the notion of Ireland from its archipelagic context. The charged, petty rivalries of these islands make little sense in a world where hatred is fluid enough to allow for even a Hitler–Stalin pact (102). Donal, describing his homeland to the German officer, cautions him that only the naive would place the island of Ireland fifty miles or so off the coast of Britain when, in fact, its true coordinates can only be found in the mysterious western reaches of the medieval imagination (75). Yet, even this is not enough of an explanation given how Irish neutrality at the time was impossible to separate from the nation's historical relationship with Britain.[39] The notion of 'England's difficulty' familiar from Una's theatrical freeze in *The Past* reappears in this novel, with Jordan fictionalising the real-life IRA's efforts to make contact with German intelligence.[40] It is only when Donal invents himself a past and explains his Spanish misadventure with a yarn about his father's incomplete revolution that Hans, his Abwehr contact, begins to take him seriously (62). The notion that an Irishman could be indifferent to politics, as Donal is, is unbelievable to the novel's continentals. In fact, it is the whole reason that the petition to release him has succeeded, for, being Irish, he is naturally expected to have a grievance with Britain and, in exchange for returning him to Ireland, the Germans expect political intelligence and contacts (68). It is, thinks Donal during his release, an odd ritual of realpolitik (77), one that the novel later mirrors, in tragicomic fashion, during the debacle off Spanish Point.

The novel's title, previously ambiguous, suddenly takes on a very concrete meaning. The Germans' attempt to land an intelligence operative and to make contact with the IRA poses a challenge to the carefully constructed pseudo-reality of Emergency-era Ireland, one which the state cannot let pass. In the appearance of the German submarine off the Clare coast, Jordan presents an anomalous entity which is not normally to be expected in Irish waters. It is a version of Fisher's presence where there should only be absence and its associated sense of threat. It is described as a monster emerging from the water (159) and so is another convincing candidate for the sea creature of the novel's title. Certainly the threat is not going to be the novel's IRA members, with Donal's connection to the republican movement being a man dressed in greatcoat carrying a fistful of pebbles and launching them into the air (112). In one way, this visitation confronting Donal outside his window in the middle of the night is broadly comedic, in another it is a satirical image of the state of an IRA reduced to throwing stones in the early 1940s. That Jordan's republican operatives speak in platitudes and exhibit only a loose relationship to logic (128) only adds to the humour; that their plan is to attack Madame Tussaud's in London – which further reinforces the interest in simulacra throughout Jordan's work – reduces the whole enterprise to farce (in many ways, *Sunrise with Sea Monster* introduces a strain of wry humour into Jordan's writing, something which weaves through the fiction from here on out).

Amid these tonal pivots, *Sunrise with Sea Monster* offers an expanding and deepening of Jordan's prior use of Irish political history. The novel depicts the end of the transitional phase between British governance in Ireland and the true beginning of the country's new self-governing status. It takes place after, as recounted by Donal, the intermediary stage of de-colonisation – best conceived of as the duration of the Irish Free State, established in 1922 (under the Anglo-Irish Treaty of December 1921) and concluded by the ratification of de Valera's *Bunreacht na hÉireann* in 1937. In this resulting funk of uncertainty, the novel depicts the civil war generation as stifling the self-expression of its inheritors in an attempt to best the British at all turns. Hence the decision of young men like Donal Gore to attempt escaping from the past and shaping new, individual destinies, in his case by enlisting with the International Brigades fighting in the Spanish Civil War. However, even this involvement is a failed attempt to muster the self-conviction that Ireland is part of Europe or, at the very least, is different from Britain. As they face execution in the fascist prison camp, the Sevillian prisoner who befriends Donal jokes that the Irishman could take his place as they look alike (50). Though Donal placates the inmate, they are not alike at all, instead possessing merits based on the relative geographies of their homelands and, even as a combatant in a foreign war, Donal's Irishness is defined by his not being English. With the war in Spain lost, and the war in Europe about to begin, Éire assumes a tactical importance that the island has not held since the Year of the French in 1798, that of the 'back door' to Britain.⁴¹ Ronan Fanning, shrewd as ever, identifies the Second World War as an existential threat to (de Valera's) Ireland because it was the only international crisis since independence that presented the possibility of breaching the nation's insular remove from world affairs.⁴² This is precisely the aspect of the Emergency that Jordan's focus on the waters around Ireland continually reaffirms. It solidifies the sea monster of the title as the vulnerability of Ireland to invasion from abroad, whether from the Germans or the British, and so the fact that the sun rises in the east – in the direction of the European conflagration – is no poetic turn of phrase.

This nexus of Irish/European allusions in *Sunrise with Sea Monster* is enhanced by how, in the novel at least, the Spanish-tinted de Valera (his birth certificate describes his father, Juan Vivion de Valera, as a Spanish artist born in the Basque Country) is held up as the near-holy originator of neutrality. The whole official nation is subsumed into the project of neutrality which, aided by censorship – the news from Europe largely passed ordinary people by (165) – generates a local pseudo-reality within the larger context of world events. Indeed, the de Valera government (for that matter the whole post-independence cultural/political project of the Irish state) is the definition of Fisher's mythic structures which derive their power from the people they assimilate.⁴³ Thus, Donal returns to what aspires to be, as Terence Brown put it, a self-sufficient nation where part of the idea of autonomy is the need to avoid martial entanglements.⁴⁴ The accompanying lack of information about the wider world allows Donal to fill the Fisher-style knowledge gap with whatever fiction he chooses about his time abroad.⁴⁵ The Irish abstention from the war effort is further reminiscent of the absence of presence which Fisher, as we have seen, defines as an aspect of the eerie, though it is not a major aspect of Jordan's novel.⁴⁶ Nonetheless, the tall tales Donal spins upon his return are the first step in his actualisation of an identity separate from that of his father's reputation. The lively pub setting of Donal's self-aggrandisements might seem at odds with commonly held perceptions of Emergency-era Ireland as a grey and lifeless place of isolationism and deprivation but, in reality, the latter is likely an exaggeration and in many respects a continuation of official policies in place since independence (in fact, much recent work has emphasised the energetic social and cultural milieu of Ireland at the time). Jordan's depiction of the agreeable social life has much more in common with how Brown, pleasingly invoking insular imagery once more, depicts the Dublin of the war years as a safe and steady port of call on tumultuous waters.[47]

Elsewhere, of course, Jordan is keen to emphasise exactly the threats that neutrality is intended to protect Ireland from. On his travels through Spain, Donal witnesses first-hand the European destruction which might potentially be visited on his homeland, most vividly (and emotionally distressing for an Irish person) the endless expanses of ruined farmland (68). Even this, however, cannot penetrate his political indifference, and his response to the German invasion of Poland is to quote Clark Gable's famous *Gone with the Wind* (1939) line of 'frankly my dear, I don't give a damn' (78). Yet, in the course of his involvement with Dublin Castle and the IRA, something changes in the character of Donal that even the horrors of Spain were unable to bring about. The notion of betrayal – of his father, of the IRA, of Ireland and of Hans – begins to obsess him. He broods on it, considering his options constantly (116, 146, 161). While Jordan presents neutrality as, in many respects, crucial to the novel's events, the innate, cultural distaste of enacting a betrayal is the only motivation for an Irishman of Donal's calibre (144). Towards the end of *Sunrise with Sea Monster*, he finally declares the German war obscene and tells his contact that a neutral country such as Ireland would never have assisted them (161). Even then his duplicity towards the German operative results as much from a sense of loyalty to a man who once saved his life as it does from any political motivation. When Jordan writes that Donal is delivering his contact into safer hands, his phonetic joke is clear: Hans ('hands') is much safer in the Curragh than he ever would be in the Abwehr (161).

Fraught with monstrous sights, Donal's earlier trip across the sea to Ireland further illustrates the external threats to the country. As his ship travels around the coast of Spain he witnesses fleets of warships massing at Gibraltar and sees submarines off Algeciras (78). Here there be monsters of a powerful and mechanical nature, creatures of industrial warfare, but they are largely hidden from Irish view, either beneath the waves or over the information horizon established by the censorship promptly imposed on the country (95). Neutrality must be protected at all costs and all coasts, as the seas crawl with the machinery of war and conflict, and Ireland – given its geographical position – is a tempting target. After de Valera, the most ardent warden of Ireland's detachment is Sam Gore himself. Metaphorically, Donal's father is both Prospero and Ariel, the wizard and the waif. His official capacity in the external relations office grants him broad authority over Ireland's foreign policy and, even after his paralysis, he continues to defend the island with a supernatural perseverance. When Donal brings his father to lay nightlines again, wheeling his chair onto the strand, the old man quietly faces off against the hulking shape of a battleship, eventually outstaring the engine of war itself (97). We are told that the sea, and fishing in particular, have always had an important meaning for him, and even his breath rises and falls in synch with the motion of the waves (137). As Donal observes, Sam Gore always enjoyed watching ships on the horizon and stories of when the world was thought to be flat (97–8). Now an active mind trapped inside a crippled body, Sam Gore seems to realise that the sea itself is key to Irish security during the Emergency (97). He is connected to it somehow, and, indeed, Donal's first meeting with his newly incapacitated father occurs as the old man is staring out to sea (81). When the storm at the midpoint of the novel finally breaks, the old man is again sitting at the window as though conducting it all with his eyes (119). Donal, who is in a boat at the time, admits to reconnecting with Sam Gore once more through the act of fishing (135). It is as though the father has called the fish to him and has them carry out his bidding (135).

Lost, finally, to the Atlantic in the fracas off Spanish Point, Sam Gore becomes a guardian of the island itself, an ethereal, supernatural counterpart to the detectives in Dublin Castle who are tasked with keeping a watchful eye on trouble coming from over the water (104). He becomes a sea-spirit, his body subsumed beneath the waves, estuarial silt banks preserving his physical form, and his soul playing over everything like a breeze perceptible only through the ripples on the water (167). Netting fish in the bay, Donal thinks he sees his father's face underneath the surface, and he imagines Sam Gore traversing the waves in the fashion of a merman (163, 167). In the phantasmagorical final section of the novel, Donal realises that it is as though the ongoing existence of the sea itself depended on Sam Gore and, in return, the sea offered his spirit a place to linger (137, 166, 168). Sam Gore is paralysed until he comes face to face with the deep blue expanse of the Atlantic (176). It is a different sea, yes, the ocean which conceals the edge of the world, but equally the reader is reminded throughout that it is the same sea (75, 157). The west coast is described by Rose as being similar to Bray but for the size of the waves (28). As in 'A Love' and 'Last Rites', water here is a continuum through which what the characters leave unsaid is finally expressed (177). Gefter Wondrich has noted this as Jordan's paean to the liminal spaces of James Joyce, though the true crepuscularity in question throughout the novel is the geopolitical opacity of Ireland itself.[48] Neutrality meant very little to German plans for European domination, though in practice Ireland was shielded from direct Nazi aggression by the island of Britain. While English cities suffered through the Blitz, the only aircraft seen by Donal is a plane which he assumes has strayed off course (112). Reflected in his eyes is the harsh truth that the price of self-determination for such a tiny nation in troubled times is constant vigilance.

TO MEASURE IS TO DEFLECT: UNCERTAINTY IN UNCERTAIN TIMES

In *Sunrise with Sea Monster*, Jordan yokes the aesthetics of literary ambiguity to the properties of physical uncertainty. He does this, in a further Joycean influence, by beginning to embrace the metaphorical and philosophical possibilities presented to an author by dabbling with ideas more at home in the physical sciences. As John Banville once wrote, such ideas engage and entice not just the scientist but the artist as well; where the former sees significance in limitation, the latter – like Jordan and indeed like Banville himself – can appreciate indeterminacy's aesthetic possibilities.[49] Yet, where Joyce in, say, *Portrait of the Artist as a Young Man* makes an explicit linkage between Stephen's political naivety and, as Katherine Ebury sees it, his cosmological uncertainty, Jordan here is more modest.[50] Donal Gore's uncertainty is domestic, at its greatest extent national, rather than cosmological. It relates not to any political ignorance, for indeed he is well educated in the facts of the independence struggle, but to his lack of political sophistication. The new physics of the 1920s and '30s, that being the youth of both

Donal and the independent Irish state, suggests a vaster universe than previously imagined, yet the inherent possibilities of reaching out for that are here seen to collapse back into, respectively, the Gore family home and the singularity of de Valera's Ireland, a historical setting which, as Terence Brown observed, expressed more than a little disgust for – let alone suspicion of – modernism.[51] Despite this resistance, the Euclidean principles so cherished by Jordan's de Valera had already been superseded by the time of the novel's setting, with the implication of relativity being that physical space itself – the geography of Ireland, if you so wish – is not Euclidean at all, and Euclidean space is a good approximation for it only over short distances (relative to the strength of the gravitational field). Thus, while the pseudo-reality of the Emergency-era state in *Sunrise with Sea Monster* projects security and certainty, *un*certainty of a political, sexual, personal and mathematical nature underpins the novel as a whole. It is apparent in the triangular relationship between Donal, Rose and Sam Gore. It is visible in the suggestion of bisexuality in Donal's quasi-erotic encounters with his male friend Mouse (31, 34, 42), how he responds to a fellow prisoner creeping into his bed in Spain, and how readily he acquiesces to playing the part of Scarlett O'Hara to the Rhett Butler of Hans, Donal's Abwehr contact. Uncertainty is further visible in Ireland's benevolently neutral stance during the war, and of course in Jordan's use of an appropriate ur-text – physicist Werner Heisenberg's paper on what is known as the uncertainty principle – which Donal and Hans use to conduct their secret communication.

Introduced in 1927, Heisenberg's uncertainty principle is a type of mathematical inequality in quantum mechanics. It asserts a fundamental limit to the precision with which certain pairs of physical properties of a particle – such as position and momentum – can be known. In layperson's terms, the more accurately we know one of these, the less accurately we can know the other.[52] On practical and metaphorical levels, the Heisenberg uncertainty principle denies even the theoretical possibility of gaining a complete knowledge of reality, that in determining one surety we must inevitably forego knowledge of another. That this is a property of all wave-like systems need not concern us here beyond the metaphorical value of Jordan setting the climax of both the novel's political and personal plots on choppy seas. More relevant is Jordan's use of Heisenberg's paper as the basis of the code by which Donal and Hans communicate. It is an apt and intriguing decision given how the uncertainty principle, as applied to language, tells us that the significance of any information depends upon that communication's recipient.[53] As Richard Schwartz put it, the mathematical descriptions of both information and noise are virtually identical, lacking anything in the way of structural differences, it is human intention – that of the transmitter and, indeed, of the recipient – that ultimately determines which is which (rather pleasingly for a discussion of Jordan, Schwartz uses the thought experiment of a cryptographer and a literary critic who both disseminate copies of a canonical text for vastly different reasons).[54] Like other contemporary authors (Banville is the obvious Irish point of reference), Jordan has a tendency to explore scientific principles like these as metaphors for human interactions. *Sunrise with Sea Monster* begins this trend, but as we shall see, it is apparent in – even intrinsic to – later work such as *Shade* and *Carnivalesque*. In the case of *Sunrise with Sea Monster*, Jordan's narrative achieves substantial power from his use of physics concepts as metaphors. More so again when you consider, say, how they can be appropriated to describe Irish politics at the time. Consider how the idea of 'complementarity' – that being light's paradoxical capacity to behave as both waves and particles, a concept developed by Heisenberg's collaborator Niels Bohr in response to the uncertainty principle – is as good a conception of Irish neutrality as any other: neutral, but benevolently so towards the Allies.

That Hans does not make this connection and so blunders his way into Irish internment is ironic (and an indictment by Jordan of Nazi arrogance). After all, Hans was once a physicist who claims to have worked on the uncertainty principle alongside Heisenberg in Leipzig (67). He glosses the remit of quantum physics for Donal, undercutting Einstein's claim that God does not play dice with the universe with his conviction that God in fact does little else (67). Jordan's running joke whereby various characters repeatedly mistake Heisenberg for Heidegger – indeterminacy mistaken for inscrutability – only reinforces the novel's sense of uncertainty and instability even among those who consider themselves knowledgeable about the world. It also serves as a nod to a similar Heisenberg-to-Heidegger spectrum in Banville's *New York Times* essay 'Physics and Fiction' (1985). There Banville, who also discusses the uncertainty principle in his novel *Eclipse* (2000), could easily be describing Emergency-era Irish neutrality when he writes of the surprising calm and straightforwardness offered by Heisenberg's principle.[55] For Banville, Heisenberg offers a means of knowing the world by consciously abandoning any pretence of perfect knowledge, an intellectual exercise with a mischievous glint in its eye.[56] Here again, one might think, is the Irish solution to an Irish problem, though Banville's essay goes on to upset this alignment: the impact of uncertainty is not confined to refined intellectual realms, he says, arguing that its real-life consequences in fact echo the aphorism about being unable to have one's cake and eat it too.[57] Coming from a perspective informed by continental literature, philosophy and history (he was, after all, writing this in the shadow of *Doctor Copernicus* and *Kepler*, both 1976), Banville foregrounds the pronounced and largely unwanted aspects of uncertainty.[58] By contrast Jordan, immersing himself in the insular, Emergency point of view of his characters, portrays a situation whereby having one's cake and eating it is exactly what benevolent neutrality ensures. De Valera's government can simultaneously show benevolence and disdain to the British. They can both stymie German military aspirations and – more controversially – express official condolences over the death of Hitler. Neutrality is a state of uncertainty which introduces fuzziness into Ireland's intentions.[59] Such a (nation) state confounds the Allies/Axis order of the day, a wartime international division more akin to the clockwork universe of Isaac Newton where everything moves in accordance with clear-cut laws and rules.[60] It is an expression of, as Donal and Hans discuss, the Irish tendency to consider implausible things to be achievable. Such a stance will increasingly become the norm in Jordan's fictional Irelands going forward. Post *Sunrise with Sea Monster*, Jordan builds upon his interest in impossible possibilities through a related principle, often confused with uncertainty: that of the observer effect. His uniquely Irish attempts to understand the influence of the observer on that which is being observed will define the structure, character and metaphysical riddle-boxes of stories such as 'The Berkeley Complex' (2003) and long-form work such as *Carnivalesque*, but it is never more apparent than in his next novel, the masterful *Shade*.

CHAPTER 6

Observation is all I am: Narration and recurrence in *Shade*

On first reading, Neil Jordan's *Shade* (2004) seems a re-tread of much that has come before. Many of the author's preoccupying themes are evident from the outset: Irish history, theatricality, fluid identities and sexualities, ruined Anglo-Irish families, and the relationship of this small island to the wider world. Yet, *Shade* is a more complicated and sophisticated text than the casual reader of historical fiction may initially surmise. Conflating myriad potent tableaux (the turn of the twentieth century, the First World War, the War of Independence and the decline of the Big Houses), *Shade* does away with the competing notions of nostalgia which typify Jordan's earlier novels and transforms the past tense into present through the use of a character with a point of view beyond linear existence. Thus, a meditation on historiography, a recreation of a lost landscape, and an introspective examination of the author's own approach to fiction, *Shade* is also an allusive text in which Jordan plays some of his most extensive games with readers and their expectations. John Banville hailed the book as a powerful and luminous novel, and it is no surprise that Ireland's accepted master of the high literary style should seek to praise the tone and elegance of the prose on display here. That being said, it is the novelist Patrick McCabe who is closer to the mark in framing *Shade* as an intricate metaphysical mystery, and it is on that aspect of the novel that this chapter will concentrate.

In *Shade*, the author revisits and revises his earlier discourse with Irish history through the character of Nina Hardy, a successful actress murdered by a childhood friend in the house on the banks of the River Boyne where she grew up. Freed from the limitations of mortal linearity, Nina's spirit simultaneously observes the events of her own funeral unfold in 1950 and her childhood and adolescence in the early 1900s. In the later timeframe she quickly realises that the spectral presence she sensed around her as a girl, the influence of whose constant observation is largely responsible for young Nina's development into an actress, was/is in fact herself. This in turn sets the stage for her eventual murder in a recurrent paradox. *Shade* is therefore a novel about time, though hardly one that is sympathetic to the temporal nature of everyday human lives. Instead, *Shade* rejects both traditional notions of linearity and popularly accepted ideas of historical fiction. Throughout the book, Jordan skilfully and stealthily organises the narrative around concepts more associated with speculative fiction than Irish literary writing: time travel, alternative timelines, the observer effect (the theory that merely observing a phenomenon inevitably changes that phenomenon), and Heisenberg's uncertainty principle (which, as a mathematical proof, played such an important role in *Sunrise with Sea Monster*). All are crucial to the narrative of *Shade*, together comprising the casual nexus of McCabe's metaphysical mystery and elevating what might otherwise have been a piece of mainstream literary fiction into a highly inventive novel about how the future influences the past, and, more specifically, how we relate to the past in Ireland.

Jordan's experiments with time are not actually as unexpected as they might seem. As Gerald Dawe wrote in 1980, Jordan has always had an interest in manipulating narrative chronology.[1] For example, 'Last Rites' – the opening story of *Night in Tunisia* – flashes forwards and backwards around the death of its protagonist, allowing for an 'afterlife' of sorts for the character through the reactions of those who discover his body.[2] So too *The Past* spends much of its time investigating how an individual's character can be moulded by their relationship to personal and political history (especially in an Irish context).[3] Yet, it is only at this advanced stage of his career that Jordan is able to find in a novel like *Shade* a mechanism to re-examine his own previous writings, particularly his approach to historiography in fiction. Allowing a character to revisit her own past grants him the opportunity to revisit his earlier described milieus and so create a more vivid, less elusive working of old ideas. This transition is clearest when one examines the perspective of *Shade* vis-à-vis those adopted in *The Past* and *Sunrise with Sea Monster*. *The Past*, in particular, is of a piece with the Great Man theory of history, implicitly linking the birth and development of the Irish state to the life of Éamon de Valera. *Shade*, by contrast, focuses on ordinary people, children for the first half of the narrative, and thus dismisses the idea that history is only concerned with noteworthy figures. This rejection of Great Man history is further signalled by both the female narrator and by the story's focus on the changing socio-economic conditions of not Dublin, not London, but the Boyne valley.

The novel is notable for its concentration on this region, a landscape to which the author has a familial connection through his mother, and which has experienced dramatic transformation over the past century.[4] Both of those aspects combine in *Shade*'s obsessive geographic focus, a deliberate choice by Jordan with the intention being to retrieve a sense of clarity from what he has described as historical sediments, the murky and ever-changing landscape of the Boyne estuary.[5] He has recalled how his mother was born in the area, and how he developed a relationship with the Boyne from childhood holidays.[6] While the region has been heavily developed in the meantime, a note of acknowledgement at the conclusion to the novel details the range of books and articles consulted by the author on the geography and history of Drogheda and the Boyne valley. The novel demonstrates an approach to geography and landscape that is sympathetic to wide definitions, encompassing whole fields dedicated to society and resource management in addition to the traditional study of physical landforms. Indeed, the density of geographical description afforded to the Boyne region in *Shade* is imposing, ranging from pure geophysical terminology about mudflats, channels and tides, to ruminations on regional economic decline such as how Nina's father's factory eventually succumbs to ruin (67, 115).

A poised and affecting ghost story, *Shade* won the Kerry Group Irish Fiction Award at the 2005 Listowel Writers' Week, beating novels by Colm Tóibín (*The Master*), Ronan Bennett (*Havoc in Its Third Year*) and Gerard Donovan (*Doctor Salt*).[7] The book was interpreted as a parable of the fall by some critics, who saw the Maiden's Tower episode of Chapter 17 as a metaphor for *Shade*'s loss of innocence narrative as a whole.[8] Reviewers also tended to label the book a Gothic fiction, no doubt because of its Big House milieu and the ghost's central role in the story. Yet, *Shade* lacks both the abiding sense of menace and the oppressive atmosphere one might normally associate with the Gothic genre. From the outset the reader knows that Nina will die, and, if anything, the power of death is itself fatally compromised by Nina's peaceful acceptance of her condition. In terms of atmosphere too, *Shade* is not typically Gothic. The novel's characters do not shirk from their mysterious landscape; rather they fearlessly explore its nooks and crannies on bright sunny days and long summer evenings. All the children, especially Nina and her half-brother Gregory, are so entirely at home in their landscape that they are imbued with a kind of imperialist mastery over the Boyne's mudflats and riverbanks.

Folklore too informs *Shade*, in particular the prelapsarian myths of early Ireland, a hazy awareness of which colours the relationship of the characters to the water itself. Crucial to the reader's understanding of the story that follows is the myth of Boinn, a story that is told to Nina – and so to the reader – early on by her father. It is, of course, a narrative divulged along the riverside, a foreshadowing tale of a beautiful woman who came to the flowing water in order to wash her hair before meeting an untimely death (9). And, of course, Boinn (literally 'cow white' in Irish) is not the only woman to be subsumed by the river in the book. The repetitious drowning of woman after woman in the Boyne reinforces the notion of temporal circularity propagated by the novel. Boinn's plight is echoed by Isobel Shawcross, the governess, whose hair is entangled in the river's weeds when her body is discovered; echoed again by Nina herself, who undergoes a more complete unification with the waters – reminiscent of Donal's father in *Sunrise with Sea Monster* – when floods flush out the contents of the septic tank and finally release her physical remains, and thereafter her implied incorporation into the hydrological cycle itself (316). With her final fate, Nina achieves complete unity with the estuary. From beyond the grave she claims to be a part of the river, with the seaweed for her hair and the barnacles for her bed (316). The manner in which body parts are continually mutating into the landscape of the Boyne valley ties *Shade* closely into Jordan's previous work and, in many ways, the novel serves as a counterpoint to the supernatural guardianship in *Sunrise with Sea Monster* and phantasmagorical evolution in *The Dream of a Beast*. Politically and socially too, *Shade* reflects Jordan's established interests. In this case Nina's upper-class, near-Ascendancy origins offer the reader a similar experience to the depiction of the Vance family in *The Past*.

Born in 1897, Nina has a distinctly colonial childhood and, even in her games, the girl chooses to call her estuarine playground Mozambique, an overseas land to be exploited (67). This core/periphery dichotomy is apparent throughout the novel, though Jordan subverts the imperial paradigm by making the provincial hinterland of Drogheda the centre of Nina's own personal empire of imagination. The world outside of Ireland is referred to only in broad strokes, such as when Gregory and George enlist to fight in the First World War, steaming from Cyprus to Alexandria to fight against Turkish forces in the Sinai, and encompassing the logistics of a vast campaign in the space of a single sentence (196). It is only when Nina herself goes abroad, to Brighton and to London, that Ireland's true position with regard to the world, and specifically to Britain, is revealed to her. In England, the adult Nina finds herself trapped by her previous peripheral behaviours; she is in fact encouraged to continue with them for the amusement of others (the cinematograph man of Chapter 37, for example, wishes to exploit her acting style, which is considered rather unsophisticated). That being as it may, *Shade* engages with the colonising power largely on its own terms. Nina's excursion abroad is, unlike Una and Michael's in *The Past*, not limited to one or two particular regions. Instead she drifts, from Liverpool to Lancashire, to Somerset and Brighton, and on to London. She witnesses the full range of British life, and not merely the artificiality of the English seaside town, itself a seasonal colony of the British upper class. A similar, if more violent, example is found in the war effort to capture the Dardanelles, where Gregory and George's unit is only one among an international collation of forces.

Always, however, the novel returns to Ireland and to the Boyne, an estuary which, as the novel progresses, is slowly transformed into a cemetery site, a resting place for shells and skeletons and dark stories alike. Identifying a Heaneyesque engagement between history and landscape, some critics have been keen to link the buried national consciousness of the Northern poet's landscapes with the flow of history through Jordan's River Boyne. Reviewing *Shade* for the *Globe and Mail*, Fiona Foster compares Jordan's imagery of submergence – specifically the many drowned women of the novel – to that found in Heaney's bog poetry.[9] Telling the tales of these hidden bodies, says Foster, allows Jordan a new avenue to interrogate Irish historical narratives on both a social and a personal level, something very much in keeping with the approach to historiography he takes throughout *Shade*. Nonetheless, the Boyne of Jordan's novel does not give up grotesquely preserved sacrifices in the way of Heaney's bogs, but rather holds within it the essence of a lost way of life. In this respect, the *Times Literary Supplement* (*TLS*) describes *Shade* as a detailed study of the Boyne's impact on those who inhabited its spatiotemporal locus during the period described, privileging this interpretation over the publisher's insistence that the book is an unforgettable portrait of childhood.[10] Thoughtful readers of *Shade* will reach not for something to dry their tears, says the *TLS*, but instead for a volume on the Boyne's landscape and archaeology.[11] The highly visual, carefully researched nature of Jordan's writing makes it easy to imagine his audience indeed seeking out the relevant further reading in geography or cartography at the close of any of his books. At the same time, however, Jordan realises that landscapes without figures lack scale, so he peoples his imaginary Irelands with a wide variety of characters – Protestants and Catholics, colonial and contemporary, natural and supernatural – who both conform to and challenge the reader's expectations of how geography and history interact to create and recreate the Irish individual.

THE WORLD OF THE DEAD AND THE DAMNED

While Jordan's use of time and narrative in concert with something of a sacred waterway in *Shade* suggests Joyce's circular 'riverrun' device in *Finnegans Wake*, this is not the last nod to the canonical texts of modern Irish literature in this highly referential novel. As Nina Hardy's ghost disturbs the ragged curtains of Baltray House, so too do the spirits of Ireland's literary greats haunt the text itself. Yeats, Joyce, Shaw, Flann O'Brien and arguably even Samuel Beckett all make their presence felt and known. Jordan's identification with, and acknowledgement of, his debt to Joyce – which has been apparent in his writing since *Night in Tunisia* – is clearly evident in the structure of *Shade*. Though a far more accessible text than *Finnegans Wake*, this novel too muddles the distinction between endings and beginnings, its conclusion underscoring not just the river running (or, if one prefers, the riverrun-ing) through it all but also how the current of the book meanders through the many recognisable pools of Irish literature.

In this way the novel echoes how Beckett, in his 1929 essay on what was then Joyce's *Work in Progress*, saw that the structure of *Finnegans Wake* relied heavily on the cyclical theories of history proposed by Giambattista Vico.[12] Vico framed historical development as successive units of four 'ages': the divine, the heroic and the human, followed by a brief fourth age which closes one cycle and heralds the next. While it is true that *Shade* is structured into five distinct sections, it is still possible to discern the four Viconian/Joycean ages: the first, the divine, the mythological age of Boinn, the drowned girl from whom the river takes its name; the second, the heroic, the childhood antics of Nina and her friends against a backdrop which they imagine is the world, and, later, their adolescent sexual encounters and Gregory and George's experiences in the First World War; third, the human, Nina and Gregory's life in London, something that approaches an everyday existence (and, coupled with this, the notion of industry and progress as it transforms the landscape of the Boyne estuary); finally, the fourth age, the present-day 1950 of the novel and the transitional period after Nina's murder when her spirit witnesses her funeral and her remains are washed out into the sea. A further oblique titular connection is to be found in that transitional period, which also concerns itself with a wake.

Elsewhere, the referential nature of the novel is more substantial. It takes its title from W.B. Yeats' poem 'To a Shade', and while this contains a certain amount of thematic relevance for a novel told from the perspective of a ghost ('If you have revisited this town, thin Shade'),[13] Jordan chooses instead to preface the book with a quotation from Yeats' 'In Memory of Eva Gore-Booth and Con Markiewicz' ('Dear shadows, now you know it all'),[14] a poem that describes the destructive impact of time on splendour. The innocent and the beautiful 'have no enemy but time', Yeats says, signalling the subject of Jordan's novel.[15] In fact, time is flagged to the reader in the very first line of *Shade*, with Nina stating that she knows exactly when she died, then continuing to muse on temporality and existence throughout the novel much as Yeats does in his later poetry. Moreover, Jordan plays games with the near anagrams of Gregory and George which embody between them the twin aspects of the 'man' from

'To a Shade'. On one level this allows the characters to exhibit the fluid identities apparent in much of Jordan's work in film (something we will see again in prose in *Mistaken* and *Carnivalesque*). In such a reading of the novel, Gregory, Nina's half-brother and the object of her forbidden love responsible for her emotional awakening, is:

> Of your own passionate serving kind who had brought
> In his full hands what, had they only known,
> Had given their children's children loftier thought
> Sweeter emotion, working in their veins.[16]

Meanwhile George, a simpleton whose unrequited love for Nina and her constant rejection sends him off to the battlefields of the First World War (service for which he is later persecuted during the Irish war of independence), is:

> Like gentle blood, has been driven from the place
> And insult heaped upon him for his pains,
> And for his open-handedness, disgrace;
> Your enemy, an old foul mouth, had set
> The pack upon him.[17]

This conflation of the characters is continued throughout the book, culminating in letters dictated by George in his distinctive syntax but written in Gregory's handwriting during their First World War experiences and whereby the pair become a single unit, thus satisfying, for a while, Nina's conflicted attraction (200). Even allowing for the personae involved, it may be a stretch to connect these letters with the so-called automatic writing famously practised by Yeats' wife, also known as 'George', but in a text otherwise strewn with quiet literary in-jokes, the reader must be aware that almost anything can be a reference. To paraphrase Flann O'Brien, any writer tackling death and damnation – where the laws of ordinary life, let alone the laws of physics, no longer seem to apply – has ample scope for cheeky retorts to the great ghosts of the past.[18]

In *Shade*, one of the most curious instances of such literary backchat occurs in Chapter 19, when Gregory and Nina are carried by a wayward racehorse into the barley field of a local monastery. There they are detained by a character named Brother Barnabas, who those versed in the intricacies of modern Irish fiction will recognise as the pseudonym under which the already pseudonymous O'Brien published an early metafictional story titled 'Scenes in a Novel (Probably Posthumous)' in a student magazine.[19] With its narrator in all likelihood deceased, 'Scenes in a Novel' is a natural touchstone for Jordan to reference in *Shade*. Nina, after all, is dead, and many of the scenes she relates to the reader – the search for her body, her funeral, her wake – have to do with her posthumous affairs. There is an affinity too between *Shade* and O'Brien's most famous work, *The Third Policeman* (published in 1967, but composed in 1939/40), the narrator of which is also dead and who, at the conclusion of the novel, appears trapped in a recurrent time-loop from which he cannot escape.

With the Barnabas episode, however, Jordan playfully signals a moment of doubt in traditional Joycean modernism, or at the least a moment of re-examination in a text predicated on reassessment. A light-hearted and reflexive interlude, the Barnabas episode begins with the entrance of the monk, a man of God and the church, presented like the Grim Reaper with a cowl on his head and a scythe held high above him. Nina's confusion at his appearance is understandable; certainly he is a reaper, in the agricultural sense, and, while not grim *per se*, he is very much in a very bad humour (142). That all of this is watched over by the child's future spiritual self adds another layer of humour to the episode. Death, it seems, is one big joke in *Shade*, and in a surprising concession to postmodernity, Barnabas warns the children that perhaps they do not really exist at all, and that maybe they are merely the dream of a drowsy abbot in the monastery garden (144). While the remark is intended to be throwaway, it sticks with Nina throughout her life (and death), and threatens her with the realisation that she and her friends are all just characters in another's fiction, a notion that reflects the deterministic philosophy found elsewhere in *Shade*. Within the context of the narrative, however, Nina utilises this conceit to escape responsibility for her actions (or non-actions): during an erotically charged moment with her half-brother, she proposes that people can only truly exist in the dreams or stories of others (169). It is a concept in which she finds a certain consolation, and at various junctures she is willing to blame the emptiness of her own life on that of an unseen creator figure

(145). While this is a far cry from O'Brien's out-of-control characters in 'Scenes in a Novel' or *At Swim-Two-Birds* (1939), Nina's dalliance with an awareness of her own fictional nature furthers the homage.

Additional hints of O'Brien – particularly of *The Third Policeman* and *The Dalkey Archive* (1964) – appear in Jordan's use of quasi-scientific inspiration in *Shade*, the appearance of which builds upon prior instances of physical or mathematical philosophising in his previous work and which anticipate those of the later *Carnivalesque*. Throughout *Shade*, Jordan deepens the metaphor of triadic ambiguity utilised so prolifically in his earlier fiction ('A Love', *The Past, Sunrise with Sea Monster*) into the quadratic ambiguity which defines the relationships of Nina, Gregory, George and their friend Janie. The author makes a further, metaphorical connection between this grouping (along with the ghost) and the traditional fifths of Ireland, four provinces bound together by spirit, or in this case, a spirit (170). Such mathematical inferences are far from accidental, as equations and measurement are a constant presence in the author's work, from James Vance and Father Beausang's friendship in *The Past* – peppered with talk of Descartes and de Valera – to the coded back-and-forth of Donal Gore and his Nazi contact in *Sunrise with Sea Monster*, a relationship that takes Heisenberg's equations as its cipher. Yet, what is notable in *Shade* is the manner in which Jordan integrates ideas from maths and physics into the structure of the novel as a whole, promoting somewhat esoteric concepts such as the observer effect from mere texture to intrinsic narrative component. While clearly he shares an interest in strange science with O'Brien (an interest that, as mentioned, will be crucial to *Carnivalesque*), Jordan does not sensationalise it for comedic effect. The authorial presence in *Shade* is deathly serious, and while the metaphysical notions which underpin Nina's condition are seldom obvious, it is Jordan's willingness to deepen the philosophical probing of his previous books that is striking here.

Other variations between *Shade* and the earlier fictions are also apparent. Heretofore, the protagonists of Jordan's novels have all been the product of single-child families. Nina, having a half-brother in Gregory, is at once something new and something similar. She endures the loneliness of a solitary childhood for nine years before Gregory's arrival and her reaction to his appearance is suitably profound (84, 145). The young Nina experiences the absence of the life they had not spent together and sheds tears for the memories this has denied her (84, 85). She sees Gregory as her missing half (90) and so wonders if the pair will ever become whole again (97). At once she comprehends that she is somehow incomplete without him, and always has been. Though the point is somewhat laboured, Gregory, as Nina's half-brother, is the missing part of herself. In many ways they share a spirit, even a ghost, and so together they create a series of histories for this shade (109, 110). In a concession to the novel's larger themes of altered temporality and circularity, Nina realises that this missing childhood, this absent space between them meant that their lives have already deviated from what they would have otherwise been (85).

Hence the litanies of deaths, which the children invent for the ghost, little knowing it is in fact one of their own, further complicate the sense of time underpinning *Shade*. On the one hand, their imaginings present a series of alternative timelines involving the same figure, while on the other their stories take the form of successive, predestined demises recurring over and over again throughout history: the ghost was young, from the Regency period, fleeing some unspecified persecution; she was an actress, from the Empire period, who had been travelling from Smock Alley; she perished while attempting to cross the Boyne or she died in childbirth (110). On and on the variations go. The inevitably tragic circumstances of her demise mirror the many drowned women of the Boyne while the repetitious nature of the deaths consistently reasserts the themes of Jordan's novel. For at the heart of this narrative is a compelling debate about free will versus determinism, with Nina's inability to change events and the children's stories about the ghost's demise arguing for the rule of destiny in an otherwise anarchic universe. Far more than *The Past*, Jordan's previous extended rumination on how people process and interpret history, *Shade* deals with the question of causality itself: without the presence of Nina's ghost, would events have transpired differently; or, alternatively, is Nina *supposed* to be murdered? Has that act been a part of established history since before she was born? All of this is part of the novel's sustained interrogation of the individual's relationship with history itself, which, unlike in *The Past*, is not something to be catalogued and collected, something once removed from the teller of the tale. In *Shade*, Nina Hardy is *present*, providing the perfect narrator for a work of historical fiction by combining first-hand participation in events with an equally first-hand observation and assessment of the same events. She is able to live in the full of her life's moments while simultaneously judging them objectively from the distance of years. One peculiar effect of this is the repeated transition from first- to third-person narration. Though *Shade* is told entirely through Nina's post-mortem first-person, the effect of third-person narration is created by her description of her younger self as 'she' throughout the bulk of the text. The resulting perturbation experienced by the reader is an artefact of the narrator's non-linearity and atemporal nature; both Ninas are the same person and yet they are two different people: one defined by a lifetime of experiences, the other a *tabula rasa*, the erosion of whose innocence is observed in the privileged company of her own older, wiser self. Their existences overlap not just in a narratological space, but in the physical, temporal spaces of Nina's early life along the Boyne (for in her later life in England and elsewhere, the ghost is conspicuous by its absence). To fully understand the complexities of this scenario, one must examine the mechanics of temporality as Jordan defines them in *Shade*.

TIME AND TIDE: CAUSALITY AND CIRCULARITY

Nina Hardy has been murdered and, as a result, should not be the ideal narrator that she is. Yet, her success is a result of her post-mortem condition. The passage of time, she claims, ended for her upon her death even if nothing else did (4). She becomes a narrator for whom the discrete divisions between the past and the present dissolve, allowing her to flit between them with supernatural ease (4). Her story, or so she claims, is subsequently endless (97). Indeed, Jordan himself admits that *Shade* is in many ways a circular story, one told from within the spherical septic tank where George dumps Nina's mortal remains (5).[20] Temporally dislocated, her spirit travels back in time to haunt her childhood, tacitly and largely unintentionally influencing her own development (and at times that of George) until both are in place for the murder to repeat itself, for the second Nina's spirit to travel back in time and the narrating Nina – the term 'original' does not seem appropriate given that these events have clearly transpired before – to be released unto the endless horizon (316). Jordan says he began with the idea of a woman remembering a presence in her life from when she was a child.[21] She recalls the clothes worn by this presence which she doesn't recognise until the day she is murdered wearing those very clothes.[22] The novel therefore rejects the limited temporal nature of human lives, transcending mere linear existence. Death is presented as vexing time's steady progress as it is perceived by the living.

The fifty chapters of the novel cover a period of just over fifty years (1897–1950), and while no single chapter covers any single year, it does suggest an overall structuring principle at work, especially with the repeated emphasis on the turn of the century being the true start of the story, with Nina's first awareness of her own ghost coinciding with that new era, as well as her father's stated pleasure at being present for the opening years of a new century (7, 8). Events in the early chapters are repeatedly dated by the number of years into the 1900s they occur (7, 24). Throughout the novel, characters are obsessed with the mechanics of this new age, though frequently such progress is portrayed quite harshly in comparison with the rural arcadia of Nina's youth (8). This is seen both in her father's dedication to new technologies in his shellfish processing plant and its Hadean conditions as well as in Gregory and George's experiences during the industrial destruction of the First World War (9, 207). However, progress and time are inescapable, at least for the living, and, to paraphrase James Joyce, history in *Shade* is a nightmare from which its characters cannot truly awaken. Though this is not to say they do not make the attempt. The character of George, mentally ill, expresses a desire to return to his childhood, something which is at least partially accomplished through his murder of Nina and her subsequent temporal dislocation (130). In fact, the history from which *Shade*'s characters cannot escape is the history of their own lives, the temporal loop in question encompassing only the time from young Nina's awareness of the ghost to her eventual release into that form herself.

Though it may at first seem straightforward, the narrative of *Shade* is thus surprisingly complex and fluid. Events frequently occur in the same place but at different times, the temporal distance between them collapsed by the narrator's nonlinear nature. The reader is left wondering to what extent the presence of Nina's ghost alters the course of events and creates an alternate Nina. How has such close scrutiny throughout her childhood impacted on the personality she develops and to what extent is this a metaphor for the interplay of Irish history and historiography in general? To what extent has the study of history in this country, and the prominent place of that subject in cultural, educational and popular contexts shaped contemporary notions of Irish identity? Through the novel, Jordan effects a critique of the relentless concentration on the heroes of the independence struggle (which previously defined his work in *The Past, Sunrise with Sea Monster* and *Michael Collins*) and how that focus has influenced the composition of contemporary ideas of Irish identity and historiography right up to the 1980s, let alone the longstanding deification of the Great Men de Valera and Collins. Having analysed himself out of the debate in previous works, Jordan here presents a story where the forward motion of time has stalled in the present as Nina's story unfolds in the past (75). His narrator very literally enters the space of her own history, while the author, in turn, explores new representations of life and society on either side of the independence era. For Nina, time is a pliable thing, and in fact the character functions as a point of temporal convergence around which all the events of *Shade* are seen to bend (65).

Yet, to what extent can this series of events be challenged by its participants? What leeway is there, if any, for the characters here to alter what will or will not be their history (127)? Between the covers of *Shade*, the answer is none at all. The ghost, for instance, wants to call out to her younger self, she wants to guide her, to let her know there are choices to how things play out, but in the end she says nothing (127). Destiny and determinism rule the day. As in *The Past*, the events here are clearly meant to happen, though unlike in the earlier novel they are largely irrelevant to any grand account of politics or nation-building. This shift of focus on Jordan's part betrays an uncharacteristic disinterest in the contested narratives of Irish history, the rivalries and revisions which characterise it as a discipline and which, through the narrator's quest for truth and accuracy, Jordan investigated thoroughly in *The Past*. What has been retained is the question of Ireland's historical relationship to Britain, an issue that was subsumed into a European context in *Sunrise with Sea Monster*. On the microscopic level, *Shade* is a novel of the Boyne and its surroundings, but, macroscopically, it is an unashamedly archipelagic text.

Shade's Drogheda is socially and economically bound to Britain as much as to Ireland, with the cattle ships and the steampacket company founded by Nina's grandfather reflecting its dependence on traffic and trade from across the Irish Sea (13, 230). This, combined with the subsequent concentration on Nina's professional experiences in Britain during the post-independence period, mark *Shade* as a rejection of the isolationist de Valera model of Irish history in favour of one predicated on the lives and experiences of ordinary individuals.

Nonetheless, it is time rather than history that provides the novel's abiding subject matter. Throughout the first section of *Shade*, there is an overwhelming sense of pieces being put in place and events being delicately nudged into motion, an impression that quickly overpowers the usual suspension of disbelief entertained by readers at the outset of any novel. The lack of subtlety with which this feeling builds suggests not predestination but, arguably, time itself consciously setting the scene for the dramas which are to follow. This is apparent in the seemingly implausible second meeting of Nina's parents, a course-correcting encounter which results in the relationship that their botched first introduction failed to instigate (14). Similarly, Nina's grandfather built the quay and the ship that, at the outset of the First World War, takes away the dearest members of her family (191). The orangeade with which the children wake Hester the doll foreshadows the whiskey of Nina's own wake, while the children's performance of *As You Like It* is curiously appropriate to their later romantic entanglements (78). Notions of eternal recurrence are detectable as well, not only in the structure of the book as a whole, but in the smaller dramas which surround the Hardys such as how Nina's friend Maggie gives birth, in a small town on the Severn, to a child of an estuary much like Nina herself (248). Again and again, events repeat themselves as time moves in great circles around the novel's characters, wrapping around itself as it will later be said to do at the conclusion of Jordan's curious 2021 sci-fi tale – which also nods to Flann O'Brien – 'Easter, 2036'.

Time is in fact everywhere in *Shade*. Witnessing the grief of her loved ones in 1950, Nina remarks that the passage of time is visible in their eyes (54). Nina's old-fashioned clothes clash quite deliberately with the uniforms of modern war at the close of Part IV (262). The megalithic tomb of Chapter 20 is as much a calendar as it is a grave, a construction for marking the passage of time (148). Elsewhere, George, en route to collect Nina, is warned not to be too early (169). As in *The Past*, *Shade* argues that Protestants think in generational timescales while Catholics are motivated by more immediate concerns. With the war of independence here overshadowed by the impact of the First World War, and the present tense of the book ending in 1950, less than twelve months after Ireland officially became a republic, *Shade* is stripped of the nationalist mythologies that underpinned Jordan's earlier novels.

Characters too are defined by their relationship to time, with Nina's back-and-forth along her lifetime – her worldline, if one wants to use the physics terminology – being merely the most obvious example. A Father Time figure (in fact his children adopt the formal 'Father' when addressing him), Nina's father abandons the futuristic promises of industry which characterised his greeting of the new century and, instead, retreats further and further into Ireland's past as he grows older. He returns to art, his first love, and undertakes a sketching tour of Boyne Valley antiquities (277); in his own way, he too is moving back and forth in time. Later, having replaced his factory with a sheaf of drawings, he considers the idea of publication by the Meath Historical Society to preserve his work for posterity, but realises that he might never complete the project (277). Cruelly, he is defeated by progress, which had been his ally earlier in life. This realisation is more affecting than the destruction of his factory during the birth-throes of the Free State, and, in the end, is revealed to be another example of the unremitting circularity expounded by the novel. He becomes estranged from the world around him once more, an old man in a house growing more and more unfamiliar (287). Which is to say that both Nina and her father are literally and figuratively unstuck in time. Gregory too seems to have inherited something of the family non-linearity, described by his sister as eternally boyish despite the greying hair of his early fifties (83). The ghost Nina, after all, sees everything.

In *Shade*, it quickly becomes apparent that this act of Nina's ghost observing herself as a child so closely has altered her development. Their interaction begins with an awareness of presence, and quickly evolves into whispering intimacies to somebody who is not there (7). The young Nina learns to exude a stoic recognition of the fact that she is always being watched and thereafter she becomes accustomed to the constant need to perform (33). This is the primary determinant in her decision to become an actress and so later be in a position to buy out Gregory's share of Baltray House, setting the scene for her murder. In physics, such an interaction is known as the observer effect, the principle whereby changes occur in the phenomenon being observed as a result of the observation itself. The reader is left to wonder how Nina's personality might have developed if her history had not been altered by the appearance of the ghost and her timeline had not diverged from its original state. The distinct separate universes of the boys' and girls' secondary schools in the novel allude to just such parallel realities coming into existence after the ghost's appearance (153). Even Gregory, we are told, experiences a digression from what his life might otherwise have been (124).

Observation is flagged early, as Nina's parents meet in an art gallery viewing a painting by Velázquez, an artist whose name comes to be a code word between the pair for lingering desires which were frustrated because of coincidences or incapacity (14, 20). Later, Nina first encounters George and Janie as they watch her from across the river while Miss Shawcross, her short-lived governess, tells her to ignore them with an instruction to not look, as if to deny them the experience of being seen is to deny them existence altogether (43). Conversely, George, in an effort to make manifest the apparition, takes the name they have given it (itself once the name of Nina's doll) and gives it to a local owl which he spots looking at them. Most tellingly of all, Nina's ghost later states that she is nothing more than observation itself, which is both correct and incorrect. While it is true that all Nina's ghost can do is watch (at several points she chooses not to intervene directly, or is prevented from doing so by the limitations of her condition), her spectral form manifests in the world and so is observable by others. Her own childhood self sees her plainly on several occasions, as does George, while Gregory and Janie both claim to have felt her presence. While the young Nina is most directly affected by the ghost, all four children are in some way altered by the incorporation of her existence into the mythologies of their childhood. The very act of watching engenders changes on the physical world of the ghost's own past (96).

Causality, the engine of progression later related through narrative as the academic discipline we call History, is thus questioned throughout the text. Even the child Nina is described as contemplating cause and effect all throughout the middle portions of the narrative (63). An interrogation of causality, this time closer to an object lesson, occurs when the young Nina wishes Miss Shawcross would drown, a demise that subsequently occurs six pages later (42, 48). The child, for a long time, is plagued by the notion that her thoughts and wishes had a material effect upon the world, and thus is haunted by a feeling of culpability in the death (64). The influence of the ghost from the future comes into question too with the hints of precognition that colour this episode. The young Nina has a vision of Miss Shawcross' hair beneath the water and it is as though perhaps the ghostly Nina and her childhood counterpart are sharing some subconscious space wherein impression, if not actual information, can be communicated (64). A hint of prescience is generated in the child's dreams by this, something that will result, years later, in Nina feeling she had somehow already experienced the emotions of loss accompanying her father's death (38, 288). In the case of Miss Shawcross, the child feels as though events are eerily familiar and that she has, somehow, glimpsed a vision of future events through her spectral self (though she lacks the ability to properly interpret this event). Could either Nina have intervened and saved the hated Miss Shawcross? Nina at least believes that some part of her could have stopped it from happening, though it is implied that her future self is shielding her from the responsibilities and burdens of true precognition (57).

The failure to save Miss Shawcross ensures that Nina's development undergoes another divergence, moving further away again from the person she might otherwise have been. Her mother decides to leave Nina's education take its own course, and Nina begins to attend the local national school, something that cements her relationship with George and Janie (66). In contrast to Shawcross' efforts to transform her into a cultured lady of high society, Nina begins to adopt the townland dialect (67). The effect is amplified by the preconceptions of her national school teacher who leaves the girl to her own imagination, convinced that her family's large house is indicative of some innate refinement (71). Any ladylike future in society which Nina may have had is thus aborted; the national school will lead to the convent school, where her love of performance and of being watched will blossom into a love of acting. The crucial factor may be Shawcross' death or, more intriguingly, may be the spirit's unwillingness or inability to warn the young Nina of her governess' impending demise.

The causation here lies with the ghost's appearance in the first place; Nina's imaginative obsession with this unseen playmate is her mother's primary motivation in hiring Shawcross to begin with. It is important to note that the presence of the spirit Nina begins to have an effect from very early on, with the baby Nina staring beyond her parents' shoulders while still in the crib (22). Equally, at her christening, the baby does not cry when she is baptised, popular belief being that if a child does not cry at the water, then bad spirits are still in her presence (22). In Nina's case, this is surprisingly accurate, and, if not bad spirits, she certainly picks up bad habits from her ghostly self until ripples from the spectre's initial presence have spread out across an entirely new history which, paradoxically, appears destined to have been created all along (137). However, while the observer effect is the chief characteristic of space and time as Jordan depicts them in *Shade*, it is not the only physical phenomenon underpinning the novel. Jordan also makes clever use of Heisenberg's infamous and closely related uncertainty principle (which is, in fact, often confused with the observer effect) and, in many respects, it structures the novel's framing story in the same way the observer effect incites the action of the main plot.

The uncertainty principle states that position and momentum cannot both be known with any great measure of precision, and the more precisely one property is known, the less precisely the other can be known. In short, you can know where a particle is or how it is moving, but you can never know both. Discovering the presence of Heisenberg in *Shade* is not unexpected given how Jordan has utilised the principle before, in *Sunrise with Sea Monster*, both as the basis for coded communications and as an allegory for Ireland's role in the Second World War and Donal Gore's role in Ireland. Indeed, the SS officer of that novel, who studied at Leipzig with Heisenberg, claims to have been an apathetic mathematician for whom metaphors counted more than equations, something that could easily be taken as a caricature of Jordan – self-described as a poor academic performer when at school – and of his use of such material throughout his fiction (*Sunrise with Sea Monster*, 67).[23] In *Shade*, Nina becomes the (un)living embodiment of Heisenberg's theory: while her story is being told, her body is missing; the gardaí diligently search for it but they cannot find it. She wonders how she can be everyplace and no place simultaneously (97). At the conclusion of the novel, the situation is reversed as her tale concludes and her body emerges from the septic tank. The reader no longer knows what Nina is doing, but knows her remains are washed out of the estuary and into the observable domain of the Irish Sea.

This final journey illuminates another central conceit of *Shade*: time and tide wait for no person, but both appear to pause long enough for Nina to tell her tale. Some readers may interpret *Shade*'s narrative as taking place entirely in the instant of Nina's death, a flashes-before-your-eyes moment in which she recalls all that has come before. This, however, is not the case. Though the child Nina declares at the funeral of her doll Hester that the dead can dream and, when they do so, they dream of those still living, the reader can easily dismiss the possibility that the past or present tense of the novel takes place entirely in Nina's memory (79). She is, quite clearly, a ghost, and the interactions between her spirit self and her childhood self indicate that she has genuinely travelled in time (otherwise the plot of the novel could not play out as it does). Her description of events that take place after her death, occurrences outside her own worldline, bolster that assertion. Refining one's understanding of *Shade* is therefore contingent not only on an understanding of the alinearity which underpins the text, but on the associated ghostly nature of the novel's narrator.

GHOST ON THE MUDFLATS: NINA AND NARRATION

An implicit linkage exists between Nina's ghostly form and the form of *Shade* itself. The looping circularity of time as it is depicted in the novel is accessible to the reader only through the sublime uniqueness of Nina's condition. She becomes her own ghost, a reassuring presence to a younger self who perceives her not as a terrifying spectre or a ghoul, but as familiar, without ever understanding just how true that is (5). Subjectivity and objectivity collapse as the two Ninas interact with each other, yet the spirit Nina appears quite localised in both time and space. She manifests primarily in the temporal locus of what might be thought of as her own existence, or perhaps more correctly the period in which her existence was in play upon the timeline. This constitutes the five decades stretching from her parents' meeting to her own funeral and the washing of her remains into the sea, limitations outside of which Nina's spirit does not stray. Geographically too, she is bounded to her childhood territories along the River Boyne, with later portions of the novel, set largely in England, taking the form of the spirit's recollections.

Jordan himself has been quite open about his personal ghostly experiences, elements of which appear to colour both the spectral representations of *Shade* and the silence of the father in *Sunrise with Sea Monster*. The author's own father used to tell him ghost stories as a child and, says Jordan, the aftermath of Michael Jordan's death left him bereft when the promise of those stories was not fulfilled.[24] He says this feeling persisted for almost half a decade before he began to feel his father's presence once again.[25] Talking to Gay Byrne, he recalled an experience on a flight from Los Angles to Dublin when, woken by turbulence, he saw his father standing in the aircraft's aisle.[26] While Jordan admits that this may have been his imagination, the vision seems to have offered inspiration, specifically in how he conceived of the ghost as stunned into silence by its demise and needing to find a way to make its being manifest once more.[27] The ghost of his father, he says, simply stood there – like Nina's spectral presence in *Shade* – appearing somewhat lost and saying nothing.[28] Jordan told Byrne that, while he was almost certainly dreaming, it felt closer to the experience of waking.[29] Dramatising such an encounter, most imaginatively from the perspective of the ghost itself, is one of the central undertakings of *Shade*.

Jordan's deceased narrator has precedents in popular culture, for example Alice Sebold's bestselling novel *The Lovely Bones*, published two years before *Shade*. With the dismemberment of its central character and the disposal of her remains in a sinkhole, somewhat reminiscent of *Shade*'s septic tank, *The Lovely Bones* may be seen as a forerunner to *Shade*, though perhaps it is Billy Wilder's film *Sunset Boulevard* that has the stronger claim. Not only is it narrated by the recently murdered Joe Gillis, but it was released in 1950, the year of Nina's death. *Sunset Boulevard* prominently features a fading actress who, like Nina Hardy, graduated from silent cinema to talkies, a character played by Gloria Swanson as something of an homage to her own earliest film roles (latter portions of Jordan's novel also investigate the development of early cinema). However, neither *The Lovely Bones* nor *Sunset Boulevard* features the prominent time-travel elements which characterise *Shade*. Sebold's novel follows events in the present tense while Wilder's film is told largely through flashback.

What *Shade* does share with these antecedents is its reliance on narration as the primary attribute of manifestation. The emphasis on self-actualisation present in Jordan's earlier novels – the narrator of *The Past* inserting himself into the metanarrative of Irish history or the protagonist of *The Dream of a Beast* literally talking himself into a new state of being – is compounded here by Nina Hardy's unusual perspective. As a non-corporal entity, self-actualisation is all she has; were Nina to stop describing herself, she would cease to exist. This is a powerful metaphor for the novelist himself, for, if Jordan were to stop describing things, where would he be as a writer? His famous remarks with regard to the prevalence of visual description in *The Past*, what he referred to as trying to force the novel form into a shape which it resisted, reveal a lack of certitude as to the role of dialogue in his earliest fiction, and this from a writer whose movies are often characterised by sharp dialogic exchanges.[30] As a result, it is perhaps worth noting that *Shade* is Jordan's 'chattiest' novel up to this point, a book in which, unlike *The Past* or *Sunrise with Sea Monster*, dialogue is as prominent as descriptive passages. Nina's narration constantly incorporates verbatim conversation into her story, with the ghost's detached presence raising the questionable objectivity of memory to something closer to documentary evidence in nature.

In a comment on the responsibilities of the writer with regard to historical literature, Jordan further allows Nina to become a familiar to Irish history itself. The child of the state motif from *The Past* is abandoned here in place of a less indulgent secret sister (33). Nina watches over the first half of the Irish twentieth century even as she lives through those same tumultuous times. Jordan admits he likes to consider the interplay of the human perception of time with the potentially supernatural, and here he does so quite literally, shunting the present of the young Nina into the memories of her ghostly future self.[31] Jordan's heightened interest in memory is wide-ranging, limited not just to narrative choices but also to the way the novel's characters interact with their world. For Janie, even in the presence of Nina's spirit, it is memories and not ghostly visitations that chill her (122). Meanwhile, Nina herself – split between time periods and wandering the expanse of time to witness her parents' courtship, her own childhood and adolescence, her mature years as an actress in London and the aftermath of her murder back in Ireland – is a ghost who literally and directly deals with memories, their production, processing and protection. The challenge, for Jordan as an author, is keeping all her dealings straight.

Alan Wall, in a substantial review for *The Guardian*, focuses on just these narratological difficulties with Nina's condition, seeing a structural tension between the deceased omniscient narrator ranging across time and space and Jordan's use of first person singular.[32] But Nina does not become an all-knowing narrator so much as an all-witnessing one; she reveals to the reader what she sees, as she sees it, and her knowledge is constrained by her limitations in both space and time. She recognises that her condition comes with rules, though she does not know what they all are (97). This results in what she describes as a sense of absence, a feeling of objects deprived of their usual associations, though this quality is not rigorously applied throughout the novel (105). In the intricacies of her drift through time, and in the way present-tense conversations weave in and out of her own memories, Nina finds that there is an enjoyable, almost poetic quality to her condition, something that puts the reader back in mind of Yeats' 'dear shadows'. Like them, Nina now seems to know it all (61, 63). Though, crucially, Jordan paraphrases Yeats by introducing an element of uncertainty; Nina is unsure that she in fact knows it all. Which is to say that, post-mortem, she does not become omnipresent but instead becomes her own familiar (4, 5, 6). Her presence and influence, rather than being boundless and all-knowing, are eventually collated with the limited perspectives of not only her younger self's doll, but with the other dead women of the Boyne valley, the drowned girl Boinn and the Maiden from the tower. As the novel progresses, she becomes the doll, the ghost and whatever the children need her to be in turn (62, 80). Both the ghostly and the living Nina identify strongly with Boinn – the river's initial victim – and her attendant mythology (9, 10). Over time (and with shades, if you will pardon the pun, of *Sunrise with Sea Monster*) the ghost becomes the watchful spirit of the river, and an early sexual encounter of the teenage Nina takes place under the eyes of a Boinn-inspired Sheelana-Gig (34, 180). Finally, when floods collapse the Victorian brickwork of the septic tank, Nina becomes part of the river itself (316).

The narrator's spectral condition further generates considerable dark irony throughout the novel. Nina is the one who gives George his job as gardener, putting him in the position to murder her, though the spirit appears to harbour no grudge against him or her own mortal self (297). Partially, this results from Nina's loneliness in her new existence, a hold-over from her time among the living. Like the Beast before her, she is the only one aware of her condition, and so it is natural that she chooses to remain close to those she loved, even to George. Complicit in this is her mortal self, and when the ghost first appears in Chapter 2 as the child's imaginary friend, the young Nina decides she must be part of a larger story, something beyond her comprehension and which began in the distant past when, in fact, the opposite is true (7). Nina's ghost forms a kind of shared world with her childhood self, much like the young Nina shares with her doll, though the ghost as she imagines it is different from the real ghost. The act of being perceived, she tells the reader, is a form of comfort in and of itself (79). Hester – after the doll – becomes the ghost's name, though as the spirit Nina reveals, a name of any kind is preferable to spectral anonymity (80, 92). This is appropriate as both die by having their heads wrenched from their bodies. Little wonder then that the children's conversations turn so frequently to decapitation and martyrdom (99, 100). Hester's demise begins their long obsession with mortality and time in so far as they can perceive such things from their perspective. To the mortal characters here, time is like the conveyer of the local farmer's threshing machine, the endlessly flowing river of grass en route to the flagellation of the thresher's wooden arms, something Jordan presents with Hellish imagery (77). As if to emphasise the point, the threshing itself takes place in a field bordering the graveyard of the local Protestant church (77).

This is the moment that Hester dies, consumed by the thresher, and it is the initial prompt for the children to question the nature of ghosts. Why, they wonder, does one person's spirit linger while another's does not (109)? They surmise that Nina's ghost has information for them, and, indeed, her testament is the novel itself (109). Certainly, the act of telling her story is more important than functioning as any kind of guardian angel to her younger self. In fact, angelic references are rare in *Shade*, especially considering Jordan's stated belief that children possess an innate religiosity.[33] The children of *Shade* do not appear particularly concerned with their immortal souls, which is again ironic considering the presence of one of those souls around them throughout their childhoods. More so, perhaps, given how Jordan has stated that he finds logic and beauty in St Anselm's proof of the existence of God: 'How can we have an idea of that which does not exist, for to have an idea of it is to bring it into some form of existence?'[34] Though over the course of *Shade*, the children's relationship to the ghost does come to resemble this reverence. They attribute random events to her intervention and they devise stories to explain her demise. Denied corporality by death, Nina derives part of her ghostly presence from their belief in her existence, something that suggests an explanation for her absence after the group disbands.

Certainly, the four children appear sensitive to spirit Nina's presence in different ways, with her manifestations taking on two forms. In the first, the spirit is seen by Nina alone, such as when the ghost goes to visit herself as a child in the hospital after her fall, appearing as a motionless figure dressed in mismatched fur coat and Wellington boots who crowds out the room behind Nina's parents and the nurse (127). The second kind of manifestation is that witnessed by others, visitations leaving physical evidence behind them. While some characters, such as Gregory, only sense the presence of the ghost (269), others, such as George, are particularly attuned. In one of the novel's strangest scenes, Janie recounts a time that George saw her – the ghost – by an old manhole, the site where forty years later he will dispose of Nina's body (133). The young George has blood on his hands but, when Janie cleans him, his skin is undamaged. It is, claims George – many decades ahead of the crime itself – the blood of the ghost. While this may seem a complication, the presence of ectoplasmic materials, manifestations of spiritual energy in the physical realms which some associate with the appearance of ghosts, actually de-problematises Nina's spectral form (and is possibly one of the few aspects of the novel that can truly be thought of as Gothic). Nina proves, in the end, to be a ghost in the traditional sense, not an entity tied only to her own mortal existence. Equally, the fact that 'Hester' tells George things, such as that she has not yet died, and so exerts an influence over his behaviour as much as her own, furthers the deterministic philosophy of the novel as a whole (136). *Shade*, a novel about the bloody spectre of Irish history and its relationship with the all too vivid memories of the past, warns us that all of this has happened before, and so is likely to happen again.

In that way, *Shade* represents an elaboration of Jordan's earlier themes and a collision of personal laws with physical laws. The novel takes a localised bubble of space as well as time from which the author extrapolates a new approach to Irish historical fiction. If the novel suffers from a weakness, it occurs in the second half, where Nina's later life is defined by the conspicuous absence of the ghost. Jordan leaves the reader wondering how he might have reconciled her presence with a more aware, older version of the character, and how their interactions might have shaped Nina's foreknowledge of her fate. That said, the novel succeeds over, and differs from, Jordan's other fiction in its constant use of socio-economic elements throughout its historical narratives, for example the importance of the Drogheda Steampacket Company (13, 14). *Shade* is also far more critical of the independence struggle than any of Jordan's other writings. Nina's father's factory is burnt during the war of independence, though it had been in decline for some time before then (269). It eventually becomes the ruined shell of the novel's 1950s era, which in itself is a poignant metaphor for the situation which prevailed in Ireland after de Valera's economic policies during the 1930s and the Emergency. Furthermore, in the transition to the Republic, the Big Houses of the state, represented by Baltray House itself, come to decay. In a further example of circularity, however, restoration is eventually attempted by Nina herself, the property being made exactly as it once was by the hand and, vitally, the memory of the older George (83). Restoring the past through the force of his memory alone, George literally unearths years gone by – old horseshoes and tin cans and coins dating back a half century or more – at the roots of an apple tree, another reminder of the fall from grace experienced both by Nina herself and by the upper class in Ireland during the 1950s (307).

The novel therefore offers a balance to the transformative myth of *The Dream of a Beast* and the mythology of decolonisation developed throughout *The Past* and *Sunrise with Sea Monster*. *Shade*, by contrast, is set largely in the pre-war, pre-independence years of early twentieth-century Ireland, a time in which the thorniness of national identity is further problematised by the country's position within the British Empire. Progress, such as education, is portrayed negatively throughout the novel. Rural electrification, when it arrives, is perceived by the children as banishing the dark, the imaginative and the mythic from their world (27). There is to be no place for these in the new century. Related to this, Miss Shawcross' first instinct on arriving at Baltray House as governess is to makes the spaces of the house seem smaller, a significant affront to a child with a tendency to pour her imagination into all available corners of the world (24, 29). She derides Nina for her childish fancy. She suggests to the girl that she has been talking to herself, little knowing that this is exactly what young Nina is doing (35). Equally, when Hester the doll's remains are consigned to the river, to an estuary already overflowing with dead women, the reader is left with the distinct impression that these figures have died through neglect of their mythologies, as much as through their drowning (79, 116).

That Jordan returns again and again to the river here is in keeping with his earlier fictions, throughout which water is a constant presence. Yet, while the Boyne at times becomes the river of Irish history itself, running with blood and tears, its most important role in *Shade* is to divide the past from the future like an eddying barrier. It also demarcates a country of the imagination from adult reality. Different rules apply on different sides, as is true of the dead Nina and her still-living family. Only at the conclusion of the novel does she undergo communion with her predecessors, one dying by drowning, another killed in a fall, and she herself killed by the dirty metal of a pair of garden shears (316). Together, they form a trinity of increasing violence through the medium of water, a feminised bastardisation of the Catholic trinity suggested by Miss Shawcross' earlier demonstration of how St Patrick used shamrock to convert the native Irish to Christianity. (40) The implication would seem clear: the heathens never truly disappeared. Yet, there is another meaning here beyond the mythological. The trinity of drowning (Boinn), falling (the Maiden) and garden shears (Nina herself) can just as easily be thought of as Isobel Shawcross (drowned in the Boyne), Hester the doll (fell into the combine harvester) and Nina who, as floodwaters carry her into the estuary, is finally allowed to disappear into the sea like Anna Livia Plurabelle embodying the Liffey at the conclusion of *Finnegans Wake*.

Nina's own wake concludes with an affirmative, creative act of the living, that being drunken sex on the crisp sheets of her own bed between Janie and the garda sergeant Buttsy Flanagan (315). Their consummation transforms a place of death into a place of life, just as Nina once did in the megalithic confines of Boinn's tomb (a symbolic and mythological encounter from which the young woman's abiding memory is of whorls carved into the lintel reminiscent of Yeatsian temporal gyres). It is an appropriate conclusion to the novel which restores the dead Nina's faith in life for, like Yeats' 'Shade', surely she 'had enough of sorrow before death'. And still, while Nina is granted release, *Shade* implies that Jordan himself remains transfixed by questions of Irish history and identity, the recurrent nature of the narrative suggesting that the author will continue to explore the territory of Irish historical fiction, circling in on how best to articulate his personal relationship to Ireland and its transformations. It is a question he will take up in his next novel, *Mistaken* (2011), and later in *Carnivalesque* (2017), works in which he splits his protagonists not between this world and the next, but into two living versions of the artist this study has been tracking since the beginning, figures of the fantastical visual world and figures of the serious literary page. Before examining these, however, is it worth considering Jordan's previous forays into the divide between his two fields: his short fiction about filmmaking.

CHAPTER 7

Jordan's Film Stories: The uncollected collection

Before he broached the collision of his written and visual selves in *Mistaken* (2011), Neil Jordan had occasionally brought both aspects of himself together in shorter works of fiction. These stories about filmmaking represent a neglected facet of an already neglected body of work and so remain the most obscure of all his published texts. In combining a fictional approach to filmic concerns, these stories allow for Jordan's two artistic worlds to overlap in a manner which he does not normally permit. The result is an unusually candid and personal interrogation of the filmmaking industry at three key points in Jordan's career: the early 1980s, when he had achieved success as a writer and was beginning his creative mitosis; the early 1990s, when he experienced a combination of mainstream success and disillusionment at the Hollywood system; and the early twenty-first century, when his international reputation was secure. The three pieces, 'She' (1980), 'Remote Control' (1993) and 'The Berkeley Complex' (2003) are available only in out-of-print or short-run anthologies and hard-to-find journals, and so lack the availability granted by collection in a single volume.[1] Even readers who follow Jordan's work may be surprised to learn of both their existence and their surprising thematic unity. Yet, the film stories serve as important transitional texts, looking back to the outsiders and crepuscular realms of *Night in Tunisia* (1976) and, at the same time, forward to the theatrical allusion of *Shade* and the creative duality of *Mistaken*. A further unifying aspect of the stories is their interrogation of key movie-industry relationships (actor/director, director/producer and actor/employment) and the manner in which they can be read as part of a larger sequence, itself suggestive of a cinematic endeavour or a three-act motion picture.

As such, the film stories are best thought of as a developing, intertextual thesis from the pen of Jordan himself. Despite the inherent possibilities of this, and the manner in which the stories allow for simultaneous consideration of Jordan's two creative spheres, criticism has steadfastly overlooked the three texts. Yet, the contribution that the stories can make as the missing link between the disparate halves of Jordan's oeuvre is important, not least in their potential to make redundant the question of whether Jordan is a writer who makes films or a filmmaker who also writes literature. Consensus on that issue, as it stands, is rare. In a somewhat exceptional comment, Desmond O'Rawe, writing in *Fortnight* in 2003, observed that Jordan at his best bridged the divide between work for the page and work for the screen, where literature is a companion to filmmaking rather than its opponent.[2] The film stories serve as trusses on the bridge which O'Rawe refers to. They frame an interface where literature and filmmaking exist symbiotically to a degree unseen throughout the rest of Jordan's output. Not even his considerable history of adapting the books of others for the screen (five out of eighteen films at time of writing) can come close to the interconnectivity that his two main art forms display in these stories. Moreover, the literary nature of the texts suggests the conscious mythologising of an intense focus on the Irish experience of filmmaking, an experience informed and privileged by Jordan's own role in the history of the industry here. Constructing an argument in this fashion allows Jordan liberties with truth and perspective not easily justified in the genres of journalism or autobiography but which, appropriately, are shared with the world of film (the historical licences taken by *Michael Collins*, for example, and discussed in his *Michael Collins: Film diary*, 1996).[3]

Jordan's personalised interplay of writing and filmmaking in these stories is comparable only to the manner in which he drew thematic material for his film *The Miracle* (1991) from the *Night in Tunisia* short stories. That picture represented a low-budget return to the craft of storytelling after Jordan's Hollywood-funded disappointments of *High Spirits* (1988) and *We're No Angels* (1989). Even this correlation, however, has been misrepresented in much of the related criticism, which continues to read Jordan's fiction as an adjunct to his work in film. A more useful reading of Jordan's fiction and his films lies in what their connection reveals of Jordan's mindset at the time. It is no coincidence that, in addition to *The Miracle*'s back-to-basics filmmaking approach (much of it was filmed in Jordan's own home), the same period also produced such a pointed critique of Hollywood as 'Remote Control'. The decidedly Jordanesque narrator of the story bemoans how investors worry that his film might have merely art-house appeal while he sits in a restaurant or drives through Los Angeles observing the decay of a depthless society ('Remote Control', 61). The character's resulting aversion is unusual for Jordan, with its manifestation taking the form of wearied curiosity in the face of Hollywood's cultural idiosyncrasies. Jordan's narrator is the stereotypical stranger in a strange land, an experience shared with the protagonists of 'She' and 'The Berkeley Complex'. The collective term 'film stories' as used here is fuelled by other similarities too. Each is narrated in the first person and each of the narrators works or has worked within the film industry. In 'She' the narrator is a young actress, in 'Remote Control' a director, and in 'The Berkeley Complex' a self-obsessed male actor. Despite their chosen professions, their relationships with the industry always take the form of outsiders looking in. They are all observers of the complicated, often self-contradictory processes by which a film is created and so all display considerable levels of confusion, amusement or discontent with the industry. The actress of 'She' is alternatively bemused and bored by her director's insistence on just the right kind of light ('She', 79). The director of 'Remote Control' is an Irishman adrift in a Hollywood of previews and playability, while the actor self-consciously narrating 'The Berkeley Complex' finds himself unemployed when offers of screen work dry up after his all too brief success and he must return to the stage.

The film stories differ from both Jordan's collected short fiction in *Night in Tunisia* and the other uncollected tales such as 'On Coming Home' (1974) and 'The Old-Fashioned Lift' (1977). They are of note in that they pepper Jordan's career from 1980 to 2003 and, by virtue of their subject matter, they chart both Jordan's development as a writer and his development as a filmmaker. One of Jordan's initial film industry experiences, serving as scriptwriter for Joe Comerford's *Traveller* (1981), is heavily suggested by the observations of 'She', while 'Remote Control' exudes the disillusionment with Hollywood projects he underwent after *High Spirits* and *We're No Angels* even as its protagonist enjoys a success comparable to that of Jordan after *The Crying Game* (1992). Simultaneously, Jordan displays a mischievous awareness of how these texts function as crossover points between the two halves of his oeuvre. 'She', for example, is subtitled '*an Unfinished Story*' (Jordan's italics) and so contains an element of ambiguity as to whether this work of fiction will ever be completed. Meanwhile, 'Remote Control' is written in such a way that the reader is left wondering if the story leans more towards fact than fiction. Viewed in isolation, 'The Berkeley Complex' is the most straightforward of these stories, but it is difficult to assess it in such light considering its loaded initial publication in a film-themed issue of a fiction magazine founded by director Francis Ford Coppola. 'The Berkeley Complex' also confounds straightforward readings through the dense web of intertextualities linking it to progenitor texts from prose, film and theatre, including, but not limited to, the work of Jordan himself.

In relating the stories to Jordan's own filmography, so intertwined with the development of filmmaking in Ireland, a parallel narrative about the indigenous film industry as a whole emerges. Like the theatrical photographs of *The Past*, the snapshots offered by the stories chart the evolution of the industry here from the country's initial use as a location for foreign filmmakers (the director of 'She' is English), to the exportation of success stories such as Jordan himself to Hollywood during the 1990s and, finally, to a self-sustaining indigenous industry of afternoon soaps and opportunities for home-grown actors in the first decade of the twenty-first century. The development of filmmaking in Ireland further reflects the wider social, economic and artistic transformations in the country during the years in question, and Jordan's position at the forefront of change in that industry – as well as his ties to the literary world – contributes to the relevance and frankness of his film stories. Taken together, these stories delineate the boundaries of an imaginative world that is more familiar and, ironically, more timeless than that of his other short fictions. The deftness with which Jordan locates these pieces among both his own work and that of other filmmakers and playwrights further textures the world of the stories with convincing details of industry-specific reference and homage.

The final story, 'The Berkeley Complex', is also notable for emphasising the important relationship between theatre and film/television in Ireland. Examples include the actor Stephen Rea, a founding member of the Field Day theatre company whom Jordan has repeatedly cast in his motion pictures (among them Jordan's most recognisable titles, *Angel* (1982), *The Company of Wolves* (1984), *The Crying Game* (1992), *Interview with the Vampire* (1994), *Michael Collins* (1996), *The Butcher Boy* (1997) and *Greta* (2018)). In similar fashion, the narrator of 'The Berkeley Complex' graduated from the playhouses of Dublin to afternoon soaps, echoing the manner in which societal changes over the last twenty years transformed the once considerable audience for the former into the natural audience of the latter. However, the inability of that character to transcend the melodramatic and unrealistic plotlines and performances, itself an implicit criticism of change in Irish culture in general, results in his extreme dissatisfaction and his unforgiving caricatures of a Celtic Tiger society disinterested in consuming challenging artistic work. The disillusionment of this character is difficult to separate from his creator, especially as 'The Berkeley Complex' was first published a year after Jordan's long-gestating *Borgia* film project fell through.[4] Jordan's plans for what would have been a lavish, epic film set in Renaissance Italy unravelled for a second time just before production was set to begin because of investor concerns over whether or not the picture would have mass market appeal (Jordan would later resurrect it as the Showtime television series *The Borgias*, which ran from 2011 to 2013).[5]

'The Berkeley Complex' portrays an actor who has fallen victim to similar market forces: when his famed theatrical run concludes he suffers from a dearth of other parts and opportunities (BC, 208). The story thus provides a natural conclusion for the film stories sequence as a whole. The self-absorption of the artist in 'She' has combined with the commodification of art in 'Remote Control' and, while the European misery of 'The Berkeley Complex' lacks the ridiculousness of the Hollywood excesses depicted in that story, the result is still an industry where the narrator's literary indulgences are valued far less than his reluctant contribution to the proliferation of television soap operas. Jordan's own, occasionally oblique, comments on the dichotomy between his fiction and his films are also illuminated by the film stories. They answer the question of how Jordan himself views the physical process of filmmaking, how he views actors, directors and producers, and how these perspectives have changed throughout his career. He claims that films fulfil a different artistic purpose for him, telling Marianne Brace that they provide an opportunity to indulge in things like dramatic tension and melodrama, which he says Joyce and Beckett excised from long-form fiction.[6] The film stories, it would seem, have allowed Jordan to restore these de-canonised aspects to his writing in short-form work that hinges upon the application of correctly accented melodrama to situations that are drawn from his own filmmaking experiences. In 'She', this sensationalism is angsty and internal, of a piece with the adolescent grievances of *Night in Tunisia*. In 'Remote Control', the melodrama is deployed in self-conscious mockery of the Jordanesque narrator's discomfort in his Hollywood surroundings, while in 'The Berkeley Complex' (the only one of the three that also successfully exhibits dramatic tension) its use is clearly satirical. Read as a sequence, the three stories resolve into a complex orchestration that would not seem out of place in a longer, novel-length endeavour. This is best illustrated by individually examining 'She', 'Remote Control' and 'The Berkeley Complex' in turn.

UNFINISHED BUSINESS: 'SHE'

Where Jordan the writer exists in the public consciousness at all, it is usually as the author of the jazz-drenched coming-of-age stories from *Night in Tunisia*. This perception reached its apotheosis with the inclusion of the title story in 1990's *Field Day Anthology of Irish Writing*, but a decade earlier the association was already heavily suggested by the publication of 'She: An Unfinished Story' alongside an artful photograph of Jordan overwhelmed by the shadow of an idling saxophone.[7] 'She', a short tale about movie production, represents an early waystation between Jordan's prose and filmmaking, a connection made explicitly by the narrative of the film-within-the-story itself. The unnamed narrator working on this project may be a young actress, but her musings on the eccentricities of film production are heavily informed by just the kind of critique we might expect from a creative practitioner whose first work in film was as a script consultant (officially a 'creative associate') on John Boorman's *Excalibur* (1979). Yet, Jordan's subjects in 'She' are not the established filmmakers of Boorman pedigree. Instead, a subtle criticism is directed towards a new generation who prioritise aesthetics over story and who eventually became the disillusioned generation depicted in 'The Berkeley Complex'.

It is most likely that the model for the story's fictional director was Joe Comerford, whose take on Jordan's first script proved to be an unwelcome departure from the writer's vision.[8] Though *Traveller* was released in 1981, a year after the story appeared, Jordan received an Arts Council Film Script Award to write the project in 1979 and the movie's production during January and February of 1980 predates the publication of 'She'.[9] The correlation between the two texts is further supported by a line in the story where the narrator describes her role, a young woman picked up by a traveller who later abandons her, as though Jordan were remarking on how he and Comerford parted ways on the completion of the project. In interviews, Jordan has stated with a certain resignation that Comerford made his own of the original script.[10] Emer and Kevin Rockett identify the issue as Comerford's tendency towards obliqueness, a trait that is a central characteristic of his filmmaking style.[11] Such an approach clashed with the more dramatic aspects of the narrative Jordan envisioned.

What Keith Hopper sees as a tension between Comerford's camera and Jordan's screenplay, the sacrifice of narrative in the face of visual suggestion, is something that recurs throughout Jordan's combative relationship with the world of professional filmmaking.[12] This is particularly true in the case of *High Spirits* (1988), where the story became subservient to the tyranny of Hollywood visual effects. The strangeness of that film within Jordan's oeuvre is acknowledged, in a seemingly self-conscious manner, by Jordan's second film story 'Remote Control', but its failures are already suggested in 'She' by the actress' confusion over her director's intention. She says she does not understand what he is trying to accomplish, her own logical considerations in conflict with the organisation of the production as a whole ('She', 79). The character's criticisms of the director are in tune with Jordan's own storytelling concerns. Which is to say that Jordan's films, though usually linear in nature, are propelled by a strong narrative drive – one predicated on the primacy of the text, on the word of the screenplay – and are a far cry from Hopper's description of Comerford's films as playing back and forth between motifs of loosely linked images and sounds.[13] Crucially, however, it was the soured collaborative experience of *Traveller* that solidified Jordan's resolve to remain in control of his material as much as possible going forward. When Channel 4 expressed interest in his script for *Angel*, Jordan refused to allow anyone but himself direct it. As the Rocketts have stated, it was the intervention of John Boorman (described by Jordan as godfathering the project) that convinced the producers to allow Jordan to have his way.[14]

There remains confusion over how exactly to acknowledge Jordan's contribution to the finished *Traveller*, particularly as he is now a much more recognisable cultural figure than Comerford. It is neither truly the work of Jordan the writer nor of Jordan the director. In the Rocketts' bibliography, for example, the film is listed under adaptations of Neil Jordan work by other directors rather than under films directed and/or written by Neil Jordan.[15] Meanwhile, one of Hopper's articles is subtitled 'Word and Image in Neil Jordan and Joe Comerford's *Traveller*', implying an acceptance of dual authorship. Hopper, however, cleverly approaches the picture as two distinct texts, one the film by Joe Comerford, the other the original treatment by Neil Jordan, and so productively sidesteps the issue. That said, it should clearly be acknowledged that Comerford was the director of the finished film and that the Jordan version exists only as typed notes in the National Library of Ireland. By convention, *Traveller* is Comerford's picture and this, combined with Jordan's distancing himself from the film in a 2006 documentary by Philippe Pilard, ought to resolve the matter.

However, at the time 'She' was written, *Traveller* remained unfinished business, something which is hinted at by the story's subtitle, though any genuine antipathy seems to have dissipated by the end of the story. In what is a relatively short text, the narrator manages to transcend her origins as a mannequin or a mouthpiece – either for her in-story director or for her author – and achieves a transformation into a fully realised character within the space of just two pages. The cutting judgements made in the final lines belong to her voice rather than Jordan's, while the egotism displayed, if viewed retroactively through the treatment of the actor's condition in 'The Berkeley Complex', is more a function of thespian psychology than an adolescent girl's self-centredness. The character tells herself that she likes both her director and her father, and, as if reviewing a performance of her own, ends with the self-congratulatory observation that her own sympathy amazes her ('She', 80). This idea, that an actor must induce an almost out-of-body experience in order to observe themselves, is something that undergoes a deeper, more metaphorical exploration in *Shade*, of course, but also in 'The Berkeley Complex'.

That story's actor reveals an obsessive identification with *Othello* (both the play and the character) on which he has constructed his rapidly self-destructing sense of self; 'She', however, utilises an allusion from closer to home. It carries from *Traveller* a narrative and thematic homage to J.M. Synge's *The Playboy of the Western World* (1907). The borrowing from Synge in *Traveller*, something that both Hopper and the Rocketts make much of, is most blatant in Jordan's original treatment. 'She', however, also hints at the homage. Being twice removed from Synge's original play, the effect here is subtler than the Shakespearian allusions of 'Remote Control' and 'The Berkeley Complex' which appear as easily identified reference or paraphrase. Here, the theatrical associations are most obvious in the actress' father, whose desire for respect in the face of self-perceived social inadequacy echoes that of Christy Mahon. The actress maintains that her father has long wanted to be the kind of person people would listen to rather than turn away from, a thin man with distinguished grey hair, and a commanding voice ('She', 79). The fact that his hair is not entirely grey, just somewhat grey along the sides, provides the first intrusion of the crepuscular into a text which itself exists in a state of intertextual flux between the author's filmic and literary concerns. This crepuscularity, which is a recurring concern throughout the film stories, is further reflected in the director's impossible desire for the perfect fading light. The narrator reports that the production has endured three days of delay for the sun to fade to the precise quality of light which the director demands of the scene ('She', 79), with the girl's repeated use of metaphors for deception or insecurity critiquing both her director's aesthetic taste and his filmic concerns.

A similar sense of disorganisation (the director endlessly wandering in circles ['She', 79]), along with the use of light to create images on film, occurs again in Jordan's 1982 novel *The Past* and it is from that book, rather than *Night in Tunisia*, that 'She' takes its stylistic cues. That the texts share a compositional relationship is implied by Jordan's publication of an extract from *The Past* as 'The Artist and the Photographer' a few months earlier in an anthology edited by William Burroughs.[16] That extract also depicts creative personalities as outsiders in Ireland. Both the artist and photographer, father and son respectively, represent the last vestiges of the Ascendancy class, while the director of the film in 'She' hails from London. The importance of the director's nationality reflects a certain state of affairs in the Irish film industry at the time. He is not just English, he is a Londoner ('She', 80). The distinction is pointedly made, as if to highlight the cosmopolitan allure of the movie business to a young person in an economically depressed Ireland. The actress' choice of Gauloises cigarettes also carries with it a certain longing for sophistication, the brand having long-standing associations with cultural figures from Pablo Picasso to Jean-Paul Sartre.

The director's extra-national origins are also representative of the Irish film industry as a whole during this time. Aside from Comerford and the likes of Cathal Black, the scarcity of indigenous filmmaking prior to the 1980s granted foreign directors a controlling interest in how the country was represented on screen. The actress of 'She', enraptured by the cosmopolitan promise of the British capital, is a victim of this situation. She, and more generally 'She', represents early Irish participation in filmmaking while simultaneously highlighting the lack of Irish control over the representations being produced. Nevertheless, it was involvement with, and inspiration by, external cinemas that anticipated the blooming of the Irish industry over the 1980s and '90s. In discussing this, the Rocketts refer to a review Jordan wrote in 1978 of Black's film *Wheels*, placing Jordan's critique within the context of a nascent indigenous film industry on the cusp of international recognition. Black's film (on which Joe Comerford served as cinematographer) was an adaptation of a John McGahern short story, and Jordan's review, titled 'Word and Image', included a discussion of the overlap between fiction and film in Irish culture. Specifically, Jordan commented on how filmic representations tended to concentrate on Northern Ireland and the Troubles, while other expressions of Irish experience remained encapsulated in literary texts. These wider experiences are, of course, reminiscent of his writings in *Night in Tunisia*, the narrative focus of which never strays far from the Republic or, in the notable exception of 'Last Rites', its emigrant communities. His script for *Traveller* – along with his 1982 script for *Angel* – specifies the use of the North and of IRA characters in a manner that suggests an almost precognitive awareness of how important the Northern trope was to become as a rallying point for an identifiable Irish film industry. The film in 'She' does not specifically take place in the North, but liminal elements such as the filling station on a deserted road between two towns can be read as suggesting a border context while, more obliquely, the presence of an obsolete Mauser pistol as a prop carries with it connotations of occupation and insurgency.

One might also interpret the metaphorical borderland of 'She' as Jordan's own representation of his position at the time. Read as such, the two towns between which the petrol station lies represent film and literature respectively. The actress, who has already been shown to at least partially represent Jordan, sits in a glass cabin which functions as a kind of transparent cage. From here, she can observe both roads but cannot escape along either of them. Her abandonment by the traveller – a personification of the filmic project itself – has marooned her between the two artistic identities. To escape, she must utilise extreme measures: she returns to her position in the cabin and, when an arbitrary man passes by, she raises the gun and shoots him through both the cabin window and the man's windshield, shattering both panes of glass along with the astonished look on the man's face ('She', 80). We might equate the shattering glass with Jordan's decision to maintain creative control over his future screenplays, while the shattering face of the motorist reads as a metafictional acknowledgement of the story's own existence, an invective perhaps aimed at Comerford's splintering of cinematic structure which is far removed from the narrative swells which Jordan believes should typify a successful film.[17] Indeed, the latter's mastery of exactly that kind of storytelling in pictures such as *Angel* and *Mona Lisa* (1986) would eventually take him to Hollywood, an experience that is the subject of 'Remote Control'.

ARS GRATIA ARTIS: 'REMOTE CONTROL'

Published in a 1993 anthology edited by Colm Tóibín, 'Remote Control' considers, in a tongue-in-cheek fashion, the flight of the artist from his native land. The narrator, a film director directly identifiable with Jordan, drifts through Los Angeles on the day his new film is to be screened before a test audience. His misadventures run from wrestling with a newspaper dispenser to appeasing his financiers, all while encountering resistance from both his studio and the landscape of Hollywood itself. The story draws on experiences from Jordan's middle period as a director, from the disappointments of *High Spirits* and *We're No Angels* to the acclaim of *The Crying Game*, a phase characterised by Jordan's own disillusionment with the Hollywood experience and his growing international reputation. In fact, with a central character so clearly autobiographical, it is hard not to see 'Remote Control' as memoir rather than fiction. A strong argument for the latter is made by context: the Soho Square anthology contains fiction and poetry, but no journalistic or memoir-type writing. Indeed, it contains no factual writing of any sort beyond a piece of academic criticism by Tom Paulin. Surreal excursions such as the coffin salesmen of the narrator's dream provide further justification for classifying the piece as fiction. Jordan himself seems aware of the categorisation difficulties that 'Remote Control' faces, and draws on this uncertainty from the outset, beginning the story with a half-recollected dream of being at either some kind of party or reception, but not being able to pin down the setting for sure (RC, 56).

The narrative also represents a break with the other film stories. The director-centric 'Remote Control' is bracketed, in the film series, by two stories about actors. This suggests, if only accidentally, both the importance of the director in bringing together the performers (reinforced by reading the actress of 'She' and the actor of 'The Berkeley Complex' as the archetypal, demographically desirable leading pair) and the importance of the actors themselves as necessary participants without whom the director would be isolated and have great difficulty in telling a conventional story. Both are necessities, but, to paraphrase George Orwell, the director is more necessary than the actor. That delicate state of imbalance is best conceptualised by David Simmons, in a passage quoted by Hopper, who praises group participation as a filmmaking ideal but nonetheless acknowledges that the reality of the situation requires a guiding hand.[18] By his own account, the narrator of 'Remote Control' is proficient in the provision of just such a hand; however, he is not naive enough to believe he is the final authority on his own film. There are producers, financiers and, crucially, studio test screenings to answer to. The title then refers to the idea of proceedings being orchestrated by powers outside of one's influence, as well as the laziness implicit in a television remote control that, in similar fashion to the directing of a film in the Hollywood studio system, delivers physical and imaginative imprisonment under the guise of freedom.

The narrator's film, a quasi-comedy (though he himself admits to being unable to tell a joke), could be either *High Spirits* or *We're No Angels*, both comedies with which Jordan has registered his displeasure. Control of *High Spirits*, in particular, was usurped by the film's producers and proved to be a particularly unpleasant experience for the director.[19] Jordan found his intended excursion into the Irish Gothic appropriated by the studio as a vehicle for a *Ghostbusters* (1984) style supernatural, effect-based comedy. The film, starring Peter O'Toole and Steve Guttenberg, did not perform well and represents one of the few creative failures of Jordan's career. More credible, though equally as unsuccessful commercially, was *We're No Angels*, a loose adaptation of an Albert Husson play (*La Cuisine des Anges*) scripted by David Mamet.[20] Together, the films comprise a particular low point for Jordan the director: *High Spirits* and *We're No Angels* unambiguously proved that Jordan's forte was not in light comedy. Indeed, Jordan has commented (about *We're No Angels*) that a comedy should not have been expected given the principal figures associated with the film: himself, Mamet, Robert De Niro and Sean Penn.[21] Jordan's Hollywood experience was followed up by the low-budget, Dublin-based project *The Miracle*, characterised by him as an attempt to return to making films that had integrity.[22] The dissatisfaction of the director in 'Remote Control' and his symbolic inability to navigate the streetscape of Los Angeles implies a similar failure, yet the story's finale (the director sitting in the dark of the theatre and deciding that things are not so bad after all; RC, 61) suggests a hopeful fate for the character – hopeful, that is, insofar as his film might recoup a significant commercial return.

Of the two potential candidates, it seems most likely that the film in the story is based on *High Spirits*. The suggestion is planted in the opening paragraph, where the narrator dreams of coffin salesmen whose commercial technique is based on palmistry. It is a sequence that, despite its disarmingly humorous nature, alludes to both the filmic inspiration for the story and the psychological state of the narrator: the salesmen read the narrator's future to estimate when he might require a coffin and so determine the payment schedule, estimating three weeks until death and so demanding cash upfront (RC, 56). The dream can in turn be interpreted as a reference to the emergence of the rotting dead from their vaults on All Hallows' Night during the climax of *High Spirits*. That this, one of the more visceral images of the picture, pervades the narrator's subconscious to such a degree bodes ill for his prospects, or, at the very least, his state of mind. Palmistry is after all a technique of divination (a primitive form of test screening, if you will), and three weeks is more than enough time for a bad movie to disappear from the theatre, and with it a directorial career. The intoxicated spectre who walks to the refrigerator, another imposition of *High Spirits* imagery on the text of 'Remote Control', further reinforces the intertextuality between the two (RC, 56). In fact, this reference, part of an extended description of how muddled a waitress looks, would be particularly enigmatic without recourse to the film.[23]

A final, particularly concrete linkage can be made via Jordan's poem 'Lines Written in Dejection', a work that originally appeared in *Producer* magazine and, shortly thereafter, in the *High Spirits* published screenplay.[24] A tongue-in-cheek indulgence in rhyming couplets (a stylistic convention Jordan has expressed a preference for in Philippe Pilard's documentary), 'Lines Written in Dejection' begins with a cutting, unglamorous depiction of financing a film in Hollywood, with unhelpful producers asking why the work isn't like the director's previous efforts and why a filmmaker known for noir stories would attempt to execute a farce. The poem goes on to describe *High Spirits*, sarcastically, as a blending of *The Quiet Man* (1952) and *The Ghost Goes West* (1935), while both it and 'Remote Control' feature protagonists who have difficulty with rental cars. In the story, the narrator drives a convertible with the hood down because he is incapable of getting it up (RC, 60). His predicament comments on the society of Los Angeles itself, which, in stereotype, is depicted as being so tech-savvy that inability to operate even the most basic of 'cachet' technology – in this case, the convertible – is equated with impotence. The comparative struggle with both vehicles suggests a common inspiration for the story and the poem that places them in a similar timeframe.

Aside from contributing to the chronological placement of the 'Remote Control' experience, 'Lines Written in Dejection' is a forgettable piece. Jordan claims to have had some enjoyment writing the poem, though he now appears slightly embarrassed by the existence of such an unconsidered response.[25] 'Remote Control', with the benefit of hindsight and Jordan's subsequent Academy Award and commercial success with *The Crying Game*, is a more measured and more mature meditation on the debacle. Incidental details, such as the car and the discussion of comedy, link the two, but 'Remote Control' is by far the more successful of the efforts. This is particularly apparent not just in the quality of the writing, but in Jordan's illumination of a Hollywood society where creativity, even life itself, is disposable. Over his newspaper, the narrator expresses an interest in the local murders, especially the classic, almost theatrical examples, as if even crime is relegated to the level of entertainment in Los Angeles. Here, more than in his other film stories, Jordan is playing games with the reader which are predicated on an insider's knowledge of cinema and of Hollywood history, yet he is also ready to subvert our expectations and comment on the rise of violent criminality in Ireland by considering if death and bloodshed are just as intimate an experience back home (RC, 59). He describes the physical cost of such violence and the kind of reconstructive medical procedures perfected in troubled cities such as Beirut and Belfast that are at a premium in LA as cosmetic surgery. The Belfast reference attracts immediate attention, as Jordan generally does not mention Northern Ireland in his fiction despite his repeated use of the conflict in films such as *Angel*, *The Crying Game* and *Breakfast on Pluto* (2005). Yet, its occurrence here is another quasi-cinematic game at the reader's expense and works not just as a shorthand for violent conflict, but also as an identifier of Irish cinema itself. One must keep in mind that 'Remote Control' was published following the resurgence in Irish cinema generated by dramas such as Jim Sheridan's *In the Name of the Father* (1993) and Jordan's own *The Crying Game*, which reinforced the filmic representation of Ireland in terms circumscribed by the Northern conflict. In saying that techniques perfected in Belfast are valued in Los Angeles, Jordan acknowledges not just the medical techniques but also the recognition afforded to Irish films and filmmakers by Hollywood, recognition including, but not limited to, the Oscar he himself received for *The Crying Game*. Certainly, that award must have come as a shock to the producers of 'Lines Written in Dejection' whose vague offer of working together with the speaker of the poem on future projects is depicted as a smug rejection.

In such a vacuous environment, Jordan's allusion to *Hamlet* within 'Remote Control' is quite telling: his protagonist is Horatio and the things undreamt of in his philosophy are teeth-whitening and orthodontic correction. He observes the perfect smile of a girl in a pink tracksuit eating in the restaurant but, despite her immaculate presentation, the reader almost expects him to tell us that something is rotten in the state of Hollywood (though, of course, that is the subtext of the piece as a whole). The empty self-centredness of the filmmaking society is represented here by Jordan's choice of mundane dentistry to represent Shakespeare's grander 'things in heaven and earth', an ironic alteration considering that Hollywood's nominal *raison d'être* is the recreation of heaven and earth for the purposes of entertainment. Dentistry also foregrounds the image-obsessed culture of Los Angeles, where appearance is depicted as being more important than substance. Thematically, this references the narrator's musings on the differences between art and commerce, and is particularly relevant to the dichotomy between director and producer. With a strong implication that the observation is based on Jordan's personal experience, the narrator watches the unease of the producers who wonder if the motion picture into which they poured so much money, and which the director fashioned with such care, might turn out to be nothing more profitable than art (RC, 61).

But why did Jordan choose *Hamlet* as a touchstone here? There are two possible reasons. First, invoking the prince of Denmark adds a certain humour to the mock-existentialist self-questioning of his narrator. Second, and perhaps more importantly, in light of the sub-Joycean day-long wandering of 'Remote Control', the *Hamlet* reference serves as an homage to the numerous references to the play in *Ulysses*. In such a light, it is impossible not to place the allusion in the context of Joyce's famous discussion of the play in the Scylla and Charybdis episode. Joyce selects *Hamlet* as an exemplifier of the highest art imaginable, something that concretely links the passage to the concerns of Jordan's narrator:

> Art has to reveal to us ideas, formless spiritual essences. The supreme question about a work of art is out of how deep a life does it spring. The painting of Gustave Moreau is the painting of ideas. The deepest poetry of Shelley, the words of *Hamlet* bring our minds into contact

with the eternal wisdom, Plato's world of ideas. All the rest is the speculation of schoolboys for schoolboys.[26]

Joyce's schoolboys are merely the previous incarnation of Jordan's youthful film executives and so, by the Joycean definition, modern Hollywood filmmaking fails to meet the criteria for art.[27] It neither revels in nor reveals ideas, nor does it spring from a deep life. Its practitioners, as the narrator realises, have no guarantee of a peaceful night's sleep after their work, giving them at least that in common with the inhabitants of Elsinore, particularly Horatio, who is roused from his bed in the opening scene to witness the restless ghost of old King Hamlet, the mighty filmmakers of old.

In phrasing his allusion the way he does, Jordan casts himself as Horatio, to whom Hamlet's original quote was addressed. The role he chooses is the man of reason and restraint, the man who survives the meltdown of the Danish kingdom just as Jordan survives the excesses of Hollywood. He endures the final showdown between Hamlet and Laertes – here echoed in the poisoned chalice of the preview – to tell the story of what has happened to Fortinbras in the same way Jordan's narrator divulges his Hollywood experience to the reader. *Hamlet* has a particular relevance to Jordan's work, especially in how the play's 'unquiet ghost', like the ever-shifting undead ghouls of the horror movie genre, suggests how the past imposes itself on the present in the form of both metaphorical and physical monstrosities.[28] Here, Shakespeare's play-within-the-play is reflected by Jordan's use of a movie-within-the-story, but where the performance that Hamlet engineers is designed to 'catch the conscience of the king', the narrator's film succeeds only in trapping himself, with the preview experience highlighting the detrimental effects Hollywood is having on his own creative independence. Given the close identification between Jordan and the narrator, 'Remote Control' thus serves to rewrite the author's own Hollywood disappointments and disillusionment, presenting instead a more dignified return to Ireland than any simple narrative of commercial failure and creative restriction (in fact, from the 1990s onwards, Jordan the director would vacillate between big-budget Hollywood-funded pictures like *Interview with the Vampire* and smaller, independent offerings such as *Ondine*).

A further literary allusion, this time to Dante by way of the American urban thriller, equates the freeway exit to LA's endless urban sprawl with Hell, with the narrator further invoking the milieu of *Night in Tunisia* by declaiming his hopes to be forsaken as he drives along the beach past gangs of kids hanging out on every corner (RC, 60). These youths are like Dante's Outcasts, those who took no part in the Christian tradition's rebellion of the angels. Neither in Hell nor out of it, the Outcasts dwell on the shores of the River Acheron in much the same way the teenagers depicted here reside on the street corners. They can be read as another of Jordan's coded references, with the rebellion of the angels corresponding to the 1992 Los Angeles riots, the Rodney King riots, sparked by the acquittal of four police officers who were videotaped beating a Black motorist. It is another hidden, but damning, indictment of LA society, and as Jordan's narrator descends deeper and deeper into this Hell, further from the small seaside towns of his childhood, he discovers – counter-intuitively – concentric circles of wealth (a gas station leads to a mall, leads to a movie theatre) culminating in the limousines and the queue of invited guests gathering in the lobby.

This journey into the disorder of the urban night is made, appropriately, down Sunset Boulevard. The crepuscular transition between light and night which sunset represents is as thematically important to 'Remote Control' as it was in 'She'. (Sunset Boulevard itself is notorious for its moral liminalities, with its wholesome Hollywood daytime appearance traditionally devolving into a red-light district by nightfall, though policing had driven the majority of sex workers away by the mid-1990s.) In 'She' the changing light represented the impractical nature of the director, but here it is utilised differently, serving as a charm by which the narrator is able to reassert his personality and values even as the Hollywood system threatens to subsume them. This is particularly true of the projector light illuminating the darkness of the film theatre during the preview, and of the dawn which greets the director just after waking from his nightmare, a sliver of silver light becoming, like a cinema screen, an elegant rectangle with stately speed, in time coming to dominate the whole room (RC, 56). Jordan's director here beholds the light alone, the tool by which he has created his own identity. For light is the means by which an image is formed on film, so it is natural that Jordan continually associates light with his fictional directors. Yet, the fact that the director can never directly observe light in the act of changing defines a key difference between his artistic convictions and the more commercial philosophy of the studio, which believes that everything can be subject to metrics and commodification.

In placing the director's comments on light at the beginning of the story, Jordan creates a natural contrast with the studio executives' test screening which occurs in the darkness during the conclusion. The studio, in essence, is seeking to measure the immeasurable, a dubious enough endeavour in the eyes of the narrator, who remarks upon the many failures of the preview process, such as films previewed with music where the score earned the highest rating or the ones that received phenomenal preview responses only to bomb at the box office (RC, 60). In his view, the filmmaking process is, like the morning light, a series of processes happening all at once. Its success or failure is as uncertain as the rectangle of light which develops in response to the individual angles of the room it enters. Indeed, Jordan himself has acknowledged the importance that luck plays in a filmmaking career – that sometimes things work out and sometimes they do not – and his comments are, unsurprisingly, similar to the thoughts of the narrator here.[29] He has spoken of the pain that accompanies the initial stages of any creative undertaking and the need to accept a certain degree of risk in the pursuit of art.[30] During his middle directorial period, Jordan discovered that one of these risks is dealing with the studios, and 'Remote Control' is more explicit and much more eloquent than 'Lines Written in Dejection' in opposing the position that there is a formula for making a hit film or that there is a mathematical accuracy to the preview system.

'Remote Control' therefore functions as an extended meditation on what the narrator calls a frisson between creativity and commerce. In the story, Jordan frames these comments as an observation about class, referring to refinement rather than economics, though herein lies the paradox of the story and, for that matter, the contradictions of Jordan the director's career as related by Jordan the writer: to stake money on a refined film is a bad idea for investors as the economics of making a picture like this are poor. Such a project immediately lacks the want-to-see of a demographic wide enough to make it financially viable; it becomes the art of which the narrator's investors are so afraid and which, in the Hollywood context depicted here, is assumed to be a synonym for failure. In making these criticisms, however, Jordan is savvy enough not to alienate future financiers, especially those whose independent contributions to his directorial projects would become so important after his repudiation of the Hollywood financing system. Funding from European production companies in particular would go on to allow Jordan a financial and creative freedom from Hollywood in the early twenty-first century which, in turn, ensured his ability to balance creative ambition and independence with a continued relevance and international commercial profile. The obscurity experienced by those arthouse directors who were once his peers offers an example of a fate which Jordan has avoided, but so too does the protagonist of the final film story, the unemployed actor and director of 'The Berkeley Complex'.

'TIS THE CURSE OF SERVICE: 'THE BERKELEY COMPLEX'

'The Berkeley Complex' is the densest and most intricate of Jordan's film stories (and also the one which stretches that categorisation the most). Effectively a long monologue, 'The Berkeley Complex' is an extended psychological investigation of an unemployed actor who enjoyed some success on television but who now is struggling to build a credible theatre career. Published in Ireland as part of the David Marcus edited *Faber Book of Best New Irish Short Stories 2004–5*, 'The Berkeley Complex' originally appeared in the United States, in the winter 2003 edition of Francis Ford Coppola's *Zoetrope: All-Story* magazine. *Zoetrope* (which takes its title from a Victorian device which creates the illusion of action from a rapid succession of static pictures) presented Jordan's story alongside work by other author-filmmakers such as Neil LaBute (*In the Company of Men*, 1997), Tamara Jenkins (*Slums of Beverly Hills*, 1998) and Abbas Kiarostami (*The Wind Will Carry Us*, 1999) in an issue themed around film–fiction intertextuality. Stories and plays published in the issue included a response to von Sternberg's *The Blue Angel* by Eric Bogosian and 'The Return of the Player' by Michael Tolkin, a sequel to the Robert Altman film of his own film-industry novel *The Player* (1988).

Obsessed with the glass eye of his deceased mother, the unnamed narrator of 'The Berkeley Complex' meanders through a Dublin which is landmarked by his personal and professional failures. He seeks absolution from Jane, his ex-girlfriend and former creative partner, and, anticipating *Mistaken* and *Carnivalesque*, falls into step behind his double, an individual who may or may not be a creation of his own fragmenting psyche. The complex referred to in the title is a piece of pop-psychology invented by the narrator, a description of the psychological condition of actors existing only in the eyes of the audience. The narrator, delighting in displays of his own erudition, bases his theory upon the writings of Kilkenny philosopher and Bishop of Cloyne George Berkeley (1685–1753), who cast doubt on the nature of physical existence. While 'The Berkeley Complex' deals with an actor who works primarily on the stage, the repeated references to his time on the afternoon soap operas (and his use of these as an excuse as to why he delayed his current production for so long) emphasises the story's concern with the work of actors before the camera. In any event, with the pool of thespian employment in Ireland being what it is, separating theatre from filmmaking is both unwise and impossible.

'The Berkeley Complex', like 'Remote Control', again alludes to Shakespeare, with the modern world and its art forms found wanting by comparison. The touchstone play in this instance is *Othello*, a drastically pared back version of which, performed by the narrator, has garnered some renown (BC, 208). Jordan usurps the key line from Othello's final speech to mock his own character's hubristic, less-than-glamorous turns upon the television screens of Ireland: he riffs on Shakespeare's tragic Moor when he recalls the service he has done for the soaps of Éire, making light of his accomplishments in the process. Soap operas, or so the narrator would have us believe, have replaced the state (subject of Shakespeare's line) as the central defining aspect of everyday life in the first years of the Irish twenty-first century. The grand politics and intricacies of Shakespearian tragedy have bequeathed the narrator's generation naught but familial antagonism, unrealistic storylines and over-acted melodrama, or so he insists in his continuing, disparaging tirade against modern Ireland (he later discovers to his chagrin that the classics now refer to Leonard Cohen rather than to the cultural treasures of Greece and Rome; it is a music choice, and by implication a cultural turnaround, that the narrator calls inevitable).

Yet, the story's concerns with *Othello* go far beyond the brief allusion made to *Hamlet* in 'Remote Control'. The narrator here talks about the play repeatedly, both the canonical text and his own interpretation. His continuing identification of characters in his life with those from the play is a defining aspect of his personality, making Jane in particular into the kind of Desdemona he sought to create on stage. Even his own identity is not immune from this and he frequently amalgamates *Othello* and Othello into a dubious self-representation of how he has been wronged by his career. In his case, the identification is fluid, slipping between first-person allusion and third-person narration in a manner reminiscent of *Shade*. Most effectively, Jordan allows his character to conclude the story with another sardonic reimagining of Shakespeare's words, directly borrowing Othello's line that 'I took by the throat the circumcised dog and smote him, thus' (BC, 220). 'Live by the sword, die by the sword' is an aphorism cited by Jordan in the Pilard documentary when discussing *Michael Collins*, and it seems an apt description for the scene where the narrator may have killed his double or, indeed, may have killed himself. The actual sequence of events is unclear. The prolonged surveillance of the double by the narrator suggests a murder; however, the unstable identity of the actor throughout the story implies a suicide. Jordan, for his part, utilises the distancing effect of the quotation to ensure the story's conclusion remains intentionally vague.

Also unclear is the narrator's reference to the pink tracksuit of the mother in the Dunnes Stores queue which seems to invoke the similarly adorned woman eating breakfast in the Hollywood diner of 'Remote Control'. Combined with the Shakespearian subtext, it is as if Jordan, with this story, begins to consciously delineate his film stories as, at least, a theoretical construction or even an uncollected collection. It may not be going too far to propose that the pink tracksuit women are the same character, or at the very least Jordan's recurring representation of innocence consumed by the industrialisation of creativity. The roughly ten-year gap between each of the stories supports the interpretation: the girl of 'She', set on her course of pursuing a cosmopolitan acting career, becomes the anonymous young woman spied in the Hollywood diner by the narrator of 'Remote Control', a stereotype of failure despite having her teeth made nicely even in order to expedite her bright new future. The woman in the Dunnes Stores queue of 'The Berkeley Complex' is the third occurrence of this inverted Cathleen ni Houlihan, an incarnation whose recent motherhood is arguably the ultimate victory of adult life and responsibilities over childhood dreams.

These women who haunt the film stories are a call-back to the many similar actresses throughout Jordan's work. In *The Past* (1980), the battle against mediocrity after the birth of her daughter is what defines Una's arc throughout the novel. As unable to secure respectable roles as is the 'Berkeley' narrator, Una redirects her energies into the area of cultural politics, though her results here are equally disappointing to her. In *Shade* (2004), the character of Maggie is journeying home to Somerset with her son to assume just such a domestic role after the abandonment of her acting ambitions. Nina, that novel's protagonist, makes the opposite decision, choosing her career over the possibility of a family and, as a result, dies in spinsterhood. That Nina and Maggie are friends and fellow travellers invites the reader to make an implicit comparison between them: in the end, it is not the domesticated Maggie whose story ends with murder and with her disposal in a septic tank. Film-wise, Renée in *The Miracle* embodies similar characteristics, having chosen to abandon her child in favour of her art. It is a decision she comes to regret, though her punishments here are not nearly as grotesque as those endured by Nina Hardy. Equally, in *The Crying Game*, Dil is a performer constrained by society's inadequate notions of gender. Yet, an actress character or figure does not exist in the key progenitor text of 'The Berkeley Complex', Jordan's 2001 play *White Horses* which, like the story, documented the fragmentation of a relationship. There are however less apparent linkages: the fascination of the play's protagonist with fossils (objects to be displayed and looked upon), for instance, is reflected in the 'Berkeley' narrator's obsession with his mother's glass eye, an item that itself symbolises themes of observation and performance (which readers will recall as playing such a part in *Shade*). Thematically, *White Horses* looks to Jordan's published writings rather than to his films and Jordan himself has admitted that the play is closer to a short story than a screenplay.[31] The stripped-down production style of *White Horses* is further echoed in the trimmed-back fashion by which the 'Berkeley' narrator re-imagines Shakespeare (BC, 208). The basic scenario of the play, the story of a man whose girlfriend has left him, is also similar to 'The Berkeley Complex', though the execution (where the protagonist discovers tape recordings made by his former girlfriend) is markedly more Beckettian than the Joycean Dublin ramble which provides the story's structure.

Moreover, the play reflects the performative milieu of 'The Berkeley Complex' in more ways than one. Alongside long-time film collaborator Stephen Rea, whose voice appears on the play's tape recorder as if in spectral acknowledgement of the author's omnipresent movie-making career, Jordan's two leads in *White Horses* are, like the story's narrator, both actors better known for their screen work (though in this case actors who have received particular attention for roles with a literary origin). Peter McDonald portrayed Stanislaus Joyce in the 2000 biopic *Nora*, while Catherine McCormack is probably best known in Ireland for her appearance in the film version of Brian Friel's *Dancing at Lughnasa* (1998) where she played Chrissy. In addition, the tripartite division between film, literature and theatre, the complete dissolution of which would appear to be Jordan's aim here, is further blurred by the Gate's production of *White Horses* as part of a three-play line-up which also included work by Brian Friel and Conor McPherson. Headlining Friel's play was Ciarán Hinds, a film and television actor now best known for his high-profile roles on the HBO series *Rome* and *Game of Thrones*, as well as Michael Mann's 2006 reworking of *Miami Vice*. McPherson, meanwhile, has also moved from theatre into filmmaking, writing and directing movies like 1997's *I Went Down* (in which McDonald also appears) and *The Actors* (2003) which, in a further link, was produced by Jordan, who also received a Story By credit.

This dense interconnectivity between *White Horses* and its contemporaneous productions, as well as its own status as a progenitor text to 'The Berkeley Complex', speaks to the world and the industry against which Jordan's story takes place. Fintan O'Toole makes much of the historical and thematic continuity of that backdrop when he notes that each writer involved in the Gate triple-bill was born about twenty years before the next.[32] By calling attention to this, O'Toole again alters our perception of both *White Horses* and 'The Berkeley Complex'. Their author now assumes the representational mantle of an entire generation of Irish writers, a burden far in excess of what Jordan's slight play could ever reasonably achieve. On the other hand, the short story finds itself imbued with new relevance as a document detailing the disillusionment of a generation of actors who were promised success within an industry that could never accommodate them all. As the reader will recall, Jordan himself experienced the actor's lot in the early 1970s and his theatrical experience seems an obvious source for the world-weariness of the 'Berkeley' narrator, representing as important a foundation for this story as does *White Horses*.

Another obvious formal progenitor for 'The Berkeley Complex' is Brian Friel's *Philadelphia, Here I Come!* (1964). It is appropriate that the story's second inspiration is also a stage-play. Adopting the terminology of Friel's work, 'The Berkeley Complex' becomes a confrontation between a kind of Narrator-Public and Narrator-Private, though here the division is more obviously Manichaean than in *Philadelphia*. Moral and Immoral would, perhaps, be better sobriquets for the two equally impaired halves of the narrator (suggestions, again, of *Mistaken*). His monstrously id-centred avatar is unrestrained by ethical considerations, while his ineffectual persona lacks the proactive capabilities of his opposite. In that respect, 'The Berkeley Complex' also contains hints of Robert Louis Stevenson's *Strange Case of Dr Jekyll and Mr Hyde* (1886). The 'Berkeley' narrator is determined to avoid Dr Jekyll's fate – subsumed by the evil personality – and, in a *Carnivalesque*-facing conclusion, he apparently dispatches what he believes to be his doppelgänger, motivated by a desire to restore his own existence by eliminating the counter-person which was cancelling out his own life. The dual nature of the narrator is one of the facets of the story that make its ancestry so fascinating. Like the potted history we receive of the narrator's career, the lineage of 'The Berkeley Complex' is not limited to theatre or television alone. We classify it, after all, as a 'film story', and while 'She' and 'Remote Control' interpret this designation much more strictly, 'The Berkeley Complex' derives its filmic credentials from allusion as much as from its nuanced treatment of actors' society and psychology. Indeed, a parallel cinematic lineage can be divined for the story, its windswept denouement a reference to Hitchcock's *Rebecca* and its foreboding maternal influence drawn from *Psycho*.

Yet, it is in the detailed examination of the narrator's psyche, presented as a microcosm of actor psychology in general, that 'The Berkeley Complex' distinguishes itself from the many texts it draws upon. The essence of this lies in the Berkeley Complex itself, the psychological affliction best illustrated by the duality of the narrator observing another version of himself (a version of the affliction which so defines Nina Hardy in *Shade* and, later, Kevin Thunder in *Mistaken*). Jordan's erudition makes this clear, particularly through his use of the quotation from Bishop Berkeley which gives the story its name: *Esse est percipi*, 'to be is to be perceived'. The need of the actor to be observed is so powerful that, in the absence of audience or employment, the narrator performs for himself. This performance is highlighted in his first sighting of the doppelgänger, who the narrator describes as though it were both himself and an actor, and is further reinforced by the confrontation with his former lover in, of course, a theatre (BC, 214). Jane and the narrator thus act out their scene in front of the empty playhouse as if they themselves were on the stage, with the narrator's repeated reference to them as Othello and Desdemona reminding us that, originally, this is exactly how they were supposed to interact. As they speak in the theatre, we again remember Shakespeare's conceit of a play-within-a-play. However, 'The Berkeley Complex' reverses Hamlet's play: Jane and the narrator, the Player Queen and King, begin their conversation in harshness and despondency, just as the play-within-the-play is seen to end. In the space of their brief exchange they soften, finishing 'very lovingly', as Shakespeare instructs his players to begin (BC, 214).

The glass eye carried by the narrator also furthers connotations of an audience. An eye looks, an eye perceives; it feeds into the narrator's self-importance, into his own Berkeley Complex and serves, quite literally, as the focal point for his steadfast belief that he is more deserving of canonical theatrical approval than the idle recognition of soap-watching Dunnes Stores patrons. His unwillingness to release the eye is a measure of just how strong his desire for acknowledgement really is. He enacts its eventual disposal with what we have come to see as his usual melodrama, describing its trajectory when he throws it away as though it were a grand and precipitous voyage (BC, 219). This is his final performance for the glass audience of the eyeball. Though, of course, what is important here is that an eye requires light in order to create images, the same principle by which images are created on film by a glass lens. As the eyeball flies through the air, the narrator describes the dimming of the light with crepuscular language which carries with it an echo of the fading sun in the opening scene of 'She' and, crucially, the lowering of the cinema house lights in 'Remote Control' that mark the beginning of the film. The implication is clear: unburdened of his theatrical expectations, the narrator is now free to find contentment through his art on film and television. Twilight in Jordan's film stories is a necessity for cinema in both its production and exhibition contexts, but we see here how it is also important for his fictional actors, creating a necessary liminal zone in which they can inhabit both their characters and their own personalities simultaneously.

Like Nina Hardy in *Shade*, the narcissism of the 'Berkeley' narrator blinds him – but not Jordan – to the socio-economic transformation Ireland has undergone since the publication of 'She'. The casual, throwaway reference to a youth of East European ancestry is a disguised measure of just this change (BC, 215). In 'She', a Londoner is considered an exotic visitor, but here the narrator considers eastern immigration so normal that he doesn't offer the boy a second glance. Simultaneously, the fact that the character is selling copies of *The Big Issue* hints at both the inequalities faced by the country's new population and the blasé attitudes whereby these inequalities are ignored by the middle classes. The narrator ignores the boy's outstretched hand in favour of a window display in a record store (BC, 215). His practised indifference only barely avoids accusations of smugness insofar as he is attempting to conceal himself from his doppelgänger at the time. Is this brief representation of modern Ireland a sideswipe from a writer who describes himself in leftist terms?[33] On the surface it seem possible, for, drawn to the capitalistic temple of the record store, the narrator pushes past the left hand of the kid in which is a rolled-up copy of the magazine. It is a moment that harks back to Jordan's earlier comments on the plight of marginal voices, and how social inclusion (and, one might say, socialism in general) has been rejected out of hand by the unbridled capitalism of modern Ireland. Moreover, the record store

(Virgin Records which, ironically, is now closed) is described in pulsating terms. It is a consumerist place that, from the narrator's perspective, seeks to take and take. It is a hungry space. It is as though it is alive.

Jordan's film stories too represent a living, growing entity, a continuum which is alive to the changes in contemporary Irish life and how that life has been represented over a period of twenty years, though it is an engagement that was not easily achieved. He says that the foremost questions for him when he began to write were about who he truly was and about the meaning of his experiences within the overwhelming weight of the Irish literary tradition.[34] In the film stories, however, the reader discovers a sequence of texts which, far from any collision with the greats of Irish fiction, provides a unique perspective on Irish identity and a subject matter for which Jordan is inimitably suited. They allow us to see how his engagements with the Irish – and world – literary traditions have evolved over the course of his writing career and how they have done so in concert with his work as a director. Read together, 'She', 'Remote Control' and 'The Berkeley Complex' demonstrate how Jordan's ease with both film and literature belongs (like the narrator of 'Remote Control') to an artist of the wider world, someone who has experienced the best and worst of multiple creative industries. In that way, the film stories provide a unique link between Jordan's two creative realms. They draw from his filmmaking experience, yes, but they are conversant with the themes and scenarios proffered by his fiction – from the coming-of-age stories in *Night in Tunisia* to the later, great novel *Shade* and, in particular, to the investigation of the bipartite artistic self which is conducted by the author in the pages of *Mistaken* and *Carnivalesque*.

CHAPTER 8

Bad Fairies and Strange, Unrealised Desires: *Mistaken, Carnivalesque* and the many Neil Jordans

This final chapter is different from those that have come before. It is the only time two long-form works by Neil Jordan are discussed in tandem. This approach has been chosen on account of the rich thematic dialogue between *Mistaken* (2011) and *Carnivalesque* (2017), a pair of novels in which Jordan interrogates notions of genre and confronts ideas of creative duality head-on. Whereas previous chapters have examined how readers and critics see Jordan's work, asking what kind of artist the field of Irish Studies considers him to be, *Mistaken* and *Carnivalesque* offer a chance to gauge the ways in which Jordan sees himself. Thus, the first half of this chapter considers *Mistaken* as an autobiographical re-examination by Jordan which mirrors *Shade*'s wider scrutiny of Irish social and political history. With his oft-confused identical protagonists Kevin and Gerry (an architect and a writer respectively) analogous to the filmic Jordan and the literary Jordan, the author consciously restages biographical material encountered by the reader of this study in the introduction and in the discussion of the film stories in Chapter 7 in highly fictionalised form. This use of Jordan's personal history contrasts with his use of national history earlier in his career. Simultaneously, *Mistaken* acknowledges Jordan's Joycean influences via a personal odyssey around Dublin, one consciously constructed to reflect both modernist and Gothic representations of the city. The novel further offers a journey through the literary Jordan's achievements and anxieties, with the central question of this study emphasised: is it possible to ever truly separate the literary and filmic Neil Jordans?

The second half of the chapter addresses *Carnivalesque*, wherein the contemporary teenager Andy loses his way in a fantastical hall of mirrors only for a simulacrum to emerge and take his place in a domestic drama redolent of literary fiction. Undercutting this, Andy – now Dany – is rescued by one of the fairy folk, themselves masquerading as carnival performers and roustabouts. He discovers a secret world of whimsy and wonder even as questions about what is real – is he the genuine article? Is life as he understood it the full story? – are problematised in such a way that they have direct bearing on a hidden aspect of Jordan's bifurcated career which this study has sought to delineate, the duality within the duality which affects both his fiction and filmmaking: how Jordan the realist relates to Jordan the fantasist. Previous chapters have made much of the author's attention to historical detail and his studied use of descriptive language to create realistic descriptions of a recognisable Ireland (the obvious exception being *The Dream of a Beast*). Yet, in *Carnivalesque*, Jordan throws himself headfirst (it is, after all, a story about acrobats) into a fantasy narrative drawing on both Irish mythology and, as we shall see, an aesthetic more at home in the subfields of speculative fiction. However, far from being out of place in the milieu of post-Celtic Tiger Irish suburban ennui as personified here by Andy's parents, Jordan the writer's overt adoption of a genre mode more at home in his films grants *Carnivalesque* a particular and successful energy.[1] More than that, and beyond even *The Dream of a Beast* or *Shade*, it makes *Carnivalesque* the fiction's strongest claim for the interconnectivity of Jordan the realist writer, Jordan the fantasist director, Jordan the realist director and Jordan the fantasist writer.

This unified Jordan exists in a kind of Venn space between all the overlapping aspects of his artistic ambitions, and it is only in novels such as *Mistaken* and *Carnivalesque* that we can come close to seeing a manifestation of this figure. As Fintan O'Toole succinctly put it, Jordan's creative interests have always been pulled in two directions, with supernatural creatures such as vampires and merfolk sharing imaginative acreage with keenly observed political, social and historical detail in both his fiction and his films.[2] O'Toole rightly goes on to say that Jordan's creative energies are at their most intense when these realist and fantastical lenses are focused on the same project (he cites, for instance, *The Butcher Boy*'s combination of recognisable small-town Ireland and apocalyptic phantasmagoria, or Jordan's skilful wielding of the uncanny in *Shade*).[3] Jordan himself, of course, is well aware that he contains multitudes, or at least one who directs films and one who writes fiction.[4] Both are attracted to sublime spectacle and both oscillate between the realistic and the fantastical, sometimes – as with *Carnivalesque* – within individual texts. Indeed, Karl Miller, describing the queerness – both in terms of sexuality and in terms of strangeness – of turn-of-the-twentieth-century doubles, could easily be writing about Jordan's work almost a hundred years later when he outlines how the destabilisation of gender binaries reflected doubts in the certainties of state and national identity; single individuals, say both Miller and Jordan, can and often do express more than one identity.[5] Certainly, duality in these forms and more has been a longstanding theme in Jordan's work, from the transformative energies of *The Dream of a Beast*, to the transgender Dill in *The Crying Game* (1992). In *Sunrise with Sea Monster*, it plays into both Donal's betrayal complex and the state of large swathes of the national psyche at the time. Jordan's engagement with ideas of duality has been lifelong and visible in all periods of his work for both page and screen.[6] In particular, *Mistaken* and *Carnivalesque* are emblematic of not just Jordan's career-shaping fascination with doubles but of how, as Jeanett Shumaker puts it, these doubles allow for the dramatisation of identity's instability and consequent unpredictability.[7]

The splits of these two books – and, for that matter, the manner in which they mirror *each other* – provide an attentive device for Jordan to conduct a process of internal examination.[8] Viewed together, *Mistaken* and *Carnivalesque* – one a work of literary fiction, one a speculative smorgasbord of folklore, fantasy and science fiction – suggest a rivalry between different parts of Jordan's artistic identity and their associated styles, a tension which is played out in the rivalries between Kevin/Gerry and Andy/Dany and across landscapes familiar from mainstream writing and romanticised fantastika.[9] The unlikely and imaginative divisions and (dis)connections visible in *Mistaken* and *Carnivalesque* lie at the heart of the more general prevalence of incongruity and, yes, uncertainty in both those novels and, for that matter, in Jordan's work more broadly. It is one of the obvious reasons that the doppelgänger concept has always been such a lure for him. As he told Caroline O'Doherty with regard to *Mistaken*, the novel draws on a universal feeling that there is another version of each one of us out there, a version who perhaps made different decisions or took different opportunities in life.[10] Though he describes this sense in terms of an almost psychological postcolonialism, his inspiration is more prosaic. There is, he has said, another Neil Jordan in Arizona, a man also born in 1950 but who he believes served a prison sentence for identity theft or wire fraud.[11]

Jordan's interest in the kind of doubling and repetition that critics like Mark Fisher see as underpinning each of the uncanny phenomena which Freud previously identified is apparent everywhere in *Mistaken* and *Carnivalesque*.[12] For Miller, too, duality is not just a term to indicate the presence of a pair of something but one which further directs that a single entity can, and perhaps should, be understood to be two:[13] Kevin and Gerry, Andy and Dany, northside and southside Dublin, the east and west coasts of Ireland, and so on. Miller links the use of such dichotomies in fiction to a conscious fostering of uncertainty which he sees as one of modern literature's defining characteristics.[14] For Miller, and for that matter for Jordan, the component parts of a dismembered whole may or may not resemble one another, they may either unite with or drive away one another.[15] They can initially be presented as collaborators or competitors, says Miller, but neither part necessarily has claim to being the genuine article.[16] Which is to say that Jordan, in many ways, is a prime example of Miller's approach to duality, exhibiting not just a split between public and private personas but – as a writer *and* a filmmaker – existing as a single individual seemingly drawing upon separate imaginative states.[17] Jordan further offers an exemplar of how, as Miller says, a single life can be observed, recorded and understood in two distinctly different critical and popular fashions.[18] Take, for example, Jordan's own reflections on how his achievements have been observed and recorded. As he described it to Sue Leonard, the result of his making *Angel* was that he became far better known as a film director than as a writer.[19] He was flown to film festivals and, to the chagrin of some older writers, found himself in considerable demand.[20] Some established literary figures, he said, perceived his turn to filmmaking as a transgression or a betrayal of the Irish writer's vocational responsibilities, the practice of a low art which they regarded as closer to property development (the latter comparison in particular is also telling when one considers the strong focus on the urban and on waste ground in *Mistaken* and *Carnivalesque* respectively).[21]

Asked after a festival appearance why he moves across so many artistic forms, Jordan replied that he enjoys working in a visual medium as much as through literary craft, and that he is repeatedly drawn to the kinds of projects he has not done before.[22] Jordan cited Yeats as a role model in this regard based on how the poet moved effortlessly between modernist verse, popular lyrics and vulgar theatre.[23] It is clear from both *Mistaken* and *Carnivalesque*, as well as contemporaneous films such as *Ondine* (2009) and *Byzantium* (2012), that Jordan remains the creator of tall tales with a supernatural flourish, not just literature in a dry, fossilised or respectable sense, but – befitting one who is also a filmmaker – of entertainment. For example, Jordan's validation of and fascination with the macabre and the pulp can be found in the strong presence of Bram Stoker's *Dracula* in *Mistaken*. Stoker and *Dracula* serve as both recurring motifs and an acknowledgement of Dublin's other – meaning non-Joycean, meaning fantastical-rather-than-realistic – literary history and heritage. He recalls often passing Bram Stoker's house on the bus when he was a child, a local landmark made unsettling by both its literary associations and its decrepitude and neglect.[24] Around that time – and from this he draws Kevin's account of the same defining experience – Jordan saw his first vampire film. He remembers it as a Bela Lugosi picture that terrified him for years afterwards and, like Kevin, he saw it in the Scouts' hall.[25] It is perhaps not surprising so that the boy who grew up to direct *Interview with the Vampire* (1994) has been critical of how dark fantasy has been neutered by the early twenty-first-century culture: the figure of the vampire, he says, has become inoffensive, even soothing, rather than genuinely terrifying (this Jordan partly ascribes to the increased prevalence of digital production techniques in filmmaking).[26] By contrast, the Dracula that *Mistaken* positions as a shapeshifting Celtic bogeyman dates to the 1890s, and, despite his atmospheric usage of Stoker's creation here, Jordan has registered his belief that the present moment would benefit from new imaginative monsters.[27]

This is something he offers in *Carnivalesque*, where Jordan draws on dualistic ideas of fairy changelings, possession by demonic beings, and even the transmigration of souls. Where *Mistaken* confronts the psychological (even narcissistic) distortions and compulsions of duality in conversation with well-worn Gothic tropes, *Carnivalesque* adopts the vernacular folklore of the stolen child conceit to examine the implications of such violations for the individual in question, with Andy becoming Dany, and his place taken by an imposter of ill intentions (though the book, says Leonard, would seem to draw just as much from the tension inside a single individual as anything else, with the same, arguably, true of *Mistaken*).[28] The simulacrum Andy in *Carnivalesque* is, in the tradition of literary dualities, made strange by his abduction and adoption into the carnival life. Most reviewers – and, for that matter, Jordan himself in interviews – connect this estrangement with the onset of adolescence and accompanying teenage distance. He said in 2017 that while he was consciously unaware of that feeling when writing *Carnivalesque*, he now acknowledges that it is something which has crept into all his recent work.[29] It is precisely the kind of self-reflection one expects from an artist who claims to live largely in his own head, though of course he also lives two different lives.[30] It is therefore fitting that both books are so heavily in dialogue with each other. Through them Jordan tells this story of duality twice, first as tragi-comedy in *Mistaken*, and second as comedic tragedy in *Carnivalesque*.

ROUND THE CIVIC OAK WE TWINE: THE FULL CIRCLE OF *MISTAKEN*

Mistaken, Neil Jordan's sixth book, is the Gothic novel that some reviewers wanted *Shade* to be. It is, moreover, not a novel he could have written at any earlier point in his writing career. An ambitious and self-consciously literary work, *Mistaken* tells the story of two identical boys – Kevin Thunder from Dublin's northside, Gerry Spain from the southside – who become aware of each other's existence through repeated incidents of mistaken identity and gradually forge a unified identity of sorts, one incorporating both the positive and negative aspects of both boys. Like *Shade*, *Mistaken* begins at the end, at a funeral. But this is a novel of the modern era, a work of historical fiction only insofar as it tells a (rather than *the*) story of Jordan's *personal* history. The novel essentially takes up where *Shade* left off. Where that book was the story of Ireland from the turn of the 1900s to the mid-century, *Mistaken* brings Jordan's fictional project from the 1950s right up to the present day, essentially taking place over the whole course of Jordan's life, or rather his two lives, for as he told Eithne Shortall, part of the reason he invented his identical protagonists was to explore the dichotomy between the visual and the literary.[31] Elsewhere, he has admitted that both characters are reflections of himself and that this offered him a way to talk about himself.[32] Indeed, in an interview with the frustrating but relevant title 'Jordan Swaps Movies for Novels', the author reiterated something which has underpinned his writing from the very start, saying that there is an authorial attempt to disguise oneself in all fiction, and that he has divided himself into two for *Mistaken* with elements of his own personality to be found in both characters.[33] The result is an elegiac study of a life not lived, twice over in fact, and of a city which is gone for good. This choice to yoke the symbolic split between Jordan the novelist and Jordan the filmmaker to a plot that is part Gothic tragedy, part thriller, results in a deepening of the author's long-established fascination with duality and with life in the city of Dublin.

With a miasmic genre idiosyncrasy, the novel portrays nuanced instances of duplication and diffusion which, while not unique to Jordan, are certainly emblematic of his career. *Mistaken* received high praise from novelist John Connelly on *The View*, who considered it perhaps Jordan's best work to date.[34] The book was awarded the Kerry Group Irish Fiction Award, worth €15,000, at the Listowel Writers' Week in 2011, making Jordan one of the few Irish authors to have won the prize twice (he previously won for *Shade* in 2005).[35] Yet, while the plot of *Mistaken* is predicated on dualities, the novel nonetheless manages to convey three distinct levels of meaning: the story of Jordan's literary life, the tension between his fictional and filmic personas, and the transformation of Dublin city from the 1960s to the early twenty-first century. Here, says Fintan O'Toole, the theme of the doppelgänger allows Jordan to unlock questions about the ambiguity of identity, with the implied elements of the fantastic enriching the result (rather than serving as a distraction from the story's humanity, a charge O'Toole levels at the similar premise of *Carnivalesque*).[36] Bookseller Des Kenny, in an online review of *Mistaken*, noted not only Jordan's outstanding contribution to Irish literature but also how the novel evidenced the author's increasing ability to unsettle the reader through a commanding use of language.[37] The defining nature of *Mistaken* saw Jordan hailed once more as a significant Irish novelist by Eileen Battersby in a passionate review of the novel for *The Irish Times*.[38] Battersby framed *Mistaken* as the culmination of Jordan's lifelong engagement with imagination, storytelling and language.[39] In particular she praised the book's precise plotting and narrative voice, artistic elements which she saw as evidence of Jordan breaking free from his contemporaries and influences.[40] Nonetheless, *Mistaken* acknowledges such inspirations openly. The book is haunted not just by Stoker (one of the boys grows up beside the house in which Stoker was born)[41] but, inevitably, by a dialogue with James Joyce, whose influence has flavoured Jordan's work from the outset. Joyce is decipherable in Jordan's use of (multiple) surrogates. He is both Kevin and Gerry. He is both author and subject, both James Joyce and Stephen Dedalus, both the anxiety and the influence. But Jordan further gestures to Joyce's presence through *Mistaken*'s strong emphasis on the depiction and geography of Dublin city. In many ways the novel amounts to a new version – a double, if you will – of the streets and social landmarks mapped out by James Joyce.[42] *Mistaken* shadows *Ulysses* in its intimate familiarity with Dublin's streets and watering holes (though Jordan has confessed to fretting over getting the bus routes correct)[43] even as it cheekily reduces the significance of that monumental novel to a memento mori of the day Nora Barnacle masturbated James Joyce in Ringsend Park (172). All of which is to say that Jordan's conflicted views about Dublin's overwhelming identification with Joyce permeate the whole of *Mistaken*. In its broad, Ulyssean portrayal of the capital, *Mistaken* is both a direct acknowledgement of the Joycean influence which has been Jordan's compass since *Night in Tunisia* and a rejection of the same. Or, as Battersby put it, the Jordan who penned *Mistaken* is considerate and respectful of Joyce before breaking away in the manner of a child stepping out from the shadow of a beloved parent.[44] In the process, Jordan commits an undeniably Joycean act by making something new of the material, utilising Dublin to depict a carefully structured conflation of physical and temporal coordinate systems. Constant juxtaposition creates a collision of space and time, with place names taking the position of chapter titles and chronological progress through the story overwritten by a geographical progress across the city.

Jordan himself has stated that when he came to write *Mistaken* his intention was to create as accurate a description as he could of not just the physical space of Dublin but also the experiential aspect of growing up in the city, particularly with an eye to issues of class distinction, not necessarily the expected distinction between working- and middle-class people but, instead, between what he thinks of as the partial and fully middle class.[45] While it is obviously a work of imaginative fiction, the novel is therefore also a product of an intimate and longstanding familiarity with the city and its inhabitants, one which transcends the author's use of autobiographical material in his prior fiction (indeed, Jordan considers *Mistaken* to be his most autobiographical work).[46] In an interview with Ciara Dwyer in 2011, Jordan recalled living on Victoria Road, close to Bram Stoker's house in Marino.[47] He spoke openly about one of the experiences that inspired *Mistaken*, riding the bus through the area and feeling that he was seeing another version of himself nearby.[48] It made an eerie impression on the young Jordan, another kind of vampiric presence flitting across the streets of the capital.

Throughout *Mistaken*, Jordan displays a great love for a city much written about but, paradoxically, seldom truly experienced in fiction.[49] In fact, with most of Kevin's relationships the result of mistaken identity, Eithne Shortall in *The Sunday Times* sees Dublin itself as the novel's only concrete character.[50] To agree wholeheartedly with this would be to do a disservice to Jordan's characterisation of Kevin (and, to a lesser extent, Gerry), though Shortall is correct in that the city's moods and mutations are central to *Mistaken*'s success. Jordan portrays Dublin, and by extension Ireland, as being in a never-ending process of transformation, developments in the social and urban fabric of the city recalling the biological metamorphosis afflicting the narrator of *The Dream of a Beast*. As with that character, the changes wrought by time on Dublin are not just inevitable, they are also impossible to offset. What's more, the impression of a city in material and demographic flux is not limited to just the fifty years covered by the novel, it is extended backwards, into the literary and cultural history of the capital (and, more tenuously, forwards into a future where the city is merely one component of a larger global village, the kind of future where Kevin thinks nothing of hopping from one continent to another). For Dublin in *Mistaken* exists in its own state of duality, not just the split between the northside and the southside, between poverty and prosperity (with, it seems, the prospect of further poverty looming on the historical horizon once again), but between the dirty old town of everyday life and a city of the imagination.

A further split occurs between the Dublin of Jordan's adolescence and that of his adult years. As he recalled during a public interview, much of *Mistaken* was inspired by how he used to cycle past Fairview cinema when he was growing up and frequently passed a nearby crescent of Georgian houses which he found to be one of the creepiest places he could imagine.[51] Additional granular elements of the novel's texture, such as Kevin's fashion sense and his predilection for clubs and popular music, draw closely on Jordan's own experience of being a teenager in Dublin. All of that is based on his own life, the novelist says, recalling teenage efforts to style himself after the mod subculture of the mid-1960s and attending clubs throughout each weekend where he enjoyed the music of artists such as Booker T. and the M.G.'s.[52] During his promotion of *Mistaken*, Jordan spoke about how writing the book was a strong reminder that the Ireland he grew up in was very different from the grim country recollected by many in his generation. At least part of Jordan's impetus in writing *Mistaken* was therefore to challenge the image of Ireland which permeates the accepted literary depiction of the country in the 1950s and '60s as a cruel and conservative Catholic corner of the world.[53] With this, another duality is apparent, that of stereotypical representation and Jordan's lived experience. His attention to detail, his emphasis on the vibrant, sexually charged nature of the city in *Mistaken* is consequently more than simply atmospheric; it is a conscious – one might say brazen – affront to the stock histories propagated by much Irish writing. *Mistaken* is a book about what he himself remembers, says Jordan, who maintains that he does not recall the pulpit-thumping theatrics of Redemptorist fathers, and definitely does not remember a pig's head in a pot at Christmas.[54] Appearing on *The Late Late Show* in 2011, he mused that perhaps he just had a more comfortable childhood than the likes of Frank McCourt in Limerick.[55]

As such, Jordan is aware that his recollections of growing up in and around the capital are at odds with the memories of others.[56] Speaking to *The Sunday Times* in 2011, he notes the disparity between the 1960s Dublin he remembers and the oppressive, impoverished, mean-spirited and Catholic-guilt-ridden place others recall it as.⁵⁷ Speaking to the *Irish Examiner*'s Caroline O'Doherty that same year, Jordan said he does not remember Ireland as a backward, grey or priest-addled place (he instead cites John Banville and Patrick McCabe as novelists whose depiction of Ireland he admires).⁵⁸ He also names John McGahern as a writer whose representation of the past does not necessarily accord with his own.⁵⁹ Speaking to Shortall, he remembers McGahern as a country teacher in Belgrove national school who simply vanished one day.⁶⁰ While Jordan found the details of the school as fictionalised in McGahern's novel *The Leavetaking* (1975) to be highly accurate, he has nonetheless stated that some other aspects of the work – the idea of curtain-twitching suburbs wherein everybody's sexual mores were subject to constant surveillance, clerical and otherwise – do not accord with his own experiences of growing up.⁶¹ His stated reason for taking Dublin as *Mistaken*'s setting is therefore to serve as a corrective to the greyish depictions of the 1960s and '70s predominating in contemporary culture and literature.⁶² Jordan instead recalls the city as a liberating place, one filled with drama, intimacy and magic.⁶³ As John Boland put it in his *Irish Independent* review of *Mistaken*, present-day Dublin is overshadowed by Jordan's affectionate recollection of the city during the 1960s, '70 and '80s.⁶⁴ Dublin is described in such detail that some reviewers saw it as a dream project of a movie set builder – and here one is reminded of Joyce's boast that one could reconstruct the city from the pages of *Ulysses* – though the reconstruction Jordan embarks on here is far from merely architectural.⁶⁵ Throughout *Mistaken*, he is at pains to give life to the inhabitants of Dublin through the evocative power of Kevin and Gerry's journeys across the city and the decades.

It is a novel in which one half of Dublin wears the livery of For Sale signage (230) and the over half is virtually abandoned (232). In a reflection of Kevin and Gerry – not to mention Jordan and Jordan – multiple versions of the same city exist side by side. Throughout the novel Dublin is forever changing and its true form is mercurial, objectively unknowable. It has, in fact, as many true forms as it has inhabitants, a figure that must be multiplied again by the intricate relationships of all those who live in the city. Just as in *Shade*, where the cartographical realities of the Boyne estuary were sublimated beneath the imaginative geographies of Nina and her friends, *Mistaken*'s conception of place and space is without absolutes. There is no such thing as a true map of Dublin, only the subjective experience of individuals interlocking and/or conflicting with those of their neighbours. In fact, Jordan's greatest innovation in the novel is perhaps to have created two characters capable of slipping from one set of these experiences to another and so, for all intents and purposes, from one *existence* to another, where existence signifies their individual, subjective interactions with the city and with others. Kevin and Gerry's exchanges, it should be noted, are not simple *Parent Trap* (1961) style tradings of Marino for Palmerstown or vice versa; they occur most often within the interface of Dublin's north- and southsides, usually in the city centre which, as with all Jordan's liminal spaces, is a domain governed by water (here, the River Liffey). Undergoing one of these exchanges, Kevin and Gerry find themselves inserted into the centre of unfamiliar social networks and particular relationships to geographic space which have formed through the other's experience. However brief these cases of mistaken identity may be, they consistently deny each character's extensive knowledge of the city they live in. The ultimate effect of this is to highlight how Dublin is less a spatial certainty and more a series of events unique to each inhabitant.

While some slight inconsistencies in the depiction of the city were criticised on RTÉ's culture show *The View*, Jordan's imaginative recreation of Dublin was widely praised.[66] Boland, for example, failed to find a false note in the novel's depiction of the capital or of its inhabitants, going on to describe *Mistaken* as a love letter to a Dublin through five decades of transformation.[67] Moreover, Kevin's constant recourse to geographical reference in his narration represents an effort on his part, perhaps even on Jordan's part, to assign literally concrete form to the amorphous memories of a lifetime, recollections of perceptions and emotions which together comprise the *gestalt* entity of Kevin and Gerry, the split soul to which they both lay claim. This leads the reader to a startling, though altogether fitting, conclusion regarding *Mistaken*, for there is a reading of the novel possible in which Kevin, Gerry and Dublin are – after the Catholic fashion – all aspects of a single entity: two halves of a spiritual soul and a physical form comprising the body of Dublin itself, the civic oak around which the others twine. If we accept that Kevin and Gerry represent aspects of Jordan himself, then why not the city too? The implication, of course, is that *Mistaken*'s Dublin, its energy and influence, is as valid an aspect of Jordan's personality as the two boys growing up within its mesmeric boundaries and flitting between the various identities that Dublin affords as both are drawn to the challenge of creating imaginary worlds. Kevin, in particular, eventually moves from architectural practice to computer game design, giving form to virtual streetscapes as a backdrop for ninjas, assassins and members of the yakuza.[68] A reader familiar with Jordan's background, and cognisant of the self-examination proffered by *Mistaken*, might well have expected the character to become a filmmaker, though such an obvious development would have been an artless turn. Kevin's job in the games industry is a more than adequate substitute in that it allows the author to assign the grammar of filmmaking – his play with completely imaginary cities – to a similarly creative, collaborative, pop-cultural undertaking (287). He describes how Kevin's use of wire-frame models takes the place of physical beams in shaping three-dimensional spaces, serving to control the interplay of shade and illumination, a concern for light which echoes Jordan's earliest depiction of film direction, in his 1980 story 'She'.[69]

On the other hand, the book's de-emphasis of Kevin's profession and his identity as a ghost in his own life – a visual artist who becomes the familiar of a writer – asks the reader to look more closely at the autobiographical content of *Mistaken*, at the soul which the author has so deviously split between Kevin and Gerry, and how it relates to the story of Neil Jordan the novelist. Kevin, it seems, only ever feels complete when he is being Gerry. For the most part there is a playfulness rather than a pain to this act of recognition, though one should remember that *Mistaken* was composed during the nine-month period Jordan was waiting for the release of his Colin Farrell picture *Ondine* (a simple, delightful story which, he acknowledges, was not seen by many people) and when his long-gestating *Borgias* screenplay mutated from the familiar shape of a motion picture project into a lavish television series for US cable channel Showtime (Jordan produced the series, directed the pilot and wrote the majority of the episodes).[70] Nonetheless, it is the past (perhaps, as we shall see, *The Past*) rather than the present that provides the novel's narrative and inspirational spine. The bifurcated life story of *Mistaken* brings Jordan right back to the start of his career as a writer. Gerry, like Jordan, chooses a pseudonym for his first published efforts (though Jordan evidently has no intention of confessing that identity), so it is not solely for comedy value that Gerry uses Kevin to speak about his self.[71] The arc of Gerry's writing career thereafter follows that of Jordan's. Gerry is given his start by the legendary David Marcus in the New Irish Writing page of the *Irish Press* (130), the same Marcus who, Jordan has said, once berated him as a twenty-one-year-old writer for what the editor found to be an irritating absence of punctuation alongside an overabundance of – and surely this is recognisable to many writers – dashes.[72] Like Jordan, Gerry becomes a writer kept by a lawyer (241). He sells a first novel called *Happiness* which, like *The Past*, is concerned with the protagonist's inherited sense of familial expectation and which, again like Jordan's book, is published through Jonathan Cape (200, 202). Gerry also publishes a collection of stories in a blue-grey colour which evokes both the mood and cover design of *Night in Tunisia* (226). For Gerry, there is little in the way of daylight between his fiction and his life (204). He dabbles in writing a screenplay (238) for which he takes a grim sojourn in Los Angeles, another attempt by Jordan to fictionalise his own Hollywood experience (and one which evokes his 1993 story 'Remote Control'). Gerry's books receive international editions (240), and eventually he achieves success and recognition at home, in this case winning the Hennessy Literary Award (273).

Yet, in Kevin's critique of Gerry's fiction, Jordan asks a metafictional question that seems at once to query the direction of contemporaneous Irish writing in general and his own back catalogue of novels in particular. Commenting on the growing conventionality of his double's writing, Kevin cites Gerry's obsession with times gone by and, indeed, with Irish fiction's broader focus on stories of the 1950s, '40s and '20s (288). That Gerry published his first writing under Kevin's name, not to mention the fact that they are both aspects of Jordan himself, transforms this into an ambiguous, quasi-authorial self-critique. It is tempting to read the '50s, '40s and '20s (even in how Jordan choses to order these) as slightly offset references (by a decade in each case) to *Shade*, *Sunrise with Sea Monster* and *The Past*, the veiled reflection of an author looking back upon his works. That said, there is also an implicit disapproval here at the curatorial perspective adopted by Irish authors of the Celtic Tiger era preceding *Mistaken*, among the output of which one finds a large number of historical novels and so-called misery memoirs (the latter a target of, as we have seen, Jordan's lively depiction of Dublin in the 1960s and '70s). *Mistaken*'s perspective on Irish writing is, in Gregory Day's view, further inseparable from the contemporary fetishisation of Joycean Dublin.[73] Jordan, says Day, has identified literary Dublin's chronic weakness as an unwillingness to concede to the reality of the present (though this is perhaps somewhat unfair to the lively twenty-first-century depictions of the city).[74] Such creative paralysis (in all the Joycean irony of that) is apparent in Gerald Spain's novels-within-the-novel, says Day, with the tougher, more practically minded northside perspective of Kevin Thunder offering disapproval.[75] Jordan/Kevin is at his most self-deprecating when he decries Jordan/Gerry's fiction for stagnation, with his subjects and titles becoming interchangeable. Kevin, as if trying to recall the title of *The Past*, cycles through names such as *Bygones* or *Remembrance* (287), while elsewhere the novel warns prospective creative practitioners about becoming too literary in their language and aesthetics (154). What either Kevin or Gerry might make of their creator later mirroring their tale with the fairies and speculative physics of *Carnivalesque* is up to the reader to decide. However, Kevin's prescient comment towards the end of the novel that gravity's rules were being rewritten (287) suggests that, on some level at least, the character is aware that the future lies in escaping from rigid notions of Irish fiction.

ORCHESTRATOR OF MIRRORS: *CARNIVALESQUE*'S SEPARATION OF THE SECOND SELF

Though an eerie double of *Mistaken*, Jordan's most successful novel to date, *Carnivalesque*, announces itself with a direct reference to one of the author's best-known big-screen works. The novel opens with a carnival, a familiar sight of amusement belying sinister undertones, with Jordan the writer evoking the slow pan across a fairground which opens Jordan the director's Oscar-winning film *The Crying Game*. This is, fittingly, a distorted reflection of what has come before. Decorative lights strung across on the waste ground (*Carnivalesque*, 1) seem to promise Jordan aficionados another contemporary tale that questions the ambiguities of the present moment's politics in insightful fashion. However, this is neither the work of Jordan the director nor of Jordan the realist. Where the politics of *The Crying Game* were national, those of *Carnivalesque* are supernatural. Here, Jordan literalises the idea of a flight of fancy through the use of fairy folk whose non-Newtonian aerial performances are a reflection of the genre acrobatics performed by their author. Unlike *Mistaken*, the novel does not look to the foundational texts of modern Irish literature such as Joyce but, instead, further back to the folklore preceding the modern state and its associated identity. A consequence of this is the freedom Jordan discovers in terms of recalibrating aspects of his fiction's geotemporal locus. While *Carnivalesque*'s split focus on Ireland east and west imitates previous Jordan work from *Night in Tunisia* to *The Past* and beyond, the author's typical emphasis on the island's archipelagic situation – on its relationship with Britain – is pushed back further in time than ever before. Previous Jordan novels have taken the independence struggle as their origin story for the modern Irish state, but *Carnivalesque* proffers the Irish Famine of the late 1840s as the inciting incident of identity politics which continue to the present day. That it does so within the framework of a fantasy narrative is one of the things that distinguishes this novel from the majority of Jordan's previous fiction.

That said, *Carnivalesque* is in many ways a reframing of the same central concept as *Mistaken*, albeit, as O'Toole says, with a stronger commitment to the grotesque and the paranormal.[76] The novel tells the story of fourteen-year-old Andy who becomes trapped within the mirror of a carnival sideshow on its visit to a Dublin suburb (though *Kirkus* commits the unforgivable error of referring to him as a British youth!).[77] What at first appears to be Andy's reflection, but is in effect a distorted simulacrum, leaves the hall of mirrors in his place to take up life with the unsuspecting parents of the original. Andy, his name now distorted into Dany, is rescued from the mirror by a circus performer, Mona, who appears to be a girl of his own age but who is really an ancient member of a long-living race with supernatural powers. Thus, where the malevolent sprite of *Mistaken* (*Mistaken*, 173) was metaphorical, those of *Carnivalesque* are, quite literally, supernatural beings. Throughout the novel, Jordan makes a sustained effort to reimagine familiar aspects of Irish mythology in line with Mikhail Bakhtin's concept of the carnivalesque.[78] He anchors this realignment in his version of the Tuatha Dé Danann, the mythological beings thought to represent the main deities of pre-Christian Ireland. In *Carnivalesque*, Jordan portrays them as self-described carnies, carnival folk who travel from town to town, a fantasy race functionally immortal until unexpectedly claimed by a fatigue which causes them to die, a people who adopt lost children into their ranks rather than procreate in human fashion. They are further compelled by circumstances to survive off the emotions of mortal beings and to conceal their superhuman abilities beyond the façade of the carnival (for example, Mona, who possesses the power of flight, plays the part of an aerial trapezist). In time, Dany becomes a carnie himself while the other Andy takes his place as the child of a housewife and a jam salesman.

Such an unusual work has, inevitably, received an uneven reception. Writing in *The Irish Times*, John Banville praised the subtle, magical aspects of the novel's pubescent parable and how it portrayed the peculiar changes that adolescence brings to the relationship between children and parents.[79] Which, on a surface level, it does, though as Jem Poster in *The Guardian* said, the interpretation of the novel as an allegorical coming-of-age story about identity and a young person's efforts to make their way through the strangeness of the world only holds up for so long.[80] The variety and complexity of the novel, she said, defies simplification in this way.[81] Indeed, defining *Carnivalesque* merely by its bildungsroman aspects is to do a disservice to a multifaceted work in which Jordan, as though one of the carnival performers who fill out his cast, is performing an authorial high-wire act. *Carnivalesque* is at once a coming-of-age narrative, a fantasy drawing on Celtic mythology, a highly stylised meditation on the cyclical disasters of Irish history, and a deft account of duality from a creator whose artistic identity is always in flux. The novel continues the trend in Jordan's work – apparent from *The Dream of a Beast* through *Sunrise with Sea Monster* and, notably, in *Shade* – of melding notions drawn from the sciences with tones and subject matter more at home on the line between fantasy and mainstream literary fiction. A consequence of this is the split between critics such as O'Toole, who expressed a scepticism rooted in Irish literary realism regarding the book's fantastical essentials,[82] and those more attuned to the sensibilities of fantasy fiction who found that the literary prose might, at times, cause reader interest to wane.[83] In many ways such a disparity of responses was inevitable for a novel which, as Bakhtin might put it, actively seeks to marry high art with low, the artistic with the asinine, the profound with the insignificant, and the intellectual with the irreverent.[84] Therein, of course, lies the novel's power, its arguable success, and perhaps the root of its multifaceted and contradictory reception. The incongruities of *Carnivalesque*, said Poster, are a challenge to those readers who demand consistency and internal order from fantasy worlds.[85] Yet, she rightly deems this unruliness to be a strength of the novel, a reflection of the diverse and evasive carnie philosophies which underpin the narrative of not just *Carnivalesque* but – and in many respects this is one of Jordan's great transpositions here – of stories about the fairy folk more generally.[86]

From its outset, *Carnivalesque* evokes traditional changeling stories or stolen child narratives, with Yeats' 'Come away, O human child!' serving as the novel's epigraph (that poem being, as O'Toole observed, a highly romanticised version of the disturbing changeling figure found in Irish folklore).[87] This concept of demonic replacement or possession further evokes what Miller sees as an indication that the subject owes something to both the pre-medieval dark ages and to the artistic concerns of the enlightenment which followed.[88] Though, as the novel progresses, the metaphorical language used by Jordan will grow closer to that of physicists than that of poets. Concepts like gravitational pull and centrifugal force are already introduced in the opening paragraph (1) while, later, the author namechecks scientific frameworks such as string theory (142). In this way Jordan prepares the reader for the fact that, though events in the novel are initially presented as akin to the kind of rite or incantation one might find in a druid's spellbook (15), this is a narrative that leans more on literalising relativity than it does on the literary revival. Moreover, it is a novel that looks back on Jordan's career in a similar manner to how *Mistaken* looked back upon his life. The image of mirrors trapping people has been with Jordan for a long time, in evidence as far back as one of the author's initial explorations of the divide between fiction and film in *The Company of Wolves* (1984). A sub-narrative of that film concerns the illegitimate son of a priest who is tricked by Terence Stamp's Devil into applying a magical ointment. The ointment causes the man to sprout ferocious hair all over his body and – with shades of this carnival's infernal machine – leaves him trapped inside a distorted mirror before the film's protagonist, Rosaleen, registers her disquiet with the unsettling tale. It is difficult so to ignore how *Carnivalesque*'s depiction of boyhood becoming manhood is an attempt – one which O'Toole deems unsuccessful – towards the male equivalent of the allegorical challenges of female adolescence so strikingly presented in *The Company of Wolves*.[89] In fact, outside of the two Ninas in *Shade*, duality in Jordan's work is largely one where rebellious male characters loom large (and it is worth noting here the shoddy manner in which the character of Andy's mother is treated by all the male figures in *Carnivalesque*).

Of note too is that Jordan chooses to address the Great Famine through this fantastical lens rather than through a realistic approach. It is not that his skills of realistic description are unequal to the task. Certainly, he has shown a talent for historical verisimilitude in previous work, such as *The Past*, the bulk of *Sunrise with Sea Monster* and *Shade*. But by contrast, in *Carnivalesque* he deliberately chooses to portray *an Gorta Mór* as *beyond* realism. It is a titanic rupture in the history of the fairies (97), it is the dividing line between their past and their present. It is a myth, it is a legend. It is an origin story with a quasi-biblical feel to it; it is a parable of the fall, a real-world horror story of death and expulsion, of vital bodies diminished to living corpses. It looms, unreal and omnipresent, in the Irish historical imagination and transcends the merely Gothic. Jordan's decision to incorporate the Famine into the fantastical pre-history of the carnie folk is therefore a deliberate artistic choice to acknowledge it as too large, too unimaginable a cataclysm for realism alone to address. Many of his peers in contemporary Irish fiction have chosen the opposite path, such as Joseph O'Connor in *Star of the Sea* (2002) or Emma Donoghue in her magnificent novel *The Wonder* (2016), both works rooted thematically and stylistically in factual accuracy. Yet, only fantasy offers an opportunity to comprehend the full magnitude of the Famine. As Timothy Morton has said, a style that foregrounds the uncanny and the fantastical in this fashion can often be superior to pure realism when it comes to depicting the full scope and scale of an environmental or economic catastrophe such as the Irish Famine: the paranormal as abnormal or beyond normal comprehension.[90]

Jordan's use of fantasy to depict this social and ecological disaster, one rarely presented – and certainly rarely presented on the same *scale* – by the accepted demarcations of Irish literary fiction, causes the reader to question reality as it is framed for them. Such scepticism about history and official narratives goes back, as we have seen, to *The Past*, though Jordan's by now deft deployment of the fantastical within the architecture of literary fiction grants *Carnivalesque* another layer. His writing here allows for the execution of fantasy's rhetorical capacities while simultaneously holding its most stereotypical expositional excess in check. Readers will recall a similar aspect of unknowability underpinning aspects of *Sunrise with Sea Monster* and *Shade*, both being artefacts of Jordan's blending of speculative themes with Irish literary fiction. In this case he dispenses with the factuality of the Famine in favour of portraying it as a mythical thing, a happening of such immensity that a full and accurate recounting of it would demand a great many pages of detailed narrative description (3). It is in fact a hyperobject in the Morton sense, one with significant ramifications for Irish historical, psychological and societal spaces.[91] It is viscous, which means it adheres to those entities involved with it (be they ordinary Irish people subject to cultural memory of the Famine, or the fairy/carnival folk who actually lived through it); it exhibits the effects of nonlocality, in other words any local manifestation of the Famine – memorials, graves, tasteless jokes about potatoes, the emigrant family of John F. Kennedy, or the backstory of fantasy novels by sometimes film directors – is not directly the Famine itself; it involves uncommonly long temporalities which range far beyond those typically experienced by human beings (represented here by the unnaturally long lifespans of Jordan's fairy folk); and it exhibits its effects in interobjective fashion, that is, its impacts are observable in those frames of reference within which the aesthetic properties of objects interact, in the criss-crossing of history and politics and capitalism and agriculture and nationalism and myths about all of the above.[92]

The fantastical backstory of the carnival folk is delivered, with Jordan's usual structural care, exactly halfway through the novel. Jordan consciously situates the carnie lore here in opposition to the realist material in which it is embedded and, by extension, against the dominant aesthetic of mainstream contemporary Irish writing. More so than even *The Dream of a Beast*, this is the only true fantastical (rather than historical) world-building Jordan performs in his writing, an effort at aesthetic stimuli more at home among the speculative fiction shelves than among contemporary Irish literature. Yet, though it is crucial to our understanding of Jordan's approach here, the carnies' fantastical Famine backstory is only one part of the novel. Definitely a post-Celtic Tiger story, *Carnivalesque* is set in 2016 (109) and, while the recession of the preceding decade was not a disaster on the same scale as the Famine, the 'Great Rupture' serves here as a mirror image to the moment from which Jordan is writing and in which the novel is set, a grotesquely distorted exaggeration of early twenty-first-century Ireland. It serves as a reminder that Ireland is enmeshed in, and highly vulnerable to, international capitalist economic systems (the global marketplace of *Mistaken* and the steam packet company of *Shade* provide other recent Jordan examples). *Carnivalesque* acknowledges that this has always been the case by presenting the Famine, a function of an international economic disaster, as part of a recurring cycle of Irish destruction and repeated recessionary incidents which result in repeated waves of immigrants arriving in the Americas and further afield (73). It stands out as the only extended use of the Great Hunger in Jordan's writing, work which generally concerns the insular politics of the twentieth and twenty-first centuries rather than the scattering of Irish emigrants on coffin ships far across the ocean. In *Carnivalesque*, the Famine is analogous to the biblical flood for the carnie characters, it is year zero for their modern incarnation. Before the Famine, these beings had been fairy tales and the stuff of myth. They had, Jordan tells us, needed no name for themselves and so had names like pooka or banshee foisted upon them by others (97). In this way fiction concealed the fact that an independent race of beings lived among humans and, in time, the carnies took advantage of these stories as a cover to go about their business (97). After the great disaster, however, which not only sundered the Irish from their crops but deprived the Tuatha Dé Danann of the mildew on which they feed (140), the fairy folk are no longer able to hide behind myths. In the process, their entire race is consigned to phase in and out of folk narratives and culture. They were cut off from the Land of Spices (140) – the carnie Byzantium to which they wish to return – and from the last remaining energies of their creation (141). Like the Irish more generally, they were forced to scatter themselves across the world and along the edges of society. They take shelter in travelling carnivals, where their unusual abilities can be passed off as performances and eccentricity, and where the patrons of the various rides and attractions leave behind precious mildew as an emotional residue.

It is in this substance, specifically in how it is generated by strong emotions such as delight, dread, terror, awe and ecstasy (140), that the novel fully reveals itself as the distorted reflection of *Mistaken*. For if we read that novel as a paean to the Dublin Gothic tradition and the seriousness of literary writing into which it has been absorbed, then the story of Dany, and specifically the fairy-sustaining mildew generated from delight and shock which he encounters, is a validation of commercial fiction's power, imaginative importance and legitimacy in the face of literary fiction's propriety notions. What many deem ephemeral is actually a crucial source of sustenance. The joy Dany eventually finds in this life is counterpointed by the tale of a boy named Walter who could not join the carnies. When this earnest student of carnie lore attempts to codify his flawed understandings of their history and existence (151, 152), he quite simply misses the point. As Mona sees it, there's something fundamentally wrong with his serious approach, with his constant irritating questions, his long-winded explanations, and his incapacity to accept that some things in the carnie universe just are.[93] As a consequence, Walter suffers from premature ageing (155) when he is excluded from carnie culture. He literally grows old before his time as he loses the ability to simply enjoy magical things for their own sake. The cautionary tale of Walter's imaginative failure is one aspect of how *Carnivalesque* fulfils the promise of its title (and, for that matter, of Jordan the writer's career trajectory) by offering us a version of Bakhtin's 'carnivalesque' as a kind of folk-humour.[94] In *Rabelais and His World* (1965), and later in *Problems of Dostoevsky's Poetics* (1984), Bakhtin defines the carnivalesque as a state wherein life is shaken loose from its rhythms and routines, and is, to at least some extent, inverted or reversed.[95] Certainly, Jordan's tendency to turn life inside out – both figuratively and literally – will be recognisable from his work in cinema (*High Spirits*, 1988, comes to mind). In *Carnivalesque*, traces of Bakhtin's carnivalesque are visible not just in the fresh presentation given to existing narrative elements evident in Jordan's use of the Tuatha Dé Danann, or in the largely grotesque depictions of the villainous Dewman, but in the way the story liberates Dany's consciousness and makes possible his new perspective on the world.[96] It surely helps that Dany, like Jordan protagonists as far back as the Beast, embraces rather than resists the new condition rather unwillingly forced upon him. But, as Bakhtin says, at the same time carnivalesque is in no way nihilistic; it imbues a sense of confidence and optimism through its philosophy of development and change, let alone through its gestures towards artistic immortality on the part of its practitioners who, in this case, are the immensely long-lived fairies.[97] Thus, the novel overturns not just socio-hierarchical structures within its storyworld (through the familial and sexual ease of the carnival folk), but, as a work of near-fantasy by an established Irish literary author, it suspends the hierarchical inequality between literary and commercial fictional forms. Dany may be working through a new mode of interrelationship with himself/his double in Bakhtinian fashion but, simultaneously, his creator is working out aspects of his interrelationship(s) with his own double(s).[98]

The expression of popular truths rooted in folk entertainments which Bakhtin identifies are echoed in Jordan's affirmation here of the validity and vitality of popular or commercial fiction. Such an accomplished avowal – there is, after all, no question that his use of the fantastic here rises to the level of art – frames the contrasting genre of literary fiction as one of Bakhtin's officially sanctioned and sanitised undertakings, one which is rivalled by the spontaneous emergence of unfettered diversions – or commercial fiction – which parallel its existence.[99] Thus, one aspect of the novel's carnivalistic blasphemy is therefore its full-throated endorsement of speculative fiction, of fairies and immortality, of space-time warping and zombies; of genres deemed 'low' but embraced by communities of readers who, in their extravagant fandoms, could themselves be said to be living Bakhtin's carnivalistic life. This fantastical and, as it progresses, almost science-fictional aspect of *Carnivalesque* may come as a surprise to the reader of *Night in Tunisia* or *The Past* (though not of *The Dream of a Beast*). Nonetheless, the attentive peruser of the bookshop will note the way the novel's back cover copy stresses how, in the carnival, 'gravity is meaningless and time performs acrobatic tricks'.[100] Like neutral Ireland in *Sunrise with Sea Monster*, Jordan's carnival folk are not subject to Newton's inconvenient rules (111). They are capable of existing on a different dimensional plane (18). In fact, they are said to have originated beyond a barrier between dimensions (166) and are as much aliens in a science-fictional sense – the reader is told that they crashed to earth at some point in the past (166) – as they are a myth in the fantasy mode. Through them, the reader is admitted to a realm of collapsible, nonlinear spacetime which routinely violates the principles of logic and the laws of gravity.[101] Jordan's innovation is how he melds the science-fictional to the fantastical, and packages the result as mainstream writing. While the possible interdimensional/interplanetary origins of the carnies tell us little about, say, Jordan's perspective on Irish history, the able and overt use of language and themes from the speculative genres by an established literary author in this fashion stands as a bold and overt statement about the merits of 'low' writing. Which should not surprise us, as the gravitational perturbations of *Carnivalesque* represent the culmination of Jordan's stylistic experiments going back as far as *The Dream of a Beast* and are informed by the blending and bending of genres which is the hallmark of his work for cinema.

In *Carnivalesque*, time and space are repeatedly seen to break down. Some of these incidents are mundane and easily explained, such as how the carnival is regularly dismantled for transport, with each component carefully slotting into another as though instinctively given to hide itself away in smaller and smaller spaces (22). Others are more esoteric, such as how the hall of mirrors is said to disappear into itself (122) and then, eventually, does exactly that at the peak of the novel's science-fictional intensity by folding into a series of multisided geometric shapes before becoming an elliptical spheroid (270). In a scene that is one part surreal, one part poetic, Jordan collapses the otherworldly machinery of the hall of mirrors into a singularity of sorts (though an imperfect one reminiscent in shape of a giant teardrop) and has the surviving carnies roll it through Liscannor to the sea cliffs high above the Atlantic. It is with this hall of mirrors – a technology inspired within the story by filmmaking, no less – that the genre-bending ambition of *Carnivalesque* reaches its zenith. Far more than merely a carnival attraction, the hall of mirrors is essentially one of a mad scientist's lunatic experiments (174) to make real Miller's thought experiment of sundering a second self from a notional original.[102] This fantastical device – one is put in mind of Arthur C. Clarke's oft-paraphrased adage that sufficiently advanced technology can often be indistinguishable from magic – is based on a real mirror maze which Jordan remembers from Bray, one which he remembers the potential for getting lost inside and which he used as a filming location for *The Miracle* (1991).[103] Crucially, its creator Burleigh – who will be cast out of carnie society for his recklessness in building the device – also has a cinema connection. He develops his infernal mirrors after witnessing initial public screenings by the Lumière brothers, some of the first presentations of projected film, in Paris (274). Like he did with the hot-house studios of *Shade*, Jordan the writer again addresses the birth of cinema in a less than positive light with Burleigh's mirrors a direct response to encountering the possibilities of filmmaking, to seeing flickering reproductions of living beings projected on a wall. Duality, says Miller as though with carnie awareness, is a kind of magical incantation, an artefact of performative misdirection and literary stagecraft or sleight-of-hand.[104] Through this, we are told by Jordan, the image has been sundered from corporeality (175).

It is sundered from time too, in honourable speculative fiction fashion, with the passage of years rendered as an echo through infinity (107). Evoking the temporal undulation of Morton's hyperobjects (and, to an extent, those of *Shade*), the reader is told again and again about how time is a mysterious process of infinite complexity (40), about how decades turn back upon themselves as though coiling inside one another (142), and about how time and light coalesce into concentric waves (17). The carnies are said to have a perception of time which differs radically from that of ordinary people (154). Some do not perceive its passage at all and, for them, time is a distorted loop (154). They dream of vast scales on the order of millennia (127), displaying an awareness of time orders of magnitude beyond that of, say, the historically focused narrator of *The Past* or Nina Hardy in *Shade*, who, in her spectral form, already exists beyond human notions of temporality. Even ghost Nina is subject to passing on after re-living her life once over whereas, for the carnies, time carries on, year after year, though very little changes in the process (79). More than that, the novel's macabre villain (and the fact that *Carnivalesque* has an overt villain – a further signifier of commercial rather than literary fiction – is unusual for a Jordan novel) is known as the Dewman (251), an evil being from the realm of the carnies (and here we might think about 'Dewman' as 'dual-man', an echo of how, as Miller points out, there is more than a little resemblance in sound and meaning between the words 'double' and 'devil').[105] He is seen to exhibit uncanny control over time and space. Jordan depicts him as drawing his powers from gravity: time itself offers little trouble to him, and he is able to distort and manipulate it at will (251). The Dewman in fact displays what Morton would call recognisably *Gaussian* temporal effects by generating vortices in spacetime in accordance with general relativity.[106] The character is said to drag the Burren landscape into uncanny motion as he moves (251). Here, Jordan is essentially describing the physical phenomenon of frame-dragging whereby a massive rotating mass literally drags the surrounding region of spacetime along with its motion. Jordan repeatedly uses language that suggests the carnies are capable of causing the manifestation of relativistic effects.[107] More than that, he often uses the terminology with reasonable if metaphorical accuracy ('dragged' being the obvious example), and this despite scientific precision being, as John Kenny warns us, not necessarily chief among the concerns of the creative practitioner when they – deliberately or otherwise – integrate or adapt specialist understanding into their work.[108]

Though the likes of *Kirkus* insist *Carnivalesque* is indeed a fairy tale, the novel concludes as an unashamedly science-fictional story, albeit it one peopled by fairy folk and set, for its conclusion, in the west of Ireland.[109] Jordan's increased use of gravitational language and metaphors – the way he consciously unites art and science – at the point of Dany's confrontation with Andy and the Dewman mirrors the way in which the disordered bodies and souls are brought back together within the narrative. The question of what is real and what is mere reflection occupies the character of Mona at one point (163). Here, in concert with *Mistaken*, it is as though Jordan is asking himself the same question, interrogating his own creative reflections – writer, director, realist, fantasist – and one might come to the exact same conclusion: no surety is ever possible. *Carnivalesque* tells us that, in a pleasing paradox, one begins with two, each a reflection of the other (144). From such an original came the Neil Jordans we know today: the novelist and the changeling who makes films, the half- and quarter-breed ones who write or direct for the theatre or the television, the snatched away and returned personas who pen stories about the making of films in Hollywood… these are all facets of the same imagination. The historical novelist and the writer who dabbles in fantasy and even science fiction coexist with the filmmaker responsible for mainstream pictures such as *The End of the Affair* (1999) or *Mona Lisa* (1986), as well as unashamedly genre work such as *Interview with the Vampire* (1994) or *Byzantium*. Dany and Andy, Kevin Thunder and Gerry Spain, Nina Hardy and her half-brother (for that matter, Nina and her own ghost), the Beast in his human and animalistic forms, the narrators of *The Past* and 'A Love' are all distorted reflections of Neil Jordan as surely as are the characters of *Ondine, The Crying Game, The Miracle* or *Angel* (1982). Reading *Carnivalesque* and *Mistaken* together tells us that the question of whether Jordan is primarily a creator of film or of fiction is, in the end, irrelevant. He is in fact all possible versions of himself. He is in the end infinitely, brilliantly Neil Jordan.

Conclusion

The archetypal Neil Jordan character stands in a liminal space. Perhaps at the entrance to a visiting carnival on waste ground at the edge of the city. Perhaps at the threshold of a damp hotel room at the limits of propriety. More often than not they are drifting through life in a seaside town. They are a performer, usually a musician or an actor, and they are more comfortable with being someone else than with being themselves. They are a loner who rambles through a large bohemian house or a moody landscape. They wrestle with questions of national and political and sexual identity. The live in the long familial shadow of stern independence-struggle veterans or artistic ascendency types or, on occasion, both. Their romantic life is a triangular Oedipal drama of unfulfilled emotion and deferred satisfaction. They are a literal monster or a ghost or an enchanted doppelgänger or a child of the nation. Nonetheless, they are always plausible as a human character, one which Jordan places credibly in their emotional situation, a character who makes decisions which resonate with their socio-economic and historical context.[1] But, as Gerry McCarthy says, a no less crucial context is the grand patterns of Jordan's larger narrative designs, an ongoing dynamic tension between formalism and naturalism, with Jordan determined to try and bring both modes into alignment.[2] Thus, the archetypal Jordan character, like their creator, is always more than the sum of their parts. They bridge worlds and forms and genres in search of more authentic aesthetic experiences. Their outsider status confers an enviable perspective which raises doubts about consensus narratives. Again and again, they confront the preconceptions of those around them, nudging the reader into questioning fundamental aspects of Irish novelistic realism and archipelagic historical impartiality. In the process, this fiction mirrors the journey of Jordan himself – from a young writer navigating dense literary and nationalist traditions with 'A Love' and *The Past*, to the wiser, internationally successful artist who tackles the knotty history of his country in *Sunrise with Sea Monster* and his decades-long investigation of Irish identity via the genre gymnastics of *Shade*, *Mistaken* and *Carnivalesque*.

In the early twenty-first century, Jordan's work is more widely available than ever before. His fiction is frequently reviewed in the mainstream press where it is no longer discussed as merely an accessory to his work for the screen but, increasingly, as the true artistic companion this study has sought to reveal it as. Writing for the *New York Times Book Review*, the film critic Tom Shore commented on how Jordan's work in fiction allows for exactly the kind of atmosphere – part folktale, part fairy tale, part fable – which the exacting gaze of the camera lens so often denies his films (Shore goes on to recommend that Jordan take advantage of this aspect of prose fiction more often).[3] Meanwhile, writing in *The Spectator*, the novelist John de Falbe dismisses the relevance of the author's filmmaking in any discussion of his writing; the gossip columnists may be interested, de Falbe says, but as a critic he resists making any connections between the filmmaking and the fiction.[4] That said, one cannot ignore – and, as we have seen, the later Jordan does not – how the young author's descriptive skill posed important questions about his future in the medium of prose. By the early 1980s, Jordan had begun to see it as futile to keep writing for the sole purpose of describing what things looked like.[5] Instead, he sought an artistic canvas less concerned with literary culture's introspection, an escape into colour and magic, into the convulsions of plot-driven storytelling and into the kinds of juxtapositions that seemed impossible in written fiction (though, ironically, these are exactly the things he would later accomplish in print with *Carnivalesque*).[6] If his description of this seems hyperbolic, it is worth noting that its context was a public interview at the Galway Film Fleadh, an audience biased by definition towards cinema to whom, with a storyteller's self-mythologising touch, Jordan described how he thought *The Past* was hobbled by concepts more at home in photography and cinema.[7] Of visual description's dominance within that novel, Jordan reflected on how he had been trying to force his fiction into a direction which it resisted, and that this was part of the experience that led him to filmmaking.[8] Elsewhere, he openly acknowledges that he has replaced writing novels with the act of writing and directing films for large portions of his career, this accounting in many ways for the long stretches of time between publications (for example, a decade passed between *Sunrise with Sea Monster* and *Shade*).⁹ Yet, even when undertaking directorial projects, Jordan thinks in literary terms. For instance, when seeking to depict early twentieth-century Dublin in *Michael Collins*, he claims he tried to recreate the city that Joyce described in *Dubliners*, *Portrait of the Artist* and *Ulysses* (a notion Jordan later attempts to *de*construct in *Mistaken*).¹⁰ Gradually, he came to realise that such an imaginative reconstruction was similar in scale to that which Joyce performed in Paris.¹¹

In recent years, Jordan's back catalogue has been reissued in handsome modern liveries. The work endures not on account of its author's success in cinema but because of the insightful, engaging sensibility Jordan offers against sweeping and richly conceived historical and imaginative backdrops, because of the psychological verisimilitude of his protagonists, and because of the sparse beauty of a prose style evoking, as much as anything else, the karst landscape of the Burren which his writing consistently revisits. Rooted in the wider physical situation of the island, the various crises of Irish history, politics and society which motivate Jordan's characters are closely linked to the author's depiction and use of recognisable settings, both rural and urban. For though Jordan writes from a contemporary perspective, from an Ireland which is part of a European and an international community, his work returns again and again to his native soil. Speaking in 2018 at the donation of his personal archive to the National Library in Dublin, Jordan was adamant that Ireland, as the place that had provided inspiration and support during his years as a novice writer and filmmaker, as well as the backdrop for his best-known films and fiction, would always be his home.¹² No wonder so that a reader coming afresh to Jordan's writing will often find, in the Ireland reflected here, a sense of humanity (and, indeed, humility) defined by generosity and surprise.

Throughout his career, Jordan has pursued a variety of subjects, tones and settings in his fiction which counterpoint his work in film. His early prose explores the familiar stylistic terrain of carefully paced Irish literary and historical fiction while, at the same time, it reconnoitres some of the more ambitious domains which his later writing will traverse. Beginning with the impressionistic and sombre stories of *Night in Tunisia* (for many readers as overt a tribute to Joyce's *Dubliners* as one might imagine),¹³ the development of Jordan's fiction more than rises to the challenge laid down by Seán O'Faoláin at the time that he possessed the potential to *become* an outstanding Irish author.[14] The ensuing critical reception of Jordan's writing has charted this development. Gerald Dawe, for instance, was exuberant upon assessing *The Past*, considering it on publication as among the standout debut novels of the previous ten years.[15] Shortly thereafter, and through an inventive if divisive blending of fantasy, science fiction and mainstream Irish realism, *The Dream of a Beast* crystallised Jordan's abilities as a craftsperson of ambiguous and unsettlingly delicate detail.[16] Though largely preoccupied with filmmaking during the 1990s and early 2000s, Jordan continued to refine his mature fictional voice by grappling with the ambiguities of Irish neutrality in *Sunrise with Sea Monster* and with questions of a mediative, fascinating and deeply compelling nature in the haunted house novel *Shade*.[17] In 2008, the editors of the *Companion to the British and Irish Short Story* saw fit to place Jordan alongside Anne Enright and Mary Dorcey as a writer who delves into the complications of money and urban living in the new Ireland.[18] While this assessment was based largely on the strength of *Night in Tunisia*, it anticipated the bold artistic rumination of the superlative *Mistaken* which was inspired not just by the author's relationship to Dublin across the decades but also by the creative tension between the Jordan who writes fiction and the Jordan who makes films which has echoed through the present study.[19]

One outlier in Jordan's development as a writer is *The Drowned Detective* (2016), which follows an English private investigator as he navigates both Mitteleuropean political intrigue and the dangerous temptations of marital infidelity. It was a novel that was poorly marketed, as the *New York Times* saw it, pitched to readers as a crime story with a romance angle but, instead, being more of a warped, long-form dream.[20] John Burnside in *The Guardian* was perhaps more attuned to the novel's intentional genre fluidity, laying out its shifts in territory from the car chases and betrayals of a fast-paced detective story, to the fantasies of a jealous and self-loathing husband, to the kind of ghost story Kafka might have written had he the inclination to dally with the genre.[21] While well received by *The Irish Times* in a review by novelist Eoin McNamee,[22] and generously blurbed by the likes of Richard Ford (who praised the deftness of the novel's noir elements, as well as the humanity of the central character),[23] *The Drowned Detective* did not achieve significant impact.

By contrast, the fantastical *Carnivalesque* offers an arresting and energising retort to how, as Jordan himself once put it, some of Irish writing's imaginative energy has drained away, with wild and daring flights of fantasy replaced by something more prosaic.[24] In many ways it is the best example of how, though the formal structure of his fiction remains largely conventional throughout his career, Jordan has displayed a growing concern with the question of genre. Through the character of Andy, now Dany, the reader comes to know not the dour realities of contemporary economic downturns but the secret history of a mythological race – the Tuatha Dé Danann – scattered by the turmoil of the Great Famine and forced to hide themselves and their inhuman abilities in the semi-wonderous spaces of carnival attractions.[25] In many ways *Carnivalesque* ranks with *The Dream of a Beast* as one of Jordan's most inventive and most misinterpreted fictions. Received mainly as a fantasy text – Kathy Sheridan, for instance, foregrounded Jordan's use of fictionalised fairy mythology and history[26] – *Carnivalesque* in fact deliberately destabilises genre divisions (even more so than, say, the predestination paradoxes of *Shade*) by drawing as much of its texture from science and science fiction as it does from mythology and fantasy. Characters frequently defy the laws of physics, while Jordan makes direct references to science fiction stories such as Philip K. Dick's 'The Father Thing' (1954). Though of course the novel's focus on flight as a metaphor for freedom is perhaps less surprising when one considers that Jordan began the book while recovering from injuring his leg when hit by a Dublin bus in 2013. As he told *The Irish Times*, he was confined to a wheelchair for several months after the accident, followed by a period on crutches, and so could not travel to meetings or direct movies.[27] In this case, to invert Eileen Battersby's famous comment about Jordan's career, filmmaking's loss was definitely fiction's gain.[28]

Though his earliest influences were primarily literary, Jordan has also been keen to point out that his mother and sisters are artists, and that he feels he shares with them a perception of freedom regarding visual art, one unconstrained by the weight of the Irish literary tradition.[29] Here, as elsewhere, he hints at what Australian novelist Gregory Day, in a particularly astute review of *Mistaken*, saw as Jordan's complex but understandable love/hate dynamic with the more soft-focus aspects of Irish literary history, one that links Jordan to another writer from a family of artists and, quite incongruously, the one most responsible for said literary tradition.[30] For Day, there is more than a touch of Yeats to *Mistaken* in particular. Jordan, says Day, permits Gerald and Kevin, as the two sundered halves of *Mistaken*'s artistic and spiritual whole, to enact – by accident as much as by design – a process not so dissimilar to the emotional and intellectual synthesis which Yeats termed 'unity of being'.[31] For Karl Miller too, the kind of opposites Yeats united could readily describe those Jordan attempts to balance in not just that novel but in his fiction overall, not just the conflicting literary and visual influences of his childhood but the disparity between the artistic and scientific, between parents and their children (particularly between fathers and sons), and between the tangled historical identities of Ireland and Britain.[32] Which is to say that in many of Jordan's books – in *The Past*, *Sunrise with Sea Monster*, *Shade*, *Mistaken* and *Carnivalesque* – duality occurs at the level on which Ireland and Irish culture itself is represented. The many dualities of the nation – the native and the British influences, the archipelagic and the continental, the folkloric and the modern, the mythic west and the commercialised east, the embrace of and rejection of the past, the simultaneous embrace of and rejection of the *present* – are all on display. More than that, however, Jordan's fiction offers versions of the modern Irish nation where realism is just a veneer for something more sublime, be that the many coincidences of *The Past*, the postcolonial biology of *The Dream of a Beast*, the ambiguous fabulism of *Sunrise with Sea Monster*, or the outright fantastical gyrations of *Carnivalesque*.

Jordan's artistic heritage elsewhere bleeds through in his claim to find significant pleasure in the sensual qualities of both visual and literary art, deeming sensory thinking to be more valuable and more profound than the analytical variety.[33] He has maintained in interviews that writing of this kind is a particularly Irish calling.[34] Indeed, he has consistently described the Ireland he came of creative age in as a literary culture, especially the obvious influences offered by early exposure to the Sligo of Yeats and the Dublin of Joyce.[35] He has often discussed the weight of precedent from under which an Irish writer must free themselves as they begin to reconnoitre this terrain, but he nonetheless believes – somewhat romantically – that the strength of imagination characteristic of Irish authors is more than equal to this challenge.[36] The Irish, he maintains, have never been empire builders in the traditional sense but instead have carved out realms of creativity and wit which, by virtue of the imaginative tools they bequeath to readers, allow for at least a partial redemption of the world (a metaphor dramatised, as we have seen, to varying degrees in work such as *The Dream of a Beast, Sunrise with Sea Monster* and *Carnivalesque*).[37] Lest one perceive a saviour complex, however, Jordan clearly remains realistic about his reputation as an author. He is cognisant and appreciative of the writers who have come after him, mentioning the likes of Colm Tóibín, Roddy Doyle and Pat McCabe in an interview with Marianne Brace, with that cohort in turn now succeeded by the subsequent waves of the Mike McCormacks and the Kevin Barrys, the Mary Costellos and Claire Keegans, the Sara Baumes and Lisa McInerneys, the Rob Doyles and Sally Rooneys.[38] All of whose work responds to the motivating impetus of the writer as Jordan describes it, the struggle to render one's experience in a manner engaging enough to merit being called literature.[39]

It is precisely this issue of literary worth or merit that underpins *Neil Jordan: Works for the Page*. One hopes that a convincing argument has been made in this volume for the value of Jordan's novels and short stories to readers and scholars alike. His fiction is not merely an interesting anecdote in discussions of his filmmaking but, far more enticingly, offers a largely unexplored realm of idiosyncratic engagement with Irish writing and modern Irish history as well as a sustained process of personal and artistic self-reflection by one of the country's best-known creative practitioners. From his thematically striking beginnings to his later experiments in subject and genre, Jordan's writing complements rather than competes with his better-known work for the screen. His stories and novels exist in a dialogue with Irish fiction over the last half century, at times an easy-going conversation, at others an insistent rejoinder to conventionality and curatorialism. Across his career, Jordan's fiction has displayed the recognisably Irish struggle for self-assertion on all levels – from language to character to publication context. His writing refreshes our perspectives about ourselves. It works in concert with his films to create new and multifaceted opportunities for those of us wishing to contemplate the repeating patterns of Irish history and identity. Therefore, at the conclusion of this study, we finally have our riposte to the question, 'Why study Neil Jordan's fiction?' and it is the most obvious answer of all: 'How could we ever not?'

Notes

INTRODUCTION

1. Eileen Battersby, 'One of God's Optimists', *The Irish Times*, 20 April 2004, *https://www.irishtimes.com/culture/one-of-god-s-optimists-1.1308785*, accessed 26 July 2020.
2. Georgie Evans, '9 Most Anticipated Books of 2017', *Cultured Vultures*, 12 January 2017, *https://culturedvultures.com/9-most-anticipated-books-of-2017/*, accessed 26 July 2020.
3. Fintan O'Toole, 'The Man Who Shot Michael Collins', *Independent on Sunday*, 3 November 1996, Magazine, p. 21.
4. D.J. Taylor, *A Vain Conceit: British fiction in the 1980s* (Oxford: Oxford University Press, 1989).
5. O'Toole, 'The Man Who Shot', p. 21.
6. John Banville, 'An Irish War of Independence', *The Observer*, 8 January 1995, p. 19; the categorisation of *The Dream of a Beast* as fantasy is Jordan's own description of the book. See Marianne Brace, 'Neil Jordan: The writing game', *The Independent*, 14 January 1995, Books, p. 27.
7. Colm Tóibín, *The Penguin Book of Irish Fiction* (London: Penguin, 2001), p. ix.
8. Seán O'Faoláin, 'Introduction', in Neil Jordan, *Night in Tunisia* (Dublin: Irish Writers Co-operative, 1976), p. 3.
9. Ibid., p. 4.
10. Neil Jordan, 'Imagining Otherwise', in Richard Kearney (ed.), *Across the Frontiers: Ireland in the 1990s* (Dublin: Wolfhound Press, 1988), p. 197.
11. Ibid.
12. Ibid.
13. Ibid.
14. John Wilson Foster, 'Irish Fiction 1965–1990', in Seamus Deane (ed.), *The Field Day Anthology of Irish Writing*, vol. 3 (Derry: Field Day Publications, 1990), p. 942; George O'Brien, 'The Aesthetics of Exile', in Liam Harte and Michael Parker (eds), *Contemporary Irish Fiction: Themes, tropes, theories* (London: Macmillan, 2000), p. 48; Gerry Smyth, *The Novel and the Nation: Studies in the new Irish fiction* (London: Pluto Press, 1997), p. 146; Roberta Gefter Wondrich, 'Exilic Returns: Self and history outside Ireland in recent Irish fiction', *Irish University Review*, vol. 30, no. 1, pp. 1–16; Robert Hogan, 'Old Boys, Young Bucks, and New Women: The contemporary Irish short story', in James F. Kilroy (ed.), *The Irish Short Story: A critical history* (Boston: Twayne, 1984), pp. 196–7.
15. Maria Pramaggiore, *Neil Jordan* (Urbana and Chicago: University of Illinois Press, 2008), p. 154.
16. Brace, 'Neil Jordan', p. 27.

17 Ruth Barton, 'Neil Jordan's Gothic Direction', *The Irish Times*, 9 August 2008, Review, p. 13.
18 Pramaggiore, *Neil Jordan*, p. 152.
19 Anonymous, 'Neil Jordan: Return to form', *Books Ireland*, vol. 183, February 1995, pp. 5–6.
20 Ibid.

CHAPTER 1. A WRITER WHO JUST HAPPENS TO MAKE MOVIES: NEIL JORDAN'S LITERARY LIFE

1 Emer and Kevin Rockett, *Neil Jordan: Exploring boundaries* (Dublin: The Liffey Press, 2003), pp. 3–16.
2 Cressida Connolly, 'Art of Darkness', *Irish Independent*, 8 May 2004, Weekend, p. 10.
3 Neil Jordan, 'The Day the Scales Fell from My Eyes', *The Guardian*, 14 May 2005, Review, p. 34; Neil Jordan in conversation with Gay Byrne, *The Meaning of Life with Gay Byrne*, broadcast 24 May 2009, produced and directed by Roger Childs.
4 Ciara Dwyer, 'Interview with the Fidgeter', *Irish Independent*, 9 January 2011, Living, p. 4.
5 John O'Mahony, 'Big Screen Visionary', *The Guardian*, 29 February 2000, Saturday, p. 6.
6 Rockett and Rockett, *Neil Jordan*, p. 3.
7 Neil Jordan in conversation with Gay Byrne.
8 Jordan, 'The Day the Scales Fell from My Eyes'.
9 Ibid.
10 Ibid.
11 O'Mahony, 'Big Screen'.
12 Dwyer, 'Interview with the Fidgeter'; Connolly, 'Art of Darkness'.
13 O'Mahony, 'Big Screen'.
14 Connolly, 'Art of Darkness'; Dwyer, 'Interview with the Fidgeter'.
15 Carole Zucker, *The Cinema of Neil Jordan: Dark carnival* (London: Wallflower Press, 2008), p. 81.
16 Dwyer, 'Interview with the Fidgeter'.
17 Jordan, 'The Day the Scales Fell From My Eyes'.
18 Ibid.
19 O'Mahony, 'Big Screen'; Connolly, 'Art of Darkness'.
20 Geraldine Bedell, 'Back to His Old Haunts', *The Observer*, 9 May 2004, Features, p. 17.
21 O'Mahony, 'Big Screen'.
22 Neil Jordan in conversation with Gay Byrne.
23 Ibid.
24 Ibid.
25 Jordan, 'The Day the Scales Fell from My Eyes'.
26 Ibid.
27 Ibid.
28 Neil Jordan, 'When We Were 10', *The Daily Telegraph*, 5 June 2004, Books, p. 8.
29 Neil Jordan in conversation with Gay Byrne.

30 Marianne Brace, 'Neil Jordan: The writing game', *The Independent*, 14 January 1995, Books, p. 27.
31 O'Mahony, 'Big Screen'.
32 Brace, 'Neil Jordan'.
33 Joe Jackson, 'Jordan Dares to Bare All', *Sunday Independent*, 9 May 2004, Review, p. 1.
34 Brace, 'Neil Jordan'.
35 Ibid.
36 Bedell, 'Back to His Old Haunts'.
37 Jordan, 'The Day the Scales Fell From My Eyes'.
38 Bedell, 'Back to His Old Haunts'.
39 Connolly, 'Art of Darkness'.
40 Mick Heaney, 'Murder He Wrote', *The Sunday Times*, 16 May 2004, Culture, p. 8.
41 O'Mahony, 'Big Screen', p. 6.
42 Guy Somerset, 'Neil Jordan: Film director and writer', *The Dominion Post*, 20 July 2004, n.p.
43 Jordan, 'The Day the Scales Fell From My Eyes'.
44 Ibid.
45 O'Mahony, 'Big Screen'.
46 Ibid.
47 Dwyer, 'Interview with the Fidgeter'; Kate Trainor, 'Neil Jordan – Prince of Darkness ... or Light?', *Univercity*, April 2003, www.univercity.com/april03/neiljordan.html, accessed 24 January 2005.
48 Dwyer, 'Interview with the Fidgeter'.
49 Ibid.
50 Ibid.
51 Jordan, 'The Day the Scales Fell from My Eyes'.
52 Ibid.
53 Ibid.
54 Ibid.
55 Brace, 'Neil Jordan'.
56 O'Mahony, 'Big Screen'.
57 Brace, 'Neil Jordan'.
58 O'Mahony, 'Big Screen'.
59 Ibid.
60 Fintan O'Toole, 'The Man who Shot Michael Collins', *Independent on Sunday*, 3 November 1996, Magazine, p. 21.
61 Jordan, 'The Day the Scales Fell From My Eyes'.
62 Neil Jordan, 'Imagining Otherwise', in Richard Kearney (ed.), *Across the Frontiers: Ireland in the 1990s* (Dublin: Wolfhound Press, 1988), p. 197.
63 Ibid.
64 Ibid.
65 Anna Simpson, 'Dark Secrets of the Psyche', *The Herald* (Glasgow), 16 June 2004, n.p.
66 Eileen Battersby, 'Return to the Fold', *The Irish Times*, 8 May 2004, Weekend, p. 5; Rockett and Rockett, *Neil Jordan*, p. 5.
67 Ibid.

68 Dwyer, 'Interview with the Fidgeter'.
69 Roberta Gefter Wondrich, 'Exilic Returns: Self and history outside Ireland in recent Irish fiction', *Irish University Review*, vol. 30, spring/summer 2000, pp. 1–16, at p. 14.
70 Ibid.
71 Dwyer, 'Interview with the Fidgeter'.
72 Ibid.
73 Heaney, 'Murder He Wrote'.
74 Caroline O'Doherty, 'Neil, an Artist of Many Identities', *Irish Examiner*, 8 January 2011, Weekend, pp. 28–9.
75 Rockett and Rockett, *Neil Jordan*, p. 4.
76 Peter Sheridan, 'The 40-Year-Old Thorn', *The Irish Times*, 28 January 2006, Weekend, p. 7; Rockett and Rockett, *Neil Jordan*, p. 16.
77 Sheridan, 'The 40-Year-Old Thorn'.
78 Ibid.
79 Ibid.
80 Ibid.
81 Jackson, 'Jordan Dares', p. 1.
82 Ibid.
83 Ibid.
84 Ibid.
85 O'Mahony, 'Big Screen'.
86 Caoimhe Fox, 'From Captain America's to Hollywood and Back', *Books Ireland*, vol. 367, May/June 2016, pp. 18–19.
87 Rockett and Rockett, *Neil Jordan*, p. 5.
88 Heaney, 'Murder He Wrote'.
89 Nicholas Wroe, 'Always Make Sure You Offend', *The Guardian*, 4 March 2000, Saturday, p. 11.
90 Ibid.
91 Dwyer, 'Interview with the Fidgeter'.
92 Ibid.
93 Ibid.
94 Ibid.
95 Claire Squires, 'Novelistic Production and the Publishing Industry in Britain and Ireland', in Brian Shaffer (ed.), *A Companion to the British and Irish Novel 1945–2000* (Oxford: Blackwell, 2005), p. 178.
96 Rockett and Rockett, *Neil Jordan*, p. 5; Heather Ingman, *A History of the Irish Short Story* (Cambridge: Cambridge University Press, 2009), p. 213.
97 Rockett and Rockett, *Neil Jordan*, p. 5.
98 Ibid., p. 9.
99 Ibid., p. 5.
100 Ibid., p. 6.
101 Ibid.
102 O'Toole, 'The Man Who Shot'.
103 Colm Tóibín, 'The *In Dublin* Interview: Neil Jordan talks with Colm Tóibín', *In Dublin*, vol. 152, 29 April 1982, p. 18.

104 Rockett and Rockett, *Neil Jordan*, p. 10.
105 Ibid., p. 31.
106 Neil Jordan, *Shade* (London: John Murray, 2004), p. 274.
107 Ibid., p. 267.
108 Somerset, 'Neil Jordan', p. 10.
109 Brace, 'Neil Jordan'.
110 Tasha Robinson, 'Neil Jordan', *AV Club*, 16 April 2003, *https://www.avclub.com/neil-jordan-1798208312*, accessed 30 December 2020.
111 Neil Jordan in conversation with Gay Byrne.
112 Ibid.
113 Ruth Barton, *Jim Sheridan: Framing the nation* (Dublin: Liffey Press, 2002), p. 3; Liam Harte and Michael Parker, 'Introduction', in Liam Harte and Michael Parker (eds), *Contemporary Irish Fiction: Themes, tropes, and theories* (London: Palgrave, 2000), p. 3.
114 Neil Jordan, *Michael Collins: Screenplay and film diary* (New York: Vintage, 1996), p. 23.
115 Robert O'Byrne, 'The Strong, Silent Type?', *The Irish Times*, 14 January 1995, p. A2; Jordan, *Michael Collins*, p. 14.
116 O'Byrne, 'Strong, Silent Type'; Jordan, *Michael Collins*, p. 14.
117 Neil Jordan in conversation with Gay Byrne.
118 Maeve Quigley, 'Neil Jordan', *Fortnight*, vol. 336, February 1995, p. 38.
119 Neil Murphy, *Irish Fiction and Postmodern Doubt* (New York: Edwin Mellen, 2004).
120 Ibid., p. 227.
121 Maurice Harmon, 'The Era of Inhibitions', in Masaru Sekine (ed.), *Irish Writers and Society at Large* (Buckinghamshire: Colin Smythe, 1985), pp. 31–41.
122 Brad Kent, 'Review of *John McGahern: From the local to the universal* by Eamon Maher', *Canadian Journal of Irish Studies*, vol. 30, no. 2, fall 2004, p. 74; Lori Rogers, *Feminine Nation: Performance, gender, and resistance in the works of John McGahern and Neil Jordan* (Lanham, MD: University Press of America, 1998).
123 Christina Hunt Mahony, *Contemporary Irish Literature: Transforming tradition* (New York: St Martin's Press, 1998), p. 242.
124 Richard Kearney, *Transitions: Narratives in Irish culture* (Dublin: Wolfhound Press, 1988), p. 88.
125 Ibid.
126 James M. Cahalan, *The Irish Novel: A critical history* (Dublin: Gill & Macmillan, 1988), p. 301.
127 Peter Fallon and Seán Golden (eds), *Soft Day: A miscellany of contemporary Irish writing* (Dublin: Wolfhound Press, 1980).
128 Ibid.
129 Jordan, 'The Day the Scales Fell From My Eyes'.
130 Jordan, 'Imagining Otherwise', p. 198.
131 Jordan, 'The Day the Scales Fell From My Eyes'.
132 Neil Jordan in conversation with Gay Byrne.
133 Ibid.

134 Maria Pramaggiore, 'The Celtic Blue Note: Jazz in Neil Jordan's *Night in Tunisia*, *Angel*, and *The Miracle*', *Screen*, vol. 39, no. 3, September 1989, p. 272.
135 Ingman, *Irish Short Story*, p. 190.
136 Connolly, 'Art of Darkness'.
137 Pramaggiore, 'Celtic Blue Note', p. 5.
138 Derek Hand, *A History of the Irish Novel* (Cambridge: Cambridge University Press, 2011), p. 267.
139 Ingman, *Irish Short Story*, p. 217.
140 Wondrich, 'Exilic Returns', p. 7.
141 For more on Jordan's thoughts about Joyce's influence, see Ferdia Mac Anna, 'The Dublin Renaissance: An essay on modern Dublin and Dublin writers', *The Irish Review*, vol. 10, spring 1991, pp. 14–30, at p. 19.
142 Roberta Gefter Wondrich, 'Survivors of Joyce: Joycean images and motifs in some contemporary Irish fiction', *Studies*, vol. 90, no. 358, summer 2001, pp. 197–206, at p. 198.
143 Connolly, 'Art of Darkness'.
144 Rockett and Rockett, *Neil Jordan*, p. 4.
145 Denise Clarke, 'Jordan Reveals Yeats' Influence on His New Movie', *Irish Independent*, 25 July 2009, *www.independent.ie/entertainment/film-cinema/jordan-reveals-yeats-infulence-on-his-new-movie-1786736.html*, accessed 26 July 2009.
146 Ibid.
147 Ibid.
148 Ibid.
149 Zucker, *The Cinema of Neil Jordan*, p. 3.
150 W.B. Yeats, 'Sailing to Byzantium', in *W.B. Yeats: The poems* (2nd edn), ed. Robert Finneran (New York: Scribner, 1997), p. 197.
151 W.B. Yeats, 'Supernatural Songs. VIII: Whence Had They Come', in *W.B. Yeats: The poems* (2nd edn), ed. Robert Finneran (New York: Scribner, 1997), p. 293.
152 W.B. Yeats, Epigraph to *Responsibilities*, in *W.B. Yeats: The poems* (2nd edn), ed. Robert Finneran (New York: Scribner, 1997), p. 99.
153 W.B. Yeats, 'In Memory of Eva Gore-Booth and Con Markiewicz', in *W.B. Yeats: The poems* (2nd edn), ed. Robert Finneran (New York: Scribner, 1997), p. 237.
154 W.B. Yeats, 'The Circus Animals' Desertion', in *W.B. Yeats: The poems* (2nd edn), ed. Robert Finneran (New York: Scribner, 1997), p. 355.
155 Kathleen Gallagher Winarski, 'Neil Jordan's *Miracle*', in James MacKillop (ed.), *Contemporary Irish Cinema: From* The Quiet Man *to* Dancing at Lughnasa (Syracuse: Syracuse University Press, 1999).
156 W.B. Yeats, 'Supernatural Songs. VIII: Whence Had They Come', in *W.B. Yeats: The poems* (2nd edn), ed. Robert Finneran (New York: Scribner, 1997), p. 293.
157 Michael Sragow, 'Beautiful Dreamer', *Salon*, 9 December 1999, *http://www.salon.com/ent/col/srag/1999/12/9/jordan*, accessed 23 March 2008.
158 Brace, 'Neil Jordan'; Jordan makes the same point again in *The Meaning of Life with Gay Byrne*.
159 Karen Jaehne, 'Interview with Neil Jordan on *The Butcher Boy*', *Film Scout*, *www.filmscouts.com/scripts/interview.cfm?ArticleCode=703*, accessed 17 November 2005.
160 Brace, 'Neil Jordan'; Bedell, 'Back to His Old Haunts'.

161 Neil Jordan in conversation with Gay Byrne.
162 Ibid.
163 Sragow, 'Beautiful Dreamer'.
164 Adrian Wootton, 'Interview with Neil Jordan, Ralph Fiennes and Stephen Woolley', *Guardian Unlimited*, 4 February 2000, republished at *www.ralphfiennes-jenniferlash.com/earev5i.htm*, accessed 17 June 2005.
165 Ibid.
166 Neil Jordan, *Sunrise with Sea Monster* (London: Chatto & Windus, 1994), p. 21.
167 Jordan. *Shade*, p. 269.
168 Rogers, *Feminine Nation*, p. 15.
169 O'Toole, 'The Man Who Shot'.
170 Val Nolan, 'If It Was Just Th'ol Book ...: A history of the John McGahern banning controversy', *Irish Studies Review*, vol. 19, no. 3, August 2011, pp. 261–79.
171 O'Toole, 'The Man Who Shot'.
172 Neil Jordan, 'A Rural Irony', *The Irish Times*, 17 June 1978, p. 13.
173 David Malcolm, *The British and Irish Short Story Handbook* (Oxford: Blackwell, 2012), p. 32.
174 John Wilson Foster, 'Neil Jordan: Night in Tunisia and other stories', in Seamus Deane (ed.), *The Field Day Anthology of Irish Writing*, vol. 3 (Derry: Field Day Publications, 1990), p. 1101.
175 Ingman, *Irish Short Story*, p. 213.
176 Ibid.
177 Ibid.
178 Grace Tighe Ledwidge, 'Netherworld: London in John McGahern's fiction', in Tom Herron (ed.), *Irish Writing London. Volume 2: Post-War to the Present* (London: Bloomsbury, 2013), n.p.
179 John McGahern, 'Wheels', in *John McGahern: The collected stories* (London: Faber, 1992), p. 8.
180 Eamon Maher, 'Circles and Circularity in the Writings of John McGahern', *Nordic Irish Studies*, vol. 4, 2005, p. 158.
181 Jordan, 'Imagining Otherwise', p. 198.
182 Pramaggiore, 'Celtic Blue Note', p. 153.
183 Battersby, 'Return to the Fold'.
184 Robinson, 'Neil Jordan'.
185 Neil Jordan in conversation with Gay Byrne.
186 Jordan, *Michael Collins*, p. 13.
187 O'Toole, 'The Man Who Shot', p. 21.
188 Ibid.

CHAPTER 2. THE ENDING OF THE DAY BRINGS RELEASE: *NIGHT IN TUNISIA*

1 Michael Dwyer, 'Neil Jordan in Conversation with Michael Dwyer', *The Fleadh Papers*, vol. 3, 1997, p. 1.
2 Ibid.
3 Richard Kearney, *Transitions: Narratives in Irish culture* (Dublin: Wolfhound Press, 1988), p. 179.

4 Guy Somerset, 'The Irish Rover', *The Dominion Post* (Wellington), 17 July 2004, Books, p. 10.
5 Heather Ingman, *A History of the Irish Short Story* (Cambridge: Cambridge University Press, 2009), p. 184.
6 Adrian Vale, 'Short Stories', *The Irish Times*, 19 February 1977, p. 8.
7 Joe Jackson, 'Jordan Dares To Bare All', *Sunday Independent*, 9 May 2004, Review, p. 1.
8 Barry Egan, 'Jordan Stars in His Own Silent Movie', *Sunday Independent*, 30 September 2007, Living, p. 4.
9 Vale, 'Short Stories'.
10 Kate Cruise O'Brien, 'The Long and the Short', *The Irish Times*, 4 August 1979, p. 11.
11 Caroline Walsh, 'Return of a Native', *The Irish Times*, 21 December 1976, p. 8.
12 Gerald Dawe, 'Writers from the South of Ireland. 4: Neil Jordan', *Fortnight*, vol. 178, October 1980, p. 19.
13 Ibid.
14 Ibid., p. 20.
15 Neil Jordan, 'Imagining Otherwise', in Richard Kearney (ed.), *Across the Frontiers: Ireland in the 1990s* (Dublin: Wolfhound Press, 1988), p. 197.
16 Ibid.
17 Walsh, 'Return'.
18 Ibid.
19 Seán O'Faoláin, 'Introduction', in Neil Jordan, *Night in Tunisia* (Dublin: Irish Writers' Co-operative, 1976), p. i.
20 Emer and Kevin Rockett, *Neil Jordan: Exploring boundaries* (Dublin: Liffey Press, 2003), p. 6.
21 Kathleen Gallagher Winarski, 'Neil Jordan's *Miracle*', in James MacKillop (ed.), *Contemporary Irish Cinema: From* The Quiet Man *to* Dancing at Lughnasa (Syracuse: Syracuse University Press, 1999), pp. 98–108.
22 No author identified, 'An Irishman's Diary', *The Irish Times*, 7 December 1979, p. 13.
23 Ibid.
24 Eileen Battersby, 'Return to the Fold', *The Irish Times*, 8 May 2004, Weekend, p. 5.
25 John O'Mahony, 'Big Screen Visionary', *The Guardian*, 29 February 2000, Saturday, p. 6.
26 Mark Hemry (ed.), *Chasing Danny Boy: Powerful stories of Celtic Eros* (San Francisco: Palm Drive Publishing, 1999).
27 'Tool', *OED Online*, Oxford University Press, March 2014. Web. 8 April 2014.
28 Jordan, 'Imagining Otherwise', p. 199.
29 Christina Hunt Mahony, *Contemporary Irish Literature: Transforming tradition* (New York: St Martin's Press, 1998), p. 239.
30 Ibid., p. 240; John Wilson Foster, 'Neil Jordan: Night in Tunisia and other stories', in Seamus Deane (ed.), *The Field Day Anthology of Irish Writing*, vol. 3 (Derry: Field Day Publications, 1990), p. 1101.
31 David Malcolm and Cheryl Alexander Malcolm, *The Companion to the British and Irish Short Story* (Oxford: Blackwell, 2008), p. 274.
32 O'Faoláin, 'Introduction', p. i.

33 Foster, 'Neil Jordan', p. 1101.
34 Ibid.
35 Mahony, *Contemporary Irish Literature*, p. 240.
36 Rockett and Rockett, *Neil Jordan*, p. 5.
37 O'Mahony, 'Big Screen', p. 6.
38 Ibid.
39 Marguerite Pernot-Deschamps, *The Fictional Imagination of Neil Jordan, Irish Writer and Film Maker: A Study of Literary Style* (New York: Edwin Mellen, 2009), p. 87.
40 Malcolm and Malcolm, *British and Irish Short Story*, p. 274.
41 Ibid.
42 Rockett and Rockett, *Neil Jordan*, p. 58.
43 Mahony, *Contemporary Irish Literature*, p. 242.
44 Samuele Grassi, 'Father's in a Coma: Father–son relationships in Neil Jordan's fiction', *Estudios Irlandeses*, vol. 3, 2008, p. 110.
45 Ibid.
46 Mahony, *Contemporary Irish Literature*, p. 240.
47 Neil Jordan, 'Night in Tunisia', in *The Field Day Anthology of Irish Writing*, vol. 3 (Derry: Field Day Publications, 1990), pp. 1101–6.
48 Neil Jordan, *Night in Tunisia* (London: John Murray, 2004); Neil Jordan, 'Night in Tunisia', in *A Neil Jordan Reader* (New York: Vintage International, 1993), pp. 33–49.
49 Fintan O'Toole, 'The Man Who Shot Michael Collins', *Independent on Sunday*, 3 November 1996, Magazine, p. 21.
50 Ibid.
51 Jordan's novel *The Ballad of Lord Edward and Citizen Small* was published as the manuscript for this book was being completed in 2021.
52 Neil Jordan, 'Interview with Colm Tóibín', *In Dublin*, vol. 152, 29 April 1982, p. 16.
53 Grassi, 'Father's in a Coma', p. 111.
54 Jordan, 'Interview with Colm Tóibín', p. 17.
55 Ibid.
56 Richard Haslam, 'Neil Jordan and the ABC of Narratology: "Stories to do with love are mathematical"', *New Hibernia Review*, vol. 3, no. 2, summer 1999, pp. 36–55, at p. 40.
57 Mahony, *Contemporary Irish Literature*, p. 242.
58 Ibid.
59 O'Toole, 'The Man Who Shot', p. 20.
60 Jordan, 'Interview with Colm Tóibín', p. 18.
61 Neil Jordan, *The Past* (London: Jonathan Cape, 1980), p. 15.

CHAPTER 3. MAKING SENSE OF THE PRESENT: LOOKING TO *THE PAST*

1 Eileen Battersby, 'Return to the Fold', *The Irish Times*, 8 May 2004, Weekend, p. 5.
2 Ibid.
3 Gerald Dawe, 'Writers from the South of Ireland. 4: Neil Jordan', *Fortnight*, vol. 178, October 1980, p. 20.
4 Battersby, 'Return to the Fold'.

5 Ibid.
6 D.J. Taylor, *A Vain Conceit: British fiction in the 1980s* (Oxford: Oxford University Press, 1989); Christina Hunt Mahony, *Contemporary Irish Literature: Transforming tradition* (New York: St Martin's Press, 1998), p. 128.
7 Battersby, 'Return to the Fold'.
8 Richard Kearney, *Transitions: Narratives in Irish culture* (Dublin: Wolfhound Press, 1988), pp. 98–9.
9 James M. Cahalan, *The Irish Novel: A critical history* (Dublin: Gill & Macmillan, 1988), p. 301.
10 Ibid.
11 Emer and Kevin Rockett, *Neil Jordan: Exploring boundaries* (Dublin: The Liffey Press, 2003), p. 62.
12 Ibid.
13 Marianne Brace, 'Neil Jordan: The writing game', *The Independent*, 14 January 1995, Books, p. 27.
14 Ibid.
15 The script for *Journal of a Hole* has never been published.
16 Thomas MacAnna, 'Nationalism from the Abbey Stage', in Robert O'Driscoll (ed.), *Theatre and Nationalism in Twentieth-century Ireland* (Toronto: University of Toronto Press, 1971), p. 91.
17 Ibid.
18 Jennifer Fisher, 'Interperformance: The live tableaux of Suzanne Lacy, Janine Antoni, and Marina Abramovic', *Art Journal*, vol. 56, no. 4, winter 1997, p. 28.
19 Oxford English Dictionary, s.v. 'id', def. 1, oed.com, accessed 10 July 2020.
20 Oxford English Dictionary, s.v., 'super ego', def 1, oed.com, accessed 10 July 2020.
21 Oxford English Dictionary, s.v., 'ego', def. 4, oed.com, accessed 10 July 2020.
22 Battersby, 'Return to the Fold'.

CHAPTER 4. TRANSFORMATIVE MYTH: INTERPRETING *THE DREAM OF A BEAST*
1 Tom Shore, 'Civil Wars', *New York Times Book Review*, 15 October 1995, p. 13.
2 Aubrey Dillon-Malone, 'Transmogrification', *Books Ireland*, vol. 79, December 1983, p. 230.
3 Anonymous, 'Neil Jordan's *The Dream of a Beast*', *Financial Times*, 22 October 1983, p. 25.
4 Christina Hunt Mahony, *Contemporary Irish Literature: Transforming tradition* (New York: St Martin's Press, 1998), p. 239.
5 Lori Rogers, 'In Dreams Uncover'd: Neil Jordan, *The Dream of a Beast*, and the Body-Secret', *Critique*, vol. 39, no. 1, fall 1997, pp. 48–54.
6 Lori Rogers, *Feminine Nation: Performance, gender, and resistance in the works of John McGahern and Neil Jordan* (Lanham, MD: University Press of America, 1998), pp. 106, 107.
7 Alain Chouinard, 'Water-sites in the Fiction and Cinema of Neil Jordan', *Wasafiri*, vol. 25, no. 2, June 2010, p. 73.
8 Matthew Ryan, 'Ourselves Alone: Solipsism in Neil Jordan's novels and films', *Bells: Barcelona English language and literature studies*, vol. 11, 2000, p. 191.

9   Patrick McCabe, '"1916 I think impossible to think about without thinking of Yeats and O'Casey": Public interview with Neil Jordan', in Seán Crosson and Werner Huber (eds), *Towards 2016: 1916 and Irish literature, culture & society* (Trier, Germany: WVT Publishers, 2015), pp. 229–54.
10 Dillon-Malone, 'Transmogrification', p. 230.
11 John Banville, 'An Irish War of Independence', *The Observer*, 8 January 1995, p. 19.
12 Roger McHugh, 'Beauty in the Beast', *Irish Press*, 12 November 1983, p. 9.
13 McCabe, '"1916 I think impossible"', pp. 229–54.
14 Neil Jordan in conversation with Gay Byrne, *The Meaning of Life with Gay Byrne*, broadcast 24 May 2009, produced and directed by Roger Childs.
15 Michael Sragow, 'Beautiful Dreamer', *Salon*, 9 December 1999, *http://www.salon.com/1999/12/09/jordan_3/*, accessed 15 March 2013.
16 Roberta Gefter Wondrich, 'Exilic Returns: Self and history outside Ireland in recent Irish fiction', *Irish University Review*, vol. 30, spring/summer 2000, p. 15.
17 John Somer and John J. Daly, 'Introduction', in John Somer and John J. Daly (eds), *The New Anchor Book of Irish Writing* (New York: Anchor, 2000), pp. xv–xvi.
18 Ibid.
19 Desmond O'Rawe, 'Origins and Orientations: An interview with Kevin Rockett, on Irish Film Studies', *Canadian Journal of Irish Studies*, vol. 29, no. 2, fall 2003, p. 59.
20 Rogers, *Feminine Nation*, p. 106.
21 O'Rawe, 'Origins and Orientations', p. 59.
22 Marianne Brace, 'Neil Jordan: The writing game', *The Independent*, 14 January 1995, Books, p. 27.
23 Eileen Battersby, 'Return to the Fold', *The Irish Times*, 8 May 2004, Weekend, p. 5.
24 McCabe, '"1916 I think impossible"', pp. 229–54.
25 Ibid.
26 Neil Jordan, 'Imagining Otherwise', in Richard Kearney (ed.), *Across the Frontiers: Ireland in the 1990s* (Dublin: Wolfhound Press, 1988), p. 198.
27 Ibid.
28 Emer and Kevin Rockett, *Neil Jordan: Exploring boundaries* (Dublin: The Liffey Press, 2003), p. 56.
29 Rogers, *Feminine Nation*, p. 126; Eileen Battersby, 'All that Glisters is Not Gold', *The Irish Times*, 29 September 2001, p. 41.
30 Anonymous, 'Review of *The Dream of a Beast* by Neil Jordan', *Gazette* (Montreal), 31 July 1993, Books, p. 13; McHugh, 'Beauty in the Beast'.
31 Steve Jenkins and Paul Taylor, 'Wolf at the Door', *Monthly Film Bulletin*, September 1984, pp. 264–5. Reprinted in Carole Zucker, *Neil Jordan: Interviews* (Jackson, MS: University Press of Mississippi, 2013), p. 49.
32 James Park, *Learning to Dream: The new British cinema* (London: Faber, 1984), p. 90.
33 Neil Jordan, 'Easter 2036', *Spoken Stories: Independence* (RTÉ Radio 1, 2021), *https://www.rte.ie/radio/radio1/clips/21912733/*, accessed 19 July 2021.
34 Jordan, 'Imagining Otherwise', p. 198.
35 Brace, 'Neil Jordan'.
36 Ibid.

37 Keith Hopper, 'Hairy on the Inside: Re-visiting Neil Jordan's *The Company of Wolves*', *Canadian Journal of Irish Studies*, vol. 29, no. 2, fall 2003, p. 18.
38 Michael Dwyer, 'Neil Jordan in Conversation with Michael Dwyer', *The Fleadh Papers*, vol. 3, 1997, p. 1.
39 Desmond O'Rawe, 'At Home with Horror: Neil Jordan's Gothic variations', *Irish Studies Review*, vol. 11, no. 2, 2003, p. 192.
40 Richard Haslam, 'Neil Jordan and the ABC of Narratology: "Stories to do with love are mathematical"', *New Hibernia Review*, vol. 3, no. 2, summer 1999, pp. 36–55, at p. 48.
41 Brace, 'Neil Jordan'.
42 Tzvetan Todorov, *The Fantastic: A structural approach to a literary genre* (trans. Richard Howard) (London: The Press of Case Western Reserve University, 1973), p. 25.
43 Stith Thompson, *The Folktale* (Berkeley: University of California Press, 1977), p. 8. Thompson defined the fairy tale as taking place in an unreal world lacking specific real-world coordinates or recognisable locations.
44 Maria Nikolajeva, 'Fairy Tale and Fantasy: From archaic to postmodern', *Marvels & Tales*, vol. 17, no. 1, 2003, p. 139.
45 Farah Mendlesohn, *Rhetorics of Fantasy* (Middletown, CT: Wesleyan University Press, 2008), p. 115.
46 Ibid.
47 Ibid.
48 Ibid.
49 Ibid., p. xxi.
50 Ibid., p. 115.
51 Brace, 'Neil Jordan'.
52 Sragow, 'Beautiful Dreamer'.
53 Adam Roberts, *The History of Science Fiction* (London: Palgrave, 2005), p. xii; Jack Fennell, *Irish Science Fiction* (Liverpool: Liverpool University Press, 2014), p. 6.
54 Roberts, *History of Science Fiction*, p. xiii.
55 Fennell, *Irish Science Fiction*, p. 7.
56 John Haffenden, 'Angela Carter', interview, in John Haffenden, *Novelists in Interview* (London: Methuen, 1985), p. 84.
57 Brace, 'Neil Jordan'.
58 Ibid.
59 Rockett and Rockett, *Neil Jordan*, p. 37.
60 Mendlesohn, *Rhetorics*, p. 136.
61 John Wilson Foster, *Cambridge Companion to the Irish Novel* (Cambridge: Cambridge University Press, 2006), p. 75.
62 Dillon-Malone, 'Transmogrification', p. 230.
63 Hopper, 'Hairy on the Inside', pp. 25, 17.
64 Ibid., p. 25.
65 Ibid., p. 17.
66 Rogers, 'In Dreams Uncover'd', p. 48.

67 Haslam, 'Neil Jordan', p. 44.
68 McHugh, 'Beauty in the Beast'.
69 Rogers, *Feminine Nation*, p. 107.
70 John Naish, 'A Novel Kind of Madness', *The Times*, 15 May 2004, pp. S3, 6.
71 Brian McIlroy, 'Irish Horror: Neil Jordan and the Anglo-Irish Gothic', in Steven Jay Schneider and Tony Williams (eds), *Horror International* (Detroit: Wayne State University Press, 2004), pp. 128–40.
72 Hopper, 'Hairy on the Inside', p. 17.
73 'Sam Stephenson', obituary, *The Times*, 22 November 2006, p. 68.
74 McHugh, 'Beauty in the Beast'.
75 W.B. Yeats, 'The Second Coming', in *W.B. Yeats: The poems* (2nd edn), ed. Robert Finneran (New York: Scribner, 1997), p. 190.
76 Mendlesohn, *Rhetorics*, p. 129.
77 Rogers, *Feminine Nation*, p. 106.
78 Neil Jordan, 'Beauty and the Beasts', *Time Out*, 13–19 September 1984. Reprinted in Carole Zucker, *Neil Jordan: Interviews* (Jackson, MS: University Press of Mississippi, 2013), p. 44.
79 Hopper, 'Hairy on the Inside', p. 18.
80 Haslam, 'Neil Jordan', p. 42.
81 Rockett and Rockett, *Neil Jordan*, p. 49.
82 Angela Carter, *The Bloody Chamber* (London: Victor Gollancz, 1979), pp. 110, 113.
83 Ibid., pp. 50, 52, 71.
84 Jordan, 'Beauty and the Beasts', pp. 40–1.
85 Sharon McCann, 'With Redundance of Blood: Reading Ireland in Neil Jordan's *The Company of Wolves*', *Marvels and Tales*, vol. 24, no. 1, 2010, p. 69.
86 Ibid., p. 70.
87 Ibid., pp. 70, 71.
88 Steve Jenkins and Paul Taylor, 'Wolf at the Door', *Monthly Film Bulletin*, September 1984, pp. 264–5. Reprinted in Carole Zucker, *Neil Jordan: Interviews* (Jackson, MS: University Press of Mississippi, 2013), p. 46.
89 Mario Falsetto, 'Conversation with Neil Jordan', *Personal Visions: Conversations with contemporary film directors* (Los Angeles: Silman-James Press, 2000), pp. 217–54. Reprinted in Carole Zucker, *Neil Jordan: Interviews* (Jackson, MS: University Press of Mississippi, 2013), see p. 11.
90 Ibid.
91 Jordan, 'Beauty and the Beasts', p. 41.
92 Jenkins and Taylor, 'Wolf at the Door', reprinted in Zucker, *Neil Jordan*, see p. 46.
93 Jordan, 'Beauty and the Beasts', p. 41.
94 Ibid.
95 Ibid.
96 Ibid.
97 Ibid.
98 Ibid.
99 Hopper, 'Hairy on the Inside', p. 21.

100 Jenkins and Taylor, 'Wolf at the Door', reprinted in Zucker, *Neil Jordan*, see p. 47.
101 Hopper, 'Hairy on the Inside', p. 17.
102 Rockett and Rockett, *Neil Jordan*, p. 37.
103 Maria Pramaggiore, *Neil Jordan* (Chicago: University of Illinois Press, 2008), p. 24.
104 Rockett and Rockett, *Neil Jordan*, p. 51.
105 Carter, *The Bloody Chamber*, p. 116.
106 Ibid., p. 110.
107 Pramaggiore, *Neil Jordan*, p. 25.
108 Ibid., p. 24.
109 Ibid., p. 25.
110 Ibid., p. 24.
111 Ibid.
112 Hopper, 'Hairy on the Inside', p. 20.
113 Chouinard, 'Water-sites', p. 73.
114 Jenkins and Taylor, 'Wolf at the Door', reprinted in Zucker, *Neil Jordan*, see p. 48.
115 Mendlesohn, *Rhetorics*, p. xiv.

CHAPTER 5. A PLACE WHERE EACH STATEMENT HAS TWO MEANINGS: *SUNRISE WITH SEA MONSTER*

1 Caroline Walsh, 'Return of a Native', *The Irish Times*, 21 December 1976, p. 8.
2 Ibid.
3 Richard Haslam, 'Neil Jordan and the ABC of Narratology: "Stories to do with love are mathematical"', *New Hibernia Review*, vol. 3, no. 2, summer 1999, pp. 36–55, at p. 39.
4 José Lanters, 'Nightlines by Neil Jordan', *World Literature Today*, vol. 70, no. 3, summer 1996, p. 692.
5 Terence Brown, *Ireland: A social and cultural history 1922–1985* (London: Fontana Press, 1985), p. 167.
6 Diarmaid Ferriter, *The Transformation of Ireland: 1900–2000* (London: Profile Books, 2004), p. 418.
7 Ibid.
8 Roberta Gefter Wondrich, 'Exilic Returns: Self and history outside Ireland in recent Irish fiction', *Irish University Review*, vol. 30, spring/summer 2000, p. 1.
9 Nicholas Wroe, 'Ireland's Rural Elegist', *The Guardian*, 5 January 2002, https://www.theguardian.com/books/2002/jan/05/fiction.books, accessed 28 July 2020.
10 Peter Guy, *As Mirrors Are Lonely: A Lacanian reading on the modern Irish novel* (Cambridge: Cambridge Scholars Publishing, 2014), p. 92.
11 Lanters, 'Nightlines', p. 692.
12 Mark Fisher, *The Weird and the Eerie* (London: Repeater Books, 2016), p. 11.
13 Ibid.
14 Ibid.
15 Ibid., p. 12.
16 Lanters, 'Nightlines', p. 692.
17 Fisher, *The Weird*, p. 12.
18 Ferriter, *Transformation*, p. 385.

19　Fisher, *The Weird*, p. 11.
20　Ibid., p. 68.
21　Ibid., p. 96.
22　Ibid., p. 61.
23　Patrick McCabe, '"1916 I think impossible to think about without thinking of Yeats and O'Casey": Public interview with Neil Jordan', in Seán Crosson and Werner Huber (eds), *Towards 2016: 1916 and Irish literature, culture & society* (Trier, Germany: WVT Publishers, 2015), pp. 229–54.
24　John O'Mahony, 'Big Screen Visionary', *The Guardian*, 29 February 2000, Saturday, p. 6.
25　Marianne Brace, 'Neil Jordan: The writing game', *The Independent*, 14 January 1995, Books, p. 27.
26　Ibid.
27　Ibid.
28　Neal G. Jesse, 'Contemporary Irish Neutrality: Still a singular stance', *New Hibernia Review*, vol. 11, no. 1, spring 2007, pp. 74–95, at p. 74.
29　John Redmond, *House of Commons Debates*, 15 September 1914, vol. 55, col. 912.
30　Gefter Wondrich, 'Exilic Returns', p. 6.
31　Robert Cole, *Propaganda, Censorship and Irish Neutrality in the Second World War* (Edinburgh: Edinburgh University Press, 2006), p. 46.
32　Fisher, *The Weird*, p. 110.
33　Elizabeth Bowen, Interview in *The Bell*, vol. 4, no. 6, September 1942, pp. 420–6, 435.
34　Keith Hopper, 'Hairy on the Inside: Re-visiting Neil Jordan's *The Company of Wolves*', *Canadian Journal of Irish Studies*, vol. 29, no. 2, fall 2003, p. 17.
35　See Ronan Fanning, 'Irish Neutrality: An historical review', *Irish Studies in International Affairs*, vol. 1, no. 3, 1982, pp. 27–38, at p. 27.
36　Geoffrey Roberts, 'Three Narratives of Neutrality: Historians and Ireland's war', in Brian Girvin and Geoffrey Roberts (eds), *Ireland and the Second World War: Politics, society and remembrance* (Dublin: Four Courts Press, 2000), pp. 165–79, at p. 179.
37　Fanning, 'Irish Neutrality', p. 27.
38　Ferriter, *Transformation*, p. 358.
39　Jesse, 'Contemporary Irish Neutrality', p. 75.
40　Brown, *Ireland*, p. 172.
41　'The back door to Britain' was one of several sensationalist headlines utilised by the *Daily Mail* in reference to Irish neutrality during 1940.
42　Ronan Fanning, *Independent Ireland* (Dublin: Helicon, 1983), p. 121.
43　Fisher, *The Weird*, p. 12.
44　Brown, *Ireland*, p. 141.
45　Fisher, *The Weird*, p. 77.
46　Ibid., p. 61.
47　See Brown, *Ireland*, p. 176.
48　Gefter Wondrich, 'Exilic Returns', p. 7.
49　John Banville, 'Physics and Fiction: Order from chaos', *New York Times*, 21 April 1985, Section 7, p. 1.

50 Katherine Ebury, *Modernism and Cosmology: Absurd lights* (London: Palgrave, 2014), p. 72.
51 Brown, *Ireland*, p. 148.
52 Alok Jha, 'What is Heisenberg's Uncertainty Principle?', *The Guardian*, 10 November 2013, *https://www.theguardian.com/science/2013/nov/10/what-is-heisenbergs-uncertainty-principle*, accessed 2 December 2019.
53 Richard Alan Schwartz, 'Cybernetics and Science Fiction' (review of *The Soft Machine: Cybernetic fiction* by David Porush), *Science Fiction Studies*, vol. 12, no. 3, November 1985, p. 333.
54 Ibid.
55 Banville, 'Physics'.
56 Ibid.
57 Ibid.
58 Ibid.
59 Jha, 'Heisenberg's Uncertainty Principle'.
60 Ibid.

CHAPTER 6. OBSERVATION IS ALL I AM: NARRATION AND RECURRENCE IN *SHADE*

1 Gerald Dawe, 'Writers from the South of Ireland. 4: Neil Jordan', *Fortnight*, vol. 178, October 1980, p. 19.
2 Ibid.
3 Ibid.
4 Bron Sibree, 'Ireland of Lost Souls', *The Daily Telegraph* (Sydney, Australia), 21 August 2004.
5 Ibid.
6 Ibid.
7 Anne Lucey, 'Jordan Wins Writers' Award at Listowel for Novel "Shade"', *The Irish Times*, 2 June 2005, p. 20.
8 Alan Wall, 'Impossible Deadlines', *The Guardian*, 22 May 2004, Reviews, p. 28.
9 Fiona Foster, 'My Spooky Colleen', *Globe and Mail*, 17 July 2004, p. D3.
10 Lucy McDiarmid, 'An Estuary Child', *Times Literary Supplement*, 21 May, 2004, p. 20.
11 Ibid.
12 Samuel Beckett, 'Dante ... Bruno. Vico.. Joyce', in *Our Exagmination Round his Factification for Incamination of Work in Progress* (Paris: Shakespeare & Company, 1929), pp. 3–22.
13 W.B. Yeats, 'To a Shade', in *W.B. Yeats: The poems* (2nd edn), ed. Robert Finneran (New York: Scribner, 1997), p. 109.
14 W.B. Yeats, 'In Memory of Eva Gore-Booth and Con Markiewicz', in *W.B. Yeats: The poems* (2nd edn), ed. Robert Finneran (New York: Scribner, 1997), p. 237.
15 Ibid.
16 Yeats, 'To a Shade'.
17 Ibid.
18 See, for example, Brian O'Nolan to William Saroyan in a letter dated 14 February 1940. Reprinted in Flann O'Brien, *The Third Policeman* (London: Flamingo Modern Classics, 1993), p. 207.

19 Keith Hopper, *Flann O'Brien: A portrait of the artist as a young post-modernist*, 2nd edn (Cork: Cork University Press, 2009), p. 36.
20 Geraldine Bedell, 'Back to His Old Haunts', *The Observer*, 9 May 2004, Features, p. 17.
21 Ibid.
22 Ibid.
23 Neil Jordan in conversation with Gay Byrne, *The Meaning of Life with Gay Byrne*, broadcast 24 May 2009, produced and directed by Roger Childs.
24 Ibid.
25 Ibid.
26 Ibid.
27 Ibid.
28 Ibid.
29 Ibid.
30 Marianne Brace, 'Neil Jordan: The writing game', *The Independent*, 14 January 1995, Books, p. 27.
31 See Eamon Delaney, 'Celtic Dreamer', interview with Neil Jordan, *Publishers Weekly*, 22 November 2004, p. 33.
32 Wall, 'Impossible Deadlines'.
33 Neil Jordan in conversation with Gay Byrne.
34 Ibid.

CHAPTER 7. JORDAN'S FILM STORIES: THE UNCOLLECTED COLLECTION

1 'She: An Unfinished Story', in Andrew Carpenter and Peter Fallon (eds), *The Writers: A sense of Ireland* (Dublin: The O'Brien Press, 1980), pp. 79–80; 'Remote Control', in Colm Tóibín (ed.), *New Writing from Ireland: A Soho Square anthology* (London: Bloomsbury, 1993), pp. 56–61; 'The Berkeley Complex', in *Zoetrope: All story*, vol. 7, no. 4, winter 2003, reprinted in David Marcus (ed.), *The Faber Book of Best New Irish Short Stories 2004–2005* (London: Faber & Faber, 2005), pp. 207–20.
2 Desmond O'Rawe, 'Review of *Neil Jordan: Exploring boundaries* by Emer Rockett and Kevin Rockett', *Fortnight*, June 2003.
3 See Neil Jordan, *Michael Collins: Screenplay and film diary* (New York: Vintage, 1996).
4 Gerry McCarthy, 'Taking a Shot at the Stage', *The Times*, 30 September 2001. DreamWorks SKG and Imagemovers, the respective production companies of Stephen Spielberg and Robert Zemeckis, were both attached to the *Borgia* project at different times. Neither resulted in a completed film.
5 Ibid.
6 Marianne Brace, 'Neil Jordan: The writing game', *The Independent*, 14 January 1995, Books, p. 27.
7 Photograph of Neil Jordan was by Mike Bunn. Published in Carpenter and Fallon, *The Writers*.
8 Neil Jordan, 'Travellers Outline', Neil Jordan Papers, Manuscript Accessions 4761, Box 2, National Library of Ireland.
9 Emer and Kevin Rockett, *Neil Jordan: Exploring boundaries* (Dublin: The Liffey Press, 2003), p. 9.

10 Philippe Pilard, *Neil Jordan: Portrait* (France: CLC Productions/Cine Classic, 2006). The film comprises an extended interview with Jordan.
11 Rockett and Rockett, *Neil Jordan*, p. 11.
12 Keith Hopper, 'A Gallous Story and a Dirty Deed: Word and image in Neil Jordan and Joe Comerford's *Traveller*', *Irish Studies Review*, vol. 9, no. 2, 2001, pp. 179–91.
13 Ibid., p. 185.
14 Pilard, *Neil Jordan*.
15 Rockett and Rockett, *Neil Jordan*, p. 290.
16 Neil Jordan, 'The Artist and the Photographer', in William Burroughs (ed.), *New Writers and Writing 16* (London: John Calder, 1979).
17 Michael Dwyer, 'Neil Jordan in Conversation with Michael Dwyer', *The Fleadh Papers*, vol. 3, 1997, p. 1.
18 See David Simmons, 'Survival? 1981 Cork Film Festival', *Film Directions*, vol. 2, no. 17, March 1982, p. 15.
19 Dwyer, 'Neil Jordan', p. 5.
20 An earlier adaptation of the same material produced a 1955 film also titled *We're No Angels*, starring Humphrey Bogart, Peter Ustinov and Aldo Ray. That film was directed by Michael Curtiz and written by Ranald MacDougall. Jordan's picture, however, features extensive changes in content from Curtiz's.
21 Rockett and Rockett, *Neil Jordan*, p. 102.
22 Dwyer, 'Neil Jordan', p. 7.
23 Furthermore, while reference to 'Steve Woolley' may contribute to the story's blurring of the distinction between fact and fiction (Stephen Woolley is Jordan's long-time producing partner, having worked on twelve of Jordan's pictures to date), it also provides the final evidence linking 'Remote Control' to *High Spirits*, as *We're No Angels* was one of the few Jordan films that Woolley did not produce.
24 'Lines Written in Dejection' appears again in the 'Hollywood' section of Philip French and Ken Wlaschin's substantial 1993 anthology *The Faber Book of Movie Verse*. Of *High Spirits*, the anthology's biographical note on Jordan simply reads 'it was not a box office success'.
25 Pilard, *Neil Jordan*.
26 James Joyce, *Ulysses* (London: Penguin Books, 2000), p. 236.
27 Neil Jordan, 'Imagining Otherwise', in Richard Kearney (ed.), *Across the Frontiers: Ireland in the 1990s* (Dublin: Wolfhound Press, 1988), p. 197.
28 See: Neil Jordan, 'Foreword', in Michael MacCarthy Morrogh (ed.), *The Irish Century* (London: George Weidenfeld & Nicolson, 1996), p. 6.
29 Bron Sibree, 'Ireland of Lost Souls', *The Daily Telegraph* (Sydney, Australia), 21 August 2004.
30 Anna Simpson, 'Dark Secrets of the Psyche', *The Herald* (Glasgow), 16 June 2004.
31 McCarthy, 'Taking a Shot'.
32 Fintan O'Toole, 'Getting Back to the Story', *The Irish Times*, 12 October 2001, Arts, p. 12.
33 Mick Heaney, 'Murder He Wrote', *The Sunday Times*, 16 May 2004, Culture, p. 9.
34 Jordan, 'Imagining Otherwise', p. 197.

CHAPTER 8. BAD FAIRIES AND STRANGE, UNREALISED DESIRES: *MISTAKEN*, *CARNIVALESQUE* AND THE MANY NEIL JORDANS

1 Jem Poster, '*Carnivalesque* by Neil Jordan Review – Nights at the Circus', *The Guardian*, 8 March 2017, https://www.theguardian.com/books/2017/mar/08/carnivalesque-by-neil-jordan-review, accessed 10 December 2019.
2 Fintan O'Toole, '*Carnivalesque* review: Neil Jordan's cirque du supernatural', *The Irish Times*, 18 February 2017, https://www.irishtimes.com/culture/books/carnivalesque-review-neil-jordan-s-cirque-du-supernatural-1.2965586, accessed 16 December 2019.
3 Ibid.
4 Sue Leonard, 'Book Review: *Carnivalesque*', *Irish Examiner*, 15 April 2017, https://www.irishexaminer.com/ireland/book-review-carnivalesque-447979.html, accessed 16 December 2019.
5 Karl Miller, *Doubles: Studies in literary history* (Oxford: Oxford University Press, 1985), p. 209.
6 Ibid., p. 159.
7 Jeanett Shumaker, 'Uncanny Doubles: The fiction of Anne Enright', *New Hibernia Review*, vol. 9, no. 3, autumn 2005, p. 107.
8 Eithne Shortall, 'Film Director Neil Jordan's Latest Novel Is, in Part, a Love Letter to Dublin, the City that Shaped Him', *The Sunday Times*, 2 January 2011, Culture, pp. 12–13.
9 'Fantastika' being a 'convenient shorthand term employed and promoted by John Clute since 2007 to describe the armamentarium of the fantastic in literature as a whole, encompassing science fiction, fantasy, fantastic horror and their various subgenres'. See John Clute and David Langford, 'Fantastika', in John Clute, David Langford, Peter Nicholls and Graham Sleight (eds), *The Encyclopaedia of Science Fiction* (London: Gollancz, updated 5 May 2020), http://www.sf-encyclopedia.com/entry/fantastika, accessed 22 July 2020.
10 Caroline O'Doherty, 'Neil, an Artist of Many Identities', *Irish Examiner*, 8 January 2011, Weekend, pp. 28–9.
11 Edel Coffey, 'People Want to Know too Much about Me …', *Irish Independent*, 7 January 2011, Lifestyle.
12 Mark Fisher, *The Weird and the Eerie* (London: Repeater Books, 2016), p. 9.
13 Miller, *Doubles*, p. 21.
14 Ibid., p. viii.
15 Ibid., p. 21.
16 Ibid.
17 Ibid.
18 Ibid.
19 Leonard, 'Book Review: *Carnivalesque*'.
20 Ibid.
21 Ibid.
22 Anonymous, 'Neil Jordan – *Mistaken*', *Listowel Writers' Week*, 2 June 2011, https://writersweek.ie/neil-jordan-mistaken/, accessed 19 December 2019.
23 Ibid.

24 Kate Muir, 'It's Lovely, Just Lovely, To Be in Control', *The Times*, 1 January 2011, Saturday Review, p. 5.
25 Ibid.
26 Ibid.
27 Ibid.
28 Leonard, 'Book Review: *Carnivalesque*'.
29 Ibid.
30 Ibid.
31 Shortall, 'Film Director'.
32 Gay Byrne, Interview with Neil Jordan, *The Late Late Show*, RTÉ 1, 7 January 2011.
33 John Spain and Majella O'Sullivan, 'Jordan Swaps Movies for Novels to Take Home Top Literary Award', *Irish Independent*, 2 June 2011, p. 9.
34 John Connelly, *The View*, RTÉ1, 18 January 2011.
35 Anonymous, 'Neil Jordan Wins Top Literary Prize at Writer's Week', *Listowel Writers' Week*, 1 June 2011, https://writersweek.ie/neil-jordan-wins-top-literary-prize-at-writers-week/, accessed 19 December 2019.
36 O'Toole, '*Carnivalesque* review'.
37 Des Kenny, 'Des Kenny Reviews *Mistaken* by Neil Jordan', 26 May 2011, https://www.youtube.com/watch?v=szdebctgtVw&feature=player_embedded, accessed 29 May 2011.
38 Eileen Battersby, 'Neil Jordan, Great Irish Novelist', *The Irish Times*, 24 December 2011, Weekend, p. 13.
39 Ibid.
40 Ibid.
41 O'Toole, '*Carnivalesque* review'.
42 Gregory Day, 'Jordan Crosses the Dublin Divide', *The Age* (Melbourne), 12 March 2011, Life and Style, p. 39.
43 Shortall, 'Film Director'; Muir, 'It's Lovely'.
44 Battersby, 'Neil Jordan'.
45 Patrick McCabe, '"1916 I think impossible to think about without thinking of Yeats and O'Casey": Public interview with Neil Jordan', in Seán Crosson and Werner Huber (eds), *Towards 2016: 1916 and Irish literature, culture & society* (Trier, Germany: WVT Publishers, 2015), pp. 229–54.
46 Muir, 'It's Lovely'.
47 Ciara Dwyer, 'Interview with the Fidgeter', *Irish Independent*, 9 January 2011, Living, p. 4.
48 Ibid.
49 Day, 'Jordan'.
50 Shortall, 'Film Director'.
51 Anonymous, 'Neil Jordan – *Mistaken*'.
52 Muir, 'It's Lovely'.
53 Shortall, 'Film Director'; Muir, 'It's Lovely'.
54 Interview with Neil Jordan, *The Late Late Show*.
55 Ibid.
56 Shortall, 'Film Director'.

57 Ibid.
58 O'Doherty, 'Neil'.
59 Shortall, 'Film Director'.
60 Ibid.
61 Ibid.
62 Anonymous, 'Neil Jordan – *Mistaken*'.
63 Ibid.
64 John Boland, 'Neil's Rare Oul' Times', *Irish Independent*, 8 January 2011, Books.
65 O'Doherty, 'Neil'.
66 *The View*, RTÉ 1, 18 January 2011.
67 Boland, 'Neil's Rare Oul' Times'.
68 Neil Jordan, *Mistaken* (London: John Murray, 2011), p. 287.
69 Ibid.
70 Shortall, 'Film Director'.
71 Linda Morris, 'Pluck of the Irish', *The Sun Herald* (Sydney), 13 February 2011, Extra, p. 4.
72 Ibid.
73 Day, 'Jordan'.
74 Ibid.
75 Ibid.
76 O'Toole, '*Carnivalesque* review'.
77 Anonymous, '*Carnivalesque* by Neil Jordan', *Kirkus Reviews*, 1 April 2017, https://www.kirkusreviews.com/book-reviews/neil-jordan/carnivalesque/, accessed 16 December 2019.
78 O'Toole, '*Carnivalesque* review'.
79 John Banville, 'Fiction, History, Humour, Emotion: The best books of 2017', *The Irish Times*, 9 December 2017, https://www.irishtimes.com/culture/books/fiction-history-humour-emotion-the-best-books-of-2017-1.3311019, accessed 10 December 2019.
80 Poster, '*Carnivalesque*'.
81 Ibid.
82 O'Toole, '*Carnivalesque* review'.
83 Mandy Jackson-Beverly, '*Carnivalesque*', *New York Journal of Books*, May 2017, https://www.nyjournalofbooks.com/book-review/carnivalesque, accessed 16 December 2019.
84 Mikhail Bakhtin, *Problems of Dostoevsky's Poetics* (Minneapolis: University of Minnesota Press, 1984), pp. 122–3.
85 Poster, *Carnivalesque*.
86 Ibid.
87 O'Toole, '*Carnivalesque* review'.
88 Miller, *Doubles*, p. 30.
89 O'Toole, '*Carnivalesque* review'.
90 Timothy Morton, *The Ecological Thought* (Cambridge, MA: Harvard University Press, 2010), p. 45.
91 Timothy Morton, *Hyperobjects: Philosophy and ecology after the end of the world* (Minneapolis: University of Minnesota Press, 2013), p. 2.

92 Ibid., p. 1.
93 Poster, *Carnivalesque*.
94 Mikhail Bakhtin, *Rabelais and His World* (Bloomington, IN: Indiana University Press, 1968), p. 15.
95 Bakhtin, *Problems*, p. 122.
96 See Bakhtin, *Rabelais*, pp. 16, 96, 274.
97 Ibid., p. 274.
98 Bakhtin, *Problems*, p. 123.
99 Bakhtin, *Rabelais*, p. 74.
100 This text can be found in the 2018 Bloomsbury paperback edition of the novel.
101 Poster, *Carnivalesque*.
102 Miller, *Doubles*, p. 49.
103 Leonard, 'Book Review: *Carnivalesque*'.
104 Miller, *Doubles*, p. 49.
105 Ibid., p. 30.
106 Morton, *Hyperobjects*, p. 1.
107 Ibid., p. 62.
108 John Kenny, *John Banville* (Dublin: Irish Academic Press, 2009), p. 105.
109 Anonymous, '*Carnivalesque* by Neil Jordan'.

CONCLUSION

1 Gerry McCarthy, 'The End of the Affair', in Carole Zucker (ed.), *Neil Jordan Interviews* (Jackson, MS: University Press of Mississippi, 2013), p. 108; originally published in *Film West*, vol. 39, February 2000, pp. 12–15.
2 Ibid.
3 Tom Shore, 'Civil Wars', *New York Times Book Review*, 15 October 1995, p. 13.
4 John de Falbe, 'A Thick Celtic Mist', *The Spectator*, 5 May 2004, *www.spectator.co.uk/books/20915/a-thick-celtic-mist.thtml*, accessed 1 December 2005.
5 Michael Dwyer, 'Neil Jordan in Conversation with Michael Dwyer', *The Fleadh Papers*, vol. 3, 1997, p. 1.
6 Ibid.
7 Marianne Brace, 'Neil Jordan: The writing game', *The Independent*, 14 January 1995, Books, p. 27.
8 Ibid.
9 Maria Pramaggiore, *Neil Jordan* (Urbana and Chicago: University of Illinois Press, 2008), p. 151.
10 Neil Jordan, *Michael Collins: Screenplay and film diary* (New York: Vintage, 1996), p. 21.
11 Ibid.
12 Anna O'Donoghue, 'Oscar-Winning Director Neil Jordan Donates Archives to National Library of Ireland', *Irish Examiner*, 9 August 2018, *https://www.irishexaminer.com/lifestyle/celebrity/arid-30861095.html*, accessed 22 July 2020.
13 Jonathan Romney, 'Sweetness and Light', in Carole Zucker (ed.), *Neil Jordan Interviews* (Jackson, MS: University Press of Mississippi, 2013), p. 51; originally published in *City Limits*, 31 May–7 June 1990, pp. 16–17.

14 Seán O'Faoláin, 'Introduction', in Neil Jordan, *Night in Tunisia* (Dublin: Irish Writers' Co-operative, 1976), p. i.
15 Gerald Dawe, 'Writers from the South of Ireland. 4: Neil Jordan', *Fortnight*, vol. 178, October 1980, p. 20.
16 Romney, 'Sweetness', p. 51.
17 Geraldine Bedell, 'Back to His Old Haunts', *The Observer*, 9 May 2004, Features, p. 17; quoted on the back cover of the 2011 edition of *Mistaken*.
18 David Malcolm and Cheryl Alexander Malcolm, *The Companion to the British and Irish Short Story* (Oxford: Blackwell, 2008), p. 253.
19 Eileen Battersby, 'Neil Jordan, Great Irish Novelist', *The Irish Times*, 24 December 2010, https://www.irishtimes.com/culture/books/neil-jordan-great-irish-novelist-1.689240, accessed 1 May 2020.
20 Éric Lambé, 'The Filmmaker Neil Jordan Has a New Novel. It's Got a Missing Girl', *New York Times*, 3 July 2016, https://www.nytimes.com/2016/07/03/books/review/the-drowned-detective-by-neil-jordan.html, accessed 21 January 2020.
21 John Burnside, '*The Drowned Detective* by Neil Jordan review – surreal, haunting and constantly surprising', *The Guardian*, 27 February 2016, https://www.theguardian.com/books/2016/feb/27/the-dronwed-detective-by-neil-jordan-review, accessed 21 January 2020.
22 Eoin McNamee, '*The Drowned Detective* by Neil Jordan review: noir like no other', *The Irish Times*, 13 February 2016, https://www.irishtimes.com/culture/books/the-drowned-detective-by-neil-jordan-review-noir-like-no-other-1.2532566, accessed 21 January 2020.
23 Blurb on the cover of the first edition of the novel.
24 Bedell, 'Back to His Old Haunts'.
25 Jem Poster, '*Carnivalesque* by Neil Jordan Review – Nights at the Circus', *The Guardian*, 8 March 2017, https://www.theguardian.com/books/2017/mar/08/carnivalesque-by-neil-jordan-review, accessed 10 December 2019.
26 Kathy Sheridan, 'Neil Jordan: "Apparently I have a terrifying temper"', *The Irish Times*, 25 February 2017, https://www.irishtimes.com/culture/books/neil-jordan-apparently-i-have-a-terrifying-temper-1.2985150, accessed 14 December 2020.
27 Ibid.
38 Eileen Battersby, 'Strike the Father Dead: Eileen Battersby on a film maker's return to fiction', *The Irish Times*, 31 Dec 1994, Weekend, p. 8.
29 Neil Jordan, 'Imagining Otherwise', in Richard Kearney (ed.), *Across the Frontiers: Ireland in the 1990s* (Dublin: Wolfhound Press, 1988), p. 198.
30 Gregory Day, 'Jordan Crosses the Dublin Divide', *The Age* (Melbourne), 12 March 2011, Life and Style, p. 39.
31 Ibid.
32 Karl Miller, *Doubles: Studies in literary history* (Oxford: Oxford University Press, 1985), p. 223.
33 Neil Jordan, 'Interview with Colm Tóibín', *In Dublin*, vol. 152, 29 April 1982.
34 See for example Christopher Bray, 'A Writer's Life: Neil Jordan', *The Daily Telegraph*, 7 May 2005, p. 12.

35 Mario Falsetto, 'Conversation with Neil Jordan', *Personal Visions: Conversations with contemporary film directors* (Los Angeles: Silman-James Press, 2000), pp. 217–54. Reprinted in Carole Zucker, *Neil Jordan: Interviews* (Jackson, MS: University Press of Mississippi, 2013), see p. 30.
36 Ibid.
37 Ibid.
38 Brace, 'Neil Jordan'.
39 Ibid.

Bibliography

WORK BY NEIL JORDAN

Jordan, Neil, 'On Coming Home', *Irish Press*, 14 September 1974, p. 6

Jordan, Neil, *Night in Tunisia* (Dublin: Irish Writers' Co-operative, 1976); republished as *Night in Tunisia* (London: John Murray, 2004)

Jordan, Neil, 'A Rural Irony', *The Irish Times*, 17 June 1978, p. 13

Jordan, Neil, 'Word and Image', *Film Directions*, vol. 1, no. 2, 1978, pp. 10–11

Jordan, Neil, 'The Artist and the Photographer', in William Burroughs (ed.), *New Writers and Writing 16* (London: John Calder, 1979)

Jordan, Neil, *The Past* (London: Jonathan Cape, 1980)

Jordan, Neil, 'She: An unfinished story', in Andrew Carpenter and Peter Fallon (eds), *The Writers: A sense of Ireland* (Dublin: The O'Brien Press, 1980), pp. 79–80

Jordan, Neil, 'Beauty and the Beasts', *Time Out*, 13–19 September 1984; reprinted in Carole Zucker, *Neil Jordan: Interviews* (Jackson, MS: University Press of Mississippi, 2013), pp. 40–5

Jordan, Neil, 'Imagining Otherwise', in Richard Kearney (ed.), *Across the Frontiers: Ireland in the 1990s* (Dublin: Wolfhound Press, 1988), p. 197

Jordan, Neil, 'Remote Control', in Colm Tóibín (ed.), *New Writing from Ireland: A Soho Square anthology* (London: Bloomsbury, 1993), pp. 56–61

Jordan, Neil, *Sunrise with Sea Monster* (London: Chatto & Windus, 1994)

Jordan, Neil, *Michael Collins: Screenplay and film diary* (New York: Vintage, 1996)

Jordan, Neil, 'Foreword', in Michael MacCarthy Morrogh (ed.), *The Irish Century* (London: George Weidenfeld & Nicolson, 1996)

Jordan, Neil, 'The Berkeley Complex', in *Zoetrope: All story*, vol. 7, no. 4, winter 2003; reprinted in David Marcus (ed.), *The Faber Book of Best New Irish Short Stories 2004–2005* (London: Faber & Faber, 2005), pp. 207–20

Jordan, Neil, 'When We Were 10', *The Daily Telegraph*, 5 June 2004, Books, p. 8

Jordan, Neil, *Shade* (London: John Murray, 2004)

Jordan, Neil, 'The Day the Scales Fell from My Eyes', *The Guardian*, 14 May 2005, Review, p. 34

Jordan, Neil, *Mistaken* (London: John Murray, 2011)

Jordan, Neil, *The Drowned Detective* (London: Bloomsbury, 2016)

Jordan, Neil, *Carnivalesque* (London: Bloomsbury, 2017)

Jordan, Neil, *The Ballad of Lord Edward and Citizen Small* (Dublin: Lilliput Press, 2021)

Jordan, Neil, 'Easter 2036', *Spoken Stories: Independence* (RTÉ Radio 1, 2021)

FURTHER AND SECONDARY WORK

Anonymous, 'An Irishman's Diary', *The Irish Times*, 7 December 1979, p. 13

Anonymous, 'Neil Jordan's *The Dream of a Beast*', *Financial Times*, 22 October 1983, p. 25

Anonymous, 'Review of *The Dream of a Beast* by Neil Jordan', *Gazette* (Montreal), 31 July 1993, Books, p. 13

Anonymous, 'Neil Jordan: Return to form', *Books Ireland*, vol. 183, February 1995, pp. 5–6

Anonymous, 'Neil Jordan Wins Top Literary Prize at Writer's Week', *Listowel Writers' Week*, 1 June 2011, https://writersweek.ie/neil-jordan-wins-top-literary-prize-at-writers-week, accessed 19 December 2019

Anonymous, 'Neil Jordan – *Mistaken*', *Listowel Writers' Week*, 2 June 2011, https://writersweek.ie/neil-jordan-mistaken, accessed 19 December 2019

Anonymous, '*Carnivalesque* by Neil Jordan', *Kirkus Reviews*, 1 April 2017, https://www.kirkusreviews.com/book-reviews/neil-jordan/carnivalesque, accessed 16 December 2019

Bakhtin, Mikhail, *Rabelais and His World* (Bloomington, IN: Indiana University Press, 1968)

Bakhtin, Mikhail, *Problems of Dostoevsky's Poetics* (Minneapolis: University of Minnesota Press, 1984)

Banville, John, 'Physics and Fiction: Order from chaos', *New York Times*, 21 April 1985, Section 7, p. 1

Banville, John, 'An Irish War of Independence', *The Observer*, 8 January 1995, p. 19

Banville, John, 'Fiction, History, Humour, Emotion: The best books of 2017', *The Irish Times*, 9 December 2017, https://www.irishtimes.com/culture/books/fiction-history-humour-emotion-the-best-books-of-2017-1.3311019, accessed 10 December 2019

Barton, Ruth, *Jim Sheridan: Framing the nation* (Dublin: Liffey Press, 2002)

Barton, Ruth, 'Neil Jordan's Gothic Direction', *The Irish Times*, 9 August 2008, Review, p. 13

Battersby, Eileen, 'Strike the Father Dead: Eileen Battersby on a film maker's return to fiction', *The Irish Times*, 31 December 1994, Weekend, p. 8

Battersby, Eileen, 'All that Glisters is Not Gold', *The Irish Times*, 29 September 2001, p. 41

Battersby, Eileen, 'One of God's Optimists', *The Irish Times*, 20 April 2004, https://www.irishtimes.com/culture/one-of-god-s-optimists-1.1308785, accessed 26 July 2020

Battersby, Eileen, 'Return to the Fold', *The Irish Times*, 8 May 2004, Weekend, p. 5

Battersby, Eileen, 'Neil Jordan, Great Irish Novelist', *The Irish Times*, 24 December 2011, Weekend, p. 13

Beckett, Samuel, 'Dante … Bruno. Vico.. Joyce', in *Our Exagmination Round His Factification for Incamination of Work in Progress* (Paris: Shakespeare & Company, 1929), pp. 3–22

Bedell, Geraldine, 'Back to His Old Haunts', *The Observer*, 9 May 2004, Features, p. 17

Black, Barbara, 'Short and Nasty Notes from Underground', *Gazette* (Montreal), 31 July 1993, Books, p. 13

Boland, John, 'Neil's Rare Oul' Times', *Irish Independent*, 8 January 2011, Books

Bolger, Dermot, 'Introduction', in Dermot Bolger (ed.), *The Picador Book of Contemporary Irish Fiction* (London: Picador, 1993), pp. xi–xii

Bowen, Elizabeth, Interview in *The Bell*, vol. 4, no. 6, September 1942, pp. 420–6

Brace, Marianne, 'Neil Jordan: The writing game', *The Independent*, 14 January 1995, Books, p. 27

Bray, Christopher, 'A Writer's Life: Neil Jordan', *The Daily Telegraph*, 7 May 2005, p. 12

Brown, Terence, *Ireland: A social and cultural history 1922–1985* (London: Fontana Press, 1985)

Burnside, John, '*The Drowned Detective* by Neil Jordan review – surreal, haunting and constantly surprising', *The Guardian*, 27 February 2016, *https://www.theguardian.com/books/2016/feb/27/the-dronwed-detective-by-neil-jordan-review*, accessed 21 January 2020

Byrne, Gay, Neil Jordan in conversation with Gay Byrne, *The Meaning of Life with Gay Byrne*, broadcast 24 May 2009, produced and directed by Roger Childs

Byrne, Gay, Interview with Neil Jordan, *The Late Late Show*, RTÉ 1, 7 January 2011

Cahalan, James M., *The Irish Novel: A critical history* (Dublin: Gill & Macmillan, 1988)

Carter, Angela, *The Bloody Chamber* (London: Victor Gollancz, 1979)

Chouinard, Alain, 'Water-sites in the Fiction and Cinema of Neil Jordan', *Wasafiri*, vol. 25, no. 2, June 2010, pp. 73–7

Clarke, Denise, 'Jordan Reveals Yeats' Influence on His New Movie', *Irish Independent*, 25 July 2009, *www.independent.ie/entertainment/film-cinema/jordan-reveals-yeats-infulence-on-his-new-movie-1786736.html*, accessed 26 July 2009

Clute, John and Langford, David, 'Fantastika', in John Clute, David Langford, Peter Nicholls and Graham Sleight (eds), *The Encyclopaedia of Science Fiction* (London: Gollancz, updated 5 May 2020), *http://www.sf-encyclopedia.com/entry/fantastika*, accessed 22 July 2020

Coffey, Edel, 'People Want to Know Too Much about Me ... ', *Irish Independent*, 7 January 2011, Lifestyle

Cole, Robert, *Propaganda, Censorship and Irish Neutrality in the Second World War* (Edinburgh: Edinburgh University Press, 2006)

Comiskey, Ray, 'Neil Jordan: Future intense perfect', *The Irish Times*, 6 September 1986, p. A9

Connolly, Cressida, 'Art of Darkness', *Irish Independent*, 8 May 2004, Weekend, p. 10

Coogan, Tim Pat, *The Man Who Was Ireland* (London: HarperCollins, 1993)

Coppola, Francis Ford (dir.), *The Cotton Club*, Totally Independent Productions/American Zoetrope/Producers Sales Organization, USA, 1984

Cruise O'Brien, Kate, 'The Long and the Short', *The Irish Times*, 4 August 1979, p. 11

Dawe, Gerald, 'Writers from the South of Ireland 4: Neil Jordan', *Fortnight*, vol. 178, October 1980, p. 19

Day, Gregory, 'Jordan Crosses the Dublin Divide', *The Age* (Melbourne), 12 March 2011, Life and Style, p. 39

De Falbe, John, 'A Thick Celtic Mist', *Spectator*, 5 May 2004, *www.spectator.co.uk/books/20915/a-thick-celtic-mist.thtml*, accessed 1 December 2005

Delaney, Eamon, 'Celtic Dreamer', interview with Neil Jordan, *Publishers Weekly*, 22 November 2004, p. 33

Dillon-Malone, Aubrey, 'Transmogrification', *Books Ireland*, vol. 79, December 1983, p. 230
Dudley Andrew, James, 'The Theatre of Irish Cinema', *Yale Journal of Criticism*, vol. 15, no. 1, 2002, pp. 23–58
Dwyer, Michael, 'Neil Jordan in Conversation with Michael Dwyer', *The Fleadh Papers*, vol. 3, 1997
Ebury, Katherine, *Modernism and Cosmology: Absurd lights* (London: Palgrave, 2014)
Egan, Barry, 'Jordan Stars in His Own Silent Movie', *Sunday Independent*, 30 September 2007, Living, p. 4
Evans, Georgie, '9 Most Anticipated Books of 2017', *Cultured Vultures*, 12 January 2017, https://culturedvultures.com/9-most-anticipated-books-of-2017, accessed 26 July 2020
Fallon, Peter and Golden, Sean (eds), *Soft Day: A miscellany of contemporary Irish writing* (Dublin: Wolfhound Press, 1980)
Falsetto, Mario, 'Conversation with Neil Jordan', *Personal Visions: Conversations with contemporary film directors* (Los Angeles: Silman-James Press, 2000), pp. 217–54; reprinted in Carole Zucker, *Neil Jordan: Interviews* (Jackson, MS: University Press of Mississippi, 2013)
Fanning, Ronan, 'Irish Neutrality: An historical review', *Irish Studies in International Affairs*, vol. 1, no. 3, 1982, pp. 27–38
Fanning, Ronan, *Independent Ireland* (Dublin: Helicon, 1983)
Fennell, Jack, *Irish Science Fiction* (Liverpool: Liverpool University Press, 2014)
Ferriter, Diarmaid, *The Transformation of Ireland: 1900–2000* (London: Profile Books, 2004)
Fisher, Jennifer, 'Interperformance: The live tableaux of Suzanne Lacy, Janine Antoni and Marina Abramovic', *Art Journal*, vol. 56, no. 4, winter 1997, p. 28
Fisher, Mark, *The Weird and the Eerie* (London: Repeater Books, 2016)
Foster, Fiona, 'My Spooky Colleen', *Globe and Mail*, 17 July 2004, p. D3
Foster, John Wilson, 'Irish Fiction 1965–1990', in Seamus Deane (ed.), *The Field Day Anthology of Irish Writing*, vol. 3 (Derry: Field Day Publications, 1990), pp. 937–43
Foster, John Wilson, 'Neil Jordan: Night in Tunisia and Other Stories', in Seamus Deane (ed.), *The Field Day Anthology of Irish Writing*, vol. 3 (Derry: Field Day Publications, 1990), p. 1101
Foster, John Wilson, *Cambridge Companion to the Irish Novel* (Cambridge: Cambridge University Press, 2006)
Fox, Caoimhe, 'From Captain America's to Hollywood and Back', *Books Ireland*, vol. 367, May/June 2016, pp. 18–19
French, Philip and Wlaschin, Ken (eds), *The Faber Book of Movie Verse* (London: Faber, 1993)
Gallagher Winarski, Kathleen, 'Neil Jordan's *Miracle*', in James MacKillop (ed.), *Contemporary Irish Cinema: From* The Quiet Man *to* Dancing at Lughnasa (Syracuse: Syracuse University Press, 1999), pp. 98–108
Gefter Wondrich, Roberta, 'Exilic Returns: Self and history outside Ireland in recent Irish fiction', *Irish University Review*, vol. 30, spring/summer 2000, pp. 1–16
Gefter Wondrich, Roberta, 'Survivors of Joyce: Joycean images and motifs in some contemporary Irish fiction', *Studies*, vol. 90, no. 358, summer 2001, pp. 197–206

Grassi, Samuele, 'Father's in a Coma: Father–son relationships in Neil Jordan's fiction', *Estudios Irlandeses*, vol. 3, 2008, pp. 101–12

Guy, Peter, *As Mirrors Are Lonely: A Lacanian reading on the modern Irish novel* (Cambridge: Cambridge Scholars Publishing, 2014)

Haffenden, John, 'Angela Carter', interview, in John Haffenden, *Novelists in Interview* (London: Methuen, 1985), pp. 76–96

Hand, Derek, 'Review of *Contemporary Irish Fiction: Themes, tropes, theories* by Liam Harte and Michael Parker; *Modernisation: Crisis and culture in Ireland 1969–1990* by Conor McCarthy', *Irish University Review*, vol. 30, no. 2, autumn 2000, pp. 388–99

Hand, Derek, *A History of the Irish Novel* (Cambridge: Cambridge University Press, 2011)

Hansard, *House of Commons Debates*, 15 September 1914, vol. 55, col. 912 (John Redmond)

Harmon, Maurice, 'The Era of Inhibitions', in Masaru Sekine (ed.), *Irish Writers and Society at Large* (Buckinghamshire: Colin Smythe, 1985), pp. 31–41

Harte, Liam and Parker, Michael, 'Introduction', in Liam Harte and Michael Parker (eds), *Contemporary Irish Fiction: Themes, tropes, and theories* (London: Palgrave, 2000)

Haslam, Richard, 'Neil Jordan and the ABC of Narratology: "Stories to do with love are mathematical"', *New Hibernia Review*, vol. 3, no. 2, summer 1999, pp. 36–55

Hemry, Mark (ed.), *Chasing Danny Boy: Powerful stories of Celtic Eros* (San Francisco: Palm Drive Publishing, 1999)

Hogan, Robert, 'Old Boys, Young Bucks, and New Women: The contemporary Irish short story', in James F. Kilroy (ed.), *The Irish Short Story: A critical history* (Boston: Twayne, 1984), pp. 169–215

Hopper, Keith, 'A Gallous Story and a Dirty Deed: Word and image in Neil Jordan and Joe Comerford's *Traveller*', *Irish Studies Review*, vol. 9, no. 2, 2001, pp. 179–91

Hopper, Keith, 'Hairy on the Inside: Re-visiting Neil Jordan's *The Company of Wolves*', *Canadian Journal of Irish Studies*, vol. 29, no. 2, fall 2003, pp. 17–26

Hopper, Keith, *Flann O'Brien: A portrait of the artist as a young post-modernist*, 2nd edn (Cork: Cork University Press, 2009)

Hunt Mahony, Christina, *Contemporary Irish Literature: Transforming tradition* (New York: St Martin's Press, 1998)

Ingman, Heather, *A History of the Irish Short Story* (Cambridge: Cambridge University Press, 2009)

Irish PEN, 'Irish PEN Annual Award for Literature', *http://www.irishpen.com/wordpress/annual-award-for-literature*, accessed 18 October 2013

Jackson, Joe, 'Jordan Dares To Bare All', *Sunday Independent*, 9 May 2004, Review, p. 1

Jackson-Beverly, Mandy, 'Carnivalesque', *New York Journal of Books*, May 2017, *https://www.nyjournalofbooks.com/book-review/carnivalesque*, accessed 16 December 2019

Jaehne, Karen, 'Interview with Neil Jordan on *The Butcher Boy*', *Film Scout*, *www.filmscouts.com/scripts/interview.cfm?ArticleCode=703*, accessed 17 November 2005

Jenkins, Steve and Taylor, Paul, 'Wolf at the Door', *Monthly Film Bulletin*, September 1984, pp. 264–5. Reprinted in Carole Zucker, *Neil Jordan: Interviews* (Jackson, MS: University Press of Mississippi, 2013), p. 49

Jesse, Neal G., 'Contemporary Irish Neutrality: Still a singular stance', *New Hibernia Review*, vol. 11, no. 1, spring, 2007, pp. 74–95

Jha, Alok, 'What Is Heisenberg's Uncertainty Principle?', *The Guardian*, 10 November 2013, *https://www.theguardian.com/science/2013/nov/10/what-is-heisenbergs-uncertainty-principle*, accessed 2 December 2019

Joyce, James, *Ulysses* (London: Penguin Books, 2000)

Kearney, Richard, *Transitions: Narratives in Irish culture* (Dublin: Wolfhound Press, 1988)

Kelly, John, et al., '*Mistaken* by Neil Jordan', *The View*, RTÉ 1, 18 January 2011

Kenny, Des, 'Des Kenny Reviews *Mistaken* by Neil Jordan', 26 May 2011, *https://www.youtube.com/watch?v=szdebctgtVw&feature=player_embedded*, accessed 29 May 2011

Kenny, John, *John Banville* (Dublin: Irish Academic Press, 2009)

Kent, Brad, 'Review of *John McGahern: From the local to the universal* by Eamon Maher', *Canadian Journal of Irish Studies*, vol. 30, no. 2, fall 2004, p. 74

Lambé, Éric, 'The Filmmaker Neil Jordan Has a New Novel. It's Got a Missing Girl', *New York Times*, 3 July 2016, *https://www.nytimes.com/2016/07/03/books/review/the-drowned-detective-by-neil-jordan.html*, accessed 21 January 2020

Lanters, José, 'Nightlines by Neil Jordan', *World Literature Today*, vol. 70, no. 3, summer 1996, p. 692

Leonard, Sue, 'Book Review: *Carnivalesque*', *Irish Examiner*, 15 April 2017, *https://www.irishexaminer.com/ireland/book-review-carnivalesque-447979.html*, accessed 16 December 2019

Lewis, Trevor, 'Paperbacks' (review of *The Penguin Book of the City*), *The Sunday Times*, 26 April 1998, Features, Books, n.p.

Lucey, Anne, 'Jordan Wins Writers' Award at Listowel for Novel "Shade"', *The Irish Times*, 2 June 2005, p. 20

Mac Anna, Ferdia, 'The Dublin Renaissance: An essay on modern Dublin and Dublin writers', *The Irish Review*, vol. 10, spring 1991, pp. 14–30

MacAnna, Thomas, 'Nationalism from the Abbey Stage', in Robert O'Driscoll (ed.), *Theatre and Nationalism in Twentieth-century Ireland* (Toronto: University of Toronto Press, 1971), pp. 89–101

Maher, Eamon, 'Circles and Circularity in the Writings of John McGahern', *Nordic Irish Studies*, vol. 4, 2005, pp. 157–66

Malcolm, David, *The British and Irish Short Story Handbook* (Oxford: Blackwell, 2012)

Malcolm, David and Alexander Malcolm, Cheryl, *The Companion to the British and Irish Short Story* (Oxford: Blackwell, 2008)

McCabe, Patrick, '"1916 I think impossible to think about without thinking of Yeats and O'Casey": Public interview with Neil Jordan', in Seán Crosson and Werner Huber (eds), *Towards 2016: 1916 and Irish literature, culture & society* (Trier, Germany: WVT Publishers, 2015), pp. 229–54

McCann, Sharon, 'With Redundance of Blood: Reading Ireland in Neil Jordan's *The Company of Wolves*', *Marvels and Tales*, vol. 24, no. 1, 2010, pp. 68–85

McCarthy, Gerry, 'Taking a Shot at the Stage', *The Times*, 30 September 2001

McCarthy, Gerry, 'The End of the Affair', in Carole Zucker (ed.), *Neil Jordan Interviews* (Jackson, MS: University Press of Mississippi, 2013), p. 108; originally published in *Film West*, vol. 39, February 2000, pp. 12–15

McDiarmid, Lucy, 'An Estuary Child', *Times Literary Supplement*, 21 May 2004, p. 20

McGahern, John, 'Wheels', in *John McGahern: The collected stories* (London: Faber, 1992)

McHugh, Roger, 'Beauty in the Beast', *Irish Press*, 12 November 1983, p. 9

McIlroy, Brian, 'Irish Horror: Neil Jordan and the Anglo-Irish Gothic', in Steven Jay Schneider and Tony Williams (eds), *Horror International* (Detroit: Wayne State University Press, 2004), pp. 128–40

McNamee, Eoin, '*The Drowned Detective* by Neil Jordan review: Noir like no other', *The Irish Times*, 13 February 2016, https://www.irishtimes.com/culture/books/the-drowned-detective-by-neil-jordan-review-noir-like-no-other-1.2532566, accessed 21 January 2020

Mendlesohn, Farah, *Rhetorics of Fantasy* (Middletown, CT: Wesleyan University Press, 2008)

Miller, Karl, *Doubles: Studies in literary history* (Oxford: Oxford University Press, 1985)

Morris, Linda, 'Pluck of the Irish', *The Sun Herald* (Sydney), 13 February 2011, Extra, p. 4

Morton, Timothy, *The Ecological Thought* (Cambridge, MA: Harvard University Press, 2010)

Morton, Timothy, *Hyperobjects: Philosophy and ecology after the end of the world* (Minneapolis: University of Minnesota Press, 2013)

Muir, Kate, 'It's Lovely, Just Lovely, To Be in Control', *The Times*, 1 January 2011, Saturday Review, p. 5

Murphy, Neil, *Irish Fiction and Postmodern Doubt* (New York: Edwin Mellen, 2004)

Naish, John, 'A Novel Kind of Madness', *The Times*, 15 May 2004, pp. S3, 6

Nikolajeva, Maria, 'Fairy Tale and Fantasy: From archaic to postmodern', *Marvels & Tales*, vol. 17, no. 1, 2003, pp. 138–56

Nolan, Val, 'If It Was Just Th'ol Book … : A history of the John McGahern banning controversy', *Irish Studies Review*, vol. 19, no. 3, August 2011, pp. 261–79

O'Brien, Flann, *The Third Policeman* (London: Flamingo Modern Classics, 1993)

O'Brien, George, 'The Aesthetics of Exile', in Liam Harte and Michael Parker (eds), *Contemporary Irish Fiction: Themes, tropes, theories* (London: Macmillan, 2000), pp. 35–55

O'Byrne, Robert, 'The Strong, Silent Type?', *The Irish Times*, 14 January 1995, p. A2

O'Doherty, Caroline, 'Neil, an Artist of Many Identities', *Irish Examiner*, 8 January 2011, Weekend, pp. 28–9

O'Doherty, Enda, 'The Son of the Father', *Irish Press*, 6 January 1995, p. 21

O'Donoghue, Anna, 'Oscar-Winning Director Neil Jordan Donates Archives to National Library of Ireland', *Irish Examiner*, 9 August 2018, https://www.irishexaminer.com/lifestyle/celebrity/arid-30861095.html, accessed 22 July 2020

O'Faoláin, Seán, 'Introduction', in Neil Jordan, *Night in Tunisia* (Dublin: Irish Writers Co-operative, 1976)

O'Mahony, John, 'Big Screen Visionary', *The Guardian*, 29 February 2000, Saturday, p. 6

O'Rawe, Desmond, 'At Home with Horror: Neil Jordan's Gothic variations', *Irish Studies Review*, vol. 11, no. 2, 2003, pp. 189–98

O'Rawe, Desmond, 'Review of *Neil Jordan: Exploring boundaries* by Emer Rockett and Kevin Rockett', *Fortnight*, June 2003

O'Rawe, Desmond, 'Ambiguities Still To Be Resolved', *Fortnight*, vol. 415, June 2003, p. 19

O'Rawe, Desmond, 'Origins and Orientations: An interview with Kevin Rockett, on Irish Film Studies', *Canadian Journal of Irish Studies*, vol. 29, no. 2, fall 2003, pp. 57–61

O'Toole, Fintan, 'The Man Who Shot Michael Collins', *Independent on Sunday*, 3 November, 1996, Magazine, p. 21

O'Toole, Fintan, 'Getting Back to the Story', *The Irish Times*, 12 October 2001, Arts, p. 12

O'Toole, Fintan, '*Carnivalesque* review: Neil Jordan's cirque du supernatural', *The Irish Times*, 18 February 2017, https://www.irishtimes.com/culture/books/carnivalesque-review-neil-jordan-s-cirque-du-supernatural-1.2965586, accessed 16 December 2019

Park, James, *Learning to Dream: The new British cinema* (London: Faber, 1984)

Pernot-Deschamps, Marguerite, 'The Narrator in Neil Jordan's Short Stories', *Journal of the Short Story in English*, vol. 36, spring 2001, pp. 82–91

Pernot-Deschamps, Marguerite, *The Fictional Imagination of Neil Jordan, Irish Writer and Film Maker: A study of literary style* (New York: Edwin Mellen, 2009)

Pilard, Philippe, *Neil Jordan: Portrait* (France: CLC Productions/Cine Classic, 2006)

Poster, Jem, '*Carnivalesque* by Neil Jordan Review – Nights at the Circus', *The Guardian*, 8 March 2017, https://www.theguardian.com/books/2017/mar/08/carnivalesque-by-neil-jordan-review, accessed 10 December 2019

Pramaggiore, Maria, 'The Celtic Blue Note: Jazz in Neil Jordan's *Night in Tunisia*, *Angel*, and *The Miracle*', *Screen*, vol. 39, no. 3, September 1989, pp. 272–88

Pramaggiore, Maria, *Neil Jordan* (Urbana and Chicago: University of Illinois Press, 2008)

Quigley, Maeve, 'Neil Jordan', *Fortnight*, vol. 336, February 1995, p. 38

Roberts, Adam, *The History of Science Fiction* (London: Palgrave, 2005)

Roberts, Geoffrey, 'Three Narratives of Neutrality: Historians and Ireland's war', in Brian Girvin and Geoffrey Roberts (eds), *Ireland and the Second World War: Politics, society and remembrance* (Dublin: Four Courts Press, 2000), pp. 165–79

Robinson, Tasha, 'Neil Jordan', *AV Club*, 16 April 2003, https://www.avclub.com/neil-jordan-1798208312, accessed 30 December 2020

Rockett, Emer and Rockett, Kevin, *Neil Jordan: Exploring boundaries* (Dublin: Liffey Press, 2003)

Rogers, Lori, 'In Dreams Uncover'd: Neil Jordan, *The Dream of a Beast*, and the Body-Secret', *Critique*, vol. 39, no. 1, fall 1997, pp. 48–54

Rogers, Lori, *Feminine Nation: Performance, gender, and resistance in the works of John McGahern and Neil Jordan* (Lanham, MD: University Press of America, 1998)

Romney, Jonathan, 'Sweetness and Light', *City Limits*, 31 May–7 June 1990, pp. 16–17

Ryan, Matthew, 'Ourselves Alone: Solipsism in Neil Jordan's novels and films', *Bells: Barcelona English language and literature studies*, vol. 11, 2000, pp. 187–98

Schwartz, Richard Alan, 'Thomas Pynchon and the Evolution of Fiction (*Thomas Pynchon et l'évolution du récit*)', *Science Fiction Studies*, vol. 8, no. 2, July 1981, pp. 165–72
Schwartz, Richard Alan, 'Cybernetics and Science Fiction' (review of *The Soft Machine: Cybernetic Fiction* by David Porush), *Science Fiction Studies*, vol. 12, no. 3, November 1985, pp. 331–4
Sheridan, Kathy, 'Neil Jordan: "Apparently I have a terrifying temper"', *The Irish Times*, 25 February 2017, *https://www.irishtimes.com/culture/books/neil-jordan-apparently-i-have-a-terrifying-temper-1.2985150*, accessed 14 December 2020
Sheridan, Peter, 'The 40-Year-Old Thorn', *The Irish Times*, 28 January 2006, Weekend, p. 7
Shore, Tom 'Civil Wars', *New York Times Book Review*, 15 October 1995, p. 13
Shortall, Eithne, 'Film Director Neil Jordan's Latest Novel Is, in Part, a Love Letter to Dublin, the City that Shaped Him', *The Sunday Times*, 2 January 2011, Culture, pp. 12–13
Shumaker, Jeanett, 'Uncanny Doubles: The fiction of Anne Enright', *New Hibernia Review*, vol. 9, no. 3, autumn 2005, pp. 107–22
Sibree, Bron, 'Ireland of Lost Souls', *The Daily Telegraph* (Sydney, Australia), 21 August 2004
Simmons, David, 'Survival? 1981 Cork Film Festival', *Film Directions*, vol. 2, no. 17, March 1982, p. 15
Simpson, Anna, 'Dark Secrets of the Psyche', *The Herald* (Glasgow), 16 June 2004, n.p.
Smyth, Gerry, *The Novel and the Nation: Studies in the new Irish fiction* (London: Pluto Press, 1997)
Somer, John and Daly, John J., 'Introduction', in John Somer and John J. Daly (eds), *The New Anchor Book of Irish Writing* (New York: Anchor, 2000), pp. xv–xvi
Somerset, Guy, 'The Irish Rover', *The Dominion Post* (Wellington), 17 July 2004, Books, p. 10
Somerset, Guy, 'Neil Jordan: Film director and writer', *The Dominion Post*, 20 July 2004, n.p.
Spain, John and O'Sullivan, Majella, 'Jordan Swaps Movies for Novels to Take Home Top Literary Award', *Irish Independent*, 2 June 2011, p. 9
Sragow, Michael, 'Beautiful Dreamer', *Salon*, 9 December 1999, *http://www.salon.com/1999/12/09/jordan_3*, accessed 15 March 2013
Squires, Claire, 'Novelistic Production and the Publishing Industry in Britain and Ireland', in Brian Shaffer (ed.), *A Companion to the British and Irish Novel 1945–2000* (Oxford: Blackwell, 2005), pp. 177–93
Taylor, D.J., *A Vain Conceit: British fiction in the 1980s* (Oxford: Oxford University Press, 1989)
Thompson, Stith, *The Folktale* (Berkeley: University of California Press, 1977)
Tighe Ledwidge, Grace, 'Netherworld: London in John McGahern's fiction', in Tom Herron (ed.), *Irish Writing London. Volume 2: Post-War to the Present* (London: Bloomsbury, 2013), n.p.
Todorov, Tzvetan, *The Fantastic: A structural approach to a literary genre* (trans. Richard Howard) (London: The Press of Case Western Reserve University, 1973)

Tóibín, Colm, 'The *In Dublin* Interview: Neil Jordan talks with Colm Tóibín', *In Dublin*, vol. 152, 29 April 1982, p. 18

Tóibín, Colm, *The Penguin Book of Irish Fiction* (London: Penguin, 2001)

Tóibín, Colm, 'The Irish Famine', in Colm Tóibín and Diarmaid Ferriter (eds), *The Irish Famine: A documentary* (London: Profile Books, 2001)

Vale, Adrian, 'Short Stories', *The Irish Times*, 19 February 1977, p. 8

Wall, Alan, 'Impossible Deadlines', *The Guardian*, 22 May 2004, Reviews, p. 28

Walsh, Caroline, 'Return of a Native', *The Irish Times*, 21 December 1976, p. 8

Wootton, Adrian, 'Interview with Neil Jordan, Ralph Fiennes and Stephen Woolley', *Guardian Unlimited*, 4 February 2000, republished at *www.ralphfiennes-jenniferlash.com/earev5i.htm*, accessed 17 June 2005

Wroe, Nicholas, 'Always Make Sure You Offend', *The Guardian*, 4 March 2000, Saturday, p. 11

Wroe, Nicholas, 'Ireland's Rural Elegist', *The Guardian*, 5 January 2002, *https://www.theguardian.com/books/2002/jan/05/fiction.books*, accessed 28 July 2020

Yeats, W.B., *W.B. Yeats: The poems* (2nd edn), ed. Robert Finneran (New York: Scribner, 1997)

Zucker, Carole, *The Cinema of Neil Jordan: Dark carnival* (London: Wallflower Press, 2008)

Zucker, Carole (ed.), *Neil Jordan Interviews* (Jackson, MS: University Press of Mississippi, 2013)

Index

Abbey Theatre, 76, 77, 78
abortion, 69
Abrahamson, Lenny, 24
Academy Awards, 2, 3, 181
Across the Frontiers (Kearney), 5
Actors, The (2003), 190
adolescence, 38, 40, 48–55, 58–9, 145, 161, 184, 195–6, 200, 211, 213
agency, 49, 52, 75, 119
agricultural movement, 70
aisling poetry, 109
Alice in Wonderland (Carroll), 89
allegory, 3, 78, 89, 94, 95, 100–107, 109, 119, 128, 157
Altman, Robert, 186
ambiguity, 6, 35, 58, 63, 89, 128–9, 135, 148, 227
Amongst Women (McGahern), 35, 116–17
Angel (1982), 1, 22, 36, 48, 92, 101, 112, 171, 174, 176, 177, 181, 198, 221
Anglo-Irish Ascendancy, 4, 6, 33, 36, 43, 64, 67, 69–71, 73, 88, 103, 125, 142–3, 176, 222
Anglo-Irish Treaty, 81, 83, 131
Anselm, Saint, 163
architecture, 105, 124, 205
art, 13, 43, 70, 71, 76, 85, 154, 155, 182–3, 226–7
Artane industrial school, 19
Arts Council, 22, 114, 173
As You Like It (Shakespeare), 19, 153
At Swim-Two-Birds (O'Brien), 148
authoritarianism, 103, 119
autobiographical material, 3, 8, 23, 38, 57–8, 159, 178, 195, 200–201, 203–9

automatic writing, 146
Autumn Journal (MacNeice), 128

BAFTAs, 2
Bakhtin, Mikhail, 210, 212, 216–17
Ballina, Co. Mayo, 72, 84
Banville, John, 2, 3, 6, 25, 26, 27, 29, 90, 135, 137–8, 139, 205, 211
Bardwell, Leland, 21
Barton, Ruth, 9
Battersby, Eileen, 2, 37, 64–5, 202, 226
Beauty and the Beast, 95, 110
Beckett, Samuel, 17, 26, 29, 36, 116, 144, 172, 190
'Beginning of an Idea, The' (McGahern), 34–5
Belton, Neil, 129
Bennett, Ronan, 141
Berkeley, George, 187, 192
'Berkeley Complex, The' (Jordan), 5, 8, 78, 138, 167–72, 174–5, 186–94
Berlin Film Festival, 2
betrayal, 56, 115, 125, 133, 197, 225
Bettystown, Co. Meath, 12
Big Houses, 24, 28, 33, 139, 141, 164
bildungsroman, 211
bisexuality, 136
Black, Cathal, 34, 176
Blake, William, 96
Bloody Chamber, The (Carter), 36, 108, 109–10, 111
Blue Angel, The (1930), 186
bodies, 28, 43–6, 94, 98, 101–2, 213
body horror, 4, 110–11
Bogosian, Eric, 186

Bohr, Niels, 137
Boinn, 142, 145, 161–2, 165
Boland, John, 205, 206
Bolger, Dermot, 21
Books Ireland, 90
Boorman, John, 22, 40, 172, 174
Borgias, The (2011–13), 36, 171, 207
Bowen, Elizabeth, 125
Boyne valley, 36, 139, 141–5, 152–4, 159, 161
Brace, Marianne, 14–15, 32, 95–6, 98, 121, 171–2, 228
Bray, Co. Wicklow, 36, 67, 69–72, 85, 123, 124, 127, 135, 219
Breakfast on Pluto (2005), 36, 42, 181
Brighton, 143
Broken Dreams (unrealised film script), 22
Brown, Terence, 132–3, 136
Burnside, John, 225
Burren, 40, 61, 66, 125–7, 220, 224
Burroughs, William, 175
Butcher Boy, The (1997), 2, 36, 171, 196–7
Byrne, Gay, 24, 25, 28, 32, 159
Byzantium (2012), 32, 98, 199, 221

Cahalan, James, 27, 65–6
capitalism, 193–4, 214, 215
carnivalesque, 210, 212, 216–17
Carnivalesque (Jordan)
    adolescence, 195–6, 200, 211, 213
    autobiographical elements, 23
    changelings, 199, 212
    cinema, 219
    critical responses, 201, 211–12, 226
    demonic possession, 199, 212
    double identities, 8–9, 146, 187, 191, 195–8, 200, 210–11, 217–21
    epigraph, 212
    fairy folk, 8–9, 196, 199, 209, 210–20
    fairy tales, 8–9, 95, 215, 220
    fantasy, 4, 27, 115, 196–7, 201, 210–18, 226, 227
    folklore, 197, 200, 210, 212
    gravitational theory, 95, 212, 217, 218, 220
    Great Famine, 27, 210, 213–15, 226
    hall of mirrors, 8, 27, 195–6, 210, 218–19
    Irish identity, 197, 223, 227
    landscapes, 199
    myth, 196, 210–11, 213–15, 218, 226
    observer effect, 138
    realism, 196–7, 211–12, 214
    recession, 27, 215, 226
    relation to *Mistaken*, 195, 197–8, 200, 209, 216, 221
    representations of women, 213
    science fiction, 27, 95, 197, 217–20, 226
    scientific metaphors, 95, 137, 148, 211, 212, 217–20, 226
    sexuality, 217
    simulacra, 8, 196, 200, 210
    supernatural, 199, 210–11
    temporality, 218, 219–20
    transformation, 27, 217
    uncanniness, 198, 213, 219
    uncertainty, 197, 198
    west of Ireland, 27, 30, 210, 220
Carroll, Lewis, 89
Carter, Angela, 36, 90, 92, 99, 107–11
Casement, Roger, 69, 74
Cat and the Moon, The (Yeats), 30
Cathleen ni Houlihan, 51, 61, 76–7, 189
Catholic Church, 14–15, 19–20, 32, 34, 84
Catholicism, 7, 28, 32–4, 38, 47, 70–73, 84, 99, 109, 115–17, 125, 153, 165, 204–5
causality, 8, 149–50, 155–8
Celtic Tiger, 7, 24, 171, 208–9
Celticism, 76, 79
censorship, 13, 20, 21, 34, 116, 118–19, 129, 132, 133
Central Bank building, Dublin, 94, 105
changelings, 4, 199, 212
Channel 4, 109, 173–4
chaos, 97–8
child abuse, 19–20
children, 14, 19–20, 96, 105–6, 139–66, 200
children of the nation, 71–2, 129, 160, 222

Index

Children's T Company, 19
children's television, 19
Chouinard, Alain, 90
cinema *see* film
circularity, 29, 32–3, 42–3, 47, 51, 142, 144–5, 147, 149–54, 158, 164
'Circus Animals' Desertion, The' (Yeats), 31
civil war *see* Irish Civil War; Spanish Civil War
Clarke, Arthur C., 218–19
class, 7, 70, 124–5, 142–3, 176, 185, 203; *see also* Anglo-Irish Ascendancy
Cohen, Leonard, 187
Collins, Michael, 152
colonialism, 4, 6, 8, 66, 67–8, 71–3, 100–107, 122–4, 143
'Come away, O human child!' (Yeats), 212
comedy, 76, 131, 179
Comerford, Joe, 22, 169, 173–4, 176, 177
Companion to the British and Irish Short Story (Malcolm and Malcolm), 52, 225
Company of Wolves, The (1984), 20, 32, 36, 90, 91–2, 95, 98, 101, 107–13, 171, 212–13
'Company of Wolves, The' (Carter), 108, 109
complementarity, 137
Connelly, John, 201
Connemara, 70–71
Conradh na Gaelige, 68
conscription, 75
Coppola, Francis Ford, 170, 186
Cornwall, 67, 69, 73, 75
Cosgrave, W.T., 125
cosmopolitanism, 29, 35, 176
'Courtship of Mr. Lyon, The' (Carter), 108
COVID-19 pandemic, 95
Creature from the Black Lagoon (1954), 90
Crying Game, The (1992), 1, 3, 18, 36, 42, 48, 50, 56, 101, 112, 169, 171, 178, 181, 189, 197, 209–10, 221
'Crying Game, The' (song), 48, 50
Cuisine des Anges, La (Husson), 179

cultural nationalism, 70, 71, 76, 79–80
Cumann na nGaedheal, 125

Dáil Éireann, 81, 82
Dalkey Archive, The (O'Brien), 148
Daly, John J., 91
Dancing at Lughnasa (1998), 190
Dante, 184
Dark, The (McGahern), 13, 34
Dawe, Gerald, 39, 64, 140, 225
Day, Gregory, 209, 226–7
de Falbe, John, 223
De Niro, Robert, 179
de Valera, Éamon, 3, 19, 56–66, 73, 75, 80–84, 114–15, 123–32, 136, 138, 140, 152–3, 164
death, 8, 40, 42–8, 60, 115, 118–21, 126, 139–42, 147–51, 156–66, 179–81, 188; *see also* funerals; murder; suicide
decay, 5, 70, 100, 106, 112, 127, 169
Deliverance (1972), 40
demonic possession, 199, 212
Descartes, René, 148
description, 9, 20, 40, 64, 74, 92, 94, 98, 141, 160, 196, 213, 223
determinism, 119, 147, 149–50, 152, 164, 226
dialogue, 92, 120, 160
Dick, Philip K., 128, 226
Dillon-Malone, Aubrey, 90
Doctor Copernicus (Banville), 138
Doctor Salt (Donovan), 141
documentaries, 22, 174, 180, 188
Dollymount Strand, Dublin, 16, 28, 30
Donoghue, Emma, 213
Donohue, Walter, 109
Donovan, Gerard, 141
doppelgängers, 1, 191–2, 193, 197–8, 201, 222; *see also* double identities
Dorcey, Mary, 35, 225
double identities
    in 'The Berkeley Complex', 187, 188, 191–2
    in *Carnivalesque*, 8–9, 146, 187, 191, 195–8, 200, 210–11, 217–21

double identities (*continued*)
    doppelgängers, 1, 191–2, 193, 197–8, 201, 222
    Jordan's dual artistic identities, 1–2, 8–9, 11, 22–5, 37, 92–3, 107–8, 112, 168–72, 177, 194–201, 207–9, 217, 220–21, 223–4
    in *Mistaken*, 8, 11, 28, 93, 146, 187, 191, 192, 195–201, 205–9
    in *Shade*, 145–6, 192
Doyle, Roddy, 228
Dracula (Stoker), 30, 199
dramatic tension, 172
Dream of a Beast, The (Jordan)
    allegory, 3, 89, 94, 95, 100–107, 109
    critical responses, 26, 89–90, 93, 98, 102, 225
    depiction of Dublin, 5, 36, 89, 94, 96, 98, 100–107
    epigraph, 96
    fairy tales, 95–6, 105
    fantasy, 4, 6, 7, 27, 89, 94–102, 106, 110, 112, 115, 118, 214, 225
    Gothic, 92, 94–5, 97, 100, 102
    influence of Joyce, 89, 91
    influence of Yeats, 106, 110
    Irish identity, 103
    landscapes, 7, 13, 36, 94, 96, 98, 100–107
    magical realism, 91, 117
    modernity, 7, 96, 99
    myth, 94, 96–7
    postcolonialism, 6, 7, 88, 89, 90, 94, 100–107, 227
    prevalence of description, 92, 94, 98, 196
    realism, 27, 225
    relation to *The Company of Wolves*, 91–2, 107–13
    religious symbolism, 99–100
    return, 97
    science fiction, 225
    sexuality, 111
    supernatural, 98, 101, 112
    transformation, 6, 7, 27, 37, 89–113, 197, 203
    water, 90, 98, 100, 112
dreams, 41, 51, 106, 109, 110, 118, 120–21, 156, 158–9, 178–80
Drogheda, Co. Louth, 141, 143, 152–3
Drowned Detective, The (Jordan), 4, 225
Dublin
    in 'The Berkeley Complex', 187, 190
    in *The Dream of a Beast*, 5, 36, 89, 94, 96, 98, 100–107
    Dublin bombing, 18
    funeral of de Valera, 56, 63
    Jordan's early life in, 12–16, 93, 199, 202, 204–5
    Joyce's depictions of, 28–30, 89, 190, 195, 202, 205, 209, 224, 227
    launch of *Sunrise with Sea Monster*, 25
    in *Mistaken*, 28, 29–30, 36, 195, 199, 201–7, 209, 224, 225
    in *Night in Tunisia*, 47, 58, 59–60
    in *The Past*, 69–70, 122–3
    in *Sunrise with Sea Monster*, 123–4, 133
Dublin Castle, 119, 133, 134
Dubliners (Joyce), 28, 29, 224
Dwyer, Ciara, 203
Dwyer, Michael, 21, 95

Easter Rising, 69, 78, 81, 122
'Easter 2036' (Jordan), 95, 153
Eclipse (Banville), 138
economic policies, 4, 125, 164
economic recessions, 4, 27, 215, 226
eeriness, 62, 117–19, 122, 132, 156, 203; *see also* uncanniness
Einstein, Albert, 32, 137
election posters, 126–7
Eliot, T.S., 118
'Emergency' *see* Second World War
emigration, 35, 215; *see also* exile
Emmet, Robert, 78
employment, 33, 169, 171, 187, 192
End of the Affair, The (Greene), 36
End of the Affair, The (1999), 36, 221
Enlightenment, 96, 212

Enright, Anne, 225
epigraphs, 31, 96, 145, 212
Euclid, 32, 129, 136
everyman figures, 42, 45, 107
Excalibur (1981), 22, 40, 172
Excalibur: Myth into Film (1981), 22
exile, 5, 18, 24, 29, 35–6, 42, 57, 62, 67–8, 116

Faber Book Of Best New Irish Short Stories, 186
fairy folk, 8–9, 196, 199, 209, 210–20
fairy tales, 8–9, 20, 95–6, 98, 99, 105, 110, 215, 220, 223; *see also* folklore
'Faith, Hope and Charity' (McGahern), 35
Fallon, Peter, 27
Fanning, Ronan, 128, 132
fantasy
    in *Carnivalesque*, 4, 27, 115, 196–7, 201, 210–18, 226, 227
    in *The Dream of a Beast*, 4, 6, 7, 27, 89, 94–102, 106, 110, 112–13, 115, 118, 214, 225
    intrusion fantasy, 97–8, 100, 106, 118
    in *Shade*, 4, 7, 115, 214
    in *Sunrise with Sea Monster*, 7, 114–15, 117–18, 128, 214
Farewell to Prague (Hogan), 18
Farrell, Colin, 207
Farrell, J.G., 100
fascism, 115–16, 117, 131; *see also* Nazism
father–son relationships, 14–15, 18, 20, 35–6, 40, 48–9, 53, 59–62, 115–17, 120–21, 129, 134–5, 227
'Father-thing, The' (Dick), 128, 226
feminism, 25, 89–90, 111
Fennell, Jack, 99
Ferriter, Diarmaid, 116, 129
Fianna Fáil, 82, 125, 127
Field Day Anthology, 35, 48, 50, 55, 172
Field Day theatre company, 170–71
film
    cinema and filmmaking in Jordan's fiction, 3, 8–9, 22–3, 74–6, 87–8, 159–60, 167–94, 219

    critical studies of Jordan's films, 1–2
    early cinema, 3, 159–60, 219
    film editing, 74, 75
    Hollywood, 31, 167, 168–9, 170, 171, 173, 177–86, 208, 221
    Irish film industry, 170–71, 176–7, 181
    Jordan develops an interest in, 16
    Jordan's awards and nominations, 2, 181
    Jordan's film reviews, 34, 176
    Jordan's films *see individual titles*
    relation to theatre, 170–71
    silent films, 159
Financial Times, 89
Finnegans Wake (Joyce), 29, 144–5, 166
First World War, 7, 36, 68, 79–80, 122, 139, 143, 145, 146, 151, 153, 154
Fisher, Mark, 117–20, 130, 132, 198
Fitzgerald, F. Scott, 55
flashbacks, 35, 59, 85, 115, 140, 160
flash-forwards, 45, 140
Fly, The (1958), 90
folklore, 20, 36, 95–6, 142, 197, 200, 210, 212, 223, 227; *see also* fairy tales
Ford, Richard, 225
Fortnight, 168
Foster, Fiona, 143–4
Foster, John Wilson, 6, 35, 50
frame-dragging, 220
Franco, Francisco, 115
free will, 119, 149
Freud, Sigmund, 198
Friel, Brian, 190, 191
funerals, 33, 56–8, 60, 63, 80, 81–2, 139, 145, 147, 166, 200

Galway Film Fleadh, 223
Game with Sharpened Knives, A (Belton), 129
Gate Theatre, 190–91
Gefter Wondrich, Roberta, 6, 18, 29, 91, 135
gender, 24, 40, 52–3, 102, 111–12, 141, 189, 197, 213; *see also* women
genre, 8, 9, 94–100, 107, 195, 196, 217–18, 225–6

Getting Through (McGahern), 34–5
Ghost Goes West, The (1935), 180
Ghostbusters (1984), 179
ghosts, 4, 91, 108, 139–42, 149–66, 183, 222, 225
Gillespie, Dizzy, 48
globalisation, 4, 203–4, 215
God, 32, 82, 99, 137, 163
Gogol, Nikolai, 14
Golden, Seán, 27, 65
Golden Globes, 2
Golon, Sergeanne, 14
Gonne, Maud, 78, 79
Good Thief, The (2002), 11
Gort, Co. Galway, 72, 87
Gothic, 4, 5, 92, 94–7, 100, 102, 109, 141–2, 163, 179, 195, 200, 216
Grassi, Samuele, 53, 57
gravitational theory, 4, 95, 209, 212, 217, 218, 220
Great Famine, 4, 27, 210, 213–15, 226
Great Men theory of history, 140–41, 152
Greene, Graham, 36
Greta (2018), 171
Griffith, Arthur, 75
Guardian, 14, 15, 21, 161, 211, 225
Guardian Fiction Prize, 2, 21, 41, 109
Guttenberg, Steve, 179
Guy, Peter, 116

Hamilton, Hugo, 35
Hamlet (Shakespeare), 182–3, 192
Hand, Derek, 29
Harmon, Maurice, 25
Haslam, Richard, 60, 95–6, 101, 108
Havoc in its Third Year (Bennett), 141
Healy, Dermot, 27
Heaney, Seamus, 25, 143
'Hearts of Oak and Bellies of Brass' (McGahern), 35
Heidegger, Martin, 137
Heisenberg, Werner, 136–8, 140, 148, 157–8
'Her Soul' (Jordan), 52
heroism, 39, 60, 123, 145, 152

Higgins, Aidan, 6, 25
High Spirits (1988), 32, 36, 42, 98, 101, 168, 169, 173, 178, 179–80, 216
Hinds, Ciarán, 190
historiography, 139, 140–41, 144, 152
Hitchcock, Alfred, 191
Hitler, Adolf, 128, 138
Hogan, Desmond, 5–6, 18, 19, 20, 29, 38
holiday resorts, 12, 36, 38, 40, 41, 49, 51, 57, 62–3, 67, 68, 71–2, 73, 124, 143, 222
Hollywood, 31, 167, 168–9, 170, 171, 173, 177–86, 208, 221
home, 5, 35, 48
home rule, 67, 68–9, 70, 75, 122
homoeroticism, 43
Hopper, Keith, 90, 100–101, 102, 108, 110, 128, 173, 174, 175, 178
horror, 4, 90–91, 95, 102, 109, 110–11, 183
House of Hunger, The (Marechera), 21
Howth, Co. Dublin, 12
Husson, Albert, 179

I Went Down (1997), 190
identity *see* double identities; national identity
imaginative crisis, 26
'Imagining Otherwise' (Jordan), 5
immigration, 193
imperialism *see* colonialism
Improbable Frequency (Riordan), 128–9
In Dreams (1999), 31, 42, 53–4
'In Memory of Eva Gore-Booth and Con Markiewicz' (Yeats), 31, 145
In the Name of the Father (1993), 181
independence struggle, 4, 7, 33, 58, 61–2, 67–9, 79–82, 114–17, 122–5, 129, 152, 164, 210, 222; *see also* Easter Rising; Irish civil war; war of independence
Independent, 16, 74, 93, 95
industrial schools, 19
industry, 5, 72–3, 90, 141, 145, 154, 164
inequality, 193–4
infinity, 50, 219
infrastructure, 100, 105, 106, 124

Inghinidhe na hÉireann, 79
Ingman, Heather, 29, 35
insularity, 4, 7, 114, 121–8, 132–3, 138, 215
International Brigades, 116, 131
Interview with the Vampire (Rice), 36
Interview with the Vampire (1994), 32, 36, 98, 101, 110, 111, 112, 171, 183, 199, 221
intrusion fantasy, 97–8, 100, 106, 118
isolationism, 4, 7, 88, 123–5, 132–3, 153
Irish Censorship Board, 21
Irish civil war, 4, 56, 59, 61–2, 80, 83, 115, 122, 125
Irish Examiner, 205
Irish film industry, 170–71, 176–7, 181
Irish Free State, 8, 19, 33, 64, 69, 125–7, 131–3, 154
Irish identity
    in *Carnivalesque*, 197, 223, 227
    in *The Dream of a Beast*, 103
    in Jordan's film stories, 194
    in McGahern, 34, 35
    in *Mistaken*, 7, 197, 223, 227
    in *Night in Tunisia*, 27, 35, 38, 39, 58, 62
    in *The Past*, 7, 66–7, 78, 88, 123, 227
    in *Shade*, 7, 152, 165, 223, 227
    in *Sunrise with Sea Monster*, 7, 114, 123–4, 131, 227
    traditional constructions of, 3, 9–10, 27, 38, 62, 152
Irish Independent, 205
Irish language, 71, 124
Irish literary revival, 76, 212
Irish PEN association, 2
Irish Press, 21, 102, 208
Irish Republican Army (IRA), 80, 125, 130–31, 133
Irish Times, 2, 34, 36–7, 39, 41, 64–5, 72, 85, 114, 202, 211, 225, 226
Irish University Review, 29
Irish Writers' Co-operative, 20–21

jazz, 29, 40, 48–51, 53, 172
Jenkins, Tamara, 186
Jesse, Neal, 122
John Bull, 76, 79

Johnston, Denis, 81
Johnston, Fred, 20
Jordan, Michael, 12, 13, 14–15, 20, 38–9, 159
Jordan, Neil
    awards and nominations, 2, 21, 41, 109, 141, 181, 201
    develops interest in films, 16
    dual artistic identities, 1–2, 8–9, 11, 22–5, 37, 92–3, 107–8, 112, 168–72, 177, 194–201, 207–9, 217, 220–21, 223–4
    early life, 11–16
    early writings, 15, 16
    education, 13, 15–17
    establishes Irish Writers' Co-operative, 20–21
    film reviews by, 34, 176
    films *see individual titles*
    influences, 28–35, 106, 110, 144–8, 195, 199, 202, 226–7
    interviews, 6, 12, 15, 25, 38, 63, 93, 95, 110, 201, 203, 204–5, 223, 228
    lack of scholarly attention for fiction, 1–2, 6, 168
    in London, 16, 17–18, 42
    marriage and family, 17–18, 114
    music projects, 13, 17, 50–51
    novels and short stories *see individual titles*
    radio plays, 17
    reading, 14, 28
    and religion, 32–3, 99–100, 163
    scholarly studies of fiction, 5–6, 25–7
    scholarly studies of films, 1–2
    television projects, 19, 21–2, 36, 48, 171, 207
    theatre projects, 17, 19–20, 30, 77, 189–91
Journal of a Hole (1971), 19–20, 77
Joyce, James
    influence on 'The Berkeley Complex', 190
    centenary celebrations, 109

Joyce, James (*continued*)
   depictions of Dublin, 28–30, 89, 190, 195, 202, 205, 209, 224, 227
   influence on *The Dream of a Beast*, 89, 91
   Dubliners, 28, 29, 224
   Finnegans Wake, 29, 144–5, 166
   influence on Jordan in general, 26–7, 28–30, 224, 227
   influence on *Mistaken*, 28, 29–30, 195, 202
   influence on *Night in Tunisia*, 29, 45, 47, 55, 202, 224
   Portrait of the Artist as a Young Man, 28, 47, 55, 135, 224
   influence on 'Remote Control', 182–3
   influence on *Shade*, 29, 144–5, 166
   influence on *Sunrise with Sea Monster*, 29, 135
   Ulysses, 28, 29, 30, 91, 182–3, 202, 205, 224
Judaism, 28, 70

Kafka, Franz, 89, 90, 105, 225
Keane, John B., 2
Kearney, Richard, 5, 25, 26, 65
Kenny, Des, 201–2, 220
Kepler (Banville), 138
Kerry Group Irish Fiction Award, 141, 201
Kiarostami, Abbas, 186
Kiberd, Declan, 116
Kirkus, 210, 220
'Korea' (McGahern), 35

LaBute, Neil, 186
Lahinch, Co. Clare, 61–2
Lambay Island, 124
landscapes, 7, 13, 17, 28, 30, 36, 40, 94, 96, 98, 100–107, 123–7, 139, 141–4, 199, 222, 224
Lanters, José, 118
'Last Rites' (Jordan), 5, 7, 18, 33, 35, 36, 41–8, 53, 54, 135, 140
Late Late Show (RTÉ), 204
Leavetaking, The (McGahern), 13, 205

'Leda and the Swan' (Yeats), 110
Leonard, Sue, 198, 200
light, 107, 137, 169, 175, 184–5, 193, 207, 219
liminality, 29, 42–4, 46–7, 51, 114, 121, 135, 177, 184, 193, 222
linearity, 5, 120, 139–40, 173
'Lines Written in Dejection' (Jordan), 180–81, 185
Lisdoonvarna, Co. Clare, 57, 58–9, 61, 62, 67, 72, 73, 126
Listowel Writers' Week, 141, 201
Little Theatre, UCD, 19
London, 16–18, 21, 35, 38, 40, 42–3, 57, 58, 59, 67–8, 75, 143, 145, 176
Los Angeles, 169, 177–84, 208
'Love, A' (Jordan), 18, 23, 26, 30, 33, 35–6, 38–9, 53, 56–63, 82, 125, 126, 135, 148, 222
Lovely Bones, The (Sebold), 259–60
Lucas, George, 94–5
Lugosi, Bela, 199
Lumière brothers, 219

MacAnna, Thomas, 78
McCabe, Patrick, 2, 29, 36, 90, 93, 139, 205, 228
McCann, Joseph, 15
McCann, Sharon, 109
McCarthy, Gerry, 222
McCormack, Catherine, 190
McCourt, Frank, 204
McDonagh, Steve, 20
McDonald, Peter, 190
McGahern, John, 2, 13, 15, 20, 25–6, 29, 34–5, 116–17, 125, 176, 205
McHugh, Roger, 90, 102
McIlroy, Brian, 102
McKenna, David, 19
McNamee, Eoin, 225
MacNeice, Louis, 128
McPherson, Conor, 190
Maffey, Sir John, 123
magic, 13, 32–3, 219
magical realism, 91, 117, 120–21

Index

Magritte, René, 110
Maher, Eamon, 35
Mahony, Christina Hunt, 26, 48, 53, 55, 62, 65, 89
Malcolm, Cheryl Alexander, 52, 225
Malcolm, David, 34–5, 52, 225
male gaze, 52
Mamet, David, 179
Man and Superman (Shaw), 14
Mann, Michael, 190
Marcus, David, 21, 186, 208
Marechera, Dambudzo, 21
marginal places *see* liminality
Mary, Virgin, 52, 62
Master, The (Tóibín), 141
masturbation, 42, 43, 44–5, 46, 47, 55
mathematics, 59, 62, 84, 136–7, 140, 148, 157
melodrama, 171, 172, 187, 192
memory, 17, 63–5, 73, 87, 103, 116–17, 120, 158, 160–61, 164, 214
Mendlesohn, Farah, 97, 100, 106
metamorphosis, 54, 89–93, 99, 103, 105, 107, 108, 110, 203; *see also* transformation
Metamorphosis, The (Kafka), 90
Michael Collins (1996), 1, 25, 36, 56, 58, 81, 168, 171, 188, 224
Michael Collins: Film Diary (Jordan), 36, 168
Miller, Karl, 197, 198, 212, 218, 219, 227
Miracle, The (1991), 22, 31, 36, 48, 112, 168–9, 179, 189, 219, 221
Miracles and Miss Langan (Jordan), 17, 21
mirrors, 8, 27, 195–6, 210, 212–13, 218–19
Mistaken (Jordan)
    autobiographical elements, 8, 23, 195, 200–201, 203–9
    critical responses, 201–2, 226–7
    depiction of Dublin, 28, 29–30, 36, 195, 199, 201–7, 209, 224, 225
    double identities, 8, 11, 28, 93, 146, 187, 191, 192, 195–201, 205–9
    funerals, 200
    Gothic, 95, 195, 200, 216
    influence of Joyce, 28, 29–30, 195, 202
    influence of Stoker, 199, 202
    influence of Yeats, 227
    Irish identity, 7, 197, 223, 227
    landscapes, 199
    relation to *Carnivalesque*, 195, 197–8, 200, 209, 216, 221
    representations of Jordan's fiction, 208–9
    sexuality, 204
    supernatural, 199
    transformation, 6–7, 201, 203, 206
    triangular relationships, 36
    uncanniness, 198
    uncertainty, 197, 198
    water, 206
    wins Kerry Group Irish Fiction Award, 201
modernism, 25, 26, 136, 147, 195, 199
modernity, 5, 7, 25, 33, 58, 72–3, 77, 96, 99, 165, 193–4, 227
Mona Lisa (1986), 101, 112, 177, 221
Monaghan bombing, 18
Monsarrat, Nicholas, 14
Moon in the Yellow River, The (Johnston), 81
Morton, Timothy, 213, 214, 219, 220
Mosney holiday camp, 49, 53
motherhood, 52–3, 60, 188–9; *see also* pregnancy
murder, 8, 23, 28, 80, 123, 139–40, 149, 150–51, 159, 162, 181, 188
Murphy, Neil, 25
music, 13, 16, 17, 29, 40, 48–51, 53, 59, 172, 187–8, 204
myth, 3, 20, 39, 61, 71–3, 82, 94–7, 112, 142, 145, 161–2, 165, 196, 210–15, 218, 226–7

narrative structure, 28, 29, 45, 50, 55–6, 150–51
national identity *see* Irish identity
nationalism, 7, 19, 33–4, 40, 59, 67–84, 103, 109, 115–16, 122–5, 129–31, 214, 222

Nazism, 119, 121, 125, 135, 137, 148
Neil Jordan Reader, A, 56
neutrality, 123, 124, 127, 128–38, 217, 225
New York Times, 137–8, 225
New York Times Book Review, 89, 223
Newton, Isaac, 138, 217
Nightlines (Jordan) *see Sunrise with Sea Monster* (Jordan)
Nightlines (McGahern), 117
Night in Tunisia (Jordan)
   adolescence, 38, 40, 48–55, 58–9
   autobiographical elements, 23, 38, 57–8
   betrayal, 56
   Catholicism, 33, 47
   critical responses, 26, 27, 29, 39, 41, 48, 225
   death, 40, 42, 44–8, 60, 140
   depiction of de Valera, 56 63
   depiction of Dublin, 47, 58, 59–60
   depiction of women, 52–3, 59–60
   exile, 5, 18, 35, 36, 42, 57, 62
   father–son relationships, 35, 36, 40, 48–9, 53, 59, 60–62
   funerals, 56–8, 60
   gender politics, 40
   holiday resorts, 12, 36, 38, 40, 41, 49, 51, 57, 62–3
   home, 7, 35, 48
   influence of Beckett, 29
   influence of Joyce, 29, 45, 47, 55, 202, 224
   influence of McGahern, 35
   Irish identity, 27, 35, 38, 39, 58, 62
   landscapes, 40
   masturbation, 42–7, 55
   modernity, 58
   music, 48–51, 53, 59, 172
   nationalism, 40, 59, 222
   O'Faoláin's introduction, 3, 40, 49–50, 225
   prevalence of description, 40
   relation to *The Miracle*, 22, 36, 112, 168
   representation of in *Mistaken*, 208
   ritual, 33, 45–7

   sexuality, 33, 35, 38, 40, 43, 45–6, 48, 50–52, 54–5, 57–9
   suicide, 42, 44–8, 51, 54
   transformation, 38
   triangular relationships, 36, 56, 59–61
   water, 43–7, 48, 51, 53–4, 58, 59, 62, 121, 135
   west of Ireland, 30, 40, 61, 82, 125, 126, 210
   wins *Guardian* Fiction Prize, 21, 41, 109
   see also 'Her Soul'; 'Last Rites'; 'Love, A'; 'Night in Tunisia'; 'Outpatient'; 'Sand'; 'Seduction'; 'Skin'; 'Tree'
'Night in Tunisia' (Jordan), 21, 23, 26, 35, 36, 40, 43, 48–56, 172
Nikolajeva, Maria, 96
nonlinearity, 32–3, 149–54, 218
Nora (2000), 190
Northern Ireland, 24, 109, 176–7, 181
nostalgia, 7, 17, 64, 65, 139
Not I (Beckett), 36
Not I (2006), 36

oath of allegiance, 81
O'Brien, Edna, 2
O'Brien, Flann, 26, 144, 146–8, 153
O'Brien, George, 6
O'Brien, Kate Cruise, 38, 39
observer effect, 138, 140, 148, 154–7
O'Casey, Seán, 17, 22, 77
O'Connor, Frank, 38
O'Connor, joseph, 213
O'Connor, Pat, 21, 48
O'Doherty, Caroline, 198, 205
O'Duffy, Eoin, 116
Oedipus Rex (Sophocles), 20
O'Faolain, Julia, 38
O'Faoláin, Seán, 3, 40, 49–50, 225
'Old-Fashioned Life, The' (Jordan), 169
O'Mahony, John, 12, 13
'On Coming Home' (Jordan), 21, 169
Ondine (2009), 36, 115, 183, 199, 207, 221
O'Rawe, Des, 92, 95, 168
origin stories, 79, 102, 210, 213

Orwell, George, 14, 178
Oscars *see* Academy Awards
Othello (Shakespeare), 175, 187–8, 192
O'Toole, Fintan, 2, 34, 37, 56, 190, 196–7, 201, 210, 211, 212, 213
O'Toole, Peter, 179
'Outpatient' (Jordan), 52, 61, 126

paralysis, 29, 40, 102, 118, 125, 134–5
Parent Trap (1961), 206
Parker, Charlie, 48, 53
Past, The (Jordan)
    Anglo-Irish Ascendancy, 6, 33, 36, 43, 64, 67, 69–71, 73, 103, 125, 142, 176
    autobiographical elements, 23
    Catholicism, 33, 70, 71–2, 73, 84, 125, 153
    cinema, 74–5, 87–8, 223
    critical responses, 26, 64–6, 225
    dedicated to Jordan's parents, 15
    depiction of de Valera, 19, 56, 58, 59, 64, 66, 73, 75, 80–82, 83–4, 140
    depiction of Dublin, 69–70, 122–3
    determinism, 119, 152
    epigraph, 31
    exile, 67–8
    extracts published in anthologies, 27, 175
    father–son relationships, 36, 53
    First World War, 68, 79–80, 122
    funerals, 80, 81–2
    holiday resorts, 36, 67, 68, 71–2, 73
    influence of Yeats, 31–2
    Irish identity, 7, 66–7, 78, 88, 123, 227
    memory, 64, 65, 73, 87
    modernity, 72–3, 77
    motherhood, 189
    murder, 80, 123
    myth, 71, 72–3, 82
    nationalism, 7, 19, 33, 67, 69, 70, 72, 74–6, 78–82, 83–4, 122–3, 222
    nostalgia, 7, 64, 65
    photography, 64–6, 70, 73–80, 87–8, 175–6, 223
    politics, 65, 66, 73, 77, 78–82, 122
    prevalence of description, 64, 74, 160, 223
    Protestantism, 6, 33, 36, 67, 68, 69–72, 73, 125, 153
    representation of in *Mistaken*, 208, 209
    temporality, 74, 87, 219
    theatre, 7, 19, 43, 65, 66, 72, 73, 75–83
    transformation, 6, 101, 122
    triangular relationships, 36, 148
    west of Ireland, 30, 64, 67, 70–71, 72–3, 82–4, 87, 123, 125, 126, 210
    wins Rooney Award for Literature, 2
patriarchy, 21, 102, 111
Patrick, Saint, 165
Paulin, Tom, 178
Pearse, Pádraig, 75, 124
Penn, Sean, 179
Pernot-Deschamps, Maguy, 52
Philadelphia, Here I Come! (Friel), 191
photography, 60, 63–6, 70, 73–80, 87–8, 175–6, 223
physics, 4, 32, 95, 135–8, 148, 155–8, 209, 212, 220, 226
'Physics and Fiction' (Banville), 137–8
Pilard, Philippe, 174, 180, 188
Playboy of the Western World, The (Synge), 175
Player, The (1988), 186
popular culture, 4, 7, 16, 17, 29, 48–50, 56, 207, 217–18
Portmarnock, Co. Dublin, 12
Portrait of the Artist as a Young Man (Joyce), 28, 47, 55, 135, 224
postcolonial biology, 7, 100–107, 227
postcolonialism, 6, 7, 25, 88, 89, 90, 94, 100–107, 131, 198, 227
Poster, Jem, 211, 212
postmodernism, 91, 111, 147
poverty, 46, 70, 193, 204
Pramaggiore, Maria, 11, 29, 110
predestination *see* determinism
pregnancy, 68–9, 72, 75, 78, 83; *see also* motherhood

Problems of Dostoevsky's Poetics (Bakhtin), 216
Proclamation, 69
Producer magazine, 180
Project Arts Centre, Dublin, 19
Protestantism, 6, 7, 28, 31, 33, 34, 36, 67–73, 99, 125, 127, 154
Psycho (1960), 191
'Puss-in-Boots' (Carter), 108

Quiet Man, The (1952), 180

Rabelais and His World (Bakhtin), 216
race, 24, 43
radio plays, 17, 109
Rea, Stephen, 170–71, 190
Readers' and Writers' Co-operative, 21
realism, 4, 7, 27, 76, 98, 114–15, 196–7, 211–12, 213, 214, 222, 225
Rebecca (1940), 191
recessions, 4, 27, 215, 226
redemption, 228
Redmond, John, 67, 68, 75, 122
Redmond, Lucille, 21
relativity theory, 32, 136, 212, 220
religion, 32–3, 39, 71–2, 82, 98–9, 124–5, 163; *see also* Catholicism; Protestantism
'Remote Control' (Jordan), 5, 8, 167–72, 177–86, 188–9, 193, 194, 208
repression, 18, 33, 40, 45, 46, 86, 102
Responsibilities (Yeats), 31
return, 18, 29, 97, 116, 119–21, 128
Rice, Anne, 36
Riordan, Arthur, 128–9
ritual, 33, 45–7, 116–17
Roberts, Adam, 99
Rockett, Emer, 5, 11, 25, 52, 73–4, 93–4, 100, 108, 110, 173–4, 175, 176
Rockett, Kevin, 5, 11, 25, 52, 73–4, 93–4, 100, 108, 110, 173–4, 175, 176
Rogers, Lori, 25–6, 34, 89–90, 101, 102, 112
'Róisín Dubh', 109
Romanticism, 96

Rooney Award for Literature, 2
Rosses Point, Co. Sligo, 12, 28, 125
RTÉ, 17, 19, 21–2, 48, 206
rural electrification, 165
Ryan, Matthew, 90

'Sailing to Byzantium' (Yeats), 31
St Anne's Park, Dublin, 13, 15
St Lawrence O'Toole (SLOT) Players, 19
St Patrick's College, Drumcondra, 12
St Paul's College, Raheny, 13, 15
'Sand' (Jordan), 41, 43, 54, 58
Sandymount, Dublin, 69
saxophone, 17, 29, 49–50, 53, 172
Schwartz, Richard, 137
'Scenes in a Novel' (O'Brien), 147, 148
science fiction, 3–4, 27, 94–6, 99, 153, 197, 217–20, 225, 226
scientific metaphors, 4, 95, 135–8, 140, 148, 155–8, 209, 211, 212, 217–20, 226
sea, the, 12, 15, 48, 51, 59, 71, 98, 118, 120–24, 127–31, 133–5, 145, 158; *see also* holiday resorts; water
Seán (RTÉ), 22
seaside towns see holiday resorts
Sebold, Alice, 159–60
Second World War, 4, 7, 102, 118–19, 121–2, 123–5, 128–38, 157
'Seduction' (Jordan), 43, 52, 58
self-determination, 119, 123, 135
sexuality, 12, 19, 29, 33–5, 38, 40, 43–59, 111, 136, 145, 161, 166, 197, 204, 205, 217
Shade (Jordan)
    Anglo-Irish Ascendancy, 6, 33, 36, 70, 88, 142–3
    autobiographical elements, 23, 159
    Catholicism, 33, 153, 165
    causality, 8, 149–50, 155–8
    cinema, 3, 23, 75–6, 159–60, 219
    circularity, 142, 144–5, 147, 149–54, 158, 164
    colonialism, 8, 143
    critical responses, 141–2, 143–4, 161
    death, 8, 42, 139–42, 147–51, 156–66

determinism, 119, 147, 149–50, 152, 164, 226
dialogue, 160
double identities, 145–6, 192
epigraph, 31, 145
fantasy, 4, 7, 115, 214
First World War, 7, 36, 139, 143, 145, 146, 151, 153, 154
folklore, 142
funerals, 33, 139, 145, 147, 166
ghosts, 7, 91, 108, 139–42, 149–66
Gothic, 95, 141–2, 163
and historiography, 139, 140–41, 144, 152
industry, 5, 141, 145, 154, 164
influence of Flann O'Brien, 146–8
influence of Joyce, 29, 144–5, 166
influence of Yeats, 145–6
Irish identity, 7, 152, 165, 223, 227
landscapes, 36, 139, 141, 142, 143–4
memory, 158, 160–61, 164
motherhood, 189
murder, 8, 23, 28, 139–40, 149, 150–51, 159, 162
myth, 142, 145, 161–2, 165
narrative structure, 27–8, 29, 150–51
observer effect, 138, 140, 148, 154–7
prevalence of description, 141, 160
Protestantism, 6, 33, 36, 70, 154
representations of women, 213
science fiction, 95
scientific metaphors, 95, 137, 140, 148, 155–8, 211
sexuality, 33, 145, 161, 166
supernatural, 28, 98, 101
theatre, 19, 23, 75–6, 78
time travel, 7, 95, 140, 158, 160
temporality, 7, 8, 23, 28, 95, 139–40, 142, 145–6, 149–59, 160–61, 219
transformation, 6
triangular relationships, 19, 36, 148, 153
uncanniness, 8, 197
uncertainty, 140, 157–8, 161
water, 142, 145, 161–2, 165–6

wins Kerry Group Irish Fiction Award, 141, 201
Shadow of a Gunman (O'Casey), 77
Shakespeare, William, 19, 72, 152, 175, 182–3, 187–8, 190, 192
Shaw, George Bernard, 14, 23, 144
'She: an *Unfinished Story*' (Jordan), 8, 22, 167–77, 184, 188, 193, 194, 207
Sheehan, Ronan, 21, 25
Sheridan, Jim, 17, 19–20, 24, 30, 181
Sheridan, Kathy, 226
Sheridan, Peter, 17, 19–20, 30
Shields, Vivienne, 17–18, 114
Shumaker, Jeanett, 197
Shore, Tom, 223
Shortall, Eithne, 201, 203, 205
'Sierra Leone' (McGahern), 34
Simmons, David, 178
simulacra, 8, 119, 131, 196, 200, 210
'Skin' (Jordan), 26, 29, 41, 52
Smyth, Gerry, 6
soap operas, 170, 171, 187
socialism, 193–4
Soft Day miscellany (Fallon and Golden), 27
Somer, John, 91
Spanish Armada, 125
Spanish Civil War, 18, 114–16, 129–30, 131
Spanish Point, Co. Clare, 119, 125, 130–31, 134
Spectator, 223
Spillane, Mickey, 14
Star of the Sea (O'Connor), 213
Star Trek franchise, 95
Star Wars (1977), 94–5
Stephenson, Sam, 105
stereotypes, 9, 30, 46, 76, 90, 180, 204
Sternberg, Josef von, 186
Stevenson, Robert Louis, 90–91, 191
Stoker, Bram, 30, 199, 201, 203
Stokes, Niall, 50
Strandhill, Co. Sligo, 72, 84, 125
'Strandhill, the Sea' (McGahern), 125
Strange Case of Dr Jekyll and Mr Hyde (Stevenson), 90–91, 191

string theory, 212
Stuart, Francis, 26
suicide, 39, 42, 44–8, 51, 54, 188
Sunday Independent, 20
Sunday Times, 203, 205
Sunrise with Sea Monster (Jordan)
    allegory, 119, 128, 157
    Anglo-Irish Ascendancy, 6, 33, 36, 125
    betrayal, 115, 125, 133, 197
    Catholicism, 33, 115–17, 125
    comedy, 131
    critical responses, 29
    death, 42, 115, 118–21
    depiction of de Valera, 56, 58, 114, 115, 123–9, 132, 136, 138
    depiction of Dublin, 123–4, 133
    determinism, 119
    Dublin launch, 25
    eerieness, 117–19, 122, 132
    exile, 5, 18, 36, 116
    fantasy, 7, 114–15, 117–18, 128, 214
    father–son relationships, 18, 36, 53, 60–61, 115, 116–17, 120–21, 129, 134–5
    holiday resorts, 36, 71, 124
    influence of Joyce, 29, 135
    influence of McGahern, 35, 116–17, 125
    insularity, 7, 114, 121–8, 132–3, 138
    Irish identity, 7, 114, 123–4, 131, 227
    landscapes, 123–4, 126–7
    magical realism, 91, 117, 120–21
    memory, 116–17, 120
    nationalism, 115–16, 125, 129–31
    neutrality, 123, 124, 127, 128–38, 217, 225
    postcolonialism, 103, 131
    Protestantism, 6, 33, 36, 125, 127
    realism, 114–15, 213
    return, 18, 119–21, 128
    ritual, 116–17
    scientific metaphors, 135–8, 211
    Second World War, 7, 102, 118–19, 121–2, 123–5, 128–38, 157
    sexuality, 136
    Spanish Civil War, 18, 114–16, 129–30, 131
    supernatural, 101, 128, 134
    temporality, 120
    transformation, 6, 123–4, 126
    triangular relationships, 36, 115, 116, 136, 148
    uncertainty, 115, 119, 129, 131, 135–8, 140, 157
    violence, 115, 121–2
    water, 118, 120–24, 127–8, 133–5
    west of Ireland, 30, 82, 121, 125–7, 135
'Sunrise with Sea Monsters' (Turner), 117
Sunset Boulevard (1950), 159–60
supernatural, 3, 28, 32, 53, 85–6, 98, 101, 112, 128, 134, 179, 196, 199, 210–11
'Supernatural Songs' (Yeats), 31–2
superstition, 32–3, 36
Swanson, Gloria, 159–60
Synge, J.M., 123, 175

tableaux vivants, 79–80
Taylor, D.J., 2, 65
teenagers *see* adolescence
television, 19, 21–2, 36, 48, 170, 171, 187, 207
temporality
    in *Carnivalesque*, 218, 219–20
    and circularity, 29, 32–3, 42–3, 47, 51, 142, 144–5, 147, 149–54, 158, 164
    flashbacks, 35, 59, 85, 115, 140, 160
    flash-forwards, 45, 140
    linear time, 120
    non-linear time, 32–3, 149–54, 218
    in *The Past*, 74, 87, 219
    in *Shade*, 7, 8, 23, 28, 95, 139–40, 142, 145–6, 149–59, 160–61, 219
    in *Sunrise with Sea Monster*, 120
    time travel, 7, 95, 140, 158, 160
theatre, 7, 17, 19–20, 23, 30, 36, 43, 65, 66, 72, 73, 75–83, 170–71, 189–93, 199
Third Policeman, The (O'Brien), 147, 148
Thompson, Stith, 96
'Tiger's Bride, The' (Carter), 108
Time Out, 109, 110

Index

time travel, 7, 95, 140, 160
Times Literary Supplement, 144
'To a Shade' (Yeats), 145–6, 166
Todorov, Tzvetan, 96
Tóibín, Colm, 3, 63, 141, 177, 228
Tolkin, Michael, 186
transformation, 6–7, 26–7, 34, 37–8, 89–113, 122–6, 197, 201, 203, 206, 217; *see also* metamorphosis
Traveller (1981), 22, 169, 173–5, 176–7
'Tree' (Jordan), 61, 126
Trevor, William, 2
triangular relationships, 19, 34, 36, 56, 59–61, 115, 116, 136, 148, 153, 222
Troubles, 24, 109, 176–7, 181
Troubles (Farrell), 100
Tuatha Dé Danann, 3, 91, 210–11, 215, 216, 226
Turner, J.M.W., 117
twilight, 51, 135, 193, 175, 184, 193

Ulysses (Joyce), 28, 29, 30, 91, 182–3, 202, 205, 224
uncanniness, 8, 129, 197, 198, 213, 219; *see also* eerieness
uncertainty, 41, 66, 115, 119, 129, 131, 135–8, 140, 157–8, 161, 197, 198
uncertainty principle, 136–8, 140, 157–8
University College Dublin (UCD), 16–17
urban landscapes, 7, 36, 94, 96, 98, 100–107, 122–4, 184, 199, 201–7, 224; *see also* Dublin

Vale, Adrian, 39
vampires, 30, 196, 199
Vico, Giambattista, 145
View, The (RTÉ), 201
violence, 8, 19, 38, 69, 111–12, 115, 121–2, 165, 181

Wall, Alan, 161
Walsh, Caroline, 39, 114
Wanderly Wagon (RTÉ), 19
war of independence, 4, 33, 35, 122, 139, 146, 154, 164
water
  in *The Dream of a Beast*, 90, 98, 100, 112
  in *Mistaken*, 206
  in *Night in Tunisia*, 43–7, 48, 51, 53–4, 58, 59, 62, 121, 135
  the sea, 12, 15, 48, 51, 59, 71, 98, 118, 120–24, 127–31, 133–5, 145, 158
  in *Shade*, 142, 145, 161–2, 165–6
  in *Sunrise with Sea Monster*, 118, 120–24, 127–8, 133–5
We're No Angels (1989), 101, 168, 169, 178, 179
west of Ireland, 12, 27, 30, 40, 61, 64, 67, 70–73, 82–4, 87, 121, 123–7, 135, 210, 220, 227
'Wheels' (McGahern), 34, 35, 176
Wheels (1976), 34, 176
White Horses (Jordan), 189–91
Wilder, Billy, 159–60
Wilhelm II, Kaiser, 76, 79
'Winter Dreams' (Fitzgerald), 55
women
  depiction of, 52–3, 59–60, 188–9, 213
  motherhood, 52–3, 60, 188–9
  pregnancy, 68–9, 72, 75, 78, 83
  as symbolic of Ireland, 60–61, 67, 68–9
  see also gender
Wonder, The (Donoghue), 213
Woolley, Steve, 109
Work in Progress (Joyce) *see Finnegans Wake* (Joyce)

Yeats, Jack B., 12
Yeats, W.B., 17, 28–33, 58, 101, 106, 110, 123, 126, 144–6, 161, 166, 199, 212, 227
young people *see* adolescence; children

Zoetrope: All-Story magazine, 186
Zucker, Carole, 11, 30